Object REXX
for Windows NT
and Windows 95

Object REXX
for Windows NT
and Windows 95

Ueli Wahli
Ingo Holder
Trevor Turton

INTERNATIONAL TECHNICAL SUPPORT ORGANIZATION
SAN JOSE, CALIFORNIA 95120

PRENTICE HALL PTR
UPPER SADDLE RIVER, NEW JERSEY 07458

This edition applies to Object REXX running under Windows NT and Windows 95.

Comments about ITSO Technical Bulletins may be addressed to:
IBM Corporation ITSO, Almaden Research Center, QXX/80-E2, 650 Harry Road, San Jose, California 95120-6099

For information about redbooks
http://www.redbooks.ibm.com/redbooks

Send comments to
redbooks@vnet.ibm.com

Published by Prentice Hall PTR
Prentice-Hall, Inc.
A Simon & Schuster Company
Upper Saddle River, NJ 07458

Acquisitions Editor: Michael E. Meehan

Manufacturing Manager: Alexis R. Heydt

Cover Design: Ueli Wahli, Ingo Holder, Design Source

Copy Editor: Maggie Cutler

Editorial/Production Supervision: Joe Czerwinski

The publisher offers discounts on this book when ordered in bulk quantities. For more information, contact:
Corporate Sales Department, Prentice Hall PTR, One Lake Street, Upper Saddle River, NJ 07458
Phone: 800-382-3419; FAX: 201-236-7141; E-mail (Internet): corpsales@prenhall.com

For book and bookstore information

http://www.prenhall.com

Printed in the United States of America

10 9 8 7 6 5 4 3 2 1

ISBN   0-13-858028-6

Prentice-Hall International (UK) Limited, *London*
Prentice-Hall of Australia Pty. Limited, *Sydney*
Prentice-Hall Canada Inc., *Toronto*
Prentice-Hall Hispanoamericana, S.A., *Mexico*
Prentice-Hall of India Private Limited, *New Delhi*
Prentice-Hall of Japan, Inc., *Tokyo*
Simon & Schuster Asia Pte. Ltd., *Singapore*
Editora Prentice-Hall do Brasil, Ltda., *Rio de Janeiro*

Abstract

Object orientation (OO) is a topic of great interest and concern today. Some developers who use OO claim that it significantly increases productivity; others view it as good for rocket science, not for business.

Many OO languages seem complicated and alien to programmers familiar with procedural languages, such as COBOL. This book introduces Object REXX, a new OO language that breaks the OO barrier. Object REXX is based on a tried-and-trusted language used around the world today. Because it has the most complete and easy-to-use set of OO features of any language, it offers a simple way for programmers with a procedural background to enter the new world of objects.

This book demonstrates a practical approach to using Object REXX and OO techniques to develop commercial systems that meet changing business requirements. It tells the story of how Hanna, Steve, and Curt design and implement a commercial application system step by step, using object persistence in file systems and relational databases, graphical user interface (GUI) builders, and Internet Web pages. Extensive code examples are provided to illustrate every step.

To Hanna, Curt, and Steve, the hard-working people at the fictitious Hacurs company. Originally loosely defined, they inspired the writing of real-life dialog to portray a small company trying to find a niche in the marketplace. Any resemblance to real people is completely coincidental.

To my colleagues, who work eagerly and with much personal commitment to get Object REXX outside the confines of IBM. To my dear friends, Dr. Johannes Kadel and Ronan Kieran, who inspired my interest in English. To my parents who supported me in various endeavors. To all those who like Object REXX and will help making it a well-known language on Windows platforms as well.

Ingo

To my wife Ingrid, for the love and patience she showed while her husband labored over recalcitrant programs and screeds of text.

Trevor

To my wife, Patricia, for her ongoing support and understanding of my long hours at work. To the staff at the ITSO San Jose Center for making work a joy, at least most of the time.

Ueli

Contents

Figures

Tables

Preface

In this book we describe the new object-oriented language, Object REXX. We list all the incremental improvements that Object REXX offers over and above classic REXX and describe the object-oriented features included in Object REXX. To illustrate its capabilities, we develop some fairly large applications.

REXX has long had great strengths in the area of linking to other programs and services. Here we demonstrate Object REXX's ability to link to DB2 Version 2 for Windows NT and Windows 95 to carry out sophisticated binary-large-object (BLOB) handling, as well as conventional record processing.

This book contains Object REXX for Windows NT and Windows 95 and OODialog, an object-oriented facility to build graphical user interface (GUI) applications. OODialog makes it easy to statically or dynamically create GUI applications, supporting all kinds of dialog features.

Object REXX also includes powerful facilities for concurrent programming. We show a graphical user interface (GUI) that exploits Object REXX's concurrent programming facilities.

Detailed syntax diagrams covering all of the new and changed features of Object REXX are included, with brief descriptions.

This book is intended for programmers who know and love REXX and would like to learn what the new facilities in Object REXX look like and the kinds of problems they can solve. It contains lots of sample code that we hope will provide a useful starting point for new projects. Programmers who currently use REXX to build large and complex systems will be well aware of its limitations in terms of splitting large programs into smaller, manageable components. Object REXX has excellent facilities that allow and encourage this process. We describe them and illustrate their use.

This book is also for programmers who would like to start learning and using OO techniques but do not have access to an OO language and compiler; or for those who *do* have access to one but find getting into it to be too complicated and alien. REXX is, above all, an accessible language. It is simple, obvious, and unintimidating; and Object REXX provides an easy entry into the world of objects.

How This Document Is Organized

The document is organized as follows:

❏ *Introducing the Hacurs Company*

In this section we introduce the hypothetical software company Hacurs, which is followed throughout the book as it uses Object REXX to implement an application for their customers.

❏ Part 1, *Introducing Classic REXX and Object REXX*

Part 1 is an overview of classic REXX and the object-oriented (OO) facilities of Object REXX. It is also a description of why OO, in general—and Object REXX in particular—are such valuable and important technologies.

➤ Chapter 1, *Introducing Classic REXX*

In this chapter we introduce classic REXX for readers without any knowledge of REXX. We listen as a Hacurs professional teaches classic REXX to a group of developers of a software company.

➤ Chapter 2, *Introducing Object REXX*

In this chapter we introduce Object REXX and describe the importance of OO.

➤ Chapter 3, *How Does Object REXX Implement OO?*

In this chapter we describe how Object REXX implements OO through objects, classes, and methods, including support for inheritance and polymorphism. It also touches on the Object REXX-provided class library.

❏ Part 2, *The Car Dealer Scenario*

In Part 2 we illustrate a broad range of Object REXX's facilities by describing the way that a hypothetical software company might use them to design and implement a fairly realistic application for various car dealers.

➤ Chapter 4, *The Car Dealer Application*

In this chapter we describe the car dealer application that Hacurs wants to develop and the process that Hacurs goes through to design the system, using OO techniques. This chapter presents the Object REXX facilities that Hacurs decides to use in support of the implementation. Extracts of source code are included for illustrative purposes, while comprehensive source listings are included in Appendix B.

➤ Chapter 5, *ASCII User Interface*

In this chapter we describe how Hacurs designs and builds Object REXX classes and methods to implement a simple ASCII character-oriented user interface for the system. The company builds one class to manage the display of information on the user's screen and another to store, display, and interpret the many menus that the system requires. Anticipating the need for a future GUI interface, Hacurs uses OO design principles to isolate the application code from the user-interface code.

➤ **Chapter 6,** *Persistent Objects on Disk*

In the base car dealer system, all updates to objects are lost when the application terminates. In this chapter, Hacurs designs and builds Object REXX classes and methods to add persistent storage behavior to the objects within the system. The object data is stored in flat ASCII files.

➤ **Chapter 7,** *Graphical User Interfaces with OODialog*

Chasing a new opportunity to sell its car dealer application, Hacurs builds and implements a GUI to it. The company uses the OODialog GUI builder provided with Object REXX.

➤ **Chapter 8,** *Persistent Objects in DB2*

Seeing yet another opportunity to market the application, Hacurs develops new classes that give objects persistent storage in a DB2 database. The new methods can support large volumes of data by selectively loading only when needed and caching frequently used data in storage as objects.

➤ **Chapter 9,** *Using Advanced DB2 Facilities*

Hacurs further extends the car dealer application by adding multimedia facilities. The code makes use of the powerful new BLOB handling facilities of DB2 Version 2 to store and retrieve the multimedia data. Audio, bitmaps, and video facilities are incorporated.

➤ **Chapter 10,** *Data Security with Object REXX and DB2*

A serious concern that arises over the security of DB2 data accessed by dynamic SQL from client PCs is resolved by developing code that exploits DB2 Version 2's stored procedure mechanism.

➤ **Chapter 11,** *Configuration Management with Object REXX*

A proliferation of different versions of the code required to meet different customers' needs threatens to get out of hand and result in a big code-maintenance burden. Hacurs develops a sophisticated system for managing many different code configurations within a multiple subdirectory structure, using different configuration files to pull the right pieces together. This allows common code to be reused without being cloned.

Hacurs develops a GUI Object REXX program that allows users to select the application configuration they need, and installs it.

> ➤ **Chapter 12,** *Object REXX and the World Wide Web*

Hacurs decides to advertise its car dealer application on the World Wide Web, often called the *Internet*. It installs a Web server and creates a simplified version of the application to present car dealer data as Web pages. It uses the Common Gateway Interface (CGI) to invoke Object REXX programs from the Web server. The Object REXX programs dynamically create Web pages with the information from the database.

Any Web browser can point to the Hacurs server and interact with the car dealer application. An extension of the application even enables a Web browser user to add a car to the database and create a work order.

❑ **Part 3,** *Object REXX and Concurrency*

> ➤ **Chapter 13,** *Object REXX and Concurrency*

In this part we describe the concurrent-processing facilities of Object REXX. After a short introduction, we solve with Object REXX the problem of the dining philosophers, a classic illustration of concurrent processing. The code to build a GUI application illustrating five philosophers sitting down to dine is developed and discussed. The GUI is developed using OODialog.

❑ **Part 4,** *Installing Object REXX, DB2, and the Sample Applications*

> ➤ **Chapter 14,** *Installing Object REXX, DB2, and the Sample Applications*

In this part we describe how to install Object REXX, DB2, and the sample applications on Windows NT and Windows 95. Installation of the code and the setup of DB2 for the sample application are explained in detail, including instructions on how to run the examples.

❑ **Part 5,** *Reference Information*

This part contains reference information that should help users write GUI applications with OODialog, access the Windows Program Manager and the Windows Registry from Object REXX, and use the Object REXX Demonstration Workbench.

> ➤ **Chapter 15,** *OODialog Method Reference*

This chapter contains the reference manual for the OODialog GUI builder. It explains all classes and methods that can be used to create GUI applications for Windows NT and Windows 95 with Object REXX.

➤ **Chapter 16, *Windows Program Manager and Registry***

In this chapter we briefly describe the two Object REXX classes provided to access the Windows Program Manager and the Windows Registry.

➤ **Chapter 17, *Object REXX Demonstration Workbench***

In this chapter we introduce a workbench that can be used to debug Object REXX programs. With the workbench users can interactively run programs, watch and modify values of variables, set breakpoints, and trace programs.

❑ **Part 6, *Appendixes***

The appendixes contain additional information about new features in Object REXX, migration from OS/2 REXX, an extract of source listings of the car dealer application, instructions on how to read the syntax diagrams, special notices, and information about related publications and ITSO redbooks.

➤ **Appendix A, *New Features in Object REXX and Migration***

This appendix contains a comprehensive set of syntax diagrams that show the new instructions, functions, classes, and methods that are a part of Object REXX, as well as the extensions made to REXX. The syntax diagrams are accompanied by explanatory text.

The differences between classic REXX and Object REXX are explained in a small migration section.

➤ **Appendix B, *Car Dealer Source Code***

This appendix contains a listing of the sample data and an extract of the source programs of the car dealer application. The base classes and the classes for file and DB2 persistence are listed.

➤ **Appendix C, *Definition for Syntax Diagram Structure***

This appendix describes the notation of the syntax diagrams used in Chapter 15, *OODialog Method Reference* and in Appendix A, *New Features in Object REXX and Migration*.

➤ **Appendix D, *Special Notices***

This appendix contains special notices about IBM products and trademarks.

➤ **Appendix E, *Related Publications***

This appendix contains a listing of related publications of the International Technical Support Organization (ITSO) and other sources, information about *How to Get ITSO Redbooks*, and a reference to *Sample Code on the Internet*.

The Team That Wrote This Redbook

Ueli Wahli is a Consultant AD Specialist at the IBM International Technical Support Organization in San Jose, California. He writes extensively and teaches IBM classes worldwide on application development and object-oriented technology. Before joining the ITSO 12 years ago, Ueli worked in technical support in IBM Switzerland as a Systems Engineer. He has 30 years of experience in application development. He holds a degree in Mathematics from the Swiss Federal Institute of Technology. His areas of expertise include many programming languages and visual development environments, as well as data dictionaries, repositories, and library management. He has been involved with many redbooks on these topics. His e-mail address is *wahli @ vnet.ibm.com*.

Ingo Holder is a Software Engineer at the German Software Development Lab in Böblingen, Germany. He has six years of experience in application development. He holds a degree in business management specializing in computer science from the Württembergische Verwaltungs- und Wirtschaftsakademie Stuttgart, Germany. His areas of expertise include many programming languages, such as C++, Pascal, PL/I, and Assembler. He wrote his graduation paper about object-oriented programming. Since October 1995 he has been responsible for the Object REXX interpreter on the Windows NT and Windows 95 platforms. You can reach him at *iholder @ vnet.ibm.com*.

Trevor Turton works as an IT Architect in the area of Network Computing for IBM South Africa. He has a BSC in Mathematics and Physics and 33 years of computer experience—29 of these with IBM. This experience spans dozens of operating systems, languages, and database managers. Trevor started designing and implementing distributed computer systems over 20 years ago, and has stayed with this mode of computing through its client/server and Internet/Intranet phases. Trevor had the great idea of writing most of the book in the dialog style—Hanna, Curt, Steve, and the Hacurs company are his inventions. You can reach him at *trevort @ vnet.ibm.com*.

This book is based on a similar redbook on Object REXX for OS/2, written by Trevor Turton and Ueli Wahli.

Acknowledgments

This book would not have been possible without the help of the following people who contributed to the content of the book:

- ❑ **Jiri Andress** from IBM Germany worked on the DB2 implementation under Windows NT and Windows 95 and wrote the reference manual for the OODialog GUI builder.

- ❑ **Karel Michek** from IBM Czech ported the OS/2 car dealer application to Windows NT and Windows 95 using the OODialog GUI builder. He also worked on the sample OODialog programs distributed with Object REXX for Windows.

Many thanks to Maggie Cutler for editing the book and making the dialog interesting. Thanks also to Jens Tiedemann, former manager of the ITSO San Jose, for the investment of resources into the Object REXX projects on OS/2, Windows NT, and Windows 95.

Ueli Wahli

Comments Welcome

We want our redbooks to be as helpful as possible. Should you have any comments about this or other redbooks, please send us a note at the following address:

redbook@vnet.ibm.com

Your comments are important to us!

Introducing the Hacurs Company

It is all too easy to make a book about a computer language read like a catalog of washing machine parts. As we go through the features of classic REXX and Object REXX we are going to try to bring them to life by showing how useful they are to a fictional, but not unrealistic, small software company called *Hacurs*. This company was started one year ago by three friends—**Hanna**, **Curt**, and **Steve**. They studied computer application design and programming together at college, and after graduation they all joined the same company and worked in its IT department. They often spoke of starting their own little software company, and after two years of corporate life, they agreed to do it. They decided to design and develop applications for OS/2 and Windows. They had used C and C++ for some of their college assignments, but most of their corporate experience was based on coding REXX. They recognized that REXX is an extremely powerful and easy-to-use language and chose it as their preferred development language.

Their company name is derived from their own names but also stands for their main business—Handy Applications Coded Using REXX.

Hacurs signed up with the IBM Developer Assistance Program (DAP) and the Developer Connection for OS/2 (DEVCON). This gave them access to lots of useful information, as well as some very useful development tools.

In this book we follow the Hacurs company as they:

❑ teach classic REXX to another software company;

❑ design an object model for a car dealer application and implement it in Object REXX;

❑ design and implement a simple ASCII window user interface;

❑ use flat files to implement object persistence;

❑ design a graphical user interface using OODialog (the GUI builder shipped with Object REXX);

❑ implement object persistence in DB2;

❑ use advanced DB2 facilities to store multimedia data in binary large objects (BLOBs);

❑ overcome data security concerns about dynamic SQL using stored procedures;

❑ design a sophisticated configuration management system using Object REXX's requires facility;

❑ put the car dealer application on the World Wide Web by dynamically creating Web pages using Object REXX; and

❑ prove how easy it is to implement concurrent processes using Object REXX.

Part 1

Introducing
Classic REXX
and Object REXX

1

Introducing Classic REXX

In this chapter we pick up the story of how Hacurs teaches a company a few features of classic REXX. This chapter is for readers not familiar with REXX and serves as an introduction to the simplicity and function of the language. In subsequent chapters we introduce the object-oriented facilities of Object REXX.

A Lesson in Classic REXX

Steve arrived safely in Seattle, although, to get a better price, he had to choose one of the smaller airlines. He claimed his baggage, walked through the hallway to the taxi rank, and took a cab. He then told the driver where he wanted to go and sat back and relaxed. It did not take long before the driver stopped and asked for the fare. Steve paid the driver well and stood in front of a modern-looking building. Above the main entrance was a big sign in flashing green letters that read *DIGITAL SOLUTIONS*.

Steve had been invited to Seattle by an old school friend, Bob, who was responsible for employee education at Digital Solutions. Always seeking to keep its employees up to date with state-of-the-art programming languages, Digital Solutions wanted to teach them Object REXX. The only problem was that the company worked exclusively on the Windows platform, so its employees did not even know classic REXX. Steve's job—a well paid one—was to introduce Digital Solutions' staff to classic REXX, so that they would have less difficulty learning Object REXX later.

Bob welcomed Steve and gave him a quick tour of the building. Then he led him to the classroom and helped prepare the room for Steve's workshop. Five minutes before the official start, the first employees came in. It took approximately 10 minutes until the last member arrived and Steve had been introduced to the group by his friend. After this, Steve took over, made a few introductory remarks, and then uncovered the blackboard and showed the goals of the lesson [see Figure 1].

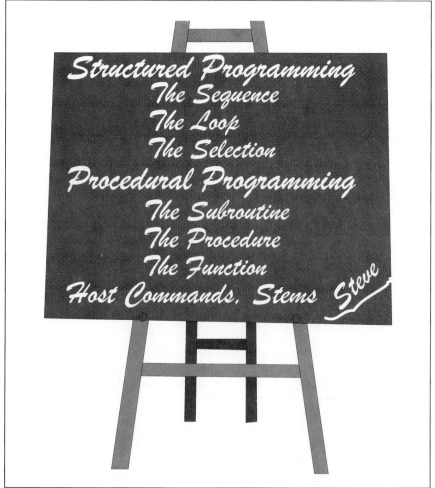

Figure 1. *Goals of the Lesson*

Structured Programming

Steve began his lesson: "For those of you who have already done some programming with other programming languages, this day will be refreshing. For those of you who do not have any experience in programming, it won't be easy, but it won't be a big deal either. The good thing about REXX is that it is so easy to use. It doesn't take much effort to learn the language, because it uses common English words and is an *untyped* language [variables are not declared to be of a certain *type*]. For the nonprogrammers among you, *untyped* might be meaningless, but don't let that bother you. However, the experienced C or Pascal developer will discover the simplification of an untyped language. This morning we will cover the three major aspects of structured programming—sequence, loop, and selection— and in the afternoon we will look at the different types of subroutines—normal subroutine, procedure, and function—and a few other important concepts, such as host commands and stems."

The Sequence

"Normally, each introduction of a programming language starts with the famous *Hello World* program. For us, this is reason enough not to do it. Instead, our first program will display some numbers." Steve went to the blackboard, picked up the chalk, and wrote a few lines of code on it [see Figure 2].

```
/* Our first REXX script */
say "The first 3 numbers of the multiplication table up to ten"
i = 1
say i
i = i + 1
say i
i = i + 1
say i
say program finished
```

Figure 2. *The First REXX Program*

"This doesn't look too complicated, does it?" asked Steve rhetorically. "The first line of our program is a comment, which means that the line is ignored during program execution. Some of you might wonder why the comment says *script* instead of *program*. Well, REXX belongs to the category of scripting languages, but you can call it a program or a script; it's up to you. It is recommended that you start a REXX script with a comment, for compatibility reasons. The comment in the first line is necessary on other systems like OS/2 or MVS. One major advantage of classic REXX and Object REXX is that your scripts are easy to port to different systems. If you forget to make the first line a comment, it cannot be ported unchanged to other systems.

"Let's go on to the second line. *Say* is an instruction to display a line of text on the screen. The text you want to display should be enclosed in quotes. You can use either double quotes or single quotes. The only restriction is that the quotes match. If you start the text with a single quote, you must end it with a single quote. If you're using special symbols in your text, such as +, !, /, *, $, and &, you have to enclose the text in quotes. The *say* instruction automatically executes a line feed at the end of the output. By the way, REXX isn't case sensitive with regard to symbols. Case sensitivity is enabled only for strings in quotes.

"In the third line, the number 1 is assigned to symbol *i*. If we now display *i* in the next line, 1 will appear on the screen. In the fifth line, the variable *i*—the symbol became a variable by the assignment—will be increased by 1. You can see that it's possible to assign a value of an expression to a variable that's used in the expression itself. In the sixth line, the variable will be displayed and the same procedure will be repeated one more time. The last line finally displays the text *PROGRAM FINISHED* in upper case."

Steve drew a frame on the right side of the blackboard and wrote the output of his program in it [see Figure 3].

```
The first 3 numbers of the multiplication table up to ten
1
2
3
PROGRAM FINISHED
```

Figure 3. *Output of the First REXX Program*

"Why is *program finished* displayed in upper case, although you wrote it in lower case?," a well-dressed man in the second row asked. "Is it because of the quotes?"

"Yes, it is," answered Steve, glad that there was some participation. "That's an important issue in REXX. The text in the first line is treated by REXX as one text string because of the quotes. The text in the last line, however, isn't a text string at all. For us human beings, it's recognizable as a text string, but for REXX, *program* is a potential variable, as is *finished*. What the last line of the program does is to display the potential variables *program* and *finished* in one line. The exception here is that REXX returns the name of a potential variable in upper case if no value has been assigned. In that case the potential variable becomes a string. Everything placed within quotes is no longer treated as a potential or real variable, but as a text string. I know that this sounds a bit complicated, but you'll soon discover that this is a good way of treating symbols. Now you can switch on your computers, because you're going to write a REXX program."

Suddenly there was a lot of noise. One could hear the power switches of the PCs clicking like machine guns, and then the ventilators started to hum. Steve was hoping that the air conditioning worked properly; otherwise, in half an hour, the room would feel like a sauna!

"To write your program you can use whatever text editor you want. Notepad isn't the best choice, because there is no line counter, but for smaller programs it is sufficient. I haven't yet mentioned how to execute your program. When you're finished editing, save the file and type `rexx program.rex` on the command prompt, where *program.rex* stands for the name you gave your REXX program. `.REX` is the recommended file extension for REXX scripts on Windows. If you use `.REX` or `.CMD` as the file extension for your script, you can leave it out when executing the program with the *rexx* command. You have to be careful using `.CMD` on Windows NT, because if you try to execute your program and you forget *rexx* in front of it, the system will interpret the script as a command file. If you're familiar with REXX on OS/2, I guarantee that you'll make this mistake. Now let's come to your first exercise. Your task is to write a REXX program that works with symbols and produces the output shown on the blackboard." [See Figure 4.]

```
This program has been written by Steve
 5
 +
 7.5
 ----
 12.5
 ====
5 multiplied by 7.5 is 37.5
25 / 5 = 5
Program finished!
```

Figure 4. *Exercise 1: Symbols*

"The requirement for your script is that all of the calculations must be done by REXX and not typed in directly. The symbol for multiplication is the *asterisk* [*], the symbol for the division as shown in the exercise output is the *slash* [/]. Go to work."

Steve's students started an editor and began to write the script. During that time, Steve prepared the solution. It's recommended that you—the reader—also create a REXX program that solves the problem described above.

After 15 minutes Steve could see that most of the students were doing something else, so he decided to conclude the first exercise and present his solution. "It seems to me that most of you are done with the program. I'm going to show you my solution and we'll discuss it. It may vary from yours, but that's to be expected, because most of the time, there is more than one algorithm to solve a specific problem."

Steve switched on the overhead projector and the tablet that was connected to his ThinkPad. He had to adjust the sharpness a bit to make his script readable on the wall [see Figure 5].

```
/* Exercise 1 */                                            1
a = 5                                                       2
b = 7.5                                                     3
author = "Steve"                                            4
say "This program has been written by" author              5
say; say " "a                                               6
say " +"                                                    7
say " "b                                                    8
say "----"; say a+b; say "===="; say                        9
say a" multiplied by "b "is" a*b                           10
say; say "25 /" a "=" 25/a                                 11
say; say "Program finished!"                               12
```

Figure 5. *Solution for Exercise 1*

"This is not the easiest way to solve the problem," began Steve, explaining his script, "but the way I did it, it is easy to take numbers other than 5 or 7.5. In lines 2 through 4, I assign numerical values to variables *a* and *b*, and my name to *author*. In line 5, the first output line will be displayed. It's important to notice that the blank between *by"* and *author* is displayed although it is not between the quotes. The stand-alone *say* without any parameters in line 6 is for the blank line. The semicolon [;] tells REXX that a new statement begins. Usually each REXX statement is coded in a separate line, but with the semicolon it's possible to circumvent this. In the same program line, the third line of the output is produced. Instead of the number 5, *a* is used to display 5. Then the + sign is printed—notice that it's between quotes. After that, 7.5 is displayed using variable *b*; then the dashed line. You can see in line 9 that it's even possible to use four statements in one line, separated by semicolons. The second statement in this line calculates 5 + 7.5 and displays the result. Lines 10 and 11 on the screen follow the same pattern. Whenever an operator has to be displayed, it must be within quotes. It's not too difficult, is it?"

Nobody seemed to take this as a serious question, so there was hardly any reaction. Steve then suggested that his students try running the same program without coding the operators in quotes. He also gave them a few minutes to correct their programs and instructed them to use variables instead of the hard-coded numbers. After the students were done with the editing, Steve continued with the next point on the agenda.

"All we have done so far is to put data to the screen. For the next program, we're going to interact with the user by asking him or her for the numbers to add, multiply, or divide. My solution for Exercise 1 is really easy to extend to user interaction. The statement to read a line from the keyboard is *PULL*. I forgot to tell you that for REXX there's no difference between a number and a string. If you type say 7.5, the string 7.5 will be displayed on the screen. The difference between the string *Hello* and *7.5* is that 7.5 can be treated as a numerical value and therefore used in a formula. When you code *pull var*, the program reads a string from the keyboard into the named variable. If the user enters a number, this variable can be used for a calculation. To make the above script [see Figure 5] user interactive, you just have to replace a = 5 and b = 7.5 by say "a?";pull a and say "b?";pull b. Try to solve the next problem. The screen output should look like the right side of the blackboard, and the values should be prompted from the user. Let's go." [See Figure 6.]

```
Please enter your name:
Steve
How old are you?
24
Steve, you'll be "74" in 50 years.
```

Figure 6. *Exercise 2: User Interaction with Pull*

Steve presented his solution for the problem and found no need to describe it in detail [see Figure 7]. All he emphasized was how to get the age within double quotes. "It's slightly difficult to read the last line, because there's a mixture of single and double quotes. To display single quotes, you must put them between double quotes ["'"]. To display double quotes, put them in single quotes ['"']. All you have to verify is that an opening single or double quote matches with a closing single or double quote."

```
/* Exercise 2 */
say "Please enter your name:"
pull name
say "How old are you?"
pull age
say name", you'll be" '"'age+50'"' in 50 years.'
```

Figure 7. *Solution for Exercise 2*

"It's time for the first break now," said Steve, feeling the need for it. "Have a coffee or a hot chocolate and be back in 15 minutes. After the break, we'll discuss how computers are majorly superior to man."

The Loop

As usual it took a few minutes longer than specified for everyone to return and be seated. "Before the break, I promised you that you would see how computers are superior to man. What I was thinking about was the speed with which a computer can repeat instructions that humans prepare. If we go back to the program with which we started, we see that we only coded the first three numbers of the table.

It would have been too much effort to code all of the remaining 97 numbers manually. Now we're going to extend the program and display the complete multiplication table up to 100. What we need for this is a *loop*. There are three types of loops:

❑ the *repetitive loop*, which is characterized by a fixed number of repetitions,

❑ the *top-driven loop*, which checks whether or not to stop the execution of the loop at the top of the loop, and

❑ the *bottom-driven loop*, which checks for the stop condition at the bottom of the loop.

"I have prepared a graphic to show you these three loops as Nassi Schneidermann charts, together with the matching REXX notation." [See Figure 8.]

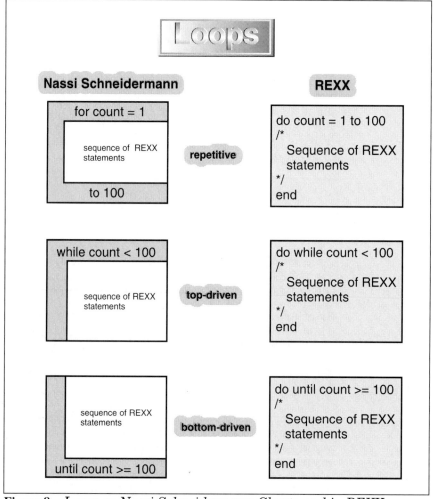

Figure 8. *Loops as Nassi Schneidermann Charts and in REXX*

"The number of repetitions for the *repetitive loop* is controlled by an index variable that is defined after the keyword *do*, assigned an initial value, and then counted up to the maximum given after the keyword *to*. In the diagram the index variable is called *count*, its initial value is 1, and the sequence surrounded by the *do ... end* is repeated 100 times.

"Both *top-driven* and *bottom-driven loops* check the specified condition after each repetition to determine whether the loop should be repeated. The *top-driven loop* checks the condition first. If the condition is true, the sequence within *do ... end* is processed, that is, the condition is a *continuation* condition. The *bottom-driven loop* first processes the sequence within *do ... end* and checks the condition afterward before the next repetition, that is, the condition is a *termination* condition. The condition for both loops is specified in front of the sequence in the *do* statement."

"What exactly are *conditions*?" one of the students asked.

"In this context, a *condition* is an expression that evaluates to 0 or 1, where 0 stands for false and 1 for true," answered Steve. "You should look up the topic *REXX General Concepts - Comparison* and *REXX General Concepts - Logical (Boolean)* in the Object REXX Online Reference. Here is an extract of the list of comparison operators:

=	True if the terms are equal
\=, !=	True if the terms are not equal (inverse of =)
<>, ><	True if the terms are not equal
>	Greater than
<	Less than
>=	Greater than or equal to
\<, !<	Not less than
<=	Less than or equal to
\>, !>	Not greater than

"Now you're familiar with the three types of loops and their REXX notation," Steve said, switching off the overhead projector and facing the audience again. "It shouldn't be difficult to write a script that lists all numbers from 1 to 100. You can choose whatever type of loop you want, but I have to say that I'd prefer the repetitive loop for this kind of problem. You have 10 minutes." The level of noise increased again.

Most of the students finished their exercise before the 10 minutes were up, or at least they stopped trying. While the others were solving the problem, Steve turned the left side of the blackboard over, where he had prepared the solution [see Figure 9].

```
/* Exercise 3 */
say "The multiplication tables up to 100:"
do i = 1 to 100
    say i
end

say "Press any key to continue..."
pull

/* now let's do it backward */
say "The numbers from 100 back to 1:"
do i = 100 by -1 to 1
    say i
end
```

Figure 9. *Solution for Exercise 3: Loops*

"Because the program would have been so short, I did a second loop that counts the numbers back from 100 to 1," explained Steve. "You could almost take the first loop directly from the graphic. All you would have to add was the *say* within the loop. Those of you who used the *while* or *until* loop noticed that two more lines were required, one to initialize the index variable to 1, and one to increase it. Well, the statements for the second loop tell REXX to start with i=100 and count down to 1. It's necessary to use *by -1*, otherwise the loop isn't executed a single time."

"Can only 1 or -1 be used for *by?*" a young lady in the first row on the left side asked, a little bit shyly.

"Good point," Steve tried to encourage her. "You can use any number as the *by* value. Even zero is possible, but you should avoid using it, or you'll get an infinite loop. *Infinite* loop means that the condition check, whether or not to repeat the loop, returns true all the time, which causes the loop to run ad infinitum. I hope that some of you have already discovered how easy it is to develop programs with REXX."

The Selection

"Selection is the third element of structured programming. Think about your daily life," Steve invited the audience. "You'll discover that you encounter selection throughout the day. Immediately after you wake up, you must decide whether to get up or go back to sleep for a couple of minutes. If you choose the uncomfortable alternative, you must move your body out of bed and decide whether to take a shower before or after breakfast. For breakfast, you have to decide whether you want to have ham or jam on your toast. And so on. You can do a single selection in REXX with the *if ... then ...* statement. To do a multiple selection, you can use a *select* group. On the graphic you can see the Nassi Schneidermann charts and the corresponding REXX notation." Steve loaded the necessary file into Freelance, went toward the projector, and switched it on [see Figure 10].

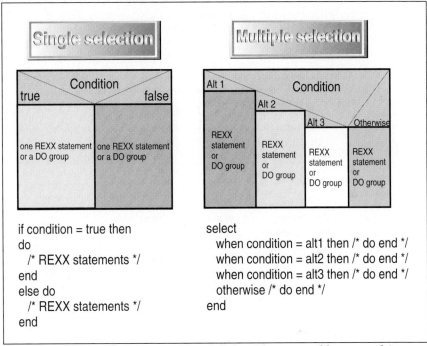

```
if condition = true then
do
    /* REXX statements */
end
else do
    /* REXX statements */
end
```

```
select
    when condition = alt1 then /* do end */
    when condition = alt2 then /* do end */
    when condition = alt3 then /* do end */
    otherwise /* do end */
end
```

Figure 10. *The Selections as Nassi Schneidermann Charts and in REXX*

"To challenge your brains a bit, let's do Exercise 4," said Steve, smiling. "The output will look like this." Steve pointed toward the blackboard where he wrote down the output of the exercise [see Figure 11].

```
/* scenario for a male person */       /* scenario for a female person */
Please enter your name:                 Please enter your name:
Steve                                   Sheila
Steve, are you male or female?          Sheila, are you male or female?
male                                    female
Steve, as a man, do you like sports?    Sheila, as a woman, do you like cooking?
yes                                     no
Steve is a man and he likes sports!     Sheila is a woman and she doesn't like cooking!
```

Figure 11. *Exercise 4: Using the Single Selection*

"On the blackboard you can see the output of two scenarios. The scenario on the left is for a male who likes sports, and the scenario on the right is for a female who doesn't like cooking. Your program should be able to handle all possible scenarios for male or female, and like or not like. By the way, to help prevent syntax errors, because *else* and *end* are two separate statements, you cannot placed them on the same line, unless you separate them with a semicolon. The values of your program must again be prompted from the user. Good luck!"

Steve gave them 30 minutes to solve Exercise 4. He walked around the classroom to see how his students were doing. Some of them wrote the program without problems, but others didn't know what to do at all. Then he said, "I forgot to tell you that it's possible to use an *if* statement within a part of another *if* statement. This might help you solving the problem. If you manage to solve the problem without using nested *if* statements, it would be great."

"Let me first show you the easier solution, which most of you I'm sure could figure out," started Steve, explaining the solution for Exercise 4 [see Figure 12].

```
/* Exercise number 4 */
say "Please enter your name:"
pull name
say name", are you male or female?"
pull sex
if sex = "MALE" then do
    say name", as a man, do you like sports?"
    pull likeit
    if likeit = "YES" then
        say name "is a man and he likes sports!"
    else
        say name "is a man and he doesn't like sports!"
end; else do
    say name", as a woman, do you like cooking?"
    pull likeit
    if likeit = "YES" then
        say name "is a woman and she likes cooking!"
    else
        say name "is a woman and she doesn't like cooking!"
end
```

Figure 12. *Solution for Exercise 4: Single Selection—Easy Solution*

"As some of you might have discovered, the value that the user types in by will be assigned to the variable in upper case. This is because *pull* is the short term for *parse upper pull*, which parses the string that is read from the keyboard into the variable. To read a string in mixed case, you can use *parse pull* followed by a variable. We're going to talk more about parsing after we finish discussing this exercise. As you can see on the test, if *likeit* is 'YES', the branch of an *if* statement can be a single statement instead of a *do ... end* group.

"Well, what I don't like about this solution," continued Steve, "is that the same algorithm is written once for a male and once for a female. In our example, the logic that has been placed in the branches of the *if* statement is not too complex, but it's worth writing the program in a different way, nevertheless."

Steve uncovered the other side of the blackboard and presented his second solution [see Figure 13].

```
/* Exercise number 4 */
say "Please enter your name:"
pull name
say name", are you male or female?"
pull sex
if sex = "MALE" then do
   kind = "man"; hobby = "sports"; pronoun = "he"
end; else do
   kind = "woman"; hobby = "cooking"; pronoun = "she"
end
say name", as a" kind", do you like" hobby"?"
pull likeit
if likeit = "YES" then
   say name "is a" kind "and" pronoun "likes" hobby
else
   say name "is a" kind "and" pronoun "doesn't like" hobby
```

Figure 13. *Solution for Exercise 4: Single Selection—Clever Solution*

"You can easily see that I made extensive use of variables, and that I didn't have to place an *if* statement into the branch of another *if* statement. If the sex is male, I set the necessary variables to fit for a man, otherwise I set them to fit for a woman. The following algorithm is the same for both male and female. The difference in the logic is handled by variables. Please use the next five minutes to go through this program so that you can understand what's going on. After this, we'll talk about parsing and then we will use multiple selection."

Steve wiped off the blackboard and prepared the multiple selection exercise. "Before we use multiple selection, I'd like to show you the way *parse* works in REXX. With *parse* you can assign data from various sources to one or more variables. One of the possible sources is the default input stream, which is used by our *pull*—short for *parse upper pull*. Another source can be a variable, which makes it possible to assign the contents of a variable to various other variables. There are still other sources, but it would be a mistake to mention them all at this time. Because *parse* is a major element of REXX, I recommend that you look up this topic in the Object REXX reference manual. To demonstrate the rules of parsing, I did a graphic that describes sample processes of parsing." Steve searched for the graphic in the current directory and called it into Freelance [see Figure 14].

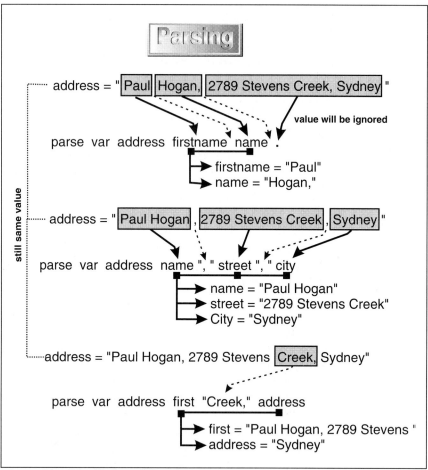

Figure 14. *The Rules of Parsing*

Steve didn't say much about the chart. He mentioned that the dotted arrows indicate the separation characters for the parsing; in the first *parse* statement the separators are blanks, in the second the separators are the comma and a blank [", "], and in the third the separator is "Creek, ". He also told them not to forget that blanks are just like other characters, except that multiple blanks are treated as one. After five minutes he closed the file and switched off the overhead and the tablet. He then gave instructions for the next exercise, "On the blackboard you can see the output of our next example." [See Figure 15.]

```
------------------------------------------------------------------
                    Multiple Selection Example
------------------------------------------------------------------
Please enter a number between 0 and 9:
6
The number you entered was 6, in letters SIX
------------------------------------------------------------------
```

Figure 15. *Exercise 5: Using Multiple Selection*

Steve went on, "What the program should do is to display the number that the user entered in letters. You are required to check for the numbers between 0 and 9 only. The lines in the output consist of 50 dash characters. Try not to use say "----------------..." to display these lines, but do it in a more clever way. You should be able to solve the problem within 20 minutes. One piece of information you might need is that the double splitbar [| |] is used to concatenate text strings."

The 20 minutes passed by quickly, and Steve discussed his solution with his students [see Figure 16].

```
/* Exercise 5 */
i = 0; s = ""
do while i < 50
    s = s||"-"
    i = i +1
end
say s; say "            Multiple Selection Example"; say s; say
say "Please enter a number between 0 and 9:"
pull number
select
    when number = 0 then letnum = "NULL"
    when number = 1 then letnum = "ONE"
    when number = 2 then letnum = "TWO"
    when number = 3 then letnum = "THREE"
    when number = 4 then letnum = "FOUR"
    when number = 5 then letnum = "FIVE"
    when number = 6 then letnum = "SIX"
    when number = 7 then letnum = "SEVEN"
    when number = 8 then letnum = "EIGHT"
    when number = 9 then letnum = "NINE"
    otherwise letnum = "UNKNOWN"
end
say "The number you entered was" number", in letters" letnum
say s
```

Figure 16. *Solution for Exercise 5: Using Multiple Selection*

"Look at the blackboard," said Steve. "The *do while* loop at the beginning of the program uses the concatenation operator [double splitbar] to build a string *s* that consists of 50 dash characters. All I have to do to display the lines is to code say s. Because the say instructions are really short, I wrote them in one line. The user input is assigned to the variable *number*, which is checked in the select group. All possible conditions must be placed within the select block between *when* and *then*. The expression after *then* is processed if the condition is true. Because only one condition can match in a *select* group, the expression of the first condition that is true will be executed. If none of the conditions is true, the *otherwise* branch is processed. Leaving out the *otherwise* will cause an error if none of the conditions matches. If the user enters a string that is none of the listed ones, the letters *UNKNOWN* will be displayed. No magic, is it?"

Steve was looking at his Swiss watch and said, "It's time for lunch now. So far we have progressed well in time and covered all elements of structured programming. After the break, we are going to learn something about procedural programming. We'll meet again in one hour. Take care."

The room emptied quickly. Steve went to Bob's office and took him out for lunch. He didn't really like to have lunch with his workshop students because, from his experience, the talking always turned to the issues of the lecture and, hey, what's a break for?

Procedural Programming Using Subroutines

After lunch, most of the students went for a short walk in the park area around the office building, and nearly all managed to return at the designated time. Steve started the second part of the day with these words: "I know that it's not easy to pay attention after lunch, so I brought you a demonstration about what it is possible to do with Object REXX. For the next 15 minutes, you can sit back and relax." Steve showed the students his demonstration, and they seemed to be astonished at what they could do with a scripting language.

"I hope you enjoyed the demonstration and digested your food," Steve continued the lecture. "Now we can start with procedural programming. With procedural programming, your program consists of a main program and one or more subprograms—also called subroutines. The main program is executed in a sequence and can call the subprograms any time to execute them. Once the algorithm in the subprogram is finished, the next instruction of the main program is processed. This graphic illustrates the behavior in a diagram," Steve said, while loading the file and switching on the projector and tablet [see Figure 17].

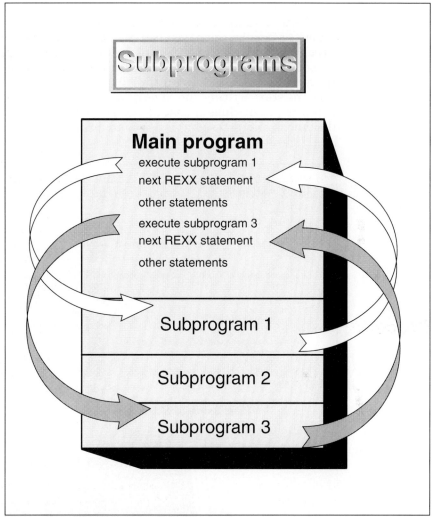

Figure 17. *The Concept of Subprograms*

"The command to call a subprogram is, as you would expect in REXX, *call*. For example, to call the *DoTheLine* subprogram, you have to code `call DoTheLine`. The subprograms must be defined after the main program. To ensure that the subprograms won't be executed after the end of the main program has been reached, you should end a main program with *exit* or *return*."

The Subroutine

"To define a subroutine, code the name of the subprogram followed by a colon. After the colon, you can code the optional keyword *procedure*, which we'll discuss later. For now, we are going to use a subroutine without the *procedure* keyword. For example, to define the *DoTheLine* subroutine, code DoTheLine: after the main program. In the next line you can start writing the algorithm of the subroutine just as in the main program. Have a look at the graphic coming up." Steve moved the mouse and pressed a few keys to display a new chart on the wall [see Figure 18].

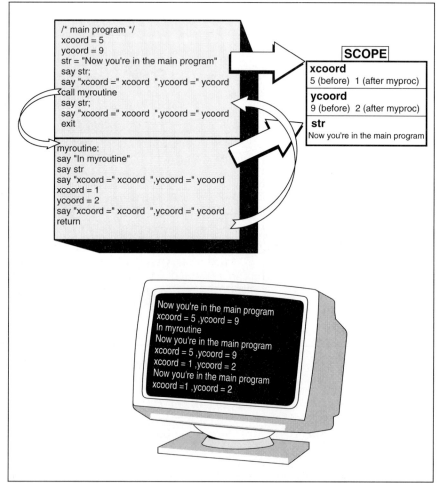

Figure 18. *A Main Program and a Subroutine Share Their Symbols*

"On the graphic you can see a REXX script in the grey box. The upper part of the box contains the main program and the lower part contains the *myroutine* subroutine. The output of the program can be seen on the computer screen. The main program assigns the value 5 to *xcoord*, 9 to *ycoord*, and "Now you're in the main program" to *str* and then displays them. The first two lines of the screen output are produced by the main program, before it calls the subroutine. The so-called scope of the program after the assignments is sketched on the right side of the main program. When the *myroutine* subroutine is called, *In myroutine* is displayed on the screen [third line]."

"The subroutine displays the variables *xcoord, ycoord,* and *str* [see lines 4 and 5 of the screen]. Because a subroutine shares all its symbols with the main program—it uses the same scope—the *say* instructions display lines 4 and 5 of the output, using the values that were assigned to the variables in the main program. Therefore, the "Now you're in the main program" string logically is incorrect. After the assignment in lines 4 and 5 of the subroutine, the *say* instruction in line 6 displays the new assigned values [see line 6 of the screen]. When the procedure returns to the main program, the new values are displayed again [see lines 7 and 8 of the screen]."

"If you look at your program from a logical point of view, it doesn't make sense," one of the typical I'm-smarter-than-you students threw in cheeky.

"Yes," Steve agreed with him, "but it demonstrates the sharing of symbols in an easy and understandable way. Are there any questions on this subject?"

Steve waited for a few seconds, then said, "Good, I didn't think so. This is probably the way most of you would expect it. It's time to do a small exercise again, before you forget what you learned in the morning," said Steve. He took the chalk and wrote down the output of the exercise, while explaining it [see Figure 19].

```
------------------------------------------------------------------
XXX                    THE MONTHS HAVING 31 DAYS                XXX
------------------------------------------------------------------
                          --> January <---
                          --> March <---
                          --> May <--
                          --> July <--
                          --> August <--
                          --> October <--
                          --> December <--
------------------------------------------------------------------
XXX                       End of the program                    XXX
------------------------------------------------------------------
```

Figure 19. *Exercise 6: Using Subroutines*

Steve instructed his students: "To learn how to use subroutines, the task is to use one subroutine to display the header and the footing, and one subroutine to display each month, one month per call."

The students went to work. Most of them had to switch on their screens again because they hadn't wanted to heat up the room unnecessarily. It took the best of them 10 minutes to write the program. The average time was about 20 minutes. After approximately 30 minutes, Steve presented his solution [see Figure 20].

```
/* main program for the 31 day months */
HeadBodyText = "THE MONTHS HAVING 31 DAYS"
call DoHeadBody
month31 = "January";  call DoMonth
month31 = "March";    call DoMonth
month31 = "May";      call DoMonth
month31 = "July";     call DoMonth
month31 = "August";   call DoMonth
month31 = "October";  call DoMonth
month31 = "December"; call DoMonth
HeadBodyText = "   End of the program    "
call DoHeadBody
exit

DoHeadBody:
    if s="S" then do     /* check if s was already initialized */
        s = ""
        do i = 1 to 65
            s = s||"-"
        end
    end
    say s
    say "XXX                      "||HeadBodyText||"                 XXX"
    say s
    return

DoMonth:
    say "                            -->" month31 "<--"
    return
```

Figure 20. *Solution for Exercise 6: Using Subroutines*

"Take your time to examine the solution," Steve said. After a while he asked, "Are there any questions about the script?"

"Could you explain why you are checking whether or not *s* equals *S* in upper case?" one of the male students asked Steve.

"Well," answered Steve, "as I tried to explain with the comment in the code, the *s="S"* checks whether or not the dashed line has been assigned to *s*. If the line has already been built, there's no need to build it a second time. If nothing is assigned to *s*, the value is the symbol itself in upper case."

"Anybody else?" Steve asked the students a second time. There were no further questions, so Steve went on with his topic. "If all subprograms were to use global variables—variables that are shared with the main program—this would be all I have to say on this issue. Unfortunately, the variables used in subroutines can be either local or global. Of course, the *unfortunately* refers only to the educational point of view. The choice between local and global offers significant advantages. If you read the Object REXX reference manual, you'll find the term *scope*. I mentioned it already in the context of the previous example. A scope is the range in which an Object REXX symbol is known. If you define a normal subroutine like that described above, all symbols used within the subroutine are global."

The Procedure

"If you're using a procedure instead, all symbols within the procedure are local. *Local* means that the symbols in the procedure can have the same name as the symbols of the main program, but they point to another object."

"How is a procedure defined?" the young lady in the first row asked charmingly.

"A procedure is defined in the same way as a normal subroutine, except that you specify the additional keyword *procedure* after the subroutine name and the colon," Steve answered, looking deeply into her eyes, but he realized in time that he was here for business and not for pleasure. "To define, for example, a procedure named *PrintBill*, you must code `PrintBill: procedure.`"

"Because all symbols are local," Steve continued, "the modifications made to them within the procedure don't affect the symbols within the main program. Whenever the procedure is entered, all of the symbols used in the procedure are reset. The scopes of the procedure and the main program are different." Steve started his Freelance, selected *open* in the *file* menu, and searched for the particular chart. After a few seconds he found it and displayed it in full screen size [see Figure 21].

"In this graphic the same main program is used as in the previous chart [see Figure 18 on page 22], except that *myproc* will be called instead of *myroutine*. The scope of the procedure at its entrance is shown on the right side below the scope of the main program. The procedure displays the variables *str*, *xcoord*, and *ycoord* [see lines 4 and 5 of the screen]. Because the subroutine uses its own scope and nothing has been assigned to these symbols within the subprogram, the *say* instructions display the symbols themselves in upper case. After the assignment in lines 4 and 5 of the procedure, the *say* instruction in line 6 displays the new assigned values [see line 6 of the screen].

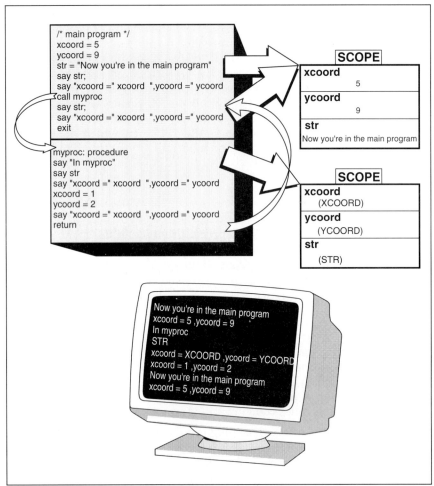

Figure 21. *Scopes of a Main Program and a Procedure Using Local Symbols*

When the procedure returns to the main program, the scope of the procedure is removed. Thus the changes to *xcoord* and *ycoord* didn't affect the variables with the same name in the main program. The values are the same as before [see lines 7 and 8 of the screen]."

"What happens if the procedure is called a second or third time?" one of the students asked.

"When the procedure is called again," explained Steve, "a new scope is created and the symbols will be uninitialized again. The procedure will produce exactly the same output the second time around."

"What's the *return* statement for?" the guy next to the charming lady asked.

"*Return* must be used to go back to the main program," answered Steve, who then went on with the topic. "Using local symbols, you cannot pass values to a procedure by setting them in the main program before calling the subprogram. There are special instructions to pass values from the main program to a procedure. To pass values to a subprogram, you must list them behind the subprogram name in the *call* statement. The symbols or variables are usually separated by a comma. For example, to pass *6, age*, and *name* to the *DisplayData* procedure you would code `call DisplayData 6, age, name.`"

"To retrieve the arguments from the main program, you use *parse arg* in the subprocedure. *Arg* is another source for the *parse* instruction. The *parse arg* instruction follows the normal parsing rules. To retrieve the values of the example, you would code `parse arg number, age, dspname`—the names of the variables in the parse list may be different. Remember that as long as your procedure does not use global symbols, *age* in the main program and *age* in the subprogram are different symbols."

"To clarify the way a procedure and arguments can be used, we are going to discuss the following program, which produces the same output as Exercise 6," Steve said, while searching for the right text file on his ThinkPad. He found it, loaded it into an editor, and switched on the tablet [see Figure 22].

```
/* main program for the 31 day months */
call DoHeadBody "THE MONTHS HAVING 31 DAYS"
call DoMonth "January"
call DoMonth "March"
call DoMonth "May"
call DoMonth "July"
call DoMonth "August"
call DoMonth "October"
call DoMonth "December"
call DoHeadBody "   End of the program     "
exit
DoHeadBody: procedure
   parse arg text
   s = ""
   do i = 1 to 65
      s = s||"-"
   end
   say s
   say "XXX               " || text || "               XXX"
   say s
return
DoMonth: procedure
   parse arg month31
   say "                        -->" month31 "<--"
return
```

Figure 22. *Solution for Exercise 6: Using Procedures with Arguments*

Steve gave them some time to look at the program and then emphasized that this was a more natural way to pass values to a subroutine than using global variables. The same student, who asked before about *s="S"*, asked why this time the check was not done. Steve explained to him that the variable *s* is local and therefore the value of the first processing is not preserved when the subroutine is called the second time. He then said, "If you'd like to pass more than one argument, you must separate the arguments with a comma in both statements; that is, when the procedure is called, and in the *parse* statement."

Steve asked his standard question—whether anyone had a question—and, after waiting a few seconds, he continued. "Well, so far we've discussed the entire sharing of variables and the complete separation of variables. We also have discussed how to pass arguments from the main program to a procedure. There's also a way to share only particular variables between two program parts. The instruction to share symbols between scopes is called *expose*. It must be placed immediately after the subprogram header—in our case after the *procedure* keyword. *Expose* is followed by a list of the symbols that are shared between the main program and the subprogram. A symbol that is exposed keeps the value of the main program when the subprogram is entered, and it keeps the value assigned in the subprogram when control is returned. An exposed symbol is located in the same scope for both the main program and the procedure." Steve closed the old file and loaded the new file into Freelance [see Figure 23].

"The graphic is similar to the previous two. The symbols *xcoord* and *ycoord* are exposed. When the procedure is called, these two symbols will still be positioned in the same scope. Because of this, the *say* instruction in line 4 of the procedure displays the values that have been assigned to the symbols in the main menu. In contrast to this, the symbol *str* has not been exposed and therefore belongs to another scope, the local scope of the procedure. This scope will be created whenever the procedure is entered. For this reason *STR* is displayed by the subprogram [see line 4 of the screen]. After the procedure is executed, *xcoord* and *ycoord* keep their values [see line 8 of the screen]. In contrast, the scope containing *str* is destroyed, but, because the symbol *str* of the main program is different from the local symbol *str*, it is not affected by the execution of the procedure. Therefore, 'Now you're in the main program' is displayed [see line 7 of the screen]."

Steve turned to the student who had asked the questions about the dash line variable and said, "If you remember the last exercise, in the first solution I tested whether or not the dashed line was already assigned to *s*, and in the second I did not. If *s* were exposed, I could do the same test in the solution with the procedures."

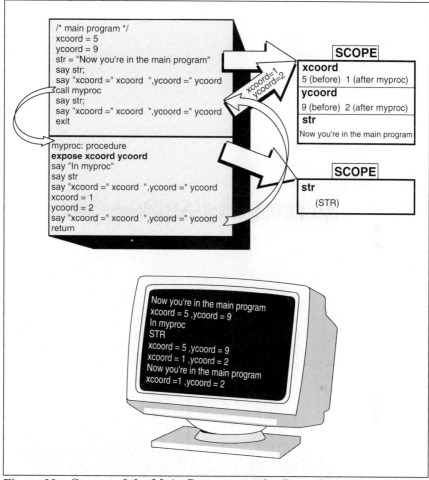

Figure 23. *Scopes of the Main Program and a Procedure Exposing Global Symbols*

The Function

"To bring the subject of subroutines to a close, we're going to discuss another type of subroutine, the *function*. Looking at the procedure, you'll notice that it's only possible to pass values to the procedure, but not to return a value from the procedure, unless you're using global symbols that have been exposed. Using functions is a way of getting a value back from a subroutine, although no global variables are used. This isn't the only advantage of functions; you can assign the return value to another symbol or you can even use them within a term to do calculations with the return value."

Steve walked to the blackboard, picked up the eraser, and erased the old stuff. He then wrote say GetSquareSize() * 2 * GetSquareHeight() on the board. Pointing to the text, Steve said, "This is a term to calculate the volume of a cuboid. What is special in this statement is that functions are called instead of providing numerical values for the length of the edges. That way it is possible to retrieve the values by an algorithm. The length values could be loaded from a file or prompted from the user, or calculated. You can do whatever you want within a function. All that matters is that they return a value for the statement in which they are used. A function can be used instead of a variable anywhere."

"What are the parentheses for?" a student in the last row asked. He had a weak voice, which made it difficult for Steve to understand him.

"Sorry," said Steve, "there was a lot of noise, so I'm not sure if I got you. You asked about the parentheses, is that right?"

"Yes," the student answered.

Steve explained, "The parentheses indicate that it is not a symbol but a function. REXX knows by the parentheses that it has to process the algorithm defined for the function and use its return value. Within the parentheses it is possible to pass arguments—separated by commas— to the subroutine. The convention is that the left parenthesis must be adjacent to the name of the function. The arguments and the right parenthesis can be separated by blanks. Now, let's see how a function is defined. Look at the board and you'll see the definition of a really simple function." Steve said this while he was writing on the board [see Figure 24].

```
/* main program */
a = input()
say a
exit

input: procedure   /* procedure is optional */
   parse pull inp
   return inp
```

Figure 24. *How to Define a Function*

After Steve was done with the function, he turned to the group again and said, "The important distinction between a subroutine and a function is the fact that *return* is followed by a term. This term is the return value of the function and is used to replace the function name within the calling statement. If you write a subroutine that doesn't return a value, and you call it as a function, you get the error message, *Function or message did not return data.*"

"Who knows what this function does, or who has a clue?" Steve asked the group, after he gave them a few seconds to study it.

More than one hand was raised, and Steve pointed to an older gentleman, who hadn't participated yet. "It expects the user to enter data and returns whatever the user enters. The return value is assigned to *a* and then displayed" the gentleman said.

"Very good," Steve encouraged him. "Actually this is not a good sample because very little is done within the function. You would rather place the *parse pull* instruction directly in the main program. But as soon as we start using arguments, this function can be really an improvement." Steve kept the function header and wiped out the rest. He then wrote a few new lines on the board [see Figure 25].

```
/* main program */
say "You are" input("Please enter your age") "years old"
exit
input: procedure
  parse arg text
  say text
  parse pull inp
  return inp
```

Figure 25. *A Function Using Arguments*

"What's the function doing now?" Steve asked again. He waited a short time to give the slower students a chance to answer as well. Finally a middle-aged woman on the left side of the room dared to raise her hand. Steve felt that she must have overcome a lot to participate, so he chose her. "The function displays the text that is given to it and then reads data from the user."

"Good," said Steve, "and do you know what the whole program does?"

"I think it asks the user for the age and then displays it in a sentence," the woman said, somehow uncertain.

"Excellent," said Steve. "In this example one can see that functions simplify programming. In my main program I just use the function without worrying about the implementation of the function. All I have to know is how I have to call the function. If I use the function twice or more in the main program, it saves me lines of code, as the procedure and the subroutine do. Once I decide to change the processing of the function, I can do that without touching the main program. And I can use the function within a term, which is also done in this example. You couldn't use a procedure within the *say* instruction. You could call a procedure beforehand, save the value in a global variable, and then use this variable to display the output."

Steve moved his mouse to interrupt the sleep mode of his ThinkPad and then loaded the two samples into his editor. "Let me briefly show you two programs to illustrate the benefit of functions." [See Figure 26.]

```
/* The benefit of functions */

/* implementation with a procedure */
call squareA 3
say "Square of 3 is" ret
call squareA 5
say "Square of 5 is" ret
call squareA 7
say "Square of 7 is" ret

/* implementation with a function */
say "Square of 3 is" squareB(3)
say "Square of 5 is" squareB(5)
say "Square of 7 is" squareB(7)

exit

squareA: procedure
    expose ret
    parse arg number
    ret = number*number
    return

squareB: procedure
    parse arg number
    return number*number
```

Figure 26. *The Benefit of Using Functions*

"Not only is the calling of the function easier, but also the definition of the function is shorter than the definition of the procedure, and you are not limited to the symbol *ret*. To make it more impressive, try to implement this construction with procedures." Steve wrote the following term on the board:

```
say "Square of 3,5,7, and 9 =" square(3)"," square(5)"," square(7)", and" square(9)
```

"It would take quite a lot of coding to do it," Steve concluded. "REXX is a powerful language. Apart from writing self-defined functions, it provides a bundle of so-called built-in functions. These functions are provided by the interpreter itself. Some of them are just to simplify programming by providing algorithms users could implement themselves, but that would mean a recurring effort by many programmers. These are, for example, the text processing functions like *delword()*, *subword()*, *word()*, *wordindex()*, *wordlength()*, *wordpos()*, and *words()*.

"Other functions implement basic elements, which cannot be assembled by using other REXX statements. These are, for example, the file manipulation functions or the type conversion functions like *charin()*, *charout()*, *chars()*, *linein()*, *lineout()*, *lines()*, *stream()*, *c2d()*, *c2x()*, *d2c()*, and *d2x()*. This next script demonstrates some of the built-in functions of REXX." Steve positioned the track point of his ThinkPad on the file icon and double-clicked the left button to load it into his editor [see Figure 27].

```
/* Using built-in functions */
call SysCls
day = DATE("W")
date = DATE("L")
say "It is" day "the" date
say
say "Please try to figure out which animal I'm thinking of."
say
say "Possible animals are: elephant, rhinoceros, goat, ant,"
say "lion, sealion, moose, owl, mouse, cat, and shark."
say "The animal is?"
ran = RANDOM(1,11,TIME("S")*TIME("M"))
pull guess
say "You answered the question at" TIME()
ani = SUBWORD("ELEPHANT RHINOCEROS GOAT ANT LION SEALION MOOSE OWL MOUSE" ,
             "CAT SHARK",ran,1)
if WORDPOS(ani, guess) > 0 then do
   call BEEP 440, 500
   say "You found the animal"
   end
else do
   outs = "You didn't know that I was thinking of a" ani
   if POS(LEFT(ani,1),"AEIOU")>0 then
      outs = INSERT("n",outs,LENGTH(outs)-LENGTH(ani)-1,1)
   say outs
end
```

Figure 27. *Using Built-in Functions*

"To understand the preceding example should be no problem. The built-in functions that are used are *beep()*, *date()*, *insert()*, *left()*, *length()*, *pos()*, *random()*, *subword()*, *time()*, and *wordpos()*. *Syscls* is not a built-in function, but belongs to the *RexxUtil* functions that are Windows operating system REXX functions. It is used to clean the console window and reset the cursor to the upper left corner. I just want to explain four more lines of this example:

❑ "The *time* function is used to generate a seed for the *random* function.

❑ "The *subword* function extracts one animal name using the random number. If you remember Exercise 5 [see Figure 16], this would be a simpler way to retrieve the name of the entered digit without using the *select* block.

❑ "The *wordpos* function is used to check whether or not the user typed in the right animal. This function makes it possible to answer with a whole sentence, such as *The animal is an elephant*. The statement simply checks for the existence of *ani* in the reply.

❑ "And now the longest statement in the third from last line. It is used to change the word *a* in the reply to *an* for animals starting with a vowel, for example, "You didn't know that I was thinking of an owl." Function *left* returns the first character of *ani*, which is used in function *pos* to check whether or not it is a vowel. If it is a vowel, function *insert* adds the letter *n* after the *a*, before the name of the animal after calculating the proper position using function *length*.

"This information should be enough to understand the script."

Steve offered his students 10 more minutes to study the example and asked them to look up some of the built-in functions in the Object REXX Online Reference. He used that time to prepare the next script on the blackboard and to have one of his beloved chocolate bars. One of Steve's failings is to eat sweets whenever there is time to relax. After he gobbled down his chocolate and licked his fingers, Steve tried to get the students' attention.

"All we have done so far is call a subroutine, procedure, or function from the main program. To make it a bit more complicated but much more powerful, it is also possible to call a subroutine from another subroutine. The same is true for procedures and functions, and naturally calls between subroutines, procedures, and functions are allowed as well."

"How often can it be done?" a well-dressed man in the second row asked.

"You mean how deep can the subroutines be nested, right?" Steve asked back, in order to give the correct answer.

"Yes, that's what I meant," the man replied.

"The nesting level of subroutines is restricted only by the resources of the REXX interpreter—the so-called stack saves information about which subroutine has been called from where. Calling a subroutine from another subroutine is just like calling them from the main program. Just use the *call* instruction together with the name of the subroutine or the function name together with parentheses within a subroutine. Notice that each subroutine still has its own scope.

"To add to the confusion, it is even possible to call a function from itself. This process is called *recursion*. Using recursive functions can help solve particular problems in a much easier way. Some problems, however, can only be solved by using recursive functions."

Steve went to the blackboard and presented the script he wrote down earlier, while the others were studying the example with the built-in functions [see Figure 28].

```
/* main program to calculate factorials */
call SysCls
say "Please enter a number up to 2000"
pull nr
if (nr > 2000) ¨ (nr < 0) then exit
say "The factorial of" nr "is" factor(nr)
```

Figure 28. *Calculating Factorials: Main Program*

Steve explained his thinking. "On the left side you can see the main program of a script that calculates the factorial of a number given by the user. The main program is transparent for both solutions, the sequential one in the middle of the board [see Figure 29] and the recursive one on the right side of the board [see Figure 30]. The main program asks the user for a number between 0 and 2000 and then displays the factorial of that number by calling the *factor* function, which can be implemented in one of two ways."

```
/* sequential calculation of factorials */
factor: procedure
  parse arg fact
  result = fact
  do i = fact-1 to 2 by -1
     result = result * i
  end
  return result
```

Figure 29. *Calculating Factorials: Sequential Function*

"In the sequential solution, a *do* loop is used to calculate the factorial by multiplying the given number by the next smaller number, and the result of this multiplication by the next smaller one again, and so forth, until the program reaches the number 2."

```
/* recursive calculation of factorials */
factor: procedure
  parse arg fact
  if fact = 1 then return 1
  else return fact * factor(fact-1)
```

Figure 30. *Calculating Factorials: Recursive Function*

"The philosophy used for the recursive solution is a different one. The approach is the following: take, for example, the factorial of 7. The factorial of 7 can be calculated by multiplying 7 by the factorial of 6. The factorial of 6 on the other hand is 6 multiplied by the factorial of 5, and so forth, until you calculate the factorial of 2 by multiplying 2 by the factorial of 1, which is 1. This is where the recursion stops, and the number 1 is returned as the value for the factorial of 1.

"Before we have another break, I just want to add that the statement *call* can not only be used to call subroutines, but you can also call external REXX programs by specifying the program name after *call*. If you want to make sure that the file name is treated correctly, I recommend enclosing the file name within quotes. An external program called as a subroutine has the same scope as a procedure, meaning that all the caller's variables are hidden. You can get complete information about *call* by reading the chapter on *call* in the Object REXX Online Reference. For now, that's enough and we'll have a short coffee break."

Host Commands

"The next topic is host commands," Steve continued after the coffee break. "Host commands are an important issue because REXX is a scripting language that offers easy access to other environments, such as the command processor of Windows NT or Windows 95. A command in the Object REXX Online Reference is defined as *a clause consisting of only an expression; the expression is evaluated and the result is passed as a command string to some external environment*."

"Such a command is, for example, *dir*, assuming that no value has been assigned to the symbol before. If no other subcommand handler has been installed, *dir* is passed on to the Windows command processor and lists the contents of the current directory—the display of the command processor is visible in the text console interface [REXX.EXE]. If *dir* is used as a variable by previously having assigned any value to that symbol, the value of *dir* is passed on to the command processor. To make sure that the desired command is processed by the system, you should always code the command enclosed in quotes. The following small program demonstrates how commands are handled by REXX." [See Figure 31.]

```
dir = "copy c:\windows\*.txt d:\tmp"
dir
"dir"
date("S")
```

Figure 31. *Invoking Host Commands in REXX*

"This script consists of one assignment and three commands. In line 2, *dir* is not a symbol but a variable containing the value *"copy c:\windows*.txt d:\tmp"*. Therefore the copy command is executed by the command handler. In line 3, because of the quotes, the literal string *dir* is passed on to the subcommand handler. Line 4 picks up on an issue that causes confusion among a lot of REXX programmers. *Date()* as you already know is a built-in function, and the characteristic of a function is that it returns a value. Usually the returned value is assigned to a variable or passed on to a REXX keyword instruction like *say*. In this particular case, the return value is neither assigned to a variable nor used in an instruction, so it is passed on to the command handler. Therefore whenever you see the message 'Bad command or file name' in your output, check whether you are using a function in your program without handling its return value."

One of the students asked, "Is it possible to call real applications from REXX, or are the commands that can be passed on to the system limited to those the Windows command handler can handle?"

Steve was surprised at that well-formulated question and answered, "There is no limitation regarding the commands you can address to the system. If the system doesn't recognize the command, you'll get the error message I mentioned before. It's no problem to invoke Notepad or Write or some other application."

"Are there any further questions concerning this topic?" Steve asked, while he was looking around. He waited for a few seconds and then continued "OK, let's come to the next issue, the stems."

"Actually I do have one more question regarding host commands," the same student interrupted Steve. "How, if at all, do I get back information from the command processor?"

"Thank you," said Steve. "I forgot to mention that issue. Indeed there are two ways to receive data back from the subcommand handler. The first way is to check the special REXX variable, *rc*, which contains the result that the subcommand handler returns. If you have to get more data than just one result, you can use *rxqueue* to redirect the output of the subcommand handler to the specified queue. A command to retrieve all files located in the current directory, for example, would look like this."

Steve took the chalk and wrote a few lines on the board [see Figure 32].

```
/* Using RXQUEUE */
"dir *.* | RXQUEUE" /* DOS command to redirect the output of DIR */
                    /* to the program RXQUEUE */
do while queued() > 0
   pull fname; say fname
end
```

Figure 32. *Communication with a Command Processor Using RXQUEUE*

"What I have done here is to redirect the output of *dir* to *rxqueue*, which pushes the incoming data into the session queue of the current process. After the host command is processed, you can retrieve the data by pulling the individual lines from the queue. The *queued* function returns the number of lines that are left in the queue. The *do while* loop of the script pulls all of the data items from the queue until the queue is empty. If you want to know more about host commands or queuing, see the Object REXX Online Reference or the Object REXX Programming Guide," Steve concluded, finishing the lesson about host commands.

Linking up to the next topic, Steve continued: "I'm nearly finished with my schedule. There is only one issue left—stems and compound variables—that we're going to deal with briefly."

Stems and Compound Variables

"A compound variable or compound symbol contains at least one period and one character on both sides of the period. Let me write down a few examples of compound symbols," Steve said, while scribbling the following list on the blackboard:

```
CAR.1
Car.chassis
Car.engine.cylinders
car.engine.1
truck..color.7
```

Steve explained the list: "If you look at compound symbols as a separate unit, this type of symbol is useful for structuring things that belong together, like the chassis and the engine of a car. A compound symbol can become a compound variable just like any other symbol by assigning it a value, for example, car.1 = "Porsche", car.chassis = "P-STG 78956", or car.engine.cylinders=6."

"A *stem* is a symbol that contains only one period, which must be the last character of the symbol. Our compound symbol list contains two stems, one is *car.*, and the other is *truck..* Stems and compound variables together provide an excellent way of bundling information. The total information in a stem can be assigned to other stems just by one expression, and a stem also can be passed on to a subroutine as an argument. This example demonstrates the use of stems and compound variables." Steve opened the display of his ThinkPad, loaded the appropriate file and switched on the overhead projector and tablet to reveal a script for using stems and compound variables [see Figure 33].

```
/* How to use stems */

call SysCls                    /* clear the window */
A_Privat. = ""                 /* initialize all fields of the stem with blank */
A_Business. = ""

call ReadAddress A_Privat., "Private Address"
                               /* copy contents of A_Privat. into A_Business. */
do i over A_Privat.
   A_Business.i = A_Privat.i
end

call ReadAddress A_Business., "Business Address"

call SysCls
say "Press any key to continue..."
call SysGetKey("NOECHO")  /* wait until a key is pressed */
call SysCls
call DisplayAddress A_Privat., "Private Address"
call DisplayAddress A_Business., "Business Address"
exit
```

Figure 33. *(Part 1 of 2) Using Stems and Compound Variables*

```
ReadAddress: procedure
   use arg Addr., OutText              /* USE needed to access stem. */
   say OutText
   say Copies("-",40)
   parse value SysCurPos() with row col /* get the current cursor position */
   say "Name?"
   call DisplayValue Addr.Name, row+1
   pull tmp
   if tmp \= "" then Addr.Name = tmp   /* only assign data to compound */
   say "Street?"                       /* variable if input is not empty */
   call DisplayValue Addr.Street, row+3
   pull tmp
   if tmp \= "" then Addr.Street = tmp
   say "Zipcode and City?"
   call DisplayValue Addr.City, row+5
   pull tmp
   if tmp \= "" then Addr.City = tmp
   say "Country?"
   call DisplayValue Addr.Country, row+7
   pull tmp
   if tmp \= "" then Addr.Country = tmp
   say Copies("-",40)
   return

DisplayValue: procedure
   parse arg Value, Row
   ret = SysCurPos(21, 79)             /* clear old lines */
   say Copies(" ",160)
   ret = SysCurPos(23, 1)              /* set cursor to bottom line */
   if Value \= "" then
      say "--> current value:" Value
   else
      say "--> empty field"
   ret = SysCurPos(Row,1)             /* set cursor below prompt */
   return

DisplayAddress: procedure
   use arg Addr., OutText              /* USE needed to access stem. */
   say Copies("-",Length(OutText)+4)
   say "|" OutText "|"
   say Copies("-",Length(OutText)+4)
   say Left("Name:",15) || Addr.Name
   say Left("Street:",15) || Addr.Street
   say Left("ZIP and City:",15) || Addr.City
   say
   say Left("Country:",15) || Addr.Country
   say
   say
   return
```

Figure 33. *(Part 2 of 2) Using Stems and Compound Variables*

"Stems are a bit tricky to handle," Steve explained, pointing to his sample script, "and this program may not be self-explanatory. Therefore let me clarify a few things you have to know about stems. I will also explain the new *RexxUtil* functions. The expressions A_Privat. = "" and A_Business. = "" are used to initialize all possible compound variables of the two stems to a null string. Initialized in this way, the assigned value of *A_Privat.Name* or *A_Privat.Any.Field.1* is a null string. To give another example, if you set `MyStem.` = `"empty"` then `say MyStem.MyField` displays the value `empty`.

"In line 8, *ReadAddress* is called to fill *A_Privat.* with the user's input. *ReadAddress* expects two arguments, a stem that receives the input and text that is displayed as a prompt for the input. The *do over* construct in lines 10 through 12 is new to Object REXX and is used to copy each individual entry of *A_Privat.* to *A_Business.*. Assigning `A_Business.=A_Privat.` directly would in fact cause *A_Business.* to return the same values as *A_Privat.*, but modifying a compound variable of *A_Business.* would cause *A_Privat.* to be modified as well because they refer to the same stem. Using the *do over* construct still keeps *A_Privat.* and *A_Business.* as different stems, but with the same compound variable values.

"After the stem copy, the input for *A_Business.* is read from the user.

"*ReadAddress* asks the user for the name, street, city, and country and assigns the input to the compound symbols of the given stem. If the input is empty—only the Enter key was pressed—the compound variable is not changed. *ReadAddress* calls *DisplayValue* to display the current value of a particular compound variable on the bottom of the screen. The *SysCurPos* function of the *RexxUtil* package is used to retrieve or set the cursor position. If no arguments are passed to *SysCurPos*, the current cursor position is returned [row blank col], but not modified.

"In the main program, *SysGetKey("NOECHO")* is used to wait until any key is pressed. After a key is pressed, *DisplayAddress* is used twice to display the data of both stems. The output is formatted using the built-in functions *copies(), length(),* and *left().*

There is still one matter left that I have to mention. There is one statement that we didn't cover yet. Does anybody know which?" Steve asked, scanning the audience for an answer. "Yes, you," Steve said, pointing to one of the students who had raised his hand.

"The *use* is new," the student said. "Up to now we used *parse arg* to retrieve subroutine arguments."

"Fine, thank you," replied Steve. "*Use* is a new statement and in accordance with the Object REXX Online Reference, it is used to perform a direct, one-to-one assignment of arguments to REXX variables. If we were to use `parse arg Addr., OutText` instead of the *use arg*, any compound variable of *Addr* would return the string value of *A_Privat.* or *A_Business.*, which is a null string, because *parse* retrieves the string value of the given stem and assigns it to the subroutine variable *Addr.*, instead of retrieving the whole stem. Changing any compound variable of *Addr.* does not affect the outer stem used as an argument. This is different from using *use*, because *use* retrieves a reference to the outer stem and assigns it to *Addr.*. Each modification of *Addr.* also affects the stem parameter *A_Privat.* or *A_Business.*.

"I know that this sounds a little bit strange, and I think it would be best if we played around with stems and compound variables for a few more minutes. Before I give you time to let your imagination run wild and write your own program that uses stems, I want to show you one more program that illustrates the connection between a stem and a counter." Steve wrote some lines of code on the blackboard [see Figure 34].

```
/* Numbers from 100 to 1 */
do i = 1 to 100
    MyStem.i = 101-i
end
do i over MyStem.
    say "MyStem." || i "=" MyStem.i
end
```

Figure 34. *Stems and Counters*

"If you run this script, you'll notice that the output is not sorted. It isn't sorted because of the *do over* that doesn't process the compound variables in order. The first do-loop fills the variables from MyStem.1 to MyStem.100 with the values from 100 to 1. The important issue here is that the different values are not assigned to MyStem.i, but the value of *i* is resolved first and then the corresponding compound variable is set. So, that's all I have to say about stems and compound symbols. For the next 15 minutes I'd like you to write your own program that uses stems. Please also use subroutines in your program that retrieve stems as arguments and switch between *parse arg, use arg*, and *arg*. After you have finished your program, you'll have some time to ask questions."

Steve switched off the overhead projector and closed his ThinkPad. He then sat down and read his computer magazine. His students seemed eager to write their program. After a while Steve put aside his magazine and started to walk around to answer individual questions. After about 15 minutes, he walked to the front of the room and offered to answer questions his students still had. As usual, there were only a few questions. A half-hour later, Steve ended his lesson and thanked his students for their attentiveness. He put away his materials, cleared the classroom, and went to Bob's office.

Steve and Bob decided to go to the baseball game that evening. Because of all the work with his new company, Steve hadn't had time for sports events for a while, and he missed singing the national anthem, drinking beer, and eating popcorn while laughing at the team mascot. Steve's plane wasn't scheduled to leave until 11 p.m., so there was plenty of time to attend the game. [The Mariners did beat the Yankees that night!]

Hints and Tips

Here are a few hints and tips for beginners:

❑ Use the .CMD or .REX file extension for your executable source programs.

❑ To execute a source program, type:

```
rexx progname
```

REXX automatically looks for .CMD and .REX files.

❑ You can also double-click on the program in the Explorer list. The .CMD and .REX extensions are registered and invoke the REXX interpreter.

❑ You might want to use a file extension other than .CMD or .REX for subroutines that cannot be executed by themselves.

❑ REXX performs a syntax check before executing a program. If it finds any syntax errors, it will not start the program.

❑ REXX generates a tokenized image in memory before executing the program. See *Tokenizing Object REXX Programs* on page 75 for information about saving the tokenized image for performance.

❑ REXX provides a *TRACE* instruction to debug programs by tracing each statement during execution:

```
trace 'r'              /* more options are available */
```

❑ Use the *REXXTRY* program to experiment interactively with REXX statements. Each statement you enter is executed immediately:

```
C:\>rexx rexxtry
 C:\OBJREXX\rexxtry.REX lets you interactively try REXX statements.
    Each string is executed when you hit Enter.
      Enter 'call tell' for a description of the features.
 Go on - try a few...          Enter 'exit' to end.
say '5 times 6 is' 5 * 6
5 times 6 is 30
```

❑ Object REXX for Windows includes a workbench that allows interactive debugging of programs. See *Object REXX Demonstration Workbench* on page 457 for more information.

2

Introducing Object REXX

Object REXX for Windows NT and Windows 95 is a new implementation of the procedures language, REXX. Apart from numerous detailed improvements, this version of REXX includes a full set of OO facilities. It is now called *Object REXX*. This chapter outlines some of the good things that have been added to REXX with the OO version of the language.

Object REXX was available first in OS/2, and now also in Windows NT and Windows 95, and possibly other operating systems and platforms in the future. *in beta on AIX November 1998*
, available on Linux since Summer 1998.

What's New in Object REXX?

Object REXX has many important new facilities; indeed, it is almost a new language. Appendix A, *New Features in Object REXX and Migration,* on page 463 describes these in detail, and Chapter 3, *How Does Object REXX Implement OO?,* on page 57 contains an overview of how Object REXX has implemented its OO facilities. The concurrency capabilities of Object REXX are described in Chapter 13, *Object REXX and Concurrency,* on page 267.

Here are a few of the highlights. Object REXX has:

- A full set of OO facilities
- Concurrency—the ability to do several things at once
- Improved ability to create subroutines with private variables
- Ability to embed source files using the *requires* command
- Ability to handle the error conditions that might arise in a called subroutine
- A *do over* command that visits every variable defined on a stem
- A *parse* command that has more case-handling options
- A *signal* command that can handle five new conditions
- Direct access to SOM objects under OS/2

Object REXX has been designed to be upward-compatible with the previous versions of REXX. With a few minor exceptions described in *Migration Considerations* on page 485, all existing REXX programs should run under Object REXX with no change.

Despite its upward compatibility with prior versions, however, Object REXX is radically different from its predecessors. In classic REXX, every variable that the programmer created is conceptually a character string—even numbers appear to be stored this way. We say *conceptually* because, under the covers, REXX implementations are at liberty to store numbers in either integer or floating-point format, so long as they are always presented in string format when the programmer asks to see them. Since humans represent both numbers and text in string format when they communicate with one another, why shouldn't they continue to do so when talking to computers? This makes programming in classic REXX very simple and intuitive.

In Object REXX, every variable now refers to an object! String objects behave just as they have always done in classic REXX, and arithmetic can still be performed on strings that happen to contain numeric values; but Object REXX introduces a number of new object types and includes facilities for programmers to create even more of their own. We will be looking at these in some detail later. So while the internals have changed a great deal, Object REXX behaves very much the same as classic REXX used to—if you ask it to do the same things.

Perhaps we should mark the end of classic REXX's reign and the beginning of the reign of Object REXX with the proclamation that traditionally greets the death of a monarch and the automatic, immediate succession of his heir:

"The King is dead! Long live the King!"

Why REXX?

The REXX language is only about 15 years old but is already very widely used on IBM operating systems. The first version ran under VM/CMS only, but since then IBM has made REXX a standard component of the following operating systems:

- ❏ VM/ESA
- ❏ MVS/ESA
- ❏ OS/400
- ❏ OS/2
- ❏ PC DOS Version 7
- ❏ AIX (as a PRPQ)
- ❏ Netware (as a PRPQ)

Object REXX, the new and enhanced REXX, is now available on OS/2, Windows NT, and Windows 95.

Other vendors have developed REXX interpreters for various other operating systems. Also, many vendors have developed packages that are coded in REXX and/or generate REXX programs automatically.

The thing that makes REXX so popular is that it is very easy to learn, and REXX code is easy to read and understand—compared to most other computer languages, that is! The language is *interpretive* in style, which means that there is no requirement to pass the source code through a compiler or linker before executing it. REXX programmers can change their code and test the changes immediately. The other great advantage to programmers is that REXX is nondeclarative. Programmers do not have to tell REXX how to store the variables they create. Conventional compiled languages such as COBOL and C do require declarations of this sort, and this roughly doubles the number of lines of code that have to be developed.

Even if we ignore the OO features that Object REXX contains, this new version of the language contains a number of significant improvements that make REXX easier to use and capable of producing more robust code.

Why Object Orientation?

Object orientation is the flavor of the year, perhaps of the decade. Most new language announcements that hit the press include the magic OO phrase, even if the applicability of OO to the product in question is sometimes unclear. Old languages such as C, COBOL, and Pascal have been extended to include OO features. Is OO a silver bullet that will solve all our programming problems, or is it just a fad?

The computer language that introduced OO concepts to the world is Smalltalk. This was originally designed in the 1970s as part of an experiment to see whether children could learn to use computers. We now know that the answer to that question is a resounding "yes!" (It is less clear, however, whether their parents can do likewise.) Smalltalk underwent significant change, but by 1980 it had the features that are indelibly associated with OO today:

❏ Objects grouped in classes
❏ Inheritance
❏ Polymorphism

These concepts are described in Chapter 3, *How Does Object REXX Implement OO?,* on page 57. But before we get into the nuts and bolts of how OO works, we should spend some time discussing the question of whether OO is worth doing at all.

The Productivity Problem

A clinical discussion of OO features does very little to explain *why* they are valuable. There is much talk today of the need for programmers who have been trained in conventional procedural languages such as COBOL to undergo a paradigm shift before they can start to understand and exploit the benefits that OO has to offer.

The benefits claimed for OO design and programming include much greater reuse of code, as well as simpler programs that are easier to understand and modify. Electronic computers have been around for about 50 years. Programmer productivity has improved radically over this time. Even so, the biggest inhibitor to the more extensive use of computers remains our inability to produce good, reliable code quickly enough to meet our users' needs. The tools and techniques that we use today to develop computer applications are still very labor-intensive, when compared to those in other industries. Most people have heard the proud boast of the computer hardware industry:

"If the airline industry had been able to improve its technology as rapidly as has the computer hardware industry, today's airliner would be able to fly anywhere in the world in half an hour and carry 10,000 passengers at a cost of $1."

Sounds impressive. Unfortunately, we in the computer software industry have not nearly as much to boast about. It has been said that:

> "If the airline industry had improved its technology at the same rate as has the computer software industry, today's airliner would be built from parts on the runway by the crew each time it flew, fueled with the finest Scotch whiskey, and used to haul garbage."

Things are not really that bad in the software industry. Our technology has advanced rapidly and consistently since the advent of computers, at a rate that is impressive when measured against any criterion except one—our users' needs. The biggest problem facing software developers is that computer hardware keeps getting cheaper and faster all the time. Applications that were technically possible but completely unaffordable 10 years ago are more than just affordable today; they are compulsory if a business is to compete in the current market.

Fortunately, there is a vast and rapidly growing number of off-the-shelf computer packages. Smaller businesses can often meet all their application needs from these packages. Larger businesses also make extensive use of packages but often need to supplement them with applications that support their core business. In many cases, a company's core computer applications give it the competitive edge that enables it to grow and prosper.

The Reuse Solution

To summarize the previous section: There are not enough programmers and there is not enough time to handcraft all the code required to meet our users' needs. The challenge is to deliver much more function, much more quickly. The only way out of the dilemma is not to try to develop all the code we need but to reuse existing code instead.

Programmers have been reusing code for a very long time. Early operating systems included subroutines to handle the complexities of driving I/O devices, and early languages such as Fortran (first built in 1957) included extensive libraries of subroutines that implemented the complex algorithms needed to calculate trig functions and logs. Most languages allow programmers to develop their own subroutine libraries to handle common requirements, and most information technology (IT) departments make use of these facilities (every installation has at least one date-handling subroutine, for example).

So if we already practice code reuse, what is so special about OO? Properly used, OO allows us to change the way we design and code applications, but to do so we must make a fundamental shift from the *procedural* to the *object-oriented* approach. Changing from procedural to OO application design can be difficult. The experiments in teaching children to use Smalltalk, referred to in *Why Object Orientation?* on page 46, showed that children can learn and use OO concepts quite easily, but for those of us who have been conditioned to design and code with procedural languages, the change to OO requires some unlearning.

Let us try to illustrate the differences between classic procedural design and OO design.

The Waterfall Method

Procedural design has converged on a process called the *waterfall method*. This consists of a series of steps. In theory, each step should be completed before the next is started. The steps are:

- ❏ Gather the business requirements
- ❏ Analyze the requirements
- ❏ Produce a high-level design
- ❏ Produce detailed specifications
- ❏ Code and unit test the specified modules
- ❏ System test the modules together

It has long been known that this approach has a serious drawback, inasmuch as the users have to express their needs fully and formally on paper and then wait 6 to 18 months before they get to see what the IT specialists thought they wanted. It is, in fact, very difficult for anyone to envisage an IT solution to a business need using just paper specs. Usually, the system has to be modified once the users understand how it works. However, the limitations of procedural languages strongly encourage this approach, and it is the norm.

The Spiral Method

Object-oriented tools can be used with the waterfall technique, but a more common approach is the *spiral method*. In this, IT specialists and the users plan to go through the design and implementation phases many times over before the project is complete. The analysts work with the users to identify the various business procedures they need to automate. They then work through the details of each procedure and document them in what is generally called a *use case*. Next, the coders build a small and simple prototype that implements the user interface with just enough logic behind that to make the interface behave as expected. There are no databases or even data models at this stage. The IT specialist and the users then work through the use case with the prototype. The users get an early idea of how the proposed system will help or hinder them in the execution of their responsibilities. They tend to become very involved and excited, then identify changes and new features that they need. In this way, it is also easier to see which features deserve a lower priority.

On the basis of this feedback, the designers revise their use cases and designs, and the coders modify the prototypes to implement the new behavior. The users work with the new prototypes and identify more changes. The entire process repeats several times, then the final version is fleshed out into a robust and reliable application, and delivered to the users. Experience shows that applications designed in this way fit the users' real needs far better than is normally achieved with the waterfall approach.

Prototyping

Prototyping is not a new concept. The idea has been around for a long time. The problem has always been that the classic procedural languages such as COBOL, PL/I, C, and Assembler are not well suited to developing prototypes. It takes too long to build a prototype, and, once developed, the investment in the prototype code is so large that the programmers cannot afford to abandon it. It is very hard to make extensive design changes to procedural code, so the first prototype often ends up being the final product, regardless of how well it fits the users' needs. Further problems arise when several independently prototyped components must be integrated to form the complete application. They often do not fit together, and extensive changes may be required. It is exactly because of these problems that the waterfall method was developed. The users and analysts are required to anticipate every code module that will be needed and to ensure that all the components will fit together. Many experienced users view this as a shrewd maneuver on the part of the IT department, designed to shift the blame for humanity's inability to predict the future from the shoulders of the IT department to those of the users.

Object-oriented languages enable programmers to take a very different approach to building prototypes. Experience shows that OO prototypes are easier to modify and extend and can be changed to meet the users' changing perceptions of what they really need. While the parts of the overall application may be developed independently of each other, OO languages allow these different components to be integrated, forming a working whole with little disruption to any of the parts. The transition from prototype to production code is a smooth process, with few ugly surprises.

The Paradigm Shift

The fundamental difference between procedural and OO designs arises from the fact that procedural languages cannot be extended. Procedural language programmers can use only those features that were built into the procedural language by the vendor that supplies it. The programmer cannot add new commands or data types to the language, no matter how much these may be needed in a given situation.

Object-oriented languages, on the other hand, *are extensible*. Designers and programmers can add new data types to the OO language to meet their unique business needs. These are called *objects*. They can add new operations, called *methods,* to the OO language to manipulate existing or new data types. New objects can be built on top of existing data types within the OO language, and on top of other objects that the programmers have already defined.

If, for example, OO COBOL had been available 20 years ago, life would have been much simpler for the software vendors who introduced major new database management systems (DBMSs) at that time. They could have extended COBOL's capabilities to include support for their DBMSs by developing new class libraries. Lacking this ability, many chose to create completely new computer languages, called *4GLs*, to allow easy access to the features of their DBMSs. A new computer language is a major investment for the vendor that builds it, the programmers who learn to use it, and especially the companies that accumulate legacy code in it.

Procedural languages force the designer and programmer to follow a process known as *stepwise refinement*. The designer first specifies a business requirement at a high level. There are no features in the procedural language that can directly implement the objects described in this design or the actions that must be performed on them. The designer must break each object down into a collection of simpler objects and each action into a series of simpler steps. This process has to be repeated until the objects are so simple that they can be directly represented in the primitive data types supported by the procedural language and the actions can be equated to the primitive operations implemented by the procedural language. The entire stepwise refinement procedure takes place on paper, not in code. Only the final step in the process is captured as code and appears in the application. All prior steps in the process are captured on paper and are not delivered as part of the running application.

Suppose we compare the design and coding of an application in a procedural language to the growth of a tree. The high-level design would correspond to the trunk and major branches of the tree. The detailed designs would correspond to its smaller branches, spreading out into twigs. The actual code would correspond to its leaves. When the application is handed over to the maintenance programmers, they regard the code as the most important thing they get. The design documents usually do not correspond exactly to the code, because the users ask for changes late in the implementation process, and changing the design document is usually low on everyone's priority list. As time goes by and the application undergoes maintenance, the design documents are seldom updated. After a while they are so far out of step with the code that they are useless and are ignored.

To go back to our tree analogy, the maintenance programmers can now see only the leaves, not the branches or twigs that were used to join them all together. From the outside (the users' view) it still looks and behaves like a tree—for a while, but from the inside it becomes increasingly difficult to see how the whole thing hangs together.

Is this gradual loss of visibility and understanding of the program's structure important? Yes it is, vitally so. Every program has an invisible component that we can call the *flow of control*. It's the way the computer sees the program when it executes. This is the most important view of the program, because it determines absolutely what the program does, regardless of what the programmers think it should do. Well-structured programs help the programmer to see what the flow of control will be and, hence, what the program will do. Most programs are not well structured—not so much because their contents are badly structured, but because of what they do *not* contain—the tree's trunk, branches, and twigs, to return to our analogy. Maintenance changes start to have unexpected side effects. Someone saws off a branch without knowing what leaves it supports, someone bends a branch to support new leaves and inadvertently cuts off the flow of sap to some other leaves. After a while, the tree no longer looks anything like a tree from the inside—it looks like a bowl of spaghetti. Then it is time to throw the whole thing out and start again from scratch—and that is a waste of time and money.

Suppose we now compare the design and coding of an application in an OO language to the growth of a tree. Once again, the design would correspond to the trunk and branches of the tree. This time, however, the components of the design *can and should* be written into the code of the final application, rather than written on paper and then discarded. Because OO languages are extensible, the objects and actions described in the design can be written directly into code. If the design speaks of customers ordering, taking delivery, and paying for products, the programmers should create new object types called *Customer* and *Product*, as well as methods that allow product objects to be ordered, delivered, and paid for by customer objects. The high-level program logic can then reflect the high-level design because it talks about exactly the same objects and actions (methods) as does the design document.[1]

In essence, we can turn the design and coding process on its head when we build OO applications. Instead of proceeding with stepwise refinement from a high-level design through successively lower-level, paper-based designs until we get down to the level of the procedural language and then writing the code, we can start by writing the design in code as if all the objects and actions it requires were already part of our target language. Then we use the language's OO facilities to *define* what these objects are, and how they behave. As we define these objects and their behavior, we often find that there is still a gap between the level of abstraction at which we are working and the built-in features of our language. Once again, we boldly code our new

---

[1] People with experience of real-life application construction may at this stage be throwing up their hands in horror. Building new applications tends to generate a huge volume of paper, usually referred to as *The Documentation*. We do not suggest that a 1,000-page mound of paper be shoveled into the code. Most of the documentation exists to explain, criticize, measure, report, and mend the design. Entity-relationship diagrams, data-flow diagrams, action diagrams, and their ilk are a good way of representing design concepts graphically. Gantt charts are a good way of representing plans and progress graphically. All these things generate an amazing amount of paper (which is often pasted up on the walls to show the users how productive the designers have been), but they are not the design. It is our belief that a well-structured OO program that contains its own design will be no bigger than the equivalent program coded with no embedded design in a procedural language. The OO programmers will write much of their logic at a high level against smart objects, while procedural languages constrain us to write all our logic at a low level against dumb objects.

definitions in terms of lower-level objects and actions *as if they already existed.*[2] We will come back later and define these lower-level objects and actions and continue in this way until, at last, all the objects and actions we need are actually present in the OO language we are using.

Please note the use of the word *can* in the preceding paragraph. It is unfortunately quite possible for programmers trained in procedural languages to ignore the capabilities of OO languages to preserve design and to use OO in exactly the same way that they previously used COBOL or C to produce only the low-level code. Proper training and motivation are required if the transition to OO is to be fruitful.

Better Reuse from the OO Approach

The way we design and build applications using OO languages should, therefore, be very different from the way we build them using procedural languages. This change is the biggest one that procedural programmers and analysts must make when moving to OO. Why do we do it this way? What are the benefits?

❑ The biggest long-term benefit is that most of the application's design is encapsulated in its code. It cannot be discarded or ignored. All changes to the application automatically update the detailed design document because it is a living part of the code. This makes long-term maintenance of the application easier and more accurate.

❑ Much of the application logic is written in terms of high-level objects that correspond directly to the objects with which the users work. Programmers and users can speak the same language because they are speaking about the same objects and actions (methods).

❑ Less code is required because it deals with high-level smart objects, such as products, that can do complex things like get ordered by customers, rather than with dumb objects, such as integers, that can do only simple things like arithmetic.

❑ Objects like customers have their data and associated actions (methods) neatly packaged together in OO language definitions. It becomes much easier to locate and reuse customer objects and their associated behavior in other applications.

---

[2] We are not suggesting that we should embark on the design and implementation of a major system without careful analysis and planning. If we simply write a program as thoughts pop into our heads, the results will be as poor with OO languages as they are with procedural ones. We will get "stream of consciousness" programs, or what we might call *Kerouac code.* It may make for entertaining reading, but trying to make it work correctly will be much less fun. Good methods and tools are available to help the OO analyst identify the objects and methods that should form the basis of a new system. However, in this section we are trying to identify what is *different* about OO analysis and design, not what is the same.

❏ When programmers reuse an object, they do not need to know how it works internally. The author of the object can carry out maintenance on it to add new data or functions without impacting any of the programs in which this object is used.

❏ OO languages all come with an extensive library of built-in classes, which can be used to define new objects. These inherit a wealth of high-level function. Much of the tedious low-level coding required to build an application can be eliminated by making use of these class libraries.

Communities of Cooperative Objects

In dealing with the benefits of OO, we have so far restricted ourselves to those that are currently being enjoyed and reported by installations that have made the switch. However, there is a sea of change taking place right now in how objects will be exploited in the future, and it is going to affect all of us.

Bloated PC Software

It is a well-known fact that "shrink-wrap" applications are getting bigger and better every year—with most of the emphasis falling on *bigger*. Ten years ago, the most sophisticated spreadsheet package came on a single floppy. Now it takes a diskette caddy to load the simplest package. Have our needs changed that much over the past 10 years? Has life really become 10 times more complex? Why is shrink-wrap software so bloated? It costs the vendors a fortune to build applications of this size and complexity, so you can be sure they are not doing it for fun. Also, a fact of life with software is: the bigger, the buggier.

Ten years ago, PC enthusiasts sneered at the "big, clumsy, slow" programs that ran on mainframes and rejoiced in their tiny, nippy applications. They have stopped talking about it. Many are watching what is happening in numb silence.

PC software is suffering from "creeping featuritis." One vendor puts in a great new feature, all the competitors put it in, too, as well as a few more unique features of their own. More bullets on the side of the shrink-wrap box. More check-boxes in the endless assessments that PC software magazines run. More entries in the already crowded menu bar. More chapters in the phone-book-sized product manual. More days on the education program. More space on the hard drive. More RAM tied up. More bucks on the bill. Where is it all going? Is this trip really necessary? Most of us use only a fraction of the features of the PC software we run.

Standard Software Components

There is another way, and it is based on the notion of building software from a host of standard, reusable components. We touched on this in *The Productivity Problem* on page 46, with those not-so-funny comparisons between the IT and airline industries. When hardware engineers want to build a system, they pick standard parts out of a catalog and wire them together. Little or none of the componentry that they need has to be invented on the fly. The parts are highly standardized and uniform in their behavior, and there are few surprises when they are clicked together. Generally, the new system works.

Software engineering is light-years away from this model. The way we handcraft code today is reminiscent of the way our ancestors used to manufacture[3] products before the industrial revolution. Programming is still in the "cottage industry" phase of development.

Liberating Objects from Applications

All this is due to change soon—indeed, is changing already. Objects have shown that they can deliver specific functions while encapsulating all their internal workings so that the programmers using them do not have to know what goes on inside. Currently, the object's horizon is limited to the application that contains it. If you want to build a lot of function into an OO application, you have to put a lot of objects into it. About six years ago, the folk in the emerging world of objects realized that objects would become much more useful if objects could be used across different applications, even if the applications were written in different languages—and even if they ran on different computers, maybe even under different operating systems (this democratic vision is not shared by all in the industry).

The CORBA Standard

To make any of this happen, standards are an absolute necessity. A cross-industry standards group called the *Object Management Group* (OMG) was formed in 1989 to develop and publish standards in this area. The OMG has been very industrious and successful, and its membership has risen to over 500. Almost every company involved in building objects is in the OMG and is busy enabling its object software to conform to the OMG standards. The biggest "umbrella" standard from OMG is called the *Common Object Request Broker Architecture* (CORBA). As with all standards, the longer the name, the more arguments and reconciliations went into its formation. The CORBA standard was widely and hotly debated by the members of the OMG, and what came of the crucible is case-hardened steel.

---

[3] *Manufacture:* verb, from Latin *manus,* "a hand," and *facto,* "I make."

IBM's CORBA-compliant object broker implementation is called the *System Object Model* (SOM). It is a standard component of OS/2, AIX, and MVS/ESA. Probably every popular operating system will have a CORBA-compliant object broker from one vendor or another by the end of 1996.

The topic is far too big to fit into the confines of this book. Several excellent publications already exist on this topic alone. We particularly recommend *The Essential Distributed Objects Survival Guide* by Robert Orfali, Dan Harkey, and Jeri Edwards (see full reference in *Related Publications* on page 533).

Note: Object REXX for OS/2 contains support for SOM, whereas Object REXX for Windows NT and Windows 95 does not contain SOM support in its first release.

So Why Object REXX?

In the preceding sections we have reviewed how successful REXX has been and how useful OO facilities are. The marriage of the two is an obvious and welcome step, bringing to the programmer a language with the strengths of both. Object REXX is likely to be widely and enthusiastically embraced by the REXX programming community for the following reasons:

❑ It's free! Everyone is talking about OO nowadays, but getting access to an OO language costs money. Object REXX is available at no extra charge, and Object REXX is a full-function OO language. What better way to get your feet wet in the OO puddle than by using the language you know and love?

❑ Object REXX lets you learn about OO incrementally. While it enables you to build totally nonprocedural code, you can also start adding OO features to existing procedural programs. You do not have to abandon your legacy REXX code or your existing skill base.

❑ The standard REXX trace and debug facilities are still available, even for OO code. You can step through your programs line by line, displaying and setting variables as you go. This makes it easy to understand what is going on.

❑ Object REXX includes new features that make it much easier to build structured and modular applications. REXX is being used to build some very large and complex systems, and these new structuring capabilities are most welcome.

❑ One of the key benefits that OO gives is reuse. REXX programmers are, in general, very familiar with the reuse approach. Programs coded in other languages can be invoked directly from within REXX programs. Commands for other programming environments, such as XEDIT under VM, DB2/2 under OS/2, and DB2 for Windows NT and Windows 95, can be embedded in REXX code. Most REXX programmers are comfortable with a "mix-and-match" approach. Object REXX extends the range of resources available to the REXX programmer to include objects developed in Object REXX

Learning how to exploit OO does not have to be a white-knuckle experience. Object REXX provides an easy path into the world of objects, building on and enhancing existing REXX skills.

3

How Does Object REXX Implement OO?

Object REXX has a very comprehensive set of OO facilities, including multiple inheritance and meta classes (see *Methods* on page 68). It has support both for static class and method construction through embedded declaratives, and for dynamic class and method construction through messages that may be issued at runtime to the built-in Class and Method classes. Here we use only the static, declarative forms.

The Object REXX manuals referenced in *Related Publications* on page 533 contain an excellent description of OO concepts and how Object REXX implements them. We give only a brief and incomplete outline of these capabilities here for the reader's convenience.

We need to start by emphasizing that the magic of OO does not lie in its definition. Many people have labored over descriptions of OO, seeking the philosopher's stone that will transform dull gray code into glistening gold in the concepts of objects, classes, inheritance, and polymorphism. Try as you will, you will not find it there. What is important about OO is the changes it *allows*—but does not *require*—

designers and programmers to make in the way they structure programs. We have tried to explain this in *Why Object Orientation?* on
page 46.

Objects

All of us deal with objects every day of our lives. Things like faucets,
toasters, refrigerators, cars, telephones, photocopiers, fax machines,
and televisions are objects. We use objects to do things. We give commands to objects. We might open a faucet, push down the cook lever on
a toaster, start a car, depress an accelerator or a brake pedal, turn a
steering wheel, dial a number on a telephone or fax machine, or press
a channel change or mute button on a TV remote control.

Objects must be able to obey the commands we issue. They need some
built-in, predefined behavior. In the OO world these are called *methods*.

Object REXX uses the ~ (tilde) operator to invoke a method on an
object.

```
┌─── Invoking methods on an object ─────────────────────────
│
│  car~start
│  car~turn('right')
│  car~speed(55)
│
```

The word preceding the tilde is the object, and the word following it is
the method. Those familiar with classic REXX can think of invoking a
method as something similar to invoking a function. Consider the following code:

```
┌─── Invoking methods compared to functions ────────────────
│
│  aString = 'Hello, World'
│  say aString          (gives:   Hello, World)
│  say reverse(aString) (gives:   dlroW ,olleH)
│  say aString~reverse  (gives:   dlroW ,olleH)
│
```

If every object we encountered differed from all others and had its own
unique set of commands, we could never cope with the daily demands
of living. Humans have learned to standardize the way similar objects
behave and are controlled. Different car models made by different
manufacturers in different countries all have similar controls and
respond in a similar way when these controls are used. Even if we
have to fly to a distant country, we can still operate the cars we find
there with reasonable success. Every car is different. Each has a
unique number plate and engine and chassis serial numbers. Each
has its own unique collection of scratches and bumps and little quirks,

such as the way it hesitates when you floor the accelerator at 50. But cars, and trucks for that matter, behave similarly enough that drivers can move from one to another and cope.

Classes

The world in which programmers must operate is also populated by objects. These objects, too, have their own unique attributes and built-in behavior. Programmers cannot cope with the diversity of objects that they must manage unless they simplify and standardize the behavior and appearance of these objects as much as possible. Quite often, programmers will impose a greater degree of standardization than exists in the real world. A program may insist, for example, that every human has a surname and one or more given names. While this is a common practice in some European countries, in Nordic countries it is not, and the people on other continents have very different practices. We have learned to live with generalizations like these so that programmers need cope only with a subset of the problems the real world contains.

In order to cope with the innate complexity of the world, programmers must seek and impose similarities in behavior across groups of related objects. In OO terminology, a group of related objects is called a *class* or *type*. Once they have identified a class of objects, programmers can define and code the routines, or *methods*, that give these objects their common behavior.

Object REXX uses *directives*, placed at the end of the program, to define classes and methods. A directive starts with two colons (::).

Directives for a class definition

```
::class Car
::method start
   ...
::method turn
   ...
::method speed
   ...
```

Note: Class definitions can also be placed into separate files using the *::requires* directive. (See *The Requires Directive* on page 116.)

Inheritance

So far, we have done little more than coin some trendy new OO terms to describe well-established programming practice. Now we start to add something new and exciting. It's called *inheritance*. It stems from the fact that, although we want to group objects into classes and enforce a common behavior across all of them, some stubbornly refuse to fit a common mold. Cars and dump trucks have similar controls to drive them, but dump trucks have extra controls to manage the dumping mechanism. How can we cope with this irritating diversity? We might be tempted to build the code needed to manage cars, then clone it and extend it to handle trucks. It gets the job done, and we score extra brownie points if our productivity is measured in lines of code, but it creates an extra maintenance burden that will last for as long as the code runs.

Object-oriented languages offer an elegant way of coping with the problem of similar but different classes. Given the problem described above, we could define a *Car* class that implements the behavior common to both cars and dump trucks (for example, starting, steering, and stopping), then define a new class called *DumpTruck* that is a subclass of the *Car* class (see Figure 35).

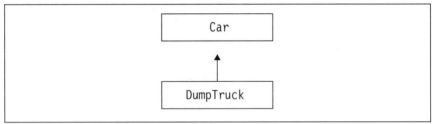

Figure 35. *Car and DumpTruck Class Inheritance Diagram*

The Object REXX class directives might look like the following:

```
┌─── Class directives for inheritance ──────────────────────
::class Car
::method start
    ...
::class DumpTruck subclass Car
::method dump
    ...
```

A subclass *inherits* all the behavior (attributes and methods) of its parent class but can add new attributes and methods of its own. We can add to our *DumpTruck* class just the new behavior that is unique to dump trucks—the ability to dump. So any dump truck objects that we create will automatically inherit all the methods they need to be driven and will also have the methods they need to dump. We have achieved the equivalent of cloning code without actually cloning code. Maintenance is simplified.

A nice side effect of this approach is that when we add new methods to the base *Car* class to handle new behavior such as fuel consumption, all of its subclasses automatically inherit these new methods as well.

Abstract Classes

But what would happen if we needed to add some new methods to the *Car* class that we did *not* want its subclasses to inherit? Suppose we needed to add information about a car's trunk capacities and optional extras—sidewalls, two-tone color schemes, and such? We could abstract from the *Car* and *DumpTruck* classes all the attributes and methods we want them to have in common and put them in a new *abstract* class called *Vehicle*. We would make both *Car* and *DumpTruck* subclasses of the *Vehicle* class (see Figure 36).

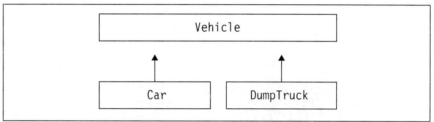

Figure 36. *Abstract Class Inheritance Diagram*

Each would inherit all the common behavior it needs from the base *Vehicle* class, and we could then add to each the behavior that it alone requires. We might never create an object directly from the *Vehicle* class. It would serve just as a handy place to keep common behavior. Since we do not change the names of the *Car* and *DumpTruck* classes, none of the code that deals with them will be affected. All the changes we make are hidden inside the class definitions. This is an example of *encapsulation*, one of the major benefits of OO.

The Object REXX directives required in this case might look like this:

```
┌─── Class directives for an abstract class ────────────────────────┐
│ ::class Vehicle                                                    │
│ ::method start                                                     │
│    ...                                                             │
│                                                                    │
│ ::class Car subclass Vehicle                                       │
│ ::method trunk_capacity                                            │
│    ...                                                             │
│                                                                    │
│ ::class DumpTruck subclass Vehicle                                 │
│ ::method dump                                                      │
│    ...                                                             │
│                                                                    │
└────────────────────────────────────────────────────────────────────┘
```

Can we take this further? Suppose the need arises to deal with trucks other than just dump trucks. How would we handle this situation? In Figure 37, we abstract the behavior that is common to dump trucks and tanker trucks and put it in a new abstract class called *Truck*. We then define *TankerTruck* and *DumpTruck* as subclasses of *Truck*. They both inherit the behavior of the base *Vehicle* abstract class and the behavior of the *Truck* abstract class, then each adds its own unique behavior to its own class.

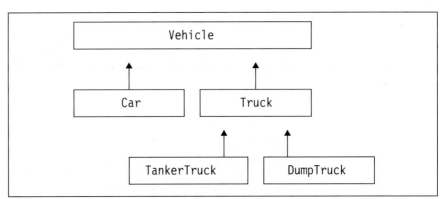

Figure 37. *Multilevel Class Inheritance Diagram*

The Object REXX directives required in this case might look like this:

Class directives for multilevel inheritance

```
::class Vehicle
::method start
   ...
::class Car subclass Vehicle
::method trunk_capacity
   ...
::class Truck subclass Vehicle
::method hitch_horse
   ...
::class DumpTruck subclass Truck
::method dump
   ...
::class TankerTruck subclass Truck
::method fill_tank
   ...
```

We can continue in this way to create as many levels of inheritance as we need.

Multiple Inheritance

The inheritance story could have ended here, but Object REXX takes it further. The Smalltalk language allows each class to have only one parent class from which it can inherit behavior. Object REXX allows classes to inherit from one or many parent classes. Only one can be the direct parent. The other parents are called *mixin* classes. Like abstract classes, they are not used to generate instances. They serve only as containers for attributes and methods that other classes can inherit from them.

Suppose we need to add information about engines to our vehicle fleet. In the old class structure, engine information was contained in the *Vehicle* class. We observe that the same sort of engine is often used in different types (classes) of trucks, and some engines are common between light trucks and cars. We want to separate out the engine information from the rest of the vehicle, which we will call the *Body*. We might do this as shown in Figure 38.

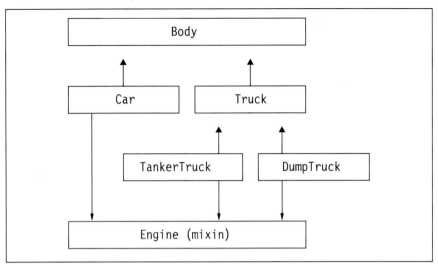

Figure 38. *Mixin Class Multiple Inheritance Diagram*

The Object REXX directives required in this case might look like this:

```
─── Class directives for multiple inheritance ────────────────
::class Body
::method rattle
   ...
::class Engine mixinclass Object
::method start
   ...

::class Car subclass Body inherit Engine
::method trunk_capacity
   ...
::class Truck subclass Body
::method hitch_horse
   ...

::class DumpTruck subclass Truck inherit Engine
::method dump
   ...

::class TankerTruck subclass Truck inherit Engine
::method fill_tank
   ...
```

The old *Vehicle* abstract class has disappeared, its attributes and methods split into two new abstract classes called *Body* and *Engine*. *Body* becomes the direct parent of *Car* and *Truck*, while *Engine* becomes a mixin class. Each vehicle now obtains its body and engine behavior from two different classes.

Object REXX Variable Pools

In classic REXX, by default each .cmd file has its own variable pool. Variables set by code within the .cmd file are available to all other code within the same .cmd file. The programmer can change this by coding the procedure instruction after a label, for example:

```
aProcedure: procedure
```

When *aProcedure* is called, REXX creates a new and private variable pool for *aProcedure*. This remains in effect until *aProcedure* terminates. In this example, none of the code within *aProcedure* can access any of the variables set by the code in the command file, and vice versa.

The programmer can obtain a limited degree of exposure of the variable pool external to *aProcedure* by using the *expose* option. For example:

```
aProcedure: procedure expose variable1 variable2 stem.
```

The variables and stems listed after the *expose* keyword map directly onto the corresponding variables in the variable pool that was active when *aProcedure* was called. Changes that *aProcedure* makes to these exposed variables remain in effect when *aProcedure* terminates. Existing REXX programs work the same way in Object REXX as they do in classic REXX, to preserve compatibility.

Objects are new in Object REXX, and they are handled differently. Each object usually has several variables, or *attributes*, associated with it. If you have 100 employee objects active, each one may have its own name, number, address, and other attributes. Object REXX associates a separate variable pool with each object.

An object's attributes can be accessed only by the methods that are defined within the object's class; in OO terminology, all data is private or *encapsulated*. Each method must specify which of the object's attributes it needs to access by listing them on an *expose* instruction immediately after the method directive (*::method*).

Example of a method

```
::method tag
   expose name address salutation
   separator = 'at:'
   return salutation name separator address
```

In this example, the variables *name*, *address*, and *salutation* are part of the associated object's variable pool. All the other methods in the class that contains this method may access and set these variables if they first expose them. Any variables a method uses that are not in its expose list are local variables and are discarded as soon as the method terminates. In this example, *separator* is a local variable.

Note: If an object inherits methods from different classes, it will have different variable pools in each class. A method defined in one class cannot share a variable with a method in another class. If methods need to share information, the owner of the variable must implement methods to get and set this variable, and the would-be sharer must invoke them.

The benefit that flows from this arrangement is that different groups can build and maintain different classes quite independently. Multiple inheritance can make bedfellows of complete strangers. If a new class claims parentage from two independently developed classes, there is no danger that the accidental use of the same variable name in the two parent classes will cause collisions and corruption of the variable. The methods of each parent class will continue to operate in its separate variable pool. This approach mirrors the way in which SOM classes manage their variables.

The down side of this arrangement is that it is a little difficult to split the definition of what the programmer may regard as a single class over more than one source file. Each class definition must be completely contained in a single file. Different files will, therefore, contain different class definitions. The methods in these files may be pooled by using inheritance, but they will not be able to gain access to one another's variables except through get and set methods created specifically for this purpose.

Object REXX provides a very simple way of creating get and set methods for a given variable. With the code:

```
::method aVariable attribute
```

Object REXX will automatically create both a *get* and a *set* method for *aVariable*. One can then get and set the value of *aVariable* by coding:

```
something = anObject~aVariable
```

```
anObject~aVariable=(aValue)
anObject~aVariable=aValue
```

Note: Unless a *SIGNAL ON NOVALUE* or a *SIGNAL ON ANY* instruction is included in the code, the methods may happily appear to use variables to which they actually have no access, if these variables happen to lie in a separate variable pool, for reasons described above. It is probably a good discipline to include the *SIGNAL ON NOVALUE* instruction in code while it is being debugged, and to leave it in while it is being used in production.

Object Instances

We have introduced objects and classes, but how do we actually create and delete objects within a class? Individual objects are often called *instances*.

Object Creation

Most OO languages provide a *new* method (operator) to create an instance of a class. This is also how object creation is implemented in Object REXX.

```
┌─── Object creation ──────────────────────────────────────
 mycar = .Car~new
    ...
 ::class Car
 ::method start
    ...
```

Note: The *Car* class defined using the class directive (*::class*) is available in the program as *.Car*, and the new method is invoked against this class object. In Object REXX, even classes are themselves objects.

We will often need to initialize the variables of a newly created object. Object REXX automatically invokes the *init* method of a new object, if an *init* method has been defined. The *init* method can accept parameters to initialize object variables and set additional variables to default values.

```
┌─── Initializing a new object ──────────────────────────────
 mycar = .Car~new(12345,'Ford','Mustang')
    ...
 ::class Car
 ::method init
    expose serialNumber make model saleDate
    use arg serialNumber, make, model        /* parameters of new  */
    saleDate = date('s')                      /* initialize variable */

 ::method start
    ...
```

Note: The new *USE ARG* statement is used to assign values to variables from the arguments. This is more effective than parsing the arguments and works for any objects passed in as parameters in the method call. See *USE (New)* on page 475 for more details.

Object Destruction

In Object REXX there is no explicit way to delete an object. Object REXX supports automatic garbage collection—that is, objects without any references (variables pointing to them) are removed from memory periodically under system control.

The program can remove references to objects by assigning another value to a variable or by dropping the variable:

```
mycar = .Car~new
...
drop mycar      /* object is subject to garbage collection */
```

Methods

Methods of a class are defined in the directives section of the program immediately after the class directive. We will often want methods to return a result that can be used by the invoking program, but this is not compulsory.

Methods can be invoked in two ways, through a single tilde (~) or through a double tilde (~~). When a double tilde is used, any result returned by the method is disregarded, and the object to which the method was applied is returned instead. This allows several methods to be applied to a single object in one statement, in a procedure known as *chaining*.

Chaining of method operations

```
car = .Car~new(...)
car~~start~~speed(55)~~for(5m)~mileage
   ...
::class Car
   ...
```

Note: Since the double tilde does not return a result, the subsequent operations work on the same car object until the *mileage* method returns the miles driven in 5 minutes.

Private and Public Methods

Methods invoked from the main program or from other classes are specified as *public* methods. They define the interface of the class, that is, all the possible operations this class can perform.

Methods used only within the class—that is, they are invoked only from other methods of the class—are *private* methods.

By default, methods are public; the *private* keyword is used to define a private method.

```
┌──── Public and private methods ────────────────────────────┐
│ ::class Car                                                 │
│ ::method milage              /* public method for users   */│
│   self~calculate             /*   - invoke private method */│
│                                                             │
│ ::method calculate private   /* private method           */│
│   expose time speed          /*   - not available to users*/│
│   return time * speed / 3600 /*   - used by other methods */│
└─────────────────────────────────────────────────────────────┘
```

Class and Instance Methods

So far, we have spoken about methods operating on objects. While this is generally the case, some methods cannot operate on specific objects because, for example, the method's purpose may be to *create* a new object, and the code calling the method cannot point it to this new object because it does not exist until after the method has run. When we deal with "normal" methods that operate on objects to do things like print them, shred them, or delete them, we speak of *instance* methods. They operate on objects, which are also known as *instances* of their class. When we deal with methods that we cannot pass a specific object to, we call them *class* methods.

This may sound rather technical, but when it comes to writing the code, the distinction will usually be very obvious. Making a method do something to an existing object requires an instance method; otherwise it must be a class method.

Instance methods usually handle the data of an individual object, whereas class methods handle data about the whole class, such as counting the number of objects in the class or managing a collection of all the objects.

Meta Classes

We have spoken about classes inheriting methods from their parents and from mixin classes. Although we did not mention it at the time, a subclass inherits both the instance and the class methods of its direct (and mixin, if any) parents. We spoke of abstract and mixin classes as a handy way to store behavior that can be inherited by a new subclass. Now we introduce meta classes. Like abstract and mixin classes, they are a handy place to store methods and attributes for other classes to inherit. The wrinkle is, when a new class inherits from a meta class, the meta class's *instance* methods become the inheriting class's *class* methods—along with any other class methods it inherits from its direct parent.

If this sounds complex, it is! But seldom will an Object REXX application programmer need to use meta classes. Direct inheritance usually gets the job done, with mixins less often required. The people who really need meta classes are the programmers who build OO languages like Object REXX. They could have kept meta classes hidden and used them for their own purposes only, but they chose to share them with the world. There are good reasons for doing this. If the feature is there, why not make it available? People have built some very complicated and sophisticated systems using OO languages in the past, and we believe that Object REXX will be no exception. It is probably a good idea for the Object REXX community to understand what meta classes are all about, and to be able to use them when required.

Polymorphism

Polymorphism is the rather cumbersome name given to a very simple idea that almost every computer language offers. It is the notion that a single operator symbol, like +, –, *, or /, can be used against operands of different types, such as short integer, long integer, short float, or long float. The language compiler (or interpreter) determines the type of operand that is involved and uses one of the many available machine instructions to carry out the appropriate operation. So whenever two numbers are added together, a plus sign is written between them, regardless of their data type.

Object-oriented languages enable programmers to define their own functions and operators (methods) for the new data types (classes) they create. For example, a *draw* method can be defined for the Shape class and, therefore, for all its subclasses (triangle, rectangle, circle, etc.). The draw method can then be invoked against an object of every subclass of the Shape class. Object REXX invokes the implementation of the draw method according to the class of each object.

A very nice example of polymorphism may be found in complex.rex in the Object REXX sample subdirectory and the associated usecomp.rex that invokes it. This code creates a class of complex numbers and defines operators to carry out simple arithmetic on them. The programmer is free to choose any method name to denote the addition of complex numbers—*complexAdd*, for example, which would require the following syntax:

```
a = b~complexAdd(c)
```

Instead, he or she wisely chooses the plus operator (+) for this purpose. This allows the programmer using the complex class to code:

```
a = b + c
```

This is, of course, a very familiar notation, and programmers will find it easy to apply these new methods to the new domain of complex numbers, even though complex numbers are not a part of standard REXX.

Just to show that Object REXX permits very useful things without much code, we show below the Object REXX method for adding complex numbers. By way of introduction for those who did not major in math, each complex number has two parts, called *real* and *imaginary*. Each of these two parts is a perfectly normal number. Combined, we can use them to do things like position a point on a graph, where we need to know how far to the right it is and how high. These two independent properties can be stored separately in the real and imaginary parts of a single complex number.

The Object REXX method for adding complex numbers

```
1  ::class complex public
2  ::method '+'
3    expose real imaginary
4    use arg adder
5    if arg(1,'o') then
6      return self
7    tempreal = real + adder~real
8    tempimaginary = imaginary + adder~imaginary
9    return self~class~new(tempreal, tempimaginary)
```

1 We use the *::class* directive to define the class of complex numbers.

2 We use the *::method* directive to start the definition of the + method.

3 We give each complex number two attributes, called *real* and *imaginary*. We *expose* them so the method can use them.

4 The + method normally works on two complex numbers. The first is the object in front of the + and the second is the object after it. We access the first object through the built-in name *self*. We access the second through the *use arg* statement and use the local variable name *adder* to reference to it.

5 If *arg(1)* is omitted, we do not have to do any addition.

6 We just return the object to which this prefix (+) applies (*self*).

7 We get the real part of *adder* and add it to the real part of the complex number we are dealing with.

8 We get the imaginary part of *adder* and add it to the imaginary part of the complex number.

9 We make a new complex number to return to the caller. We need to find the class of the object we are dealing with, because the method that makes new complex numbers is a *class* method (see *Class and Instance Methods* on page 69). *Self~class* gets the class of the object, and *class~new* invokes the *new* method of the complex class.

The class library that is supplied with Object REXX (see *The Object REXX Class Library*, below) makes extensive use of polymorphism. For example, the method name *[]* may be used to refer to an element of any type of collection, be it from the Array, Bag, Directory, List, Queue, Relation, Set, Stem, or Table class. The *[]* notation has been long and widely used in languages like C to denote subscripting of arrays, so the Object REXX convention exploits and reinforces an association that many programmers already have.

Programmers are encouraged to follow the same convention when they create new methods. If it does something analogous to an existing method of another class, give it the same name. It is easier to remember the name when needed, and it is easier to guess what the method does when only the name is known.

The Object REXX Class Library

Every OO language worthy of the name comes with a set of class definitions. These do a wealth of useful things and spare the OO programmer reinventing the wheel. Object REXX is no exception. Many of its classes relate to managing collections of data. These are called the *Collection* classes and are shown in Table 1. Another group provides a variety of useful functions to the programmer, listed in Table 2. These are very terse lists; for details, please see the Object REXX Reference manual.

Table 1. The Object REXX Collection Classes

Class Name	Purpose
Array	A sequenced collection
Bag	A nonunique collection of objects, subclass of Relation
Directory	A collection indexed by unique character strings
List	A sequenced collection that supports inserts at any position
Queue	A sequenced collection that can accept new items at its start or end
Relation	A collection with nonunique objects for indexes
Set	A unique collection of objects, subclass of Table
Table	A collection with unique objects for indexes

Table 2. The Other Object REXX Classes

Class Name	Purpose
Alarm	Generates asynchronous messages at specific times
Class	A technical class to create new classes
Message	Supports the deferred or asynchronous sending of messages
Method	A technical class to dynamically create new methods
Monitor	Manages the forwarding of messages
Object	A technical class to manage all objects
Stem	A collection indexed by unique character strings
Stream	Supports input and output operations
String	Supports operations on character strings
Supplier	Supplies the elements of a collection one by one

As with any OO language, the Object REXX class library is an extremely valuable asset and will richly repay careful study. We can never claim to know an OO language until we have a fair idea of what its class library contains.

The Object REXX Class Library Browser

Most OO languages contain a facility called a *class browser*, a program that presents the class library to the programmer on request. It supports lookup by class name or by method name. Object REXX provides this feature through its online reference books, which should be installed when Object REXX is installed. With its hypertext links, it provides far more information than does the usual class browser. Of course, it can display only the built-in Object REXX class library. There is at this stage no equivalent facility for browsing programmer-defined classes.

Experimental Class Browser

We implemented two simple experimental class browsers in Object REXX. They are available as browscls.rex and browser.rex in the Xamples subdirectory of the car dealer application.

The DOS window class browser, browscls.rex, is interactive and asks the user for the name of a class and then displays its subclasses, superclasses and methods.

OODialog Class Browser

The GUI class browser, browser.rex, starts with the **.Object** class and displays its subclasses and methods. The user can then choose any subclass and browse through the hierarchy of classes.

Once a class is selected, its subclasses, superclasses, and method are displayed in list boxes. The user can select any of the displayed classes and retrieve its information. The user can also type a class name and retrieve its information using the *Enter* key.

For user defined classes and the OODialog classes the user can also select a method and display the source code.

When the class browser is started it retrieves all the car dealer and OODialog classes in source format. The list of classes is defined in the browser.lst file and can be tailored by the user.

A typical screen capture is shown in Figure 39. The user has selected the *CustomerBase* class. Its superclass is *Object* and it has a subclass *Customer*. The source code of the *FindVehicle* method is displayed in the list box at the bottom.

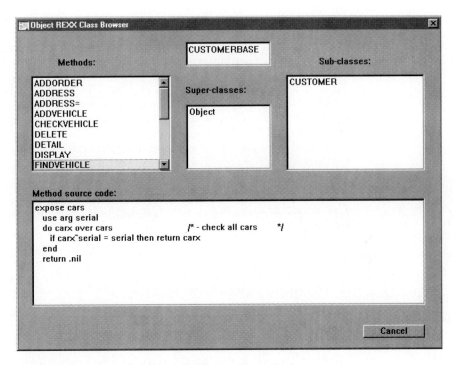

Figure 39. *Experimental OODialog Class Browser*

Tokenizing Object REXX Programs

Whenever Object REXX interprets a script, the whole file and all the required files are read, checked for syntax errors, and then translated into an internal format that the interpreter needs to execute the script, where the comments are skipped. If a syntax error is detected, the program won't be executed. Because the internal format consists of tokens, the process of the transformation is called *tokenizing*.

For larger scripts, this process can take several seconds. For very large programs contain several thousand lines of code and comment, tokenizing can take more than 15 seconds on slow machines.

To avoid this overhead every time a program is executed, Object REXX provides the *REXXC* utility (see *The REXXC Utility* on page 467) to tokenize a program to a file instead of only into memory. The Object REXX interpreter is able to execute both, the original program or the tokenized file. If a tokenized file is passed to the REXX interpreter, the syntax check and the tokenizing are skipped, which saves time.

REXXC does not resolve the *::requires* statements, but you can tokenize the required programs separately. The program in the *::requires* statement can have both formats as well.

If you tokenize, pay attention that you don't overwrite your source program. *REXXC* requires an input file name and an output file name.

```
REXXC input.rex output.rex
```

The tokenized scripts are not readable anymore, so you cannot modify them after this process. Therefore, we recommend that you keep the source program in another directory. If you want Object REXX to use tokenized versions of your program and required files, make sure that the tokenized files are found before the source programs.

Because the symbol names are not available in the internal format, tokenized programs cannot be traced. Often, you might first want to trace your scripts and then, if everything is alright, you want to use the tokenized version for faster startup.

REXXC is also a good tool to encrypt programs that are going to be delivered to customers.

Recommendations for tokenizing

❏ Put all source programs into a subdirectory, for example, *SRC*.

❏ Tokenize the source from the subdirectory into the main directory, using the same name as the output file.

```
REXXC SRC\program.REX program.REX
```

❏ Write a small program which tokenizes all the source programs of the subdirectory.

```
say 'Tokenizing directory:'
call SysFileTree 'src\*.*','files','FO'
do i=1 to files.0
    filename = substr(files.i,lastpos('\',files.i)+1)
    say "REXXC" files.i
    "REXXC" files.i filename
end
```

❏ Make sure that all *::requires* files are tokenized and found before their source files.

Automatic Tokenizing

Object REXX provides an environment variable, *RXSAVETOKENS*, to automate tokenizing of source programs. If *RXSAVETOKENS* is YES, the tokenized image of each source program is appended to the source file when the program is executed for the first time.

Note: Many editors display the appended image, and you have to manually delete the image when changing the source program; otherwise a new tokenized image is appended to the program again.

Part 2

The Car Dealer
Scenario

4

The Car Dealer Application

In this chapter, we visit the Hacurs software company and pick up the story of how it uses Object REXX to implement a car dealer application. We look at the objects required for this application and find out how the classes built into Object REXX (its class library) can be used to help construct them.

The Car Dealer Opportunity

"Hey, team," yelled Curt as he banged in through the door of the Hacurs office late one afternoon, "we've got our breakthrough! I spent most of today with Trusty Trucks looking at their requirements for a car dealer system. They are really keen to automate this part of their business, and I've pretty near convinced them that we can build a system that will meet their needs, and that we can do it fast."

"That's wonderful," said Hanna.

"Great going!" exclaimed Steve.

"What do they want?" asked Hanna.

"They service vehicles—cars and trucks," Curt answered as he put down his bag and sat at his desk. "I tried my hand at developing a use case with them to describe their business process. I captured it on my ThinkPad."

Curt pulled his ThinkPad from his bag, plugged it in and powered it on. Once it had booted up, he opened a view of his project subdirectory and dragged an icon to the Notepad editor.

"This is what we came up with," he said [see Figure 40 on page 80]. "Now, before you start criticizing, remember this is the first use case that I've built. We wrote up the steps that have to take place, and then I identified the nouns by making them bold, and all the verbs by making them underscored.

---

1. **Trusty Trucks** <u>draws up</u> a list of the **parts** it has in stock.

2. **Trusty Trucks** also <u>defines</u> the **services** it offers and <u>lists</u> the **parts** each service needs.

3. **Customers** <u>bring in</u> their **vehicles** for servicing.

4. **Trusty Trucks** <u>records</u> the **customer** and **vehicle** details on a **work order** and <u>itemizes</u> the **services** required.

5. **Service staff** <u>carries out</u> the specified **services** on the **vehicles**.

6. **Clerical staff** <u>prepares</u> **bills** based on the **work orders**.

7. The **customers** <u>pay</u> their **bills** and <u>claim</u> their **vehicles**.

Figure 40. *Car Dealer Application Use Case*

"We decided not to mark every noun," said Curt. "Some just didn't seem useful to us. All the nouns we highlighted are candidates for objects in the application design. And all the verbs we highlighted are candidates for methods."

"Well that looks very simple and straightforward to me, Curt," said Hanna, "although I'm sure it will turn out to be a lot more complicated when we get down to the details."

"Should we try to draw up a list of the objects you have identified and their related methods?" asked Steve.

"OK," said Curt. He copied the text of his use case and edited out all words except the highlighted ones. "This brings up a question," he noted. "If I can remember back to my high-school grammars, most sentences have a subject, a verb, and an object. Both the subject and the object are nouns. But when we come to attach methods to objects, does the verb get associated with the subject or the object of the sentence? For example, in the first item I've got

Trusty Trucks *draws up* a list of the **parts** it has in stock.'

"Should *draws up* be the method of 'Trusty Trucks' or of 'parts'?"

"Of 'parts', I think," answered Steve. "The Trusty Trucks object uses the method, but the parts object must implement it. It deals with parts data."

"OK, let's use that approach and see what happens," said Curt.

The Hacurs team worked together on this task. After some thought, they derived the table presented in Table 3.

Table 3. Car Dealer Objects and Methods

Object	Method
A list of parts	Draw up
Services	Define
Parts	List for each service
Vehicles	Bring in
Customer	Record the details
Vehicle	Record the details
Services	Itemize on a work order
Vehicles	Get services
Bills	Prepare
Bills	Pay
Vehicles	Claim

"It looks like we've got some nouns left over," said Hanna. "Trusty Trucks, the Stores department, Service staff, and Clerical staff acted as subjects but never as objects in the use case sentences."

"That's interesting," said Curt. "I discussed these with Trusty Trucks. We recognized that we could identify objects corresponding to various divisions within the company and store them in the database. Trusty Trucks couldn't see any point in doing so. I suggested that we could capture these in a field within each transaction, to act as an audit trail in case they ever needed to know who did what. They could see the potential value of doing that, but they plan to have a paper audit trail of each transaction and decided against keeping it in the database."

"We're starting to see the value of the use case discipline," said Steve. "It makes you take into account those loose bits and pieces that might otherwise be overlooked in the design. Even if you eventually decide to ignore them, it's good that you had to think about them."

"Good point, Steve," said Hanna. "And Curt, I think you've done a great job collecting this information and getting to understand what Trusty Trucks needs. Is this all we have to do? Do we create a class for each of the objects we've defined, and a method for each of the verbs?"

"I'm afraid there's a lot more to it than that," responded Steve. "We have to decide on the shape that we want our application to take. There's a lot of technical issues that we still need to discuss."

"Like what?" asked Hanna.

"Like what kind of user interface we must develop," Steve answered, "and what database manager we should use."

"Or if we use a database manager at all," added Curt.

The Application Model

Hanna, Curt, and Steve sat around a table together, going through the requirements for the car dealer application and trying to identify the objects they would choose to implement in Object REXX. After a couple of hours of work, they came up with five objects that seemed to play a dominant role:

❑ Customer
❑ Vehicle
❑ Part
❑ Service
❑ Work order

"This is it," said Curt. "Customers bring their vehicles in for various services. Trusty Trucks records the services each vehicle needs in a work order. Each service requires a standard amount of labor and parts. Those are the objects we have to model. The relationships between the objects look like this." Curt drew a sketch on the whiteboard [see Figure 41].

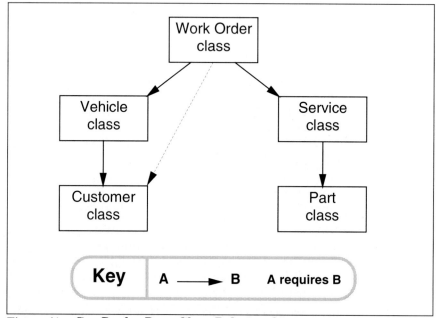

Figure 41. *Car Dealer Data Class Relationships*

"You don't need a line from the *Work Order* class to the *Customer* class," said Steve. "Each work order points to a vehicle, and each vehicle has an owner, and that's who the customer is."

"Not necessarily," said Curt. "Suppose someone rents a truck and bends a fender. He or she might decide to take the truck in to get it fixed, rather than return it, dented, to the rental company. The customer is the renter, but the owner of the vehicle is the rental company."

"That sounds pretty unlikely to me," said Steve. "Anyhow, Trusty Trucks wouldn't know that it's a rented truck. They would capture the name of the person who brought the truck to them as the owner. All they care about is who's going to pay them."

Hanna broke in with a suggestion: "We can sort out this detail later. Make the line from the *Work Order* class to the *Customer* class dotted, and let's carry on."

"How about labor—don't we need that as an object?" asked Steve.

"I don't think so," said Hanna. "The only thing we know about it is the standard labor charge for each service. We wouldn't have any attributes to store in labor if we made it an object."

"But there are different types of labor, and they charge out at different rates," said Steve.

"Maybe so, but Trusty Trucks doesn't want to record that kind of detail in its service records," said Curt. "Let's not make this more complicated than it has to be. We have to get a solution working fast if we want to get the business."

"OK, let's take those objects as our first cut," said Hanna. "What attributes do we need to store for each one?"

"I've kept a list of the attributes as we went along, and they look like this," said Curt, laying out a sheet of paper [see Figure 42].

```
01 customer                            01 service
    05 custnum      smallint               05 itemnum      smallint
    05 custname     char(20)               05 labor        smallint
    05 custaddr     char(20)               05 description  char(20)
                                           05 servpart     occurs 20 times
01 vehicle                                     10 partnum  smallint
    05 serialnum    integer                    10 quantity smallint
    05 custnum      smallint
    05 make         char(12)           01 workorder
    05 model        char(10)               05 ordernum     smallint
    05 year         smallint               05 custnum      smallint
                                           05 serialnum    integer
01 part                                    05 cost         integer
    05 partnum      smallint               05 orderdate    char(8)
    05 price        smallint               05 status       smallint
    05 stock        smallint               05 workserv     occurs 20 times
    05 description  char(15)                   10 itemnum  smallint
```

Figure 42. *Car Dealer Object Attributes*

"That looks like a mixture of COBOL and SQL," said Steve.

"Never mind, it gets the job done," said Curt.

"You've got repeating groups in service and work order," Steve noted. "We'll have to normalize[1] the data."

"Not necessarily," said Hanna. "The collection classes in Object REXX allow an object to have attributes that are arrays, lists, sets, bags, directories…"

"OK, OK—you've made the point," said Steve. "But when we come to store persistent objects in a relational database, we'll have to normalize the data."

"Also not necessary," chimed in Curt. "The new binary-large-object (BLOB) support in DB2 Version 2 would allow us to store the repeating group as an array in a single BLOB column." Seeing Steve's look of concern, he added, "I would also feel more comfortable if the database was normalized, but the objects in storage don't have to look exactly the same."

Methods and Variables

"OK, if those are the objects we have to model, what comes next?" asked Hanna.

"We need to work out which methods each object must support and the variables they need," said Curt. "I also kept a note of those as we went through the use cases. First, every object type…"

"You mean 'class,'" interrupted Steve.

"Uh—yes, class," agreed Curt. "OK, each class that manages the objects we've identified [see Figure 41 on page 82] needs the basic CRUD methods: create, read, update, and delete. Then whenever there's a relationship between two different objects, we need a method to maintain it. Who owns which vehicle, for example. We need to be able to track changes in ownership without having to delete the old vehicle and capture it all over again under a new customer."

"Why?" asked Steve. "You said we should keep it simple. Vehicles don't change ownership that often. Why not discard the old vehicle record and capture a new one?"

"What if there's a query relating to work done on the vehicle before it changed hands?" asked Hanna. "If we delete the old vehicle record we would lose any references we had to it in the work order history data."

---

[1] *Normalization* of data is a term used in database design. In simple words it makes individual tables of a database nonredundant and all columns of a table nonrepeating and dependent on the key only.

Steve nodded, so Curt carried on: "Some of these methods relate to a specific object—update and delete, for example. These would have to be implemented as *instance* methods. But others don't relate to a specific object. We would have to implement those as *class* methods."

"Can you give us an example?" asked Hanna.

"Sure," said Curt. "When we create a new object, we can't send the create message to the object because it doesn't yet exist. So we have to send the message to the object's class instead, and it returns the new object to us. And when we want to search our customer set by name, we can't send the message to a particular customer object, we have to send it to the class instead. The class method would come back with a customer object—or a list of customer objects if more than one has the search name, or maybe an empty list if the search fails."

"Speaking of searching customers, how can we find all the customer objects that exist within the customer class?" asked Steve.

"We haven't found any built-in way of doing that," replied Hanna. "We could maintain a variable for the *Customer* class that consists of the set of all customer objects. Suppose we call it *extent*. Whenever a new object is created, Object REXX automatically calls the object's *init* method. This is normally used to initialize the new object's instance variables. It could invoke a class method that puts the new object into the set of all objects created. And likewise for the other objects that we need to keep track of."

"That's smart," said Curt. "And we can have another class method that removes the reference to the object from the class's extent attribute when the object is deleted."

"Right," said Hanna. "Let's get to work and draw up tables of all of the methods we'll need for each class. We won't worry about how we store the objects on disk in this version. Let's just concentrate on managing the objects in storage." [See Tables 4–9.]

Table 4. Methods Required by Every Data Class

Method	Type	Purpose
initialize	Class	Initialize the extent variable
extent	Class	Return an array of all objects of the class
add	Class	Add a new object to the extent
remove	Class	Remove an object from the extent
init	Instance	Initialize a new object
setnil	Instance	Clear out the object record
delete	Instance	Delete the object from the class
detail	Instance	Return object details, formatted
makestring	Instance	Default ID for this object
display	Instance	Display object data on standard output

Table 5. Methods Required for Customer Class

Method	Type	Purpose
number	Instance	Return the number of the customer
findNumber	Class	Find a customer given the number
findName	Class	Return an array of customers matching name
heading	Class	Return a heading for output
name	Instance	Get or set the customer's name
address	Instance	Get or set the customer's address
update	Instance	Update the customer's data
addVehicle	Instance	Add a new vehicle to the customer
removeVehicle	Instance	Remove a vehicle from the customer
checkVehicle	Instance	Does this vehicle belong to the customer?
getVehicles	Instance	Return the customer's vehicles
findVehicle	Instance	Return a specific vehicle of the customer
addOrder	Instance	Add a work order to the customer
removeOrder	Instance	Remove a work order from the customer
getOrders	Instance	Return all work orders for this customer
ListCustomer-Short	Class	List customers on standard output
ListCustomerLong	Class	List customers with their vehicles

Table 6. Methods Required for Vehicle Class

Method	Type	Purpose
serial	Instance	Return the serial number of the vehicle
make	Instance	Get or set the vehicle's make
model	Instance	Get or set the vehicle's model
year	Instance	Get or set the vehicle's year
update	Instance	Update the vehicle's attributes
makemodel	Instance	Return make and model formatted
getOwner	Instance	Return the owner of the vehicle
setOwner	Instance	Set the owner of the vehicle
deleteOwner	Instance	Set the owner of the vehicle to nil

Table 7. Methods Required for Part Class

Method	Type	Purpose
findNumber	Class	Return the part's number
heading	Class	Return a heading for output
number	Instance	Return the serial number of the part
price	Instance	Return the price of the part
description	Instance	Return the description of the part
stock	Instance	Return the stock level of the part
increaseStock	Instance	Increase the stock level of the part
decreaseStock	Instance	Decrease the stock level of the part
ListPart	Class	List all parts on standard output

Table 8. Methods Required for Service Class

Method	Type	Purpose
findNumber	Class	Return the service's number
heading	Class	Return a heading for output
number	Instance	Return the number of the service
laborcost	Instance	Return the labor cost of the service
description	Instance	Return the description of the service
usesPart	Instance	Tell service it uses this part
getParts	Instance	Return the parts used by this service
getQuantity	Instance	Return the quantity used of this part
getPartsCost	Instance	Sum cost times quantity of parts used
getWorkOrders	Instance	Return work orders with this service
ListService	Class	List all services on standard output

Table 9. (Part 1 of 2) Methods Required for Work Order Class

Method	Type	Purpose
findNumber	Class	Return the work order's number
newNumber	Class	Issue a new work order number
findStatus	Class	Return work orders of given status
number	Instance	Return the number of the work order
cost	Instance	Return the cost of the work order
date	Instance	Return the date of the work order
setstatus	Instance	Set the status of the work order

Table 9. (Part 2 of 2) Methods Required for Work Order Class

Method	Type	Purpose
getstatus	Instance	Get the status of the work order
getstatust	Instance	Get the status of the work order as text
getCustomer	Instance	Get the customer of the work order
getVehicle	Instance	Get the vehicle of the work order
addServiceItem	Instance	Add a service item to the work order
removeService-Item	Instance	Remove a service item from the work order
getServices	Instance	Return services of this work order
getTotalCost	Instance	Compute the total cost of the work order
checkAndDecreaseStock	Instance	Issue the parts required for the services
generateBill	Instance	Return array of output lines of bill
detailcust	Instance	Return customer and vehicle details
makeline	Instance	Return work order details, formatted
ListWorkOrder	Class	List the work orders on standard output

"Wow! That's a long list of methods," said Curt, looking at the tables they had produced. "Aren't we making this much more complicated than it needs to be?"

"I don't think so," answered Hanna. "The books on object orientation warn that you need a lot of methods to get the job done, but they say that the methods must be very short. Some say that if a method is longer than 30 lines, it's too long. I read that in connection with Small-talk. I guess it's too soon to say if the same limit should apply to Object REXX."

"What's the benefit of having lots of silly little methods, each of which does very little?" asked Curt. "Why not lump functions together to make fewer, bigger methods?"

"It's like making bricks rather than prefabricating walls," said Steve. "The simpler each method is, the more likely you'll be able to reuse it for other purposes. And the more complex it is, the less likely you'll be able to use it again."

"Hmm," mused Curt. "It sounds good, but I'll reserve judgment on that until we've built our first application and I can see how it works out in practice.

Relationships Among Objects

"I know it's getting late, but I'd like to spend a little time talking about the relationships that we need to implement between the different objects," said Hanna. "This is the way I see it." She quickly constructed a list and showed it to the others. It read:

- ❏ A customer can own one or more vehicles
- ❏ A vehicle can be involved in many different work orders over time
- ❏ A customer can be involved in many different work orders
- ❏ Each work order requires one or more services
- ❏ Each service requires zero or more parts

Hanna asked, "Which of these relationships do we have to keep track of? And from which end?"

"What do you mean, 'from which end'?" asked Steve.

"If we're given a customer, do we need to know which vehicles he owns?" asked Hanna.

"Yes!" chorused Curt and Steve.

"And if we're given a vehicle, do we need to know to which customer it belongs?"

"Yes!" chorused Curt and Steve again.

"Then maybe we need to put a list of vehicles owned into each customer object, and an owner attribute into each vehicle," said Hanna.

"Wait a minute," said Curt, "that doesn't sound possible. If the vehicle object contains the customer object, which in turn contains the vehicle object, which one will really contain the other? Will we put the system into a perpetual loop trying to do what we tell it?"

"No," smiled Hanna. "Objects never actually contain each other, they just contain references to each other. The objects themselves are all kept in Object REXX's system storage. When you assign an object to a variable, you're actually just storing a *pointer* to the object in the variable."

Steve chimed in too: "And if you call a subroutine or method passing a huge BLOB as an argument, the system passes just a pointer to the BLOB."

"Cute," said Curt. "So how do we actually store the relationships that you spoke about? I seem to recall that there is a List class built into Object REXX."

The Object REXX Collection Classes

"There's a whole lot of collection classes built into Object REXX, including Array, Bag, Directory, List, Queue, Relation, Set, and Table," said Steve. "All of them can be used to store sets of related information. All of them have several methods in common, and all have their own unique capabilities. We're spoiled for choice—it's almost embarrassing!"

"OK—so which should we use?" asked Hanna.

Realizing that this would take some time, the Hacurs team phoned out for pizza and went in detail through each of the relationships that Hanna had identified.

"So this is what we've agreed," said Curt, wiping some tomato sauce from the handwritten table and presenting it to his teammates for their approval [see Table 10].

Table 10. Relationships between the Car Dealer Objects				
First Object	**Second Object**	**From 1st to 2nd**	**From 2nd to 1st**	**Type**
Customer	Vehicle	Set	Attribute	1:m
Customer	Work order	Set	Attribute	1:m
Vehicle	Work order	'none'	Attribute	1:m
Work order	Service	Relation	Relation	m:m
Service	Part	Set	'none'	m:m

"That's cryptic!" exclaimed Steve. "What does it all mean?"

"It's simple, really," replied Curt. "The first two columns list different types of object. The third column shows how we record the relationship from the object in the first column to the object in the second. If we don't, the entry is 'none'. Otherwise it's the name of the Object REXX class we agreed to use. The object that carries the relationship is stored as an attribute in the first object. The fourth column is the same as the third, except the other way around. It shows how we store the relationship in the second object back to the first. In most cases I've written just *attribute*. This means that there's only one object of type one associated with the second object, so we don't have to store a list, only a single object pointer. The fifth column shows the type of relationship we model. We distinguish between many-to-many (m:m) and one-to-many (1:m) relationships."

"Why don't we record the services that use a certain part?" asked Hanna. "Trusty Trucks is not interested in that information, so there is no need to carry it," replied Curt, "and we handle the work orders from the customer directly, without going through the vehicle," he added.

"Now that we see it all," said Steve, "do we really have to use the relation class to implement the relationship between work orders and services? Wouldn't it be simpler to use the same collection class for all our relationships?"

"Maybe, but this will look better on our CVs[2]," replied Curt with a smile.

"I'm more worried about our paychecks than our CVs!" muttered Hanna.

```
─── Example of relationship between customer and vehicle classes ───

::class Customer
  ...
::method init                /****** NEW CUSTOMER ******/
  expose customerNumber cars /* each customer object   */
  use arg customerNumber     /* has a customer number  */
  cars = .set~new            /* and a set of cars      */
  ...
::method addVehicle          /****** ADD NEW VEHICLE ***/
  expose cars                /* new cars are added to  */
  use arg newcar             /* the set of cars        */
  cars~put(newcar)
  ...

::class Vehicle
  ...
::method init                /****** NEW VEHICLE ******/
  expose serialNumber owner  /* each vehicle points to */
  use arg serialNumber, owner /* the owner (customer)   */
  owner~addVehicle(self)     /* and adds itself there  */
  ...
```

Object Creation and Destruction

"Let's talk through the life-cycle of these objects and make sure they can all be created when needed and discarded when their work is done," suggested Hanna.

"I think we've covered that," said Curt. "We listed the methods that are common to every object [see Table 4 on page 85] and these include *init* to create new objects and *delete* to throw old ones away. We also plan to define an *extent* set as a class variable in each class to keep track of all the objects we have defined within that class. And we plan to have an *add* and a *remove* method for each class. *Add* will save a pointer to each new object in the extent when it's created, and *remove* will drop it when it's discarded. The *init* and *delete* instance methods will invoke the *add* and *remove* class methods."

---

[2] CV, curriculum vitae, or resume, a short account of one's career and qualifications.

"That's fine for keeping track of objects in storage," responded Hanna, "but what happens when the user powers-off the PC? Are all the objects lost?"

"Ah! Now you're talking about object persistence," said Curt. "That's a big topic, and this isn't the right time to start getting into it. We've covered a lot of ground today, and I for one am getting tired."

Hanna glanced at her watch. "You're right, it is getting late. OK guys, let's call it a day. Thanks for giving up your time for this project. It will be a big one if we manage to close the business. And with any luck we'll be able to sell the same solution to a number of different companies. This could turn out to be the milk-cow application we need to keep our paychecks rolling in. Sweet dreams!"

Maintaining the set of objects of a class

```
.Customer~initialize                    /* prepare the class       */
cust1 = .Customer~new(101,'Steve')      /* create some customers   */
cust2 = .Customer~new(102,'Hanna')
.Customer~ListCustomerShort             /* list all customers      */


::class Customer

                                        /****** class methods ******/

::method initialize class               /* prepare the set of cust. */
  expose extent                         /* in variable "extent"    */
  extent = .set~new

::method add class                      /* add new customers to set */
  expose extent
  use arg aCust                         /* Arg passed from new/init */
  extent~put(aCust)                     /* - add it to the set     */

::method ListCustomerShort class
  expose extent                         /* list of all customers   */
  do aCust over extent                  /* iterate over extent     */
    aCust~display                       /* - call instance method  */
  end                                   /*   for each customer     */

::method init                           /****** instance methods ****/
  expose customerNumber name            /* initialize variables    */
  use arg customerNumber, name          /* - from arguments        */
  .Customer~add(self)                   /* add itself to the extent */

::method display
  expose customerNumber name            /* display cust. variables */
  say 'Customer: number='customerNumber 'name='name
```

Note: This simple example shows how instance methods can invoke class methods (*init* invokes *add*), and class methods can invoke instance methods (*ListCustomerShort* invokes *display*). The separation is very logical; operations at the class level are implemented as class methods using the *class* keyword in the method directive, and operations at the individual object level are instance methods.

Implementation of the Model in Memory

Figure 43 shows the object model with class and instance variables for the sample car dealer application.

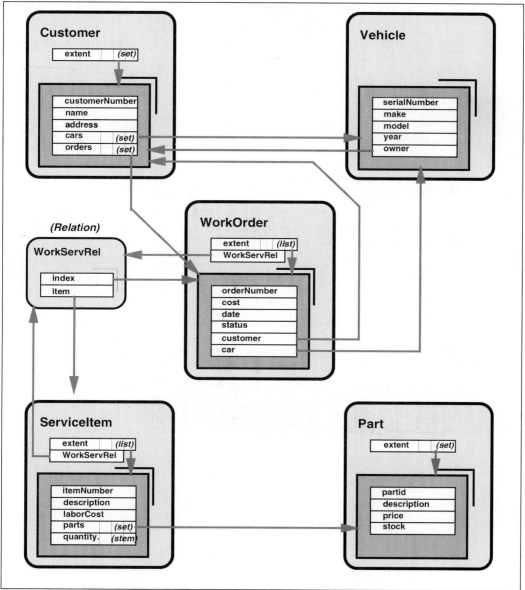

Figure 43. *Implementation of the Car Dealer Model*
The outer rounded boxes represent the classes, the inner rectangles the instances (objects) of the class. The white boxes in the outer rounded boxes are the attributes of the class; the white boxes in the inner rectangles are the attributes of the instances. Arrows indicate attributes that point to object instances.

Implementation Notes

1. We chose to use the set, list, and relation classes to experiment with the features of these collection classes. For work orders, for example, we chose to have a list so that new work orders are added at the top.

2. The relation class is well suited to implement the m:m relationship between work orders and services. It provides methods to get a list of related objects:

```
::class WorkOrder
::method addServiceItem
  use arg itemx
  workserv = self~class~getWorkServRel
  workserv[self] = itemx        /* add a service item to the work order */
::method getServices
  return self~class~getWorkServRel~allat(self)

::class ServiceItem
::method getWorkOrders
  return self~class~getWorkServRel~allindex(self)
```

The method *getWorkServRel* returns a pointer to the external relation object and the *allat* and *allindex* methods of the relation class return an array of related objects.

The relation object is implemented in the local directory (see *The Local Directory* on page 225) as

```
.local[Cardeal.WorkServRel] = .Relation~new
```

3. The methods to list all the objects of a class (*ListCustomerShort*, *ListPart*, etc.) are implemented as *routines* instead of methods. Object REXX provides the *::routine* directive to define subroutines (callable procedures):

```
::routine ListPart public
  aui~LineOut('List of' .Part~extent~items 'parts:')
  aui~LineOut(.Part~heading)
  do partx over .Part~extent
      aui~LineOut(partx~detail)
  end
  aui~EnterKey
  return
```

The decision to use routines is based on the assumption that this code is used only by the ASCII user interface and not by the GUI.

Sample Class Definition

Figure 44 shows an abbreviated listing of the *Customer* class as implemented in memory.

```
::class CustomerBase public

::method initialize class                  /*----- class methods ------*/
   expose extent
   extent = .set~new                       /* prepare set of customers */
::method add class                         /* add customer to set      */
   expose extent
   use arg custx
   extent~put(custx)
::method remove class                      /* remove customer from set */
   expose extent
   use arg custx
   extent~remove(custx)
::method findNumber class                  /* find customer by number  */
   expose extent
   parse arg custnum
   do custx over extent                    /* - look through the set   */
      if custx~number = custnum then return custx
   end
   return .nil
::method findName class                    /* find customer by name    */
   arg custsearch
   custnames = .list~new                   /* - prepare result         */
   do custx over self~extent               /* - look through the set   */
      if abbrev(translate(custx~name),custsearch) then do  /* compare name */
         custstring = custx~number~right(3)|| ,
                      '-'custx~name'-'custx~address
         custnames~insert(custstring)      /* - add one to result      */
      end
   end                                     /* - return the result      */
   return custnames~makearray
::method extent class                      /* return set of customers  */
   expose extent
   return extent~makearray
::method heading class                     /* return a heading         */
      return 'Number        Name           Address'

::method init                              /*----- instance methods ---*/
   expose customerNumber name address cars orders
   use arg customerNumber, name, address   /* initialize new customer  */
   cars = .set~new
   orders = .set~new
   self~class~add(self)                    /* add it to the set of cust*/
::method delete                            /* delete a customer        */
   expose cars orders
   do carx over cars                       /* - and all the cars       */
      carx~delete
   end
   do workx over orders                    /* - and all the orders     */
      workx~delete
   end
   self~class~remove(self)                 /* remove it from the set   */
```

Figure 44. *(Part 1 of 2) Customer Class in Memory*

Unguarded

*method is
callable
from other
methods active
on same object.
Otherwise
other methods
would be
blocked pending
completion.
(queued).*

```
::method number unguarded              /* return customer number    */
    expose customerNumber
    return customerNumber

::method name attribute                /* name, name= methods        */
::method address attribute             /* address, address= methods*/

::method update                        /* update customer info       */
    expose name address
    use arg name, address
::method addVehicle                    /* add vehicle to customer   */
    expose cars
    use arg newcar
    cars~put(newcar)
    newcar~setowner(self)
::method removeVehicle                 /* remove vehicle from cust */
    expose cars
    use arg oldcar
    oldcar~deleteOwner
    cars~remove(oldcar)
::method getVehicles                   /* return vehicles of cust. */
    expose cars
    return cars~makearray
::method findVehicle                   /* find vehicle by serial    */
    expose cars
    use arg serial
    do carx over cars
        if carx~serial = serial then return carx
    end
    return .nil
::method addOrder                      /* add order to customer     */
    expose orders
    use arg newwork
    orders~put(newwork)
::method removeOrder                    /* remove order from cust.  */
    expose orders
    use arg oldwork
    orders~remove(oldwork)
::method getOrders                      /* return all orders of cust*/
    expose orders
    return orders~makearray
::method detail                         /* return a detail line      */
    expose customerNumber name address
    return customerNumber~right(5) '     ' name~left(20) '  ' address~left(20)
::method makestring
    expose customerNumber name
    return 'Customer:' customerNumber name
```

Figure 44. *(Part 2 of 2) Customer Class in Memory*

Source Code for Base Class Implementation

The source code for the base implementation is described in Table 21 on page 301 and listed in *Base Classes* on page 493.

5

ASCII User Interface

In this chapter we look at a variety of technologies that can be used to develop the user interface for Object REXX applications. While most of the solutions that we present are graphical (GUI), we also present a simple ASCII character user interface (AUI).

Designing the User Interface

"Come on, Steve, you're late for the meeting!" called Curt.

"I'm busy working," Steve called back.

"You know that work is no excuse for missing a meeting, Steve," responded Curt.

"Meetings are work, man," grumbled Steve, gathering his ThinkPad and stopping to pour some coffee before joining Curt and Hanna in the meeting area.

"Whoops!" said Hanna. "Being late for a meeting is bad enough, but coming in late *with coffee* is a capital offense, Steve. You know the rules!"

"Yeah!" agreed Curt. "You get to buy the cookies for our mid-morning coffee break. Make mine a blueberry muffin, please."

Steve shook his head. "Someone has to do the work while you guys sit around talking to each other, or nothing would ever get done." he said. "I've been designing the user interface for the car dealer application."

"What do you mean, 'designing the interface'?" asked Curt. "You know that Trusty Trucks doesn't want a GUI front end to the application. All their existing PC applications are character-based, and they want the car dealer app to look exactly the same. Building a character-based user interface is the easiest thing in the world. We don't need to waste time designing it."

"Yes, I know," said Steve, shaking his head. "It's amazing. They've just upgraded all their PCs from DOS to Windows 95 so they can get easy file-sharing and Internet access, and they still want DOS-style interfaces. Surely you could have sold them on the benefits of a good GUI, Mr. Ace Salesman?" He looked pointedly at Curt.

"Be realistic, Steve," responded Curt. "They've got a lot of legacy DOS applications that they have to keep running. One of the main reasons they chose Windows 95 is its DOS compatibility. They don't want to redevelop all their old apps with GUI front ends. In fact, they don't even have source code for some of the older ones. They were built by a little contracting company that went out of business. Like we might, too, if we don't get a move on with this project!"

"Exactly!" said Steve. "That's why I was working on the user interface. And for your information, the reason we need to design it carefully is that we plan to sell the same application to other businesses, as well. You know that I've been talking to Classy Cars about it, and they're really interested. There's no way they will want a clunky old character interface app in their smart showrooms with the sort of cars they sell. They want the latest GUI, where the *G* stands for 'Gee Whiz'! And when I showed them some multimedia with bitmap displays, recorded audio, and even a short video clip, they were turning handsprings."

"Multimedia? With audio and video?" snapped Curt. "Steve, are you crazy? This is a simple car dealer application. It handles the booking and tracking of vehicle services. We're talking about guys in greasy overalls crawling under cars. Multimedia has absolutely nothing to offer us in this application. We've got a tight deadline to deliver working code to support a serious business operation, and you're messing around with your multimedia toys again! You're just trying to justify the company money you wasted buying that fancy multimedia Think-Pad."

Steve smirked in reply. "Your trouble is you have absolutely no imagination," he said to Curt. "Sure, we're building a vehicle servicing application. But the reason we chose to build it in Object REXX is that, as time goes by, its OO facilities will allow us to reuse the objects we build, for totally new applications. And while I was talking with Classy Cars, I found that their real hot button is the sale of cars, both new and secondhand. Sure, they need a system to manage car services, but they make more money selling cars. And when I talked through the selling process with them, I soon realized that our application already contains many of the objects needed to support selling. Like vehicles and customers, for example."

"But Steve, we have no multimedia data in our system at all as it stands," said Hanna. "And writing code to handle multimedia will be a major undertaking. Is it realistic to start with something that complicated at this stage?"

"What you guys don't realize is how easy it is to do multimedia in REXX," said Steve. "I developed a little demo on the fly at Classy Cars to show them how it could work. Just look at this."

Steve double-clicked an icon on his ThinkPad's desktop, and a folder opened. In it were several icons, each looking like a car, with captions referring to different popular brands. There were also icons labeled *Audio* and *Video* in the folder. Steve dragged one of the car icons and dropped it onto the Audio icon. After a second, they heard his recorded voice saying, "The Gazebo. An ideal outdoor car for the driver who enjoys plenty of fresh air." Steve picked up the same icon again and dropped it onto the Video icon. A window opened on his screen, and the famous IBM 'Butterfly' ThinkPad opened its top cover and expanded its keyboard.

"Is that all it does?" asked Curt. "And how many hundreds of lines of code did you waste building it?"

Hanna looked thoughtful as well. "How many lines of code did it take, Steve?" she asked.

"Hardly any," said Steve. "Look, this is just a demo to show what could be done, not a production system. I used Windows 95's facilities to put together the folder and icons. I pointed to my audio.cmd in the audio button's properties notebook. When the user drops an icon on Audio, my command gets scheduled with the name of the icon dropped on it as the parameter. I use this name to pick an audio file and play it. Here's the code."

Steve opened an editor window, and there, hiding in the top corner, were 10 lines of code. "The video works the same way," he added, and brought up the video.cmd for them to see, as well.

Hanna was excited. "Hey, Steve, that's really neat. If that's what you were building just now, I'll pay for the cookies in the next coffee break."

"This is just a red herring," said Curt. "We've got to deliver the car-servicing application soon if we want to get Trusty Truck's business. And if we want to stay in business. We don't have time to mess around building multimedia demos."

Steve looked upset and was about to respond, but Hanna cut in. "Wait, Curt. You're right that we have to deliver Trusty Trucks' application soon. But Steve's also right. We're using Object REXX precisely so that we can extend the base application to do different things for different customers in the future. We have to strike the right balance. And the key to that is to design the system right from the start so it can grow to meet new needs as they arise."

"And that was exactly what I was doing when you interrupted me to come to this meeting," said Steve. "So why don't we stop talking and get some work done?" He brought up his notes on his ThinkPad and started talking through them. "We will have to develop both character and GUI versions of our application. I've called the character version *AUI* for short. Most of the functions that we have to implement will be common to both versions, and, of course, we don't want to duplicate the code."

"Why not?" asked Curt. "That's how we've always done it in the past. It's a clean solution. You can implement a change that one customer wants without messing up the other customer's versions."

"Well, we didn't have very much choice in the past," said Steve. "Classic REXX is procedural, and it's hard to share procedural code between different versions of an application. It's even hard to segment a large application into many small files with classic REXX because of the communication barriers between different source files. And if the individual source files are big, it follows that they deliver complex functions. The key to reuse is keeping the functions small and simple. That's where Object REXX shines."

"Maybe Object REXX makes it easier to share code," said Curt, "but what's the advantage? Different customers will want different features added to the application, and it won't be long before they'll need different versions of the source."

"We have to break out of that cycle if we want to be more profitable," said Hanna. "If you look at the really successful PC software products, there isn't a different version with different features for each customer. The vendor implements only those features that will be useful to most of the customers, then they *all* get the new features. We aren't quite in that kind of business, and we will have to implement some features that only one customer requests. But we should always be on the lookout to make new features available to every customer who might possibly want them, even if it's some time out in the future."

"Yes, and Object REXX will allow us to keep a common code base in the form of common class definitions in a shared source file, and then to implement only the *differences* as source unique to a particular customer," agreed Steve. "That's why I've been trying to work out how we can implement the ASCII user interface as an object."

ASCII User Interface As an Object

"Did I hear you right?" asked Curt. "You want to implement the ASCII user interface as an object?"

"That's right, Curt," replied Steve. "We're using an object-oriented language, you know, so why not use its facilities for the user interface, too?"

"Well, I've got good news for you, Steve," Curt said. "In Object REXX, every variable and expression is actually an object, and every function is a method on an object. When you code:

```
say aString
```

"that's actually equivalent to:

```
call lineout aString
```

"and Object REXX implements that as:

```
.OUTPUT~lineout(aString)
```

"where *.OUTPUT* is a standard object in each process's directory of local values. You need struggle no longer to design an OO interface for the AUI version, Steve. Just use the *SAY* command!"

"I was trying to work at a *slightly* higher level of abstraction than that," said Steve. "Think about the menus, for example. Our old REXX programs that run in AUI mode are riddled with strings of *SAY* commands that spill menus out on the screen. Those won't work so well when we have to switch the output from the default *.OUTPUT* object to a GUI screen driver, will they, Curt? We would probably want to make use of the GUI window's menu bar instead."

"That's why we need different versions of the source for the AUI and GUI versions," replied Curt.

"Can we put the AUI-handling code and menus into a subroutine in a separate file?" asked Hanna. "The GUI version would simply not call that subroutine and not have that code."

"It's not that easy," said Steve. "The logic that handles the menu has to call the code that implements the menu option chosen by the user. The menu code has to be the main routine, and the rest of the system subroutines. If they're in separate files, it's not that easy to pass them all the data they need to run."

"That's why we need different versions of the source for the AUI and GUI versions," parroted Curt.

"We're trying to solve a problem, not score cheap points," said Hanna. "The problem of communicating with subroutines isn't that great with Object REXX—we can encapsulate all the data they need in a single object, if necessary. But tell us the approach you were working on, Steve."

The AUI Class

"Well, we could implement an AUI class to handle all output to the console. Handling the screen-full condition is always a bit messy, and in the past we've written that logic into every piece of code that produces a listing on the screen. The AUI *init* routine would be called automatically when we create the AUI object, and it could use the REXX *SysTextScreenSize* built-in function to find out how many rows can fit on the screen. Each time the *lineout* method is used, it can call the REXX *SysCurPos* built-in function to find out how many screen rows are already used, and handle the screen-full condition automatically."

"Sometimes we need to put out several related lines that we want to stay together on the screen—perhaps a customer with all of his or her vehicles," said Hanna. "How would the AUI object handle that?"

"We could build a *checkRows* method for AUI," replied Steve. "You pass it the number of lines you want together on the screen. It checks to see if there's enough space free, and if not, it invokes the screen-clearing logic. With this approach, none of the routines that generate screen output would need to know how many lines the screen has space for, or how many of its lines are already in use. All of this screen-related information would be *encapsulated* in the AUI object."

"That's neat," said Hanna.

The AUI Operations

"Let's define all the operations (methods) needed for the character interface on a sheet of paper," added Curt. Shortly afterward, they had it all ready [see Table 11].

Table 11. Methods Required for AUI

Method	Type	Purpose
init	Instance	Initialize object, store window size
getrows	Instance	Return number of rows in window
ClearScreen	Instance	Clear output window
LineOut	Instance	Output one line of text
CheckRows	Instance	Check if there is enough space for "n" rows
UserInput	Instance	Ask user for input, character or numeric
YesNo	Instance	Ask user for Yes or No input
Enterkey	Instance	Wait until user presses enter key
Error	Instance	Display error message
AckMessage	Instance	Display acknowledgment message

"Why are the methods instance methods?" questioned Curt.

"Well, Curt, it's true we could implement all methods as class methods," replied Steve, "but I think it is cleaner to create an actual *AUI* object at run time to handle the interactions."

ASCII Menus as Objects

"The other things I'd like to tidy up are the menus. In the past we have implemented them by coding a whole bunch of *SAY* instructions, outlining the options. Immediately after these come *WHEN* instructions, checking for each of the options and implementing some action if that option has been chosen. I'd like to move the menu text and associated actions right out of the REXX programs and store them as parameter files. Then we could define a menu class. Its class *init* method could read the menu parameter file and set up the menus as a list of objects in storage. It would also have a method to display a selected menu object, check which option the user chooses, and automatically implement the corresponding action."

"Often, a menu action will simply display a submenu," said Curt.

"That's right," said Hanna. "In that case, the action in the main menu would be an instruction to display the submenu. The menu display method would invoke itself. That's possible, isn't it?"

"Yes," said Curt. "I've been doing some playing around with the concurrency features of Object REXX..."

"So I'm not the only one who plays around!" interrupted Steve.

"...and methods can invoke themselves recursively," continued Curt. "Of course, we would have to make sure we don't send them into an infinite loop by linking a submenu back to one of its parent menus."

"Our menu display process would be user-driven. The user would quit soon enough if it loops back on itself," said Steve.

"That sounds like a good approach," said Hanna. "I'm still not clear on how we'll tie it all together when we build our first GUI front end, but that's not today's problem. It's time for our coffee break. I'll buy the cookies."

"Great!" said Steve. "In that case, let's go to the Golden West Coffee Shoppe."

"Oh no!" groaned Curt. "Don't tell me that I have to sit and watch him nibble his way through yet another Golden West Monster Munch Chocolate Chip Cookie!"

The Menu Operations

After the coffee break, the three sat together and developed the list of menu operations [see Table 12].

Table 12. Methods Required for Menu		
Method	**Type**	**Purpose**
initialize	Class	Read menu file and build menu objects
findMenu	Class	Find existing menu or allocate new one
init	Instance	Initialize new menu object with array of items
addItem	Instance	Add a menu item to the menu object
getname	Instance	Return name of a menu object
showMenu	Instance	Display the menu, prompt user

Implementing the Menus

The menu input file MENU.DAT has the following structure, with fields separated by tab characters (represented as ¬ signs):

```
┌─── Structure of menu data file ──────────────────────────────────┐
│ Main¬CAR DEALER - GENERAL MENU                                    │
│ Main¬List (customer, part, work order, service)¬showMenu List     │
│ Main¬Update customer and part information        ¬showMenu Update  │
│  ...                                                              │
│ List¬CAR DEALER - LISTING MENU                                    │
│ List¬List customers                      ¬call ListCustomerShort  │
│ List¬List customers and vehicles         ¬call ListCustomerLong   │
│  ...                                                              │
│ Update¬CAR DEALER - UPDATE MENU                                   │
│ Update¬Create a new customer   ¬call Newcust                      │
│  ...                                                              │
└──────────────────────────────────────────────────────────────────┘
```

The main program uses the menu class as follows to initialize the menu structure and to run the application using the menus:

```
┌─── Menu loop in main program ──────────────────────────────────────────┐
│ aui = .AUI~new                         /* allocate AUI object        */ │
│ menus=.array~new                       /* runtime level array of menus */ │
│ menus[1] = .Menu~initialize            /* build menu objects, store 1st */ │
│ level = 1                              /* start at top menu          */ │
│ do until level < 1                     /* run loop until exit        */ │
│    action = menus[level]~showMenu      /* show the current menu      */ │
│    select                              /* - user enters an action    */ │
│       when action = .nil then level = level - 1  /* previous menu    */ │
│       when action~class = .Menu then do  /* user select submenu      */ │
│             level = level +1           /* - add submenu at lower level */ │
│             menus[level] = action                                      │
│          end                                                           │
│       otherwise interpret action       /* user select an action      */ │
│    end                                 /* - run that action          */ │
│ end                                                                    │
└────────────────────────────────────────────────────────────────────────┘
```

Appearance of ASCII User Interface

The windows displayed to the user by the menu system are shown in Figure 45.

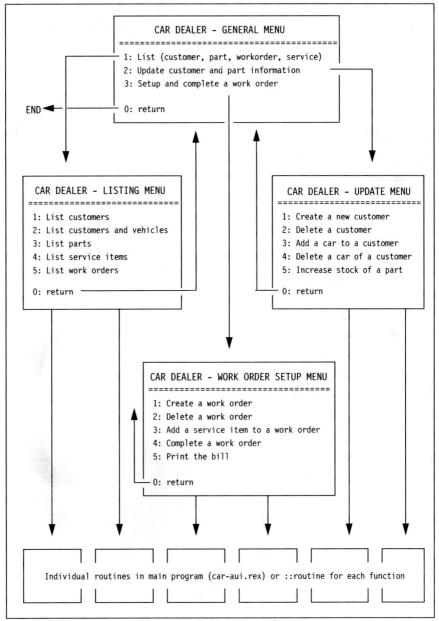

Figure 45. *Appearance of ASCII User Interface*

Source Code for ASCII User Interface

The source code of the AUI and menu implementation is not listed in the appendix; it is available in the car dealer directory on the CD, or on a hard drive after Object REXX has been installed (see Table 25 on page 302).

The source code to start the AUI program is listed in *Program to Run the Car Dealer Application* on page 527.

6

Persistent Objects on Disk

In this chapter, we find out how objects can be made persistent by storing them in conventional flat ASCII files. We want to ensure that the objects survive (even when the program that creates them ends) and are available again the next time that the program runs. For brevity, we call this the *FAT* (File Allocation Table) *option*, although, of course, the files may equally well be located on a device with another file system.

Storing Objects in FAT Files

"Great news, team—we're on the last lap of agreeing on the detailed design of the car dealer system with Trusty Trucks!" Curt strode into the Hacurs premises, stripping off his coat and beating a light dusting of snow from it.

"Wonderful!" said Hanna. "We've all spent a lot of time on this application. We need to implement it and bill for it soon."

"The only outstanding area is, How are we going to store their objects when they turn off the PC that runs the application?" asked Curt.

"Did you say 'the PC'?" asked Steve. "Aren't they going to run it on multiple machines?"

"No," replied Curt. "We did some performance evaluation with our latest prototype and worked out that they'll be able to handle their current business volumes easily on a single workstation. And Trusty Trucks is too cost-conscious to use two PCs to do the job if one will do."

"What if the one PC breaks down?" asked Steve.

"Well, that's part of what we have to discuss and implement," replied Curt. "We need to make sure that all object creations, updates, and deletes are recorded on disk, and that the system will recover its objects automatically from disk when it is brought up again. We also have to decide on some kind of disaster recovery scheme."

"The obvious way to do this is to base our object persistence on a database manager like DB2," said Steve.

"Trusty Trucks is a cost-conscious organization, Steve," replied Curt. "They're not like Classy Cars. They don't own a real database management system, and they're not about to buy one just to run our application. We're going to have to find a way of doing the job using conventional ASCII files, if that's possible."

"If only a single workstation needs to access the data, it's entirely possible to do the whole job using ASCII disk files," said Hanna. "In fact, that approach would work even if multiple PCs want to read the files at the same time, so long as only one PC has update access to the files." *and shared network access to file*

"That would be the ideal solution, Hanna," said Curt. "How would you go about it?"

"I don't think I'm going to like this!" interjected Steve, but the other two ignored him.

Hanna swept her hair back with her fingers, walked to the whiteboard and picked up a pen. Curt and Steve knew she wouldn't use the pen, just holding it seemed to help her think. "Because we're using an OO approach to the whole system, we know exactly when a new object is created, or an old one updated or deleted. It can't happen unless our object methods are called."

"Right," said Steve and Curt in unison.

"OK. So all we have to do is change the *init* method for each object to write a copy of the new object to disk as soon as it has finished initializing it. And we make similar changes to the delete methods so they can delete the objects from disk, and to the update methods so they can rewrite the objects to disk whenever they change."

"That sounds straightforward," said Curt.

"How would you delete an object from a disk file if it's in the middle of the file?" asked Steve. "You can't just leave a hole in the file."

"We could shift all the trailing objects one place to the left and leave out the deleted object," replied Hanna.

"How will we know the position of the object in the file?" asked Steve. "We can't shift the remaining objects over it unless we know where it is."

"We could give every object a new attribute called *position*," suggested Curt. "When we read the objects into storage, we could store the positions in which we found them in this attribute. Then when we need to update or delete them, we'll know where they are on disk."

"But if they keep shifting around every time you delete an object, you won't know where they are when it comes time to update them," reasoned Steve. "It would really be simpler if we used a database manager. It has all the logic needed to sort out problems of this kind."

"I've just told you, Steve..." started Curt, but Hanna interrupted.

"Hold on, guys! Curt, how many objects are there going to be?"

Curt shifted his scowl from Steve and answered Hanna. "A couple of hundred vehicles, somewhat fewer customers, and maybe a thousand service records if they keep six months' history on line."

"So why don't we just rewrite all the objects to disk any time one of them is changed?" suggested Hanna.

"That would be a huge overhead!" Steve objected.

"Not necessarily," answered Hanna. "We need to store only 30 to 40 bytes of information per object, and if there are a thousand, we have to write 30 or 40 KB. That won't take long."

"It would take forever!" said Steve. Curt began tapping on this Think-Pad's keyboard. "Anyhow," continued Steve, "if you add up all the objects of all types, it comes to a pretty big file, maybe 120 KB."

"No, we would split the different object types into separate files," said Hanna. "Otherwise we'd have a jumble of different object types in the file, and we'd have to write extra logic to separate them. So the biggest file we'd have to handle would be only about 40 KB."

"That would still take a long time to rewrite," said Steve.

"Let's time it," said Curt. "I've just written a little REXX command that takes two parameters—average record length and number of records. It writes a file of this size to disk, and measures how long it takes. So what numbers should I try?" he asked.

"Try a 30-byte record length and 1000 records," said Hanna.

No mention of relative performance of test PC relative to customer PC. →

"OK," said Curt, and he typed in the command. "That took one second," he said. "Doesn't sound too long to me," he added, looking at Steve.

Steve looked stunned for a while, then he said, "Of course! Windows 95 has a good file buffering system built-in, so records are written to disk quickly."

"That sounds great to me," said Curt. "Since the operating system takes care of that for us, we really don't have to worry about performance. And the production system will run on a server at Trusty Trucks. Its disk is faster than mine. So Hanna's approach will perform beautifully."

"Yes, but what if the system goes down while it's still writing to disk?" asked Steve. "A database manager logs all changes to disk, as well as writing the data back, so if something goes wrong while it's writing the data, it can always fix it up from the log."

"The data files for Trusty Trucks will be so small that we could easily write the data out to a different file name each time around, and cycle through the list of three or so file names for each file," said Hanna. "When we start up the system, we can use the *query timestamp* operand of the stream command to find out which version of the data is the most recent. We can write a special trailer at the end of each file, so if it's not there we know the file is incomplete and we should use the next most recent one. It's easy to solve this kind of problem."

"I agree," said Curt. "Let's get the system going against flat ASCII files and start doing user training and acceptance testing at Trusty Trucks. We can change it later to put in smart recovery logic. The users are waiting for us, and we need the money we'll get once this system is installed."

"That's fine for Trusty Trucks," said Steve, "but Classy Cars is a much bigger operation. They need to support six to eight separate locations, and they will need update facilities from multiple workstations at the same time. There's no way a simple ASCII file approach will meet their needs."

"You're absolutely right, Steve," agreed Hanna. "We'll have to build database support when it's time to implement the system for Classy Cars. And maybe in the past we would have had to try to persuade Trusty Trucks to use a database manager as well, because we couldn't afford to support two different versions of the application. But the main reason we're using Object REXX for this application is so we can customize different versions for different customers and still reuse all the common business logic. Remember?"

"Yes, I guess so," said Steve, not looking convinced. "Except that once we've got the ASCII file version going, you'll probably change your minds and decide that's the way we have to go for Classy Cars too."

"We'll do what's best for the customer, Steve," said Hanna. "That's the only way to make sure that they'll ask us for help again."

"OK." he said, "We'll build an ASCII file solution for Trusty Trucks, but I'm going to start working out how we can structure the application to get the kind of configuration flexibility we'll need in the future."

* Switch between an ASCII file and a dbms.

"That's a great idea, Steve," said Hanna. "Now, let's finish this design and get coding. What format should we use for the objects when we write them out to disk files?"

Format of the Objects

"Why not write them out as comma-delimited records, the way a spreadsheet package would export rows?" asked Curt.

"Not bad, but our data could easily include commas in things like address fields," said Hanna. "Let's use tab characters to delimit fields."

"Good idea!" said Curt. "I've got the fields we need on this piece of paper." He rifled through his work file and pulled out a piece of paper [see Figure 42 on page 83]. "All we have to do is write the files in this format."

"Just a minute," said Steve. "You've got some *smallint* fields defined there. Those are 2-byte binary integers. Either byte could easily contain the code value for a tab, the ASCII value 9. That would throw you off when you try to decode the record during loading."

"Good thinking, Steve," said Hanna. "We'll have to write the numeric values as strings. No problem, because that's the way REXX writes them out, unless you tell it otherwise."

```
┌──── Sample ASCII file for the customer class ──────────────────┐
│                                                                │
│  number name              address          (¬ = tab key)       │
│  101    ¬Senator, Dale    ¬Washington                          │
│  102    ¬Akropolis, Ida   ¬Athens                              │
│  103    ¬Dolcevita, Felicia ¬Rome                              │
│  ...                                                           │
└────────────────────────────────────────────────────────────────┘
```

Steve smiled his appreciation for Hanna's compliment and got more enthusiastic about the design. "We've also got some repeating groups in the service and work order objects," he said. "How are we going to handle those?"

"We can just attach them to the back end of the record, delimited by tabs, like the other fields," said Curt. "We'll know what they are when we read the files. There's no chance of confusion."

```
┌──── Sample ASCII file for the work order class ─────────────────┐
│                                                                │
│  number date      cost complete custmr serial  service-items (¬ = tab key) │
│  1      ¬09/06/95¬-1  ¬0        ¬101  ¬123456 ¬1               │
│  2      ¬09/06/95¬-1  ¬0        ¬103  ¬398674 ¬10¬9¬4          │
│  3      ¬09/06/95¬-1  ¬0        ¬106  ¬911911 ¬7¬6             │
│  ...                                                           │
└────────────────────────────────────────────────────────────────┘
```

"Not exactly third normal form[1]!" said Steve.

"No problem," said Hanna. "No one is going to read these files except us, while we're debugging the code."

"Hmm—I guess so," agreed Steve reluctantly.

Implementing the Changes in Code

"Well, I think we've got this all sorted out," said Curt. "We just have to modify the methods we wrote for our objects, to write updates to disk..."

"Hold it!" snapped Steve. "We've just agreed that we're going to have different versions of the system supporting both ASCII files and a database manager, and you want to start carving up our existing methods to hard-wire ASCII file logic into them. Once we've done that, we'll *never* be able to support two different versions while sharing common code."

"Be realistic, Steve!" said Curt. "How are we going to support ASCII files if we don't write some new function into the code? This OO stuff isn't magic, you know."

Steve glared at Curt, then strode to the whiteboard and took the pen from Hanna. She sat down, grateful to give her feet a rest.

"Let's start with customers," he said. "We already have a *Customer* class defined with its methods to control how customer objects behave once they're in storage."

"Right," said Hanna encouragingly, as Steve drew a box and labeled it *Customer* on the board.

"Currently, the *Customer* class is a subclass of the *Object* class by default, since we didn't say otherwise when we defined it." Steve drew a box labeled *Object* above the *Customer* box and connected the two. "Now, let's say we change the name of the *Customer* class to *Customer-Base*, and define a new class called *FAT Customer*." Steve drew a new box with this label below the *Customer* box, and drew connecting lines to show that *CustomerBase* was a child of *Object* and *FAT Customer* a child of *CustomerBase*.

"With this structure," Steve added, "we could write the additional methods that we need for object persistence in FAT files as new methods in the *FAT Customer* class. We could change the *CustomerBase* class methods to invoke these new persistent methods when object updates need to get written to disk."

"Hold on," said Curt, "*FAT Customer* isn't a valid class name."

---

[1] Third normal form does not allow repeating fields within a table. A separate table with a row for each repeating value is used in normalized tables.

"Well, the class name would actually be just *Customer*," Steve answered, "but we would have different versions of the *Customer* class definition; one for FAT, another for DB2. We would store them in separate files. I thought of giving both files the same name, but with different extensions to distinguish them—maybe `customer.FAT` and `customer.DB2`, for example."

"That looks fine, Steve," said Hanna, "but how would we switch between the FAT and DB2 versions of the code?"

"Like this," said Steve. He drew a *DB2 Customer* box next to the *FAT Customer* box, and then changed the lines [Figure 46].

"Let's suppose we need a DB2 version," he said. "We develop a totally separate class called *Customer* with its own methods to handle persistent storage in DB2 tables. We set up two different configurations. In the FAT configuration, the *FAT Customer* class inherits its persistent methods from the *CustomerBase* class, and in the DB2 configuration the *DB2 Customer* class inherits them from the *CustomerBase* class. With this approach we can use exactly the same class and method definitions for both the FAT and the DB2 implementations."

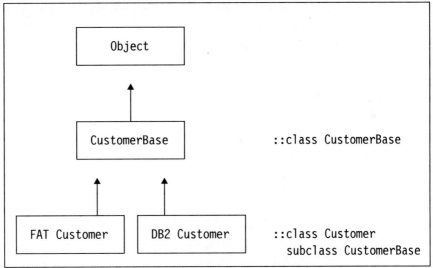

Figure 46. *Customer Class Inheritance Diagram*

"That's really neat, Steve," said Hanna. "That's using the power of inheritance in Object REXX to solve a real problem. What do you think, Curt?" she asked, turning to him.

"It sounds like it might work," said Curt, "but I think we should think it through a bit more before we decide on it."

Hanna turned back to Steve. "Why don't you try coding-up some sample code, Steve?" she said. "I'll gladly help you if you need me."

"I'll rough something out for *Customer*, and we can get together again and check it out," he replied. "If it works out the way we need, we can split the remaining classes between us and make corresponding changes to them."

"OK," said Hanna. "Do you think you'll have something ready for us to look at tomorrow?"

"Is that a question or an order?" asked Steve. "I think I'll have something for you to look at. After all, when you've seen one baseball game, you've seen them all."

"Oh Steve, you make me feel terrible!" said Hanna.

"But not as terrible as you'll feel if you don't deliver, Steve!" added Curt. And on this note they parted.

The Class Structure

The next morning, Steve was in early. When the other two arrived, Steve called them over to his ThinkPad. He had plugged it into the big screen so they could see what he was doing while he worked with the smaller screen of the ThinkPad.

"This turned out easier to do than I expected," said Steve. "I actually had time to watch the game. Too bad about the result! I've defined the new FAT Customer class to handle persistent storage on ASCII disk. It has only six methods." He pointed to the screen, which showed:

❑ A *persistentLoad* class method to load all customer objects from disk into storage when the system comes up:

```
::method persistentLoad class
   expose file
   file = 'customer.dat'
   call stream file, 'c', 'open read'
   do i = 0 by 1 while lines(file)
      parse value linein(file) with customerNumber '9'x name '9'x address
      self~new(strip(customerNumber), strip(name), strip(address))
   end
   call stream file, 'c', 'close'
   return i
```

❑ A *persistentStore* class method to write all customer objects from storage to disk when any customer object changes:

```
::method persistentStore class
   expose file
   call stream file, 'c', 'open write replace'
   do custx over self~extent
      x = lineout(file,custx~fileFormat)
   end
   call stream file, 'c', 'close'
   return 0
```

❏ Three methods—*persistentInsert, persistentUpdate,* and *persistentDelete*—that simply invoke the *persistentStore* method; for example:

```
::method persistentInsert
    return self~class~persistentStore
```

❏ A *fileFormat* method to convert the customer object into a tab-delimited string to be written to disk:

```
::method fileFormat
    return strip(self~number)'9'x || left(self~name,20)'9'x || ,
        left(self~address,20)
```

"There are only 45 lines of code in this class; it's really simple," Steve continued, showing them the code.[2]

"What did you have to do to the original Customer class?" asked Curt.

"A few things," replied Steve, and explained:

❏ "I had to change the *initialize* class method to invoke *persistentLoad*. This is the method in the *FAT Customer* class that loads all the customer objects from disk into RAM:

```
::method initialize class
    expose extent
    extent = .set~new
    self~persistentLoad
```

❏ "Then I changed the *init* method to invoke *persistentInsert* for a new customer:

```
::method init
    expose customerNumber name address cars orders
    use arg customerNumber, name, address
    cars = .set~new
    orders = .set~new
    self~class~add(self)
    if arg() = 4 then self~persistentInsert
```

❏ "And I changed the *update* method to invoke *persistentUpdate*:

```
::method update
    expose name address
    use arg name, address
    self~persistentUpdate
```

---

[2] The source code referred to by Steve is not included in this document. His application structure turned out to have some problems when Hacurs needed to introduce support for DB2. The *persistentInsert*, *persistentUpdate* and *persistentDelete* methods were moved to a separate mixin class called *Persistent*, as described in *The Persistent Class* on page 117.

❑ "Last, I changed the *delete* method to invoke *persistentDelete*:

```
::method delete
   expose customerNumber name address cars orders
   do carx over cars
      carx~delete
   end
   do workx over orders
      workx~delete
   end
   self~class~remove(self)
   self~persistentDelete
```

"And that's all I had to do. It was very simple, really," said Steve.

"I don't get it," said Curt. "Why did you define separate *persistentInsert*, *persistentUpdate*, and *persistentDelete* methods if all of them simply invoke the *persistentStore* method? That looks like a waste of time."

"Well, I'm thinking ahead to how we'll implement the DB2 support," said Steve. "With DB2 we'll use different SQL commands to handle the insert, update, and delete cases. As it happens, we plan to handle these different cases by rewriting all the customer objects to an ASCII file for Trusty Trucks. But we need to invoke different methods in the base customer class so that one version can meet both requirements."

"That's good thinking, Steve," said Hanna.

"Yes," said Curt, "so long as he doesn't waste too much time thinking about the DB2 implementation. We've got to deliver this system fast."

"I've done my bit," said Steve. "Why don't you and Hanna make the corresponding changes for the other classes? Those are the *Vehicle, Service Item*, *Part*, and *Work Order* classes. You can use my code as the basis for your changes. I've put it on the server in the project directory."

"Great! Let's go," said Hanna.

The Requires Directive

"Wait!" said Curt. "Are you planning to put the class definitions for customer, vehicle, service item, part, and work order into different files?"

"Yes," said Steve, "it makes for a nice clean implementation. None of the class files will be more than a few hundred lines of code."

"That may be so," Curt replied, "but these classes refer to one another extensively. If you put them into separate files, will they still be able to use one another?"

"That's why Object REXX has a *::requires* directive, Curt," Hanna said. "It allows the code in one file to use classes and methods defined in another. As you go through the code, make a note of the classes it refers to, and just make sure that you include a *::requires* directive for each class that isn't defined in the same source file."

Example of ::requires directive ────────────

In the *FAT Customer* class we require the definition of the *Customer-Base* class:

```
::requires 'carcust.cls'
```

The Persistent Class

Hanna and Curt settled down at their ThinkPads and started looking at the code. Pretty soon, Hanna called out, "Say Steve, we're all going to code exactly the same three *persistentInsert*, *persistentUpdate*, and *persistentDelete* methods for each of the other four classes. Isn't there a better way of doing that?"

"Come on Hanna, just cut and paste," said Curt. "It won't take long."

"But Curt," said Hanna "We talked about several different ways of implementing persistent storage and settled on our current approach for Trusty Trucks only because their file sizes are going to be small. What happens if their volumes grow, or if we find an opportunity to sell this solution to a bigger business that still wants a flat file solution but has large volumes?"

"Now you're thinking OO, Hanna!" agreed Steve. "There is an easy way to do what you're asking. I'll move the three methods out of the *FAT Customer* class and put them into a new class—let's say we call it *Persistent*. Then each of our five FAT classes can inherit these methods from the *Persistent* class."

"So we should make our FAT classes subclasses of the *Persistent* class?" asked Curt.

"Yes. No! Wait!!" said Steve. "Let's do this properly. I'll make the *Persistent* class a *mixin* class. When you define your FAT classes, use the *inherit* clause to inherit methods from my *Persistent* class. That's what mixin classes are for, after all. It's very simple, really. Look, I'll change the diagram to show how it would work."

Steve drew shadow boxes behind the *Customer* class to represent the other data classes to be handled—*Vehicle*, *Work Order*, *Service Item*, and *Part*. He then added a new *Persistent* mixin class and showed that the FAT data classes inherited some methods from it [see Figure 47].

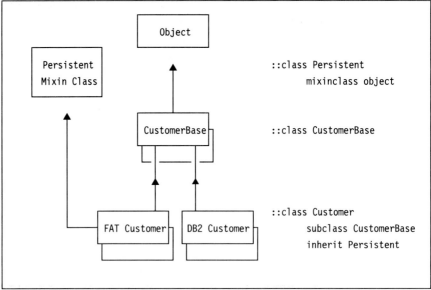

Figure 47. *FAT Data Classes Inheriting from a Mixin Class*

"What about the persistence methods for the DB2 version, Steve?" asked Hanna.

"The methods for persistence in DB2 will have to contain specific SQL statements for each object type," replied Steve. "We'll probably end up coding them directly into the DB2 classes themselves."

"Is all this messing about really worth the trouble?" asked Curt.

"If we start building it right, we'll finish building it easily," said Hanna. "If we start cutting corners while we're busy laying the foundations, there's no way we're going to get the walls square later on."

```
┌─── Sample code of the Persistent class ──────────────
│
│ ::class Persistent public mixinclass Object
│
│ ::method persistentLoad class              /* class methods */
│     return 0
│ ::method persistentStore class
│     return 0
│
│ ::method persistentInsert                  /* instance methods */
│     return self~class~persistentStore
│ ::method persistentDelete
│     return self~class~persistentStore
│ ::method persistentUpdate
│     return self~class~persistentStore
```

They all settled down to work. Their car dealer application was tested and working off persistent FAT file storage before the end of the day.

"I'm going to take this round to Trusty Trucks first thing tomorrow," said Curt. "Wish me luck—I may just come back with the specs signed off and a committed implementation plan."

"I'll bring in a bucket of ice and some sparkling wine," said Hanna. "Now don't disappoint us, or Steve and I will have to drown our sorrows—alone."

"You've got a deal!" said Curt.

Source Code and Sample Data for FAT Class Implementation

The source code for the *FAT* classes is described in Table 22 on page 301 and listed in *Persistence in Files* on page 509.

Sample flat files for the five classes of the car dealer application are described in Table 22 on page 301 (data subdirectory) and listed in *Sample Data* on page 489.

The source code of the *Persistent* class is listed in *Persistent Class* on page 507.

7

Graphical User Interfaces with OODialog

In this chapter, we look at a tool that can be used to develop a GUI for the Object REXX car dealer application.

This chapter also serves as a user's guide for the OODialog GUI builder that is part of the Object REXX code shipped with this book. Chapter 15, *OODialog Method Reference,* on page 317, contains the reference information for OODialog.

The Setup

"That was some party!" said Steve. "Do you still have the Trusty Trucks contract, Curt? I hope you didn't turn it into a paper plane."

Curt smiled. "No danger of that, Steve" he said. "This contract is going to pay our salaries for the next few months while I'm busy installing the system and training the users."

"The Trusty Trucks order was a wonderful business win, Curt," said Hanna. "It makes me feel really confident about the future of our company."

"While you're busy skinning this lion, I'll go out and catch another," said Steve. "Classy Cars is very keen on our car dealer application, and they'll feel a lot more confident once they know they won't be the only company using it. The only thing is, I'll have to develop a GUI front end for it."

"It would be great if we could sell our system to other customers," said Hanna. "That's the way to get our profits up. We spent a lot of time designing it so that we could easily customize it to different users' requirements. It would be a great shame if that were never put to the test."

"Well, I'll take care of the GUI," said Steve.

"How did you imagine to do that, Steve? We don't have the time to develop our own GUI builder, and I don't know of any graphical interface for Object REXX on the Windows systems yet. Did you find an ad while surfing?" asked Hanna surprised.

"No, I didn't. I don't think there are any tools for Windows yet. All the GUI builders I know are for OS/2 REXX. But you might remember Kevin, the German I met last year at the CEBIT conference," answered Steve.

"The guy working for IBM?" interrupted Hanna. Steve nodded approvingly. "That's right! In his last e-mail, he wrote that he's now responsible for the Windows part of Object REXX. In good foresight, I have already questioned him about some tools or products to do the same as Dr. Dialog does for OS/2 REXX."

"And what was his answer?" Hanna asked while searching the drawer of her desk for a pencil.

"He told me that they had received some inquiries on this subject before, and they decided to provide a Windows dialog interface that they named OODialog. Perhaps we could set up a video conference with Kevin, and he could tell us more about this interface," suggested Steve.

"That's a good idea," Hanna said with a little smile on her face. "I'll ask Curt to set up the environment for a video conference, and meanwhile you could contact Kevin and fix a date for it."

"I'm already in action," said Steve, leaving Hanna's cubicle and heading for his desk.

Steve began to write the request for a conference call addressed to Kevin. He was pretty sure that Kevin wouldn't be in his office. It must have been 8:30 p.m. in Germany, a time you didn't have to be ashamed of to be at home rather than working in the office. (It took Steve quite a few seconds to figure out the time in Germany, having to adjust for daylight savings time in addition to the usual time zone difference.) After Steve finished writing his request, he sent it to Kevin and returned to his usual business, which was thinking about the DB2 interface.

Steve was pretty surprised when he got an e-mail back from Kevin 20 minutes after he had sent his request. Kevin mentioned that he planned to do some overtime that day anyway, so he suggested holding the conference call in half an hour. Steve checked with Curt, who agreed to the time because he only had to make a few minor changes to the setup for the video conference. He then informed Hanna and wrote back to Kevin to confirm the time.

At the agreed upon time, Hanna joined her two colleagues, who were trying to get a connection over the Atlantic Ocean to Germany. The satellites and wires seemed to be pretty busy, so they had to try it a few times. Finally they connected to Kevin's CODEC system and could start their conference.

"Hello Kevin, how's it going. It's nice to talk to you again after such a long time. We have a pretty bad connection today," said Steve with some uncertainty about what to say.

"Hi Steve, thank you, I'm fine. Nice to talk to you, and your friends as well," said Kevin, nodding toward the camera. "After we finish our business, we have to talk about my residency in the States, but let's start talking about OODialog to save your company some money," said Kevin and grabbed his notes. "What do you want to know?" he asked. "Give me some keywords, so we don't waste time talking about subjects you're not interested in."

"We need all the information we can get. As I mentioned in the e-mail to you, we've got only a few days to create a GUI front end for our car dealer application to make an important deal with another company."

"OK." Kevin cleared his throat. "That means, we don't have to cover all available OODialog methods. I'll send you the reference guide for the dialog interface, so that you can look up the methods and their arguments that are provided with the tool."

"Well, it sounds pretty good that there's something written about your GUI builder," said Hanna with relief. "You could give us access to your machine so we can ftp it."

"No problem, already noted!" said Kevin, still writing on the paper in front of him. "Are you ready to start?"

"We're ready and waiting. Shoot," replied Steve.

"First I'll talk a little bit about the design of OODialog and later I'll introduce the dialog classes to you. Conceptually the GUI builder consists of three basic parts, the Object REXX interface to the Windows API written in C, an IBM resource editor called *Resource Workshop*, and the Object REXX dialog classes. The API is not of your concern, but the other two parts are fundamental for creating a professional front end for your application. There is also a way to create dialogs without the Resource Workshop, but I'll only mention this dynamic facility briefly at the end."

Resource Workshop

"With the Resource Workshop you can create and manipulate Windows resources. On Windows, a resource is a file or a part of a file that describes the layout of a window. You can use resources to compose the dialogs you want to execute using Object REXX. Within the Resource Workshop you can determine the size, frame type, and style of the dialog, and you can place the text, control items, and data fields that the dialog should contain."

"It would be great if we had this Resource Workshop installed on one of our machines, so we could follow you on the screen," Steve suggested.

"I'll send you all the stuff you need to use OODialog. For now, all I'm going to tell you is on a more abstract level. Once you receive the files, you can set up another conference call to talk about implementation questions. Do you agree with that?" Kevin asked, not really waiting for an answer.

"That's fine with us," the three said concurrently.

"OK, what was the last point I was talking about?" Kevin asked himself. "Ah yes, control items and data fields. I'll load a resource script on my ThinkPad and switch the video display to it, so that I can show you the available dialog items."

Kevin started the Resource Workshop on his machine, loaded an existing resource script from his hard drive, and pressed the display switch button to change the display of the video conferencing system to his computer screen. "Can you see the dialog?" Kevin asked. [See Figure 48.]

"Yes, clearly and plainly," Curt replied.

Kevin explained all of the dialog items to Steve, Hanna, and Curt.

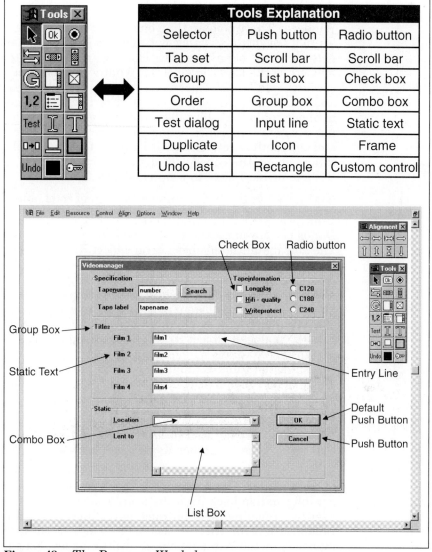

Figure 48. *The Resource Workshop*

"Now you know at least what I'm talking about," Kevin said, continuing with his lecture. "With the Resource Workshop you can add and place one or more of these items into the dialog. When you have finished your dialog design, you can save the data into a resource script, which you'll need later to execute the dialog with Object REXX. If you have no questions about the resources, I'll continue with the second part, the Object REXX dialog classes."

None of the three seemed to have any questions at the moment, so Kevin went on talking about the dialog classes.

Object REXX Dialog Classes

"The dialog classes build the interface between you—the user—and Windows. There is more than one class because there is more than one way of executing a dialog with Object REXX, and there are dialogs with different behaviors. The class we are most interested in at the moment is the *UserDialog* class. What we want to do with this class is execute a dialog that has been created with the Resource Workshop and stored into a resource script. The *UserDialog* class contains the methods to do that. I'll talk about the details of dialog execution during our next conference, when you have received the class definitions and the method reference. All I can do for now is tell you a few more things about the concept of dialog execution. Let me just get something to drink, I have to wet my whistle."

Kevin went to the fridge, snatched a can of soda, and took a long sip.

"Ahh," sighed Kevin, "that feels good. Let's continue. To use the *UserDialog* class, you must create an object—just as with every other class. The new instantiated object is an Object REXX object. At this moment you don't have a Windows object, which means that Windows hasn't created a dialog window yet or allocated memory for one. The next step will be loading the resource script. What you have now is a template describing the layout of the dialog in a Windows internal format. You still don't have a Windows object. If you call the method to execute the dialog in Object REXX, a real Windows object is created, data is transferred to the Windows object, and it is displayed. Now the user can enter data and communicate with the items of the dialog or the dialog itself. When the user is done with the dialog, the data is received in Object REXX from the dialog, and the Windows object is destroyed."

"What do you mean that *data is transferred or received*?" Curt asked, still trying to put together Kevin's last sentences.

Kevin nodded as if he expected this question. "There are two reasons to use a dialog: One is to give information to the user, the other is to get information back from the user. You can get information from the user by providing push buttons, entry lines (also called entry fields), radio buttons, or check boxes. The values of these dialog items are managed by the Windows object itself. Whenever the user changes the state of one of these dialog items, the internal data buffer of the Windows dialog is updated, but the state of the Object REXX object that has been instantiated to execute the dialog remains the same."

"That sounds pretty complicated," interrupted Curt.

"You'll see that it isn't," replied Kevin, "but I must tell you all this to prevent you from making typical errors later. OK?"

Again Kevin didn't wait for an answer, but instead continued explaining his dialog interface. "The *UserDialog* class defines some methods to transfer the data stored in the Object REXX dialog object to the

Windows dialog and vice versa. Before executing the Windows dialog, data is automatically copied from the Object REXX object to the Windows dialog, and after dialog execution, data is copied from the Windows dialog back to the Object REXX dialog object. What you should keep in mind from all of this is that there is a separation between the Object REXX dialog attributes and the Windows dialog data. Thus it is possible to keep the original data of the Object REXX dialog, if the Windows dialog has been abandoned—by pressing Cancel or Esc."

"OK! I guess I'm with you now," said Curt.

"It's good to stop at this point and continue when you have installed the GUI builder. Then we can talk about OODialog, using real method names," suggested Kevin.

"Fine. Thank you for helping. We appreciate your spending time with us," said Hanna, expressing her gratitude.

"Steve, do you have five more minutes?" asked Kevin, rushed. "I'd like to talk with you about my stay in the States."

"Certainly," Steve replied.

"Steve, at the same time you could fix the date for the next video conference," Hanna chimed in.

Steve talked for a few minutes with Kevin, who told him that he had been chosen by an American company to spend four weeks in the States to educate the employees of its software department. Steve and Kevin agreed on a time for the next video conference and settled on a date for a personal meeting.

Using the Resource Workshop

In the evening, Curt downloaded the files from Kevin's machine to his hard disk, using TCP/IP. Kevin sent Curt a short e-mail with guidance on installing the program and reference files of OODialog.

The next day, early in the morning, they got together for the second conference. Kevin didn't want to stay until 11 p.m. again, so the three Hacurs professionals had to get up at a time when the nicest part of their dreams begin—6:30 a.m.

After the usual greeting, Kevin asked Curt, "Did you manage to install OODialog?"

"Yes, I have," Curt answered proudly.

"Then let us start with the Resource Workshop right now." Kevin opened the second session. [We recommend that the reader follow this scenario online.]

"To start the Resource Workshop, enter Workshop or double-click on the icon created by the installation program. Once Workshop comes up, create a new resource by selecting the *New resource project...* in the *File* menu. The format we are interested in is a .RC, which stands for resource script. Now you can create a new dialog by selecting the *Resource - New* menu item."

"Wait, there's a dialog named *Add file to resource project*," interrupted Steve. "What shall we do with that one?"

"Use the **Cancel** button to close that dialog," answered Kevin. "Because you will use the resource scripts for Object REXX, you don't need a symbol definition file. It's useful for C or C++ programmers only—the original clientele of the Resource Workshop.

"Now, let's create a dialog. Select *New* in the *Resource* menu and *DIALOG* as the resource type. In the DialogExpert dialog you can choose between *Buttons on right* or *Buttons on bottom*. The other two choices don't apply, because you want to have a dialog and not a window."

"OK! We selected *Buttons on right* and have a new window containing a blank dialog with three buttons," said Steve.

"That's fine," said Kevin, "But before we go on, let's briefly set up the default display view of the Resource Workshop by selecting *Preferences* in the *Options* menu:

❑ "Select *WYSIWYG* drawing type. If your dialog contains owner drawn buttons, which we might discuss much later, you would select *Normal* drawing type.

❑ "Select *Use Ctl3dv2.dll* in *Selection options* so that your dialog is shown in 3D style.

❑ "Make sure that *Generate CONTROL statements only* is not selected.

"Now let's continue with the dialog. Select *Rename* in the *Resource* menu and set *New name* to the identification number you want to give the dialog, for example, 100. Symbolic IDs are allowed for C or C++ only. After that, double-click on the title bar of the dialog you created. What you get is a prompt to set the window style of your dialog. To use a resource script together with OODialog, you should disable the *Visible* check box within *Dialog style*, so that OODialog can enable the visible flag when the dialog is ready for that."

"Is it possible to enable one of the other check boxes?" asked Curt.

"Only *System menu, Thick frame, System modal, Modal frame,* and *Visible* have an effect on your dialog. By the way, the entry lines for *Class* and *Menu* must be empty, but you should enter a dialog title, for example, *Exercise Dialog*, into the *Caption* field. If later your dialog doesn't come up, check the *Class* entry line for characters that shouldn't be there. Now leave the *Window style* dialog, so that we can add a new item to the dialog. I'll do that once together with you. For all of the other items, the procedure will be the same. Add an entry line by selecting *Edit text* in the *Control* menu and clicking with the left mouse button at the position where you want to have the entry line placed. Later you can do that by selecting the corresponding icon within the tools window. Do you have an entry field within your dialog now?"

"Yes we do," answered Curt.

"Double-click on the entry line, and you get another prompt to set the style for this dialog item. What you have to do for each of your dialog items is give them a numerical identification number within the *Control ID* field. In addition, each item that is an input item—the entry line, the radio button, the check box, the combo box, and the list box—must be assigned a name within the *Caption* field. You'll need the ID for communicating with a dialog item, and the name to tell OODialog where to retrieve or store the data of the dialog item. Because there is usually no need to communicate with static items, such as text or group boxes, you can give all static members an ID of -1. Communicating includes sending and receiving data. So far that's all you have to do to make your dialog work together with OODialog."

"Kevin," said Curt, "when I leave the *Edit text style* dialog, the name I gave to the entry line is displayed within the field. I don't want that, do I?"

"It doesn't matter that the caption is displayed in the entry line, because it will not be displayed while executing the dialog with Object REXX. There are some additional comments I want to make concerning the naming of dialog items. OODialog will check your resource script for input items and create an attribute within your Object REXX dialog class to retrieve data from and store it to this object member. It could be a problem that Object REXX doesn't allow all characters within symbols. OODialog filters blanks and ampersands (&) that mark the letters that can be used together with the ALT key to select the items. Blanks within item names should be avoided. However, for radio buttons and check boxes, the text displayed and the item name are declared by the *Caption* input box within the *Item style* dialog, so blanks might be necessary within the item name. But when using blanks, you have to be aware that the name of the corresponding Object REXX attribute is without blanks."

"Wow, that's a lot," Curt said, taking a deep breath. "Is there anything else we have to know?"

"No, I think that's all you have to know about using the Resource Workshop," said Kevin, still seeking for matters he had not covered yet. "I have a meeting with my boss in 10 minutes. Call me again in two hours and we'll talk about how to execute your dialog from Object REXX. Meanwhile you could create a test dialog to experiment with the Resource Workshop."

Creating a Dialog with Object REXX

For two hours Curt and Steve played around with the Resource Workshop, and the result of a heated discussion was a small dialog containing all possible dialog items. At the arranged hour, only Steve and Curt sat together to set up the connection to Germany for the third time. Hanna said that there was a lot of work waiting for her, and two programmers would be enough.

The UserDialog Class

"Hi, so you are back to talk about dialog execution," Kevin said, without wasting time. "Did you manage to create a dialog we can use to demonstrate the execution within Object REXX?"

"Yes, we did," replied Curt, seizing the opportunity to be the first to answer. "I'll switch to our screen so that you can see it." [See Figure 49.]

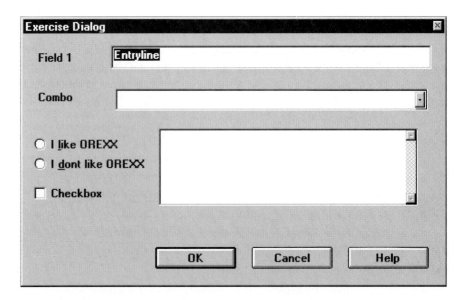

Figure 49. *The Exercise Dialog*

"Fine," continued Kevin. "That's all we need to start our third lesson. Start an editor to create a new Object REXX script. To make sure that we don't forget it, type in *::requires 'oodialog.cls'*. This statement, placed at the end of the script, embeds all of the necessary class definitions to use OODialog. For the first step, all we're going to do is display your dialog, enter some data, and quit the dialog. We won't implement any special functionality yet, so we don't have to define our own dialog subclass; we can use the existing class. The class we need for working with dialogs defined through a resource script is called *UserDialog*. I'll show you how to start your dialog on my display. What is the name of your dialog's resource script?"

"We named it *exercise.rc*," answered Curt.

"Could you show me your resource script, so I know the names you assigned to the dialog items?" Kevin asked Curt.

"Certainly, no problem," Curt said, loading the resource script into a text editor and switching the display of the video conferencing system to his monitor [see Figure 50].

```
/***********************************************************************
exercise.rc

produced by VisualAge Resource Workshop
***********************************************************************/

#define DIALOG_1         1
100 DIALOG 26, 28, 263, 163
STYLE DS_MODALFRAME | WS_POPUP | WS_CAPTION | WS_SYSMENU
CAPTION "Exercise Dialog"
FONT 8, "System"
{
 CONTROL "Entryline", 10, "EDIT", WS_BORDER | WS_TABSTOP, 56, 8, 198, 14
 CONTROL "ComboBox", 11, "COMBOBOX", CBS_DROPDOWNLIST | WS_CHILD | WS_VISIBLE | WS_TABSTOP, 59, 36, 193, 77
 AUTORADIOBUTTON "I &like OREXX", 12, 7, 66, 57, 12, BS_AUTORADIOBUTTON | WS_GROUP | WS_TABSTOP
 AUTORADIOBUTTON "I &dont like OREXX", 13, 7, 79, 72, 12
 AUTOCHECKBOX "Checkbox", 14, 7, 98, 60, 12
 CONTROL "List", 15, "LISTBOX", LBS_STANDARD | WS_TABSTOP, 86, 63, 159, 57
 DEFPUSHBUTTON "OK", 1, 83, 139, 50, 14
 PUSHBUTTON "Cancel", 2, 143, 139, 50, 14
 PUSHBUTTON "Help", 9, 203, 139, 50, 14
 LTEXT "Field 1", -1, 9, 11, 43, 8
 LTEXT "Combo", -1, 9, 37, 44, 8
}
```

Figure 50. *The Resource Script of the Exercise Dialog*

"Curt, Curt, Curt," Kevin said, sounding like a teacher. "Both of you didn't pay attention. You are using symbolic IDs in your resource script for the **OK**, **Cancel**, and **Help** push buttons."

"But they've been added by the Resource Workshop," Steve replied.

"I know that and in this particular case it's no problem because OODialog replaces these symbolic IDs for you if the resource is used together with UserDialog. *IDOK* is replaced by 1, *IDCANCEL* by 2, and *IDHELP* by 9, which are the default IDs for these buttons on Windows. To get accustomed to using numeric IDs, please change the symbolic IDs to the default values. In the meantime I'm going to write the Object REXX script."

Steve and Curt could hear Kevin typing into his ThinkPad, so they started the Resource Workshop and changed the button IDs.

"Here is the first part of what you have to do to execute your dialog," said Kevin after he stopped editing. Kevin switched the display again and started explaining the Object REXX script on his screen [see Figure 51].

```
dlg = .UserDialog~new
if dlg~InitCode <> 0 then exit
if dlg~Load("EXERCISE.RC", 100) > 0 then exit
if dlg~Execute("SHOWTOP") = 1 then do
    say dlg~EntryLine
    say dlg~ComboBox
    say dlg~ILikeOREXX
    say dlg~IDontLikeOREXX
    say dlg~CheckBox
    say dlg~List
end
dlg~deinstall
::requires "OODIALOG.CLS"                    /* OODialog classes */
```

Figure 51. *Simple Object REXX Script for the Exercise Dialog*

"The first line of the script instantiates an object of the predefined *UserDialog* class and assigns the object to the symbol *dlg*. The second line checks for an initialization error. The third line loads your resource script and creates a template for the Windows dialog. You don't have a Windows object yet. The Windows dialog will first be created within the *Execute* method. After *Load* you can set the object attributes for the dialog's data items. For example, if you'd like to fill data items of your dialog with values before the dialog pops up, you can assign these values to the attributes, using *UserDialog* methods."

"Give me an example, please," interrupted Steve. "How do I make *HANS* the default value for the first entry line of the dialog?"

"To do that, you add dlg~EntryLine = "HANS" after the *Load* method, where *EntryLine* is the entry field's caption entered in the Resource Workshop."

"Ahh, I think I got it now," Steve said, a bit hesitatingly, but with a smile on his face. "For each of the input items we added to the dialog, a method is created within our class that has the same name we assigned to the dialog items in the *Caption* field. Right?"

"You are close," Kevin replied. "There are three corrections I have to make on your statement. First, not one but two methods are added for attributes. Second, the name will be the *Caption* without '&' or blanks, or, if it isn't a valid Object REXX symbol at all, the attribute will be named *DATAx*, where *x* stands for the identification number of the dialog item. And third, the most important point, the attributes will be added to the object, not to the class."

"In our example that means *dlg* instead of *.UserDialog*, doesn't it?" Curt interjected, expecting praise.

"Exactly," replied Kevin.

"And if I want to change the value of a dialog item, or get the value back, all I have to do is assign a new value to the attribute that belongs to the item, or retrieve the value of the attribute," Curt added, not doubting for a moment that he could be wrong.

"Sorry," said Kevin, "but that's not quite right! You have to remember the separation between the data within your Object REXX object and the data within the internal buffer of the Windows dialog. Whenever you change an attribute belonging to your object, only the state of the object is modified, but not the state of the Windows dialog. To do that, you must transfer the data from the Object REXX object to the Windows dialog by using the *SetData* method. To get the data from the Windows dialog, use the *GetData* method. All data of the Windows dialog is then copied to your object and accessible by the attributes."

"What if I don't want to send or receive all dialog items, but only a single one?" asked Steve.

"There is a bundle of methods for doing that," answered Kevin. "See the OODialog Method Reference for *SetValue* and *GetValue, SetAttrib* and *GetAttrib,* and the other methods beginning with *Set* or *Get* followed by the name of the dialog item type, such as *SetEntryLine* or *GetRadioButton*."

"You didn't say anything about the *Deinstall* yet," said Curt. "What's this method for?"

"*Deinstall* is used to remove from memory the external functions needed for OODialog," answered Kevin. "It's a cleanup method."

Changing the Dialog Behavior

For a few seconds, none of the three had anything to say. Then Steve began to speak. "Kevin, at the beginning, you briefly mentioned something about our not having to implement any special functionality, and that was why we could use the predefined class, *UserDialog*. Is there a way to influence the behavior of the dialog, or what did you mean by *special functionality*?"

"Yes," said Kevin nodding. "OODialog defines more than 250 methods, and most of them are used to specify the behavior of the Windows dialog. We're going to use some of them right now. If you look at your dialog, you can see two items that don't make sense at the moment. Do you know which items I'm talking about?"

Steve and Curt were both concentrating on their dialog to figure out which items Kevin meant. Each of them has his own way of intensifying his mental ability through physical behavior. Steve was pulling at his nonexistent beard, and Curt was twiddling his hair with his index finger.

Suddenly, Steve seemed to have found a clue. "I guess you're talking about the list and the…" Steve was searching for the right word. "I don't remember what the second item is called. I mean the drop-down list."

"It's called a combo box," Curt added.

"Yes, the combo box," continued Steve. "If there are no values to select within these lists, what are they useful for?"

"Exactly!" shouted Kevin smiling. "You need to fill these lists with strings. You can do that dynamically, using methods of OODialog. Let us add a few lines to the sample program." Kevin disappeared from the screen and started to enter some code into his ThinkPad. After a minute or so, his head reappeared on the display of Steve and Curt's CODEC.

"I have added some lines," Kevin said. "Have a look at the new code." Kevin switched his display to the new code and presented the Object REXX source [see Figure 52].

Note: you must instance the subclass

```
dlg = .MyDialog~new                              Instance the subclass
if dlg~InitCode <> 0 then exit
if dlg~Load("EXERCISE.RC", 100) > 0 then exit
if dlg~Execute("SHOWTOP") = 1 then do
    say dlg~EntryLine                  /* id=10 */
    say dlg~ComboBox                   /* id=11 */
    say dlg~ILikeOREXX                 /* id=12 */
    say dlg~IDontLikeOREXX             /* id=13 */
    say dlg~CheckBox                   /* id=14 */
    say dlg~List                       /* id=15 */
end
dlg~deinstall

::requires "OODIALOG.CLS"                      /* OODialog classes */

::class MyDialog subclass UserDialog           /* my dialog class */
::method InitDialog
    self~AddListEntry(15, "Selection List 1")
    self~AddListEntry(15, "Selection List 2")
    self~AddListEntry(15, "Selection List 3")
    self~AddComboEntry(11, "Selection Combo 1")
    self~AddComboEntry(11, "Selection Combo 2")
    self~AddComboEntry(11, "Selection Combo 3")
```

Dont understand why it fails to work if you Just do the Add...Entry between ~Load & ~Execute

Figure 52. *Extended Dialog Using Subclassing*

"I defined my own class, *MyDialog*, which is a subclass of *UserDialog*," started Kevin, explaining what he did. "The definition of this class starts right after the *::requires* statement—this is a must. *MyDialog* redefines one method called *InitDialog*, which is defined in the *User-Dialog* class."

"To be correct, you overwrote this method," Curt suggested.

"Yes, I did," replied Kevin. "In my code the *InitDialog* method puts three strings into the list specified by ID 15, and three strings into the combo box specified by ID 11. There are several other methods of working with list boxes and combo boxes. I'll briefly list those for a list box. There is *AddListEntry, InsertListEntry, DeleteListEntry, Change-ListEntry, FindListEntry, GetCurrentListIndex, SetListTabulators, ListAddDirectory,* and *ListDrop.* For the combo box there are the same methods except that you have to use *Combo* instead of *List* for the method names, and there's no *SetComboTabulators.* I'll ftp my program to you right now so that you can run it to see the different behavior of the dialog." Kevin connected to Curt's ftp server by typing `ftp curt@hacurs.com`. Then he entered the user ID and password Curt gave him and copied the small Object REXX script to the hard drive of Curt's machine, using the ftp *put* command.

After Kevin left ftp, he said, "Now you can start the program by typing `REXX EXERCISE`." Steve and Curt invoked this command, played for a few seconds with the dialog, and were impressed at how easy it was to implement the new behavior of their dialog.

"If you have played long enough, please add a new button to your dialog with any identification number greater than 9, and not used already for another item," Kevin said, trying to stop them from playing around.

Curt started the Resource Workshop, intending to add the new button, when Steve interrupted him. "Let me do this, you already did most of the existing dialog. I'd like to learn more about the Resource Workshop as well." Curt didn't have the energy to fight Steve, so he decided to lean back and let Steve do the work. "You know," Curt said, struggling to avoid laughing, "I like work. I can sit there for hours and see it be done." Steve didn't react to his joke but instead tried to find the right icon on the tools window to add a button. After a while Steve saved his modifications and informed Kevin about his success. "I have added a button called **PushMe** with ID 16 to our dialog. Is there a reason for choosing an ID greater than 9?"

"Yes there is," answered Kevin. "ID 1 and 2 are reserved for the **OK** and the **Cancel** buttons. Both buttons terminate the dialog execution and call their corresponding methods. ID 9 is reserved for a **Help** button that calls the *help* method. All IDs from 10 to 9999 are available."

"Kevin," said Curt, "I executed the new dialog while you were explaining the button IDs, and I clicked on the new button, but nothing happened."

CONNECTBUTTONS

"Well, that's because you didn't connect the buttons of your Windows dialog to a method of your Object REXX object," replied Kevin. "You must tell your dialog what should happen when a button is clicked. The easy way to combine a dialog button with a method is to have it done automatically: load the resource script, using the *CONNECT-*

BUTTONS option of the *load* method. In that way, all buttons of the dialog will be connected to a method with the name given in the *Caption* field."

"The instruction to load the resource script would then look like this," said Steve, while he was switching the display to the video conference. The cursor of his editor was positioned at this line:

```
if dlg~Load("EXERCISE.RC", 100, "CONNECTBUTTONS") > 0 then exit
```

"Yes, exactly," said Kevin. "If that's not what you want to do, you can also explicitly connect a single button to a method, using the *Connect-Button* method. The code to connect your **PushMe** button to the *ButtonPushed* method is `self~ConnectButton(16, "ButtonPressed")`. After this statement is executed, the *ButtonPressed* method is called whenever you click on the button with ID 16."

What's Going On Inside

If you—the reader—think you know how to use a dialog with Object REXX and you're not curious about internals, you can skip this topic and continue with the next, *Implementing a Method for a Push Button* on page 138.

"Can you tell me more about the connection issue?" asked Steve. "I feel some uncertainty concerning this matter."

"OK," answered Kevin. "The best way is to tell you what happens internally when a button is pressed. Whenever the user pushes a button, Windows sends a message to the so-called window procedure of your dialog. Your window procedure gets the message and determines whether or not it is a message in which the dialog is interested. Because the window procedure usually is written in C, the Object REXX programmer cannot change the behavior of the dialog for an incoming message directly within the window procedure. What I implemented for OODialog instead is this: I look up the message in a table, and, if the message number is found, I send the message stored in the table entry to the Object REXX dialog object. All that *Connect-Button* does is add an entry to the message lookup table. If you don't connect the button to the dialog, the window procedure won't find an entry in the table, and the message sent by the button will be ignored. Is it clearer now?"

"That was really helpful," replied Steve. "And is it possible to connect other dialog items to methods as well?"

"Yes," said Kevin, "you can connect radio buttons and check boxes to methods by using the *ConnectControl* method and the same arguments as for *ConnectButton*. For more information about this topic, you should read about *AddUserMsg* in the OODialog Method Reference. With *AddUserMsg* you can connect any window message to an Object REXX method."

Connect any message to any method

Object REXX for Windows

Kevin had hardly finished the last sentence, when he remembered another issue. "Talking about the message table, there is another internal table that manages all the data items within the dialog. If you take the method reference, you can see the *BaseDialog* class containing an attribute called *AutoDetect*. If this attribute is 1—the default— your Windows dialog will be searched for data items, that is, entry lines, radio buttons, check boxes, list boxes, and combo boxes. There are methods to register data items manually, but usually there is no need for you to use them. Data items must be registered so that OODialog knows how to transfer data from and to the Windows dialog. For each registered data item, an attribute will be added to the Object REXX dialog—remember the *Caption* field and *DATAx*. If a stem variable is passed to the *init* method of the dialog, the stem variable is searched for the ID of the dialog items to initialize and retrieve their data. Because *SetValue*, *GetValue*, *SetAttrib*, and *GetAttrib* use information from this table, it is only possible to use these methods for dialog items that have been registered."

"OK," said Steve, "but because auto detection is enabled as the default, these methods can be used for *normal* dialogs, right?"

"Yes, that's right," answered Kevin, "but I classified you as curious programmer, and therefore wanted to tell you more than you actually need to know."

"That's nice," said Steve, blushing a bit. "Thank you. Let me see if I'm not only curious, but also able to understand. Push buttons and data items must be registered so that OODialog knows about them and the calling of methods can be enabled. The data transfer between the Object REXX object and the Windows dialog depends on the registration as well. What I didn't understand is the thing with the stem."

"The stem," began Kevin, hesitating because of an uncertainty that he went too far with this, "is the second way to transfer data. If you pass the name of a stem to the *init* method of a *UserDialog* object, data will be taken from the stem variable to initialize your Windows dialog, and it will be updated in the stem variable after the dialog execution. A stem is particularly useful when the dialog includes a lot of check boxes or radio buttons, because you can use an index variable to initialize them. I guess this explanation is deep enough and more than you must really know, but it might help you understand how to use OODialog just a little bit better."

"Yes, indeed," replied Steve. "I imagine that it will help me remember that I have to use numerical identification numbers, name the dialog items with valid Object REXX symbol names, and use the *CONNECT-BUTTONS* option or the *ConnectButton* method, if I'm using push buttons. Thanks again, it was a good lesson."

Implementing a Method for a Push Button

Kevin thought for a few seconds about how to continue and then suggested, "Let's define the *PushMe* method for our dialog and connect it to the Windows dialog. For educational reasons we're going to use the *ConnectButton* method. Within the *PushMe* method you can calculate, print something to the console or a printer, display a message box, store data in a file, or work with your dialog. Please wait a few seconds so that I can change our demo script."

Again Kevin started to hack on his keyboard to make the required changes. Curt and Steve could here the noise of keys clicking, so it was easy for them to recognize when Kevin was finished with his new script, and they were able to load the new program into their editor.

"I made the modifications," Kevin said, reappearing on the display. "You can load the new script now."

"It's already up," replied Curt [see Figure 53].

"The first part of the REXX script didn't change," Kevin started to explain his work. "I have added two methods, *PushMe* and *Validate*. Within *PushMe* I used a collection of methods provided by OODialog to demonstrate its power, so you can honor what I did by developing such a program. Here is a short description of what *PushMe* does. First, I retrieve all of the data from the Windows dialog into *dlg*'s attributes through *GetData*. Then, I check if the *I dont like OREXX* radio button is selected. If so, I disable the **OK** button, so it's only possible to leave the dialog with Cancel or Esc. I change the data within the entry line directly, I let the list box disappear, and I add a new string to the list that I hid before. If the radio button isn't selected, I enable the **OK** button, set the entry line to *You can go now* indirectly, load the attributes into the Windows dialog, and show the list."

"Does *directly* mean that you change a single dialog item and *indirectly* that you copy all of the attributes to the dialog?" asked Steve.

"Exactly!" answered Kevin.

"Why did you add the *Validate* method?" asked Curt inquisitively.

"Because I wanted to show you how dialog validation is done with OODialog," Kevin answered. "The *Validate* method is called by **OK**, and if *Validate* returns a zero value, the Windows dialog is not closed. In our case, *Validate* checks whether *I dont like OREXX* is selected, and if it is, a message box is displayed and the dialog does not disappear."

```
dlg = .MyDialog~new

if dlg~InitCode <> 0 then exit

if dlg~Load("EXERCISE.RC", 100) > 0 then exit

if dlg~Execute("SHOWTOP") = 1 then do
   say dlg~EntryLine                    /* id=10 */
   say dlg~ComboBox                     /* id=11 */
   say dlg~ILikeOREXX                   /* id=12 */
   say dlg~IDontLikeOREXX               /* id=13 */
   say dlg~CheckBox                     /* id=14 */
   say dlg~List                         /* id=15 */
end
dlg~deinstall

::requires "OODIALOG.CLS"               /* OODialog classes */

::class MyDialog subclass UserDialog    /* my dialog class */

  ::method InitDialog
     self~AddListEntry(15, "Selection List 1")
     self~AddListEntry(15, "Selection List 2")
     self~AddListEntry(15, "Selection List 3")
     self~AddComboEntry(11, "Selection Combo 1")
     self~AddComboEntry(11, "Selection Combo 2")
     self~AddComboEntry(11, "Selection Combo 3")
     self~ConnectButton(16, "PushMe")

  ::method PushMe
     self~GetData
     if self~IdontLikeOREXX = 1 then do
        self~DisableItem(1)             /* disable OK */
        self~SetValue(10, "You cannot leave the dialog" ,   ← EntryLine
                          "if you hate Object REXX")
        self~HideItem(15)               /* hide the list */
        self~AddListEntry(15, "Tried to quit")
     end; else do
        self~EnableItem(1)              /* enable OK */
        self~EntryLine = "You can go now"
        self~SetData
        self~ShowItem(15)               /* show the list */
     end

  ::method Validate                     /* called by OK */
     if self~GetValue(13) = 1 then do
        call InfoMessage "If you don't like Object REXX" ,
                         "you cannot leave"
        return 0
        end
     else return 1
```

Figure 53. *Sample Dialog Class with a Push Button Event*

Kevin loaded one of the OODialog source scripts—BASEDLG.CLS—into his editor and went through it to find methods he didn't explain yet. Reaching the end of the script, Kevin said, "I think we covered all of the fundamental methods for working with dialogs. Are there any questions?"

Steve answered this question in the negative. "No," he said, "I think Curt and I should try to do the GUI with the level of knowledge we have now, and if there are problems we can't solve, we'll send an S.O.S. and call you again. Thank you very much Kevin for the time you shared with us. I owe you a beer or two."

"It's been my pleasure," Kevin said quickly, to stop Steve from expressing his thanks. "But do me a favor. I'd rather have a hamburger than a beer because your American beer is not comparable to our German beer, which is still made with natural ingredients only."

"That's fine with me," Steve replied. "See you in eight weeks at the latest, when you're on your residency. Bye!"

"Yes, see you, Ciao," Kevin said, using one of the few Italian word he knew. "Good bye Curt, and have fun developing the GUI."

"Ciao, Kevin," said Curt, showing that he too can pronounce an Italian word. "If the design of your graphical interface is good, fun is guaranteed."

Kevin switched off his camera and so did Curt. "It's late again," said Steve, looking at his watch. "Come and join me at Wendy's for a Caesar salad. Tomorrow we can start coding the GUI."

"Thank you," said Curt, "I don't hear myself saying no."

The two shut down their systems, left the office, and drove to Wendy's to enjoy the promised salad. For the next three days, they designed the draft dialogs with the Resource Workshop and embedded them into the existing car dealer application. After the weekend, Hanna asked her two colleagues about the GUI.

"Boys, did you complete the user interface yet?" Hanna asked, like a mother asking her little children if they've done their homework.

"Yes we did," answered Curt, "but some improvements are required, and we don't know how to do them at the moment. We are going to set up one more video conference with Kevin. Is that OK with you?"

Hanna nodded. "Certainly, if you think it's necessary."

"It's not absolutely necessary to make these improvements," said Steve, "but it would be good to implement what we planned, and it's at least not a waste to get more information about OODialog."

Steve scheduled the video conference for 9 a.m. the next day.

Doing Graphics with OODialog

[To save the reader some time we jump right into the video conference the next day....]

"What problems do you have?" Kevin asked.

"We decided to make our dialogs more attractive, so we have to change the appearance of the dialogs. We'd like to use our own graphical push buttons, and it would be nice to display the car dealer's logo in the background of the main panel."

"Well," said Kevin, "that's no big deal. The method you need for using a bitmap as the background is called *BackgroundBitmap* or *Tiled-BackgroundBitmap*, depending on whether you want to show a bitmap one time or tile the whole dialog background with a bitmap. The argument for both methods is the file name of the bitmap file.

"The other method you're looking for is called *ConnectBitmapButton*. As you can see from its name, this method is used instead of *Connect-Button*. The arguments for this method are the ID of the button, the method name to be called, and four bitmap files representing the four button states *normal, focused, selected,* and *disabled*—the normal bitmap is required and the others are optional. The last argument is used for options. Valid options are *FRAME, USEPAL, INMEMORY*, and *STRETCH. FRAME* means that a 3D frame is drawn around the bitmap so that your bitmap button behaves just like a normal Windows button. *USEPAL* is necessary to correctly display bitmaps that have their own color palette instead of the system default. *INMEMORY* is necessary to indicate that the bitmap has already been loaded into memory using the *LoadBitmap* method. In this case the bitmaps are not specified by a file name but by a handle. *STRETCH* allows the bitmaps to match the size of the button rectangle exactly.

"For all of the graphical functions you can do with OODialog, you have to place a push button into your dialog and select *Owner draw* in its style dialog [double-click on the push button to get the style dialog]. The graphic methods need the so-called device context—memory to draw graphics—from the button. Even though you might not want the functionality of a button for your graphic, you must use an *owner drawn* button, but it would not be connected to a method. Also, change the drawing style to normal [*Preferences* in *Options* menu]; otherwise the push buttons are invisible when not selected."

"This means that if I'd like to display a bitmap in my dialog, I'll have to place a button with the size of the bitmap into the dialog at the position where I'd like to display the bitmap, double-click on the button and select *Owner draw* in the style dialog, and connect the button to the bitmap through *ConnectBitmapButton* without using a method name. Does this hit the core?" asked Steve.

"Hey," said Kevin, with an intense tone to his voice, "you're good, you know that?"

"I know it, but I'm not sure if Curt and Hanna know it too," Steve said, kidding.

"Back to the subject," said Kevin. He drew his lips together and stopped smiling. "Instead of using file names, you can load the bitmaps into memory by using *LoadBitmap* and then pass the return value of this method—a handle of the bitmap—to *ConnectBitmapButton* as the arguments for the *normal, focused, selected*, and *disabled* states. Loading the bitmaps into memory might be much faster if you change the bitmap within one button very often. To change the bitmap within a button, you can use the *ChangeBitmapButton* method [see Philosophers' Forks example]. If you no longer need the bitmap, you should free the memory by using *RemoveBitmap*. You can also move a bitmap within a button by using the *ScrollBitmapFromTo* method. To complete the list there are a number of other graphic methods to draw colored figures:

❑ to create drawing objects there are *CreatePen* and *CreateBrush*;
❑ to draw a line there's *DrawLine*;
❑ to draw a pixel there's *DrawPixel*, and to get the color of a pixel there's *GetPixel;*
❑ to draw a rectangle there's *Rectangle*;
❑ to draw circles and ellipses there are *DrawArc, DrawPie*, and *DrawAngleArc*; and
❑ to fill an outline with a color, there's *FillDrawing*."

"You gave me a keyword," interrupted Curt. "Is there a way to simulate a neon sign like the LED ones that are used in shops? We'd like to show the highlights of the cars that way."

"You are lucky, aren't you?" replied Kevin. "A method called *ScrollIn-Button* displays a given text with a given font within a button from right to left. For more information about this topic, you should read the OODialog Method Reference. There are other methods of writing text to a dialog as well, but it would take too much time to explain all of them."

"I guess we don't have to write text to a dialog," said Curt. "All we want to do is try the *ScrollInButton* method."

"I'll send you some sample scripts that I wrote for test reasons while developing OODialog," said Kevin, writing himself a note to send them. "These samples might give you some assistance in developing your own application. They should cover most of the methods available with OODialog, so, together with the OODialog Method Reference, you have quite enough information to use OODialog to its fullest. [See *OODialog Samples* on page 305.] Take a short glance at one of the dialogs included with the samples, and you'll be certain that you can make your user interface look really good." [See Figure 54.]

Figure 54. *A Dialog Using Bitmap Buttons*

While Steve and Curt were looking at the dialog example, Kevin sent them a diagram he had prepared to summarize the contents of the previous video conferences [see Figure 55 on page 145]. "Once you get the file I'm currently sending, I'd like you to load it into Freelance. But before that, let's briefly talk about nesting dialogs."

Nesting Dialogs

"What do you mean by *nesting dialogs?*" Curt asked curiously.

"Nesting dialogs means that you execute a dialog while running another dialog," Kevin satisfied Curt's curiosity. "You'll see that a somewhat bigger application cannot be easily structured without nesting dialogs. OODialog has a maximum nesting level of 10 dialogs. The good thing is that you don't have to care about the nesting. You just instantiate a new dialog object, create the Windows dialog, and execute it. OODialog does the dialog management for you. Running a *child* dialog from a *parent* dialog causes the parent dialog to be disabled, which means that you cannot access control items of this dialog anymore."

"That's how it should be," Steve interjected, "because a dialog should at least be application modal."

"Exactly," replied Kevin. "You don't have to disable the dialog manually, it is done automatically. The usual way is to execute the newly created child dialog with *SHOWTOP*, which causes the dialog to be the topmost window. After the dialog is finished, the parent dialog is enabled again automatically."

"Does the parent dialog become the topmost window after the child dialog is finished?" asked Curt.

"No," Kevin answered. "You have to do that yourself by calling the *ToTheTop* method in the parent dialog. To make sure that the parent dialog isn't locked by an unsuccessful execution of the nested dialog, you can invoke the *Enable* method before the parent dialog gets control back. But these two methods and the limit of 10 dialogs are all you have to know about nesting dialogs.

"The file transfer should be complete now. Because you will need some time to study the diagram, I suggest disconnecting for 30 minutes and then going on. Reconnect at a quarter to?"

"Fine," replied Curt as he popped up the menu of the video conferencing system to disconnect the current communication.

Summary of User Dialog *class.*

Figure 55 describes the way the methods of a UserDialog object must be called to create and execute a Windows dialog.

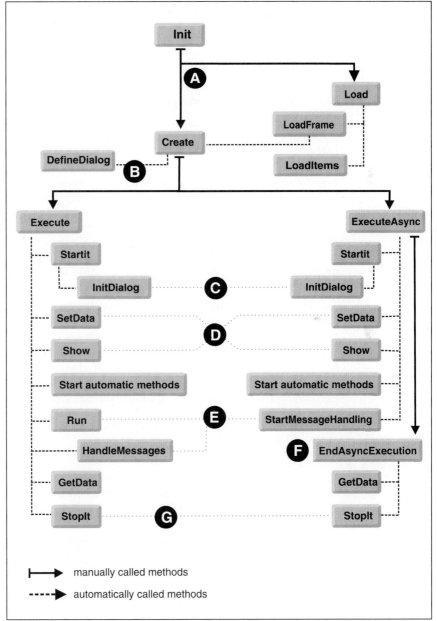

Figure 55. *How the Methods Work Together*

The first method that is called is *Init*. This is done automatically by the *new* class method when an object is instantiated. Once the object has been created, the user has the choice [A] between defining the dialog manually—using the *Create* method—and loading the dialog from a resource script—using the *Load* method. The choice is indicated by the solid lines.

If the user wants to load the dialog from a resource script, the *Load* method first calls *LoadFrame* and then *LoadItems*. *LoadItems* can also be used for a *CategoryDialog* to load all dialog items from a dialog resource into a category page. *LoadFrame*, however, calls *Create*, which means that choosing to load the dialog ends in the same branch as choosing to define the dialog manually.

The *Create* method allocates memory for a dialog template to which the dialog items can be added. The *DefineDialog* method [B], which is called by *Create*, is the right place to add items to the dialog. If the user chooses to define the dialog manually, it is recommended that *UserDialog* be subclassed and all *Add...* messages (*AddText*, *AddEntryLine*, *AddButton*) be placed into *DefineDialog*. The new attributes will be added to the OODialog object by *LoadItems* or the *Add...* methods. Therefore, the user can assign values to dialog items after *DefineDialog* is executed. The user can choose whether to send the *Execute* message or the *ExecuteAsync* message after *Create* has been processed. At this time, no Windows dialog exists, only a dialog template that contains all information about the dialog's appearance.

Once the user sends the *Execute* or *ExecuteAsync* message, the *Startit* method is called. Method *Startit* creates a real Windows dialog and calls *InitDialog* [C]. The *InitDialog* method is the right place to fill the combo boxes and list boxes—using *AddListEntry* or *AddComboEntry*—and to invoke other methods that deal with real dialog items (Windows objects). All *Connect* methods, such as *ConnectCheckBox*, *ConnectButton*, and *ConnectBitmapButton*, can also be placed in this method, but the *Init* method is the recommended place because the *Connect* methods do not deal with Windows objects. You can also prepare attributes of dialog items with values, but do not use the *Set...* methods.

In the *Execute* and *ExecuteAsync* methods the next method called is *SetData* to transfer the data from the attributes—or the stem if given—to the Windows dialog. This is why *Set...* methods in *InitDialog* have no effect because the data items are set again by *SetData*.

Next, the dialog is displayed by sending *Show* [D]. After this, all the methods that were added by using *AddAutoStartMethod* are executed asynchronously. This feature is for animated buttons.

At this point there is a difference between *Execute* and *ExecuteAsync* [E]. For *Execute* dialogs, the *Run* method is invoked next to dispatch the messages until the dialog is closed by the user. For *ExecuteAsync* dialogs the *StartMessageHandling* message is started to handle the incoming messages and dispatch them to the dialog object. Because this method is executed asynchronously, *ExecuteAsync* returns while the dialog is still up.

When the dialog is closed, the data is transferred from the Windows dialog to the OODialog object through *GetData*, and the dialog is removed from memory by *Stopit*. A second *Execute* is not possible. When using *ExecuteAsync*, you must call *EndAsyncExecution* [**F**] manually to wait until the dialog is closed by the user and to transfer the data to the object.

After *Stopit* [**G**] is called, you can no longer use methods that deal with Windows objects. You still have access to the attributes of the dialog object.

OODialog Classes

"If you remember our first video conference," began Kevin after the reconnect, "I told you that there is more than one way to execute your dialogs with OODialog. What we did all the time was use *UserDialog*, which is required when the dialogs are stored in a resource script. In some of my samples I'm using other classes that I'd at least just briefly like to mention. The class I'm going to introduce to you right now is called *ResDialog*."

The ResDialog Class

Kevin continued: "The *ResDialog* class is used when the dialogs are stored within a dynamic link library (DLL). Are you familiar with DLLs?"

"I think so," said Steve, "at least if they are the same on Windows as on OS/2."

"They serve the same purpose," said Kevin. "If you save your resources as a .RES file in binary format—you can do that with the Resource Workshop—you can link this file to a DLL. Windows provides functions to load resources directly out of a DLL, and exactly those functions are used by *ResDialog*. The advantage of using DLL resources is that they are faster. You can store bitmaps in the DLL as well, so you no longer have this heap of files, and your dialog resources are more protected."

"You mentioned that it is possible to save resources in binary format with the Resource Workshop," interrupted Steve. "What you didn't mention is how to link the resources to a DLL."

Kevin explained: "In order to link a binary resource file to a DLL, OODialog includes the IBM VisualAge C++ linker, *ILINK*. This linker enables you to create a DLL from a RES file.

"The linker must be executed within a command window. Here is the syntax to invoke the linker:

```
ilink MyDialog.res /DLL -out:MyDialog.dll
```

"This command creates `MYDIALOG.DLL` from `MYDIALOG.RES`. To minimize the keystrokes, you can also use `MAKEDLL.BAT`, which contains the same command. To create the same DLL, just enter `MAKEDLL MyDialog` on the command prompt. Notice that when using `MAKEDLL` the name of the DLL is the same as the name of the binary resource file, with a different extension."

"Do you recommend using binary resources stored in a DLL or resource scripts?" Steve wanted to know from Kevin.

"It depends on what you want to do," replied Kevin. "If your application uses dialogs with many bitmap buttons or if you use a lot of complex dialogs, it is better to store the resources in a DLL so that you have just one file instead of all those .BMP and .RC files. The management and distribution are easier as well. If your application is not too big, you don't have to bother with the link process, and it's easier to modify your resources. Notice also that the bitmaps stored in a DLL don't support different color palettes. This might force you to use bitmap files. Is that enough to answer your question?"

"Yes, thanks," nodded Steve.

"There are a few differences between using *UserDialog* and *ResDialog* that I want to list now," Kevin continued.

❑ "The *init* method needs two (additional) arguments, the name of the DLL and the ID of the dialog resource. For example, to instantiate a dialog object that can execute dialog 100 that is stored in `MYDLG.DLL`, you have to use this statement:

```
dlg = .ResDialog~Init("MYDLG.DLL", 100)
```

❑ "You don't have to call *Load* or *Create*. As a matter of fact, you must not call them.

❑ "The *DefineDialog* method is not called.

❑ "You can pass the resource IDs of bitmaps stored in your DLL to *AddBitmapButton* and *ChangeBitmapButton* instead of the file names or bitmap handles.

"The rest of the methods of *ResDialog* are the same as those of *UserDialog*. The difference, as explained, is how to initialize the dialog. Any questions?"

"I'm not sure it's clear," answered Curt, "but it might be more clear after I see one of your programs that uses *ResDialog*."

"Yes, I'm sure that would help," replied Kevin.

The CategoryDialog Class

"Now there's only one class left that I didn't mention, but it's the class I'm most proud of because you can do really nice dialogs with it. It's called *CategoryDialog*, and it is a subclass of *UserDialog*. *CategoryDialog* facilitates the use of more than one dialog within one window. It's comparable to OS/2's notebook. The best way to explain it is to show you one of these dialogs. I have already prepared a demo application for *CategoryDialog*. I'll switch the display to it, but I need a few seconds." [See Figure 56.]

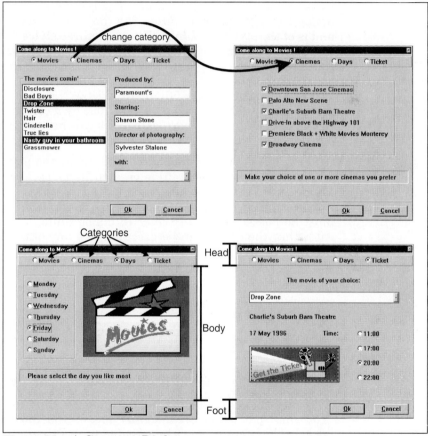

Figure 56. *A Category Dialog*

Kevin explained, "The four dialogs displayed on my screen are four pages of a *CategoryDialog*. To select another page, the user must select the corresponding radio button and the other page will be displayed—illustrated by the curved arrow. The dialog is split up into three parts, which I have named head, body, and foot. Only the body must be defined by the programmer; head and foot are created by OODialog itself. Here are the Object REXX instructions to execute this category dialog." [See Figure 57.]

```
dlg = .TicketDialog~new(data.,,,,"TOPLINE")
if dlg~InitCode \= 0 then do; say "Init did not work"; exit; end

dlg~createcenter(200, 180, "Come along to Movies !")
dlg~execute("SHOWTOP")
dlg~deinstall
```

Figure 57. *Execution of a Category Dialog*

"The first line instantiates an object of *TicketDialog*, which is a subclass of *CategoryDialog*. The initialization data will be passed to the dialog through the stem *data*. The dialog consists of four categories and is of the style *TOPLINE*. There are three styles for a *CategoryDialog*: normal—using no option—, *TOPLINE*, and *DROPDOWN*. Instantiating a normal *CategoryDialog* displays the categories in one column on the left side of the dialog. You already saw the layout of a *TOPLINE* dialog [Figure 56]. If *DROPDOWN* is specified, the category selection isn't done by radio buttons, but by a combo box. This is particularly useful when more categories are needed than would fit on one line of the dialog.

"After *InitCode* has been checked, the dialog template [see *Summary of User Dialog* on page 145] is created by using *CreateCenter*. Using *Create* or *CreateCenter* means that no resource script is used to retrieve the layout of the dialog. This is why the size of the dialog must be passed to *CreateCenter* in dialog units, not in screen pixels. After that the dialog can be executed like any other dialog with *Execute*."

"Is the third argument of *CreateCenter* the title of the dialog?" asked Curt.

"Yes, it is," answered Kevin.

"How do I know the size the dialog must have?" Curt continued questioning.

"The dialog must be big enough so that all the dialog pages fit, plus the head and the foot, which are added automatically."

"How are the single dialog pages defined?" Curt asked impatiently. "You said that using *CreateCenter* means that no resource script is loaded. Therefore it won't be possible to use the Resource Workshop, right?"

"You might find it astonishing, but you can use the Resource Workshop to define the pages. What you cannot use the Resource Workshop for is to define the category dialog itself, which there is no need for. Let me explain how the layout of a *CategoryDialog* is defined in the previous example." Kevin moved the cursor in his editor so that the necessary lines of the Object REXX script could be seen on the display he was sharing with Steve and Curt [see Figure 58].

```
::class TicketDialog subclass CategoryDialog

...

::method InitCategories
   self~catalog['names'] = .array~of("Movies", "Cinemas", "Days", ,
                                     "Ticket")
...

::method Movies
   self~loaditems("rc\movies.rc")

::method Days
   self~AddText(10,self~SizeY - 65,0,0, ,
                "Please select the day you like most")
   self~AddRadioGroup(31, 5, 5,0, "&Monday &Tuesday &Wednesday" ,
                        "T&hursday &Friday &Saturday S&unday")
   self~AddBlackRect(1, self~SizeY -68, self~SizeX -6, 14)
   self~AddBitmapButton(145, 73, 10, 125, 100, ,,"bmp\movie.bmp")

::method Ticket
   self~loaditems("rc\ticket.rc")
   self~connectBitmapButton(45, 'printTicket', "bmp\ticket.bmp",,,, ,
                        "FRAME USEPAL STRETCH")
...
```

Figure 58. *Defining the Layout of a CategoryDialog*

Kevin pointed with the mouse and said, *"InitCategories* is one of the methods that must be overwritten. To use *CategoryDialog* you have to subclass it, otherwise it's worthless. *InitCategories* is used to set the information about which categories are used. The information must be
 assigned to the Object REXX <u>directory object</u> *catalog*. The entry *names* in this directory must be assigned to an array containing the names of the categories.

"If you made the most of the last half an hour you'll have noticed that the *DefineDialog* method is called by *Create* to add dialog items to the dialog template. With a *CategoryDialog*, there's not only one dialog to be defined; there are as many as there are categories. Instead of calling *DefineDialog*, a method with the same name as the category is called to define the particular dialog page."

Kevin moved the mouse cursor to the definition of the *Days* method and said, "This is the method that is called to define the dialog page that is displayed when the *Days* radio button is selected. Below is the *Ticket* method, which is called to define the *Ticket* page."

"If I understand correctly," Curt interrupted, "the methods have the same name as the category names I added to the array in *catalog['names']*."

"Correct," answered Kevin. "In the *Days* method the dialog items are added manually instead of loading a resource script. The *Add...* methods need the positions where the dialog items ought to be located in dialog units. These methods enable you to create dialogs without using the Resource Workshop. Some of them add a whole group of items, which is much faster than adding the items with the Resource Workshop."

"Are all the methods to add dialog items manually listed in the OODialog method reference?" Steve asked, hoping that the answer would be yes.

"Yes, all of them," answered Kevin.

"We still haven't used the Resource Workshop to define the pages," interjected Curt, "even though you said it's possible."

"Slow down," Kevin replied, "and look at the *Ticket* method. It calls *LoadItems* with the name of a resource script. *LoadItems* is the same method that is used within *Load* together with *LoadFrame* to retrieve the resource. Because the *CategoryDialog* is created by means of *Create* and the pages contain only dialog items, it's not necessary to retrieve the dialog frame, only the items of the dialog. That's what is done by *LoadItems*."

"Is it possible to load items out of a resource script and then manually add more of them?" asked Curt.

"Yes," said Kevin, "you can use both ways together. Once you have defined your dialog pages, all dialog handling, such as creating the dialog, switching the pages, and transferring the data, is done by OODialog itself. The data handling is the same as with *UserDialog*. Object attributes will be added for all of the data items. It's also possible to use a stem variable to set or retrieve the dialog values. All of the data items of all pages will be copied from or into one stem."

"Let me make sure I've gotten it," said Curt. "All I have to do to use a *CategoryDialog* is to subclass it, overwrite *InitCategories* with a method that creates an array containing the category names and assign it to *catalog['names']*, and define the methods to load or add the dialog items to the pages, using method names matching the names that were stored in the array. Is that it?"

"Yes, that's it, but there's still something to be aware of," answered Kevin. "Because the dialog items are spread over more than one dialog, all of the methods that must communicate with real Windows objects, such as *GetValue*, *SetValue*, *AddComboEntry*, and *FindListEntry*, must know in which page the corresponding dialog item is. Therefore, you must use the *Category* methods instead and add the dialog page number starting with 1. Some of the *Category* methods are used in the sample." Kevin moved the scroll bar until the definition of *InitDialog* became visible [see Figure 59].

```
...

::method InitDialog
    expose films
    self~InitDialog:super
    films = .array~of("Vertigo","Taxi Driver","Superman", ,
                      "Larger than Life","Hair","Cinderella", ,
                      "True Lies","E.T.","Twister","Lawnmower Duel")
    do i = 1 to filsm~items
        self~addCategoryListEntry(31, films[i], 1)
    end
    self~setCategoryEntryLine(32,"Paramount")
    self~setCategoryEntryLine(33,"Kim Novak")
    self~setCategoryEntryLine(34,"Alfred Hitchcock")
    ...

::method PageHasChanged              /* invoked when page changes */
    expose films
    NewPage = self~CurrentCategory           /* current page */
    if NewPage \= 4 then return
        self~CategoryComboDrop(41, 4)              /* empty combo box */
        Lines = self~getCategoryValue(31, 1)    /* get selected films */
        do i = 1 to words(Lines)              /* fill combo box */
            self~addCategoryComboEntry(41, films[word(Lines,i)] ,4)
        end
        self~setCategoryComboLine(41, films[word(Lines,1)] ,4)
        ...
```

Figure 59. *Examples of Category Methods*

Kevin explained, "The methods have the same name as their equivalent in *UserDialog* with the prefix *Category* added. The arguments are the same except that it's also necessary to specify the page on which the dialog item is located.

"The *PageHasChanged* method is invoked by OODialog whenever the page changes. In the example, the names of the selected movies are filled into the combo box on page 4 and the first one is selected."

Kevin scrolled through the sample script to find something that was still important to say. He found a topic: "Please pay attention while defining the resource scripts or the layout definition methods, so that you don't use the same item ID twice. All methods that allow you to manually add a group of dialog items expect a starting ID for the first item, which will be increased for each item. The other methods are the same as for *UserDialog*."

Kevin again scanned the script and finally said, "That's it. Now we've covered all OODialog classes. Only the standard dialogs are left. Are you interested in predefined dialogs that can be used for quick user interaction? It's similar to simple GUI builders on OS/2."

"Certainly," said Steve, "Shoot."

Standard Dialog Classes

"I'm going to display the different dialogs included in STDDLG.CLS and tell you how they are executed," said Kevin. "Most of them are two-liners, so if you just need a quick interface to the user, they are pretty useful. We'll start with the timed message box dialog."

[The rest of this section does not repeat what Kevin told Curt and Steve. It is a summary of Kevin's explanations of standard dialogs.]

Standard Dialog Functions

The standard dialogs are available as Object REXX classes and as callable functions. In this section we describe the standard dialog classes. See *Standard Dialog Classes and Functions* on page 436 for a description of the standard dialog functions.

Timed Message Box

The *timed message box* is used to display a message to the user for a specified time. The first argument contains the message; the second, the box title; and the third, the number of milliseconds during which the message box is visible. As with the other dialogs, you have to call *execute* to run the dialog [see Figure 60].

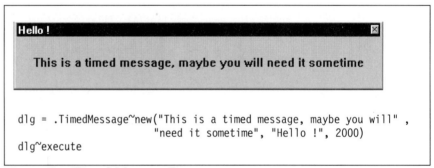

```
dlg = .TimedMessage~new("This is a timed message, maybe you will" ,
                        "need it sometime", "Hello !", 2000)
dlg~execute
```

Figure 60. *Timed Message Box*

Input Box, Integer Box, Password Box

The *input box* is used to read a text string from the keyboard, similar to what the REXX *PULL* instruction does in a DOS window. The first argument contains a message, and the second, the box title. The *execute* method runs the dialog and returns the text string [see Figure 61].

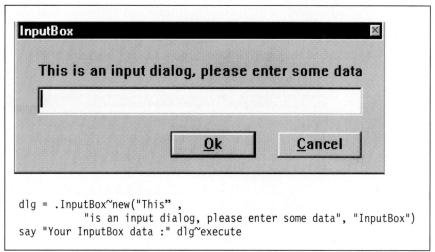

```
dlg = .InputBox~new("This" ,
          "is an input dialog, please enter some data", "InputBox")
say "Your InputBox data :" dlg~execute
```

Figure 61. *Input Box Dialog*

The *integer box* and the *password box* are similar to the *input box*, with this exception: In the *integer box* the user can return only numerical data, and in the *password box* the typed characters are displayed as asterisks [*]:

```
dlg = .IntegerBox~new("Please enter your age","IntegerBox")
say  "Your IntegerBox data: " dlg~execute
```

```
dlg = .PasswordBox~new("Please enter your password","Security")
say  "Your PasswordBox data: " dlg~execute
```

Multiple Input Box

The *multiple input box* is used to read more than one text string from the keyboard. The first argument contains a message; the second, the dialog title; the third, a stem containing the labels for the entry lines; and the fourth, a stem containing the initialization values for the entry lines. The first stem containing the labels must start with 1 and continue in one number increments. The second stem must start with 101 and continue in one number increments. The *execute* method runs the dialog. The data is placed into the second stem and into the object attributes that have the same names as the labels, with ampersands (&), colons (:), and blanks removed [see Figure 62].

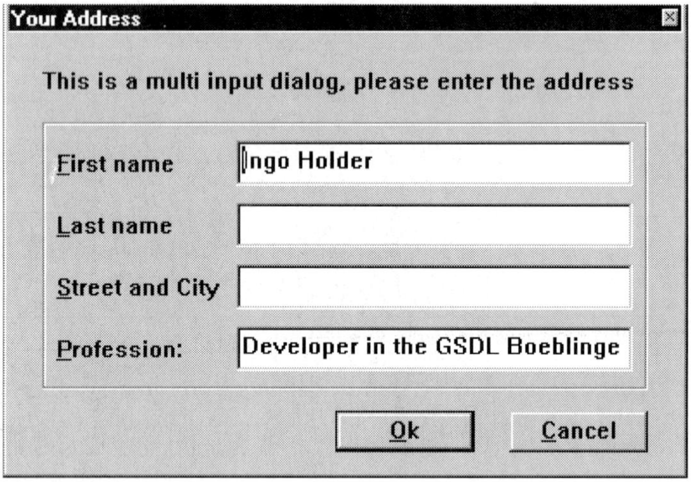

```
lab.1 = "&First name:"
lab.2 = "&Last name:"
lab.3 = "&Street and City:"
lab.4 = "&Profession:"

addr.101 = "Ingo Holder"
addr.102 = ""
addr.103 = ""
addr.104 = "Developer in the GSDL Boeblingen"

dlg = .MultiInputBox~new("This is a multi input dialog, please" ,
                         "enter the address", ,
                         "Your Address", lab., addr.)
if dlg~execute = 1 then do
   say dlg~FirstName ; say dlg~LastName ; say dlg~StreetandCity
   say dlg~Profession
end
```

Figure 62. *Multiple Input Box Dialog*

List Choice

The *list choice* dialog is used to select one entry of a list. The first argument contains a message; the second, the dialog title; and the third, a stem containing the entries for the list. The stem suffixes must be 1 to n in increments of one. The *execute* method runs the dialog and returns the selected text string [see Figure 63].

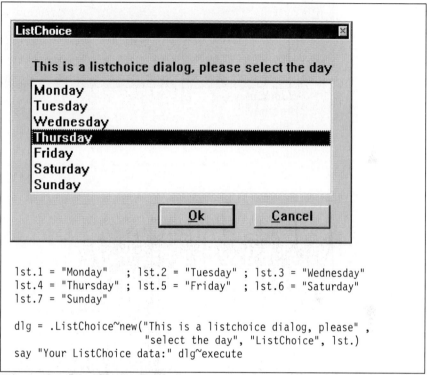

```
lst.1 = "Monday"    ; lst.2 = "Tuesday" ; lst.3 = "Wednesday"
lst.4 = "Thursday" ; lst.5 = "Friday"  ; lst.6 = "Saturday"
lst.7 = "Sunday"

dlg = .ListChoice~new("This is a listchoice dialog, please" ,
                    "select the day", "ListChoice", lst.)
say "Your ListChoice data:" dlg~execute
```

Figure 63. *List Choice Dialog*

Multiple List Choice

The *multiple list choice* dialog is similar to the *list choice* dialog, except that the user can select more than one list entry. The *execute* method runs the dialog and returns the numbers of the selected entries, separated by blanks [see Figure 64].

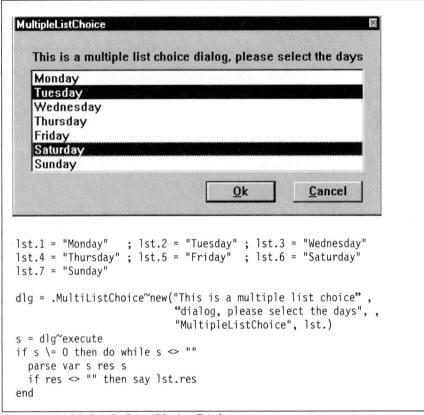

```
lst.1 = "Monday"   ; lst.2 = "Tuesday" ; lst.3 = "Wednesday"
lst.4 = "Thursday" ; lst.5 = "Friday"  ; lst.6 = "Saturday"
lst.7 = "Sunday"

dlg = .MultiListChoice~new("This is a multiple list choice" ,
                          "dialog, please select the days", ,
                          "MultipleListChoice", lst.)
s = dlg~execute
if s \= 0 then do while s <> ""
  parse var s res s
  if res <> "" then say lst.res
end
```

Figure 64. *Multiple List Choice Dialog*

Check List

The *check list* dialog is similar to the *multiple list choice* dialog. Instead of using a list to offer the alternatives, check boxes are used. The first argument contains a message; the second, the dialog title; the third, a stem containing the alternatives; and the fourth, a stem containing the initialization value of the check boxes. Optional parameters are the length of the check boxes in dialog units and the number of check boxes in one column. The first stem suffix must start with 1 and continue in increments of one. The second stem suffix must start with 101 and continue in increments of one as well. To preselect a check box, the corresponding stem entry must be assigned to 1. The *execute* method runs the dialog. The data is returned in the second stem and in the object attributes named after the check box labels. For example, chk.102 and dlg~tuesday represent the same check box. If a check box has been selected, its stem entry and the relative object attribute are 1, otherwise they are 0 [see Figure 65].

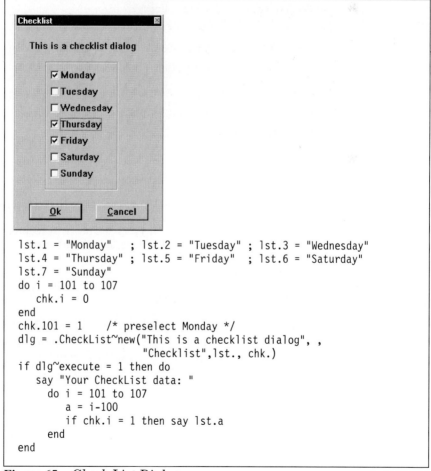

```
lst.1 = "Monday"    ; lst.2 = "Tuesday" ; lst.3 = "Wednesday"
lst.4 = "Thursday" ; lst.5 = "Friday"   ; lst.6 = "Saturday"
lst.7 = "Sunday"
do i = 101 to 107
   chk.i = 0
end
chk.101 = 1     /* preselect Monday */
dlg = .CheckList~new("This is a checklist dialog", ,
                    "Checklist",lst., chk.)
if dlg~execute = 1 then do
   say "Your CheckList data: "
     do i = 101 to 107
        a = i-100
        if chk.i = 1 then say lst.a
     end
end
```

Figure 65. *Check List Dialog*

Single Selection

The *single selection* dialog is similar to the *list choice* dialog. Instead of offering the alternatives in a list, radio buttons are used. The arguments are the same as with the *check list* dialog, except that argument number 4 is not a stem but the number of the radio button that shall be preselected—in the example, *June* is preselected. The *execute* method runs the dialog and returns the number of the selected radio button [see Figure 66].

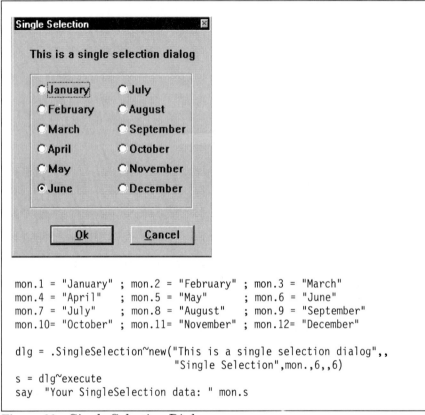

```
mon.1 = "January" ; mon.2 = "February" ; mon.3 = "March"
mon.4 = "April"   ; mon.5 = "May"      ; mon.6 = "June"
mon.7 = "July"    ; mon.8 = "August"   ; mon.9 = "September"
mon.10= "October" ; mon.11= "November" ; mon.12= "December"

dlg = .SingleSelection~new("This is a single selection dialog",,
                          "Single Selection",mon.,6,,6)
s = dlg~execute
say   "Your SingleSelection data: " mon.s
```

Figure 66. *Single Selection Dialog*

After Kevin finished his explanation of the standard dialogs, he said, "Now, we're almost done." "Give me just five more minutes to tell you something about tokenizing. Do you think you'll be able to stand it?"

"No question," replied Steve, "we're tough Americans."

Tokenizing OODialog Scripts

Kevin was in a lecturing mood. "You probably know that larger REXX scripts should be tokenized for performance. [See *Tokenizing Object REXX Programs* on page 75.] Make sure that your GUI scripts using OODialog are tokenized as well. Otherwise the load time for your interactive programs can be annoyingly long."

"I assume that the OODialog files are also tokenized," said Curt. "In that case it's not possible to learn from the code or adapt it to one's own needs."

"The required OODialog class file, OODIALOG.CLS, is in the internal format; otherwise it would take too much time to parse them," explained Kevin. "However, you also have the source scripts in the SCRIPTS subdirectory to make some modifications. After you have changed the source files, you must execute REXX BUILD to merge and tokenize the modified source scripts."

"That's good to know," said Curt. "I don't like tools where you can't change anything. What's next?"

"I'm pretty sure that we covered all that's necessary for you to develop your GUI," Kevin answered. "If there is a problem, feel free to call me."

"I appreciate what you've done for us, Kevin," said Steve. "Thanks a lot for that. We'll mention your name somewhere in the documentation of our application." Both parties switched off their video conferencing system, and it was the last time Steve would see Kevin for seven weeks.

Modifying OODialog Source Scripts

If you modify the OODialog source files to build your own merged class file, you are prompted for an output file name. The file name you provide must be a name other than OODIALOG.CLS, which is shipped with the product.

The Car Dealer GUI

After the weekend, Steve asked Curt. "Would you like to work with me enhancing the GUI of the car dealer app?" he asked.

"Yes, if you think you are familiar enough with the graphical facilities of OODialog now," Curt answered, pulling a chair across to Steve's desk.

Steve started the Resource Workshop. "Let's begin with the main dialog. We will make it as simple as possible, providing just four buttons that will start single dialogs for each task."

"Good idea," Curt mused, "and I suggest that we make all of the panels look more attractive by using the graphical features of OODialog."

Main Dialog

For the next hour, Steve designed the main window, while Curt wrote the corresponding lines of code [see Figure 67].

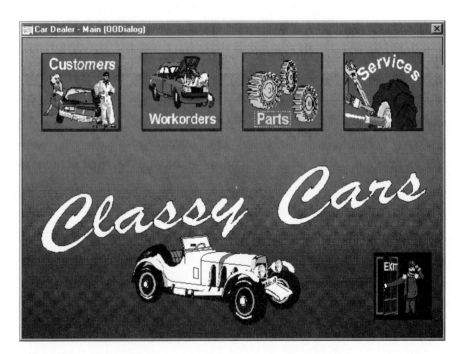

Figure 67. *Main Window of OODialog GUI Application*

Steve and Curt were so delighted by the result that they wanted to jump immediately onto the next dialog. However, Curt was called away by an urgent telephone inquiry. All he managed to say was, "Steve, why don't you design the more complex customer and work order dialogs. I will finish the logic for the main dialog and complete the simpler dialogs for the service items and parts. I want to learn more about how Object REXX is coded for OODialog."

Steve was tempted to object; he wanted the whole job for himself so that he could show off his abilities, but from Curt's determined face he understood that there was no chance of changing his mind.

Two days later, Steve was ready. "Would you like to see the beta version of the car dealer application?" he asked Hanna and Curt.

"I'd love to," Hanna answered, sitting down on the desk next to Steve's monitor. Curt joined them shortly afterwards.

Customer Dialog

Steve started the GUI application and clicked on the **Customers** button to display the newly designed Customers & Vehicles window [see Figure 68].

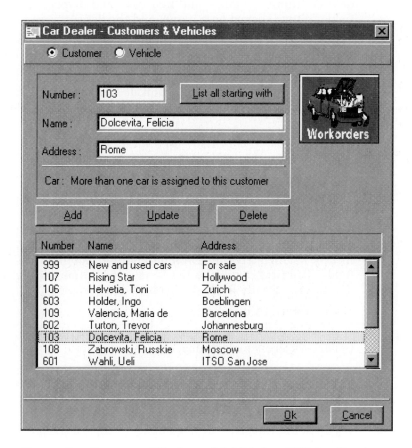

Figure 68. *Customer Window of OODialog GUI Application*

Steve started to explain his design: "I decided to provide one dialog, based on the *CategoryDialog* class, for customers and vehicles. The dialog is separated into two panels. I can switch between them, while always having consistent data, that is, all vehicles shown on the second panel belong to the selected customer on the first panel."

"So this is the first panel for the customer information," remarked Hanna.

"Right on!" replied Steve. "This is the customer dialog, and users can do a lot with it alone. The first thing they have to do is identify a customer. They can put a name, or part of a name, in the *Name* entry field, then click on the **List all starting with** button. I fetch all customers whose names match the search pattern entered and put them into the list box at the bottom."

"And if they enter no characters at all in the search field?" asked Curt.

"Then the customer *findName* class method will fetch all customers," Steve answered, demonstrating this as he spoke. "Now if the user clicks on a particular customer in the list box, I fetch that customer's details—number, name, and address—and display them in the entry fields." Steve clicked on a name, and the details were filled in.

"And how can the user get information on the customer's car or cars?" asked Hanna.

"There's nothing easier than that!" Steve exclaimed. "The user just clicks on the *Vehicle* radio button at the very top of the dialog. But before doing that, the user can see a hint in the *Car* field."

Vehicle Dialog

Steve clicked on the *Vehicle* radio button, and the second panel of the dialog replaced the first panel [see Figure 69].

Steve continued: "While switching to the second panel, I fetch the list of the cars owned by that customer and put them into the Vehicle list box at the bottom of the window. If the user clicks on a particular car in this list, I fetch that car's details and populate the *Vehicle* entry fields. The first car in the list is selected automatically, and the car's details are already fetched when the dialog comes up."

"That's neat," said Hanna.

"I've got **Add**, **Update**, and **Delete** push buttons for both the customer and the vehicle dialog," Steve elaborated.

❏ "To add a new customer, the user fills in the customer's number, name, and address and then clicks on the **Add** button.

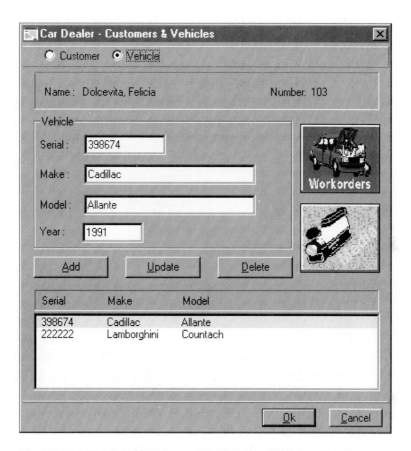

Figure 69. *Vehicle Window of OODialog GUI Application*

❏ "To update a customer, the user selects the customer, overtypes the name or address, and then clicks on the **Update** button.

❏ "To delete a customer, the user selects the customer and then clicks on the **Delete** button.

"The **Add**, **Delete**, and **Update** buttons on the vehicle panel do similar things. And I've put a **Media** button there too. It doesn't do anything yet—it's just a reminder." Steve finished. [See *Using Advanced DB2 Facilities*, Figure 87 on page 196, for the function of the **Media** button.]

"And with the **Workorders** push button you can see all of the work orders of the customer, right?" asked Hanna, excited, because the new dialogs looked much better than expected.

"Exactly!" answered Steve. "This will open a new dialog, the same dialog that is accessible through the bitmap button on the main window."

Work Orders Dialog

Steve clicked on the **Workorders** button in the main window of the OODialog GUI application and the Work Orders window appeared [see Figure 70].

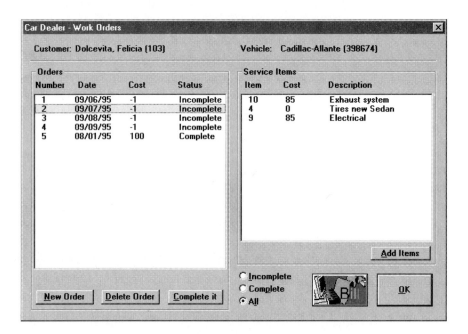

Figure 70. *Work Orders Window of OODialog GUI Application*

Steve was proud of his design of the Work Orders window. "Look on the left-hand side," he started. "The list box shows some or all work orders, depending on several things. If the dialog is started from the main window, all uncompleted work orders are listed by default. But you can force the program to list only the completed or even both completed and uncompleted work orders. Just select the corresponding radio button at the bottom of the panel." Steve selected a work order in the list, then another.

"Oh, I noticed that the fields at the very top changed when you selected another work order item," Curt observed.

"Yes," replied Steve. "That's because each work order belongs to a car of a specific customer. If the work order dialog is called from the customer or vehicle dialog, these fields never change." Steve continued, clicking as he spoke: "In that case I fetch only the work orders associated with the currently selected car and customer."

"That makes sense," Hanna agreed, "so if I want to see all work orders, I'll start this dialog directly, and if I want to view a specific car's work order, I'll go through the customer and vehicle dialog. But sorry, I didn't mean to interrupt you."

"In the list box on the right-hand side, I show the list of the service items associated with the selected work order," Steve continued.

"Wow, Steve, you've put a lot of work into this," said Hanna. "It's impressive."

Add Service Items Dialog

"There's more to come!" said Steve. "The user can click on the **New Order** button to create a new work order for that vehicle." Steve clicked the button, and a new work order appeared in the list box. It was already selected.

"There are no service items on the new work order yet. I don't have to bother with all the service item numbers because just one click on the **Add Items** button displays a multiple selection list of services available." [See Figure 71.]

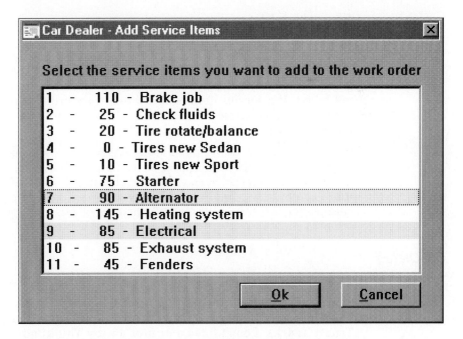

Figure 71. *Add Service Items Window of OODialog GUI Application*

Steve selected a few service items from the list and closed the dialog. The work orders window refreshed its right-hand list immediately.

"Since the Add Service Items window is that simple, I don't use the Resource Workshop, but I create it dynamically with just a few lines of code." [See Figure 72.]

```
/* prepare a stem "lst." with all service items */
i = 1
do servx over .local['Cardeal.ServiceItem.class']~extent
   lst.i = servx~number~left(3) " - " servx~laborCost " - " servx~description
   i = i + 1
end

/* now create the dialog window */
dlg = .MultiListChoice~new( ,
        "Select the service items you want to add to the work order", ,
        "Service items", lst.)

/* display the dialog */
ret = dlg~execute
/* handle returned values to add the selected service items */
...
    curorder~addServiceItem(servx,'store')
...
```

Figure 72. *Code to Create the Add Service Items Window*

"Can you delete service items from an existing work order?" asked Hanna.

"No!" said Steve emphatically. "That's a feature Classy Cars particularly *doesn't* want to have. It's suspected that some 'sweethearting' is going on in the service department, where services are performed but not billed. If a service item is added to a work order in error, the clerk responsible has to make out a whole new work order and get management approval to delete the old one."

"Once all service items on a work order have been completed, the users can mark the work order as complete," Steve continued. "They do so by selecting the work order and clicking on the **Complete it** button. I compute the final cost of the work order, based on the standard charges for the service items and parts involved, and update the work order to show that it's complete, and what the final cost is."

Bill Dialog

"What happens when you click on the **Bill** button?" asked Curt.

"This," answered Steve, clicking on the button. "This is the bill that I have to print. It has the same format as the bill you produced for Trusty Trucks. I don't have a printer for my ThinkPad at home, so I'm displaying the print image on the screen for the time being." [See Figure 73.]

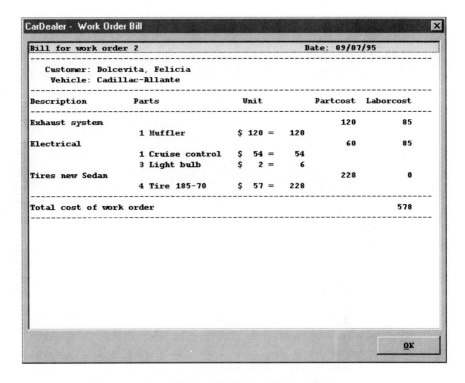

```
CarDealer - Work Order Bill                                          X
Bill for work order 2                               Date: 09/07/95
------------------------------------------------------------------------
    Customer: Dolcevita, Felicia
    Vehicle: Cadillac-Allante
------------------------------------------------------------------------
Description          Parts            Unit          Partcost  Laborcost
------------------------------------------------------------------------
Exhaust system                                        120        85
                     1 Muffler        $ 120 =   120
Electrical                                             60        85
                     1 Cruise control $  54 =    54
                     3 Light bulb     $   2 =     6
Tires new Sedan                                       228         0
                     4 Tire 185-70    $  57 =   228
                     -------------------------------------------------
Total cost of work order                                        578
                     -------------------------------------------------



                                                              OK
```

Figure 73. *Work Order Bill of OODialog GUI Application*

"And by clicking on **OK** in the Work Orders window, you always come back to the dialog from where the work orders dialog was invoked," Steve concluded.

"That's really great! I guess now it's my turn. Would you like to see what I have done?" Curt asked.

"No! I don't." Steve joked. He had already clicked on the **Parts** button in the main window of the OODialog GUI application [see Figure 67 on page 162].

"Hey, it's my turn!" Curt said, "and it doesn't work anyway since I haven't connected the button clicked event with my dialogs. I'll do it immediately. Will you be so kind and bring some coffee in the meanwhile please?"

Steve went away to fetch coffee for his friend.

Parts List Dialog

Curt added a few lines to the main dialog's code. When Steve came back, Curt started his part.

"If the user clicks on the **Parts** button, it opens a Parts List window," he explained, performing the action as he spoke [see Figure 74].

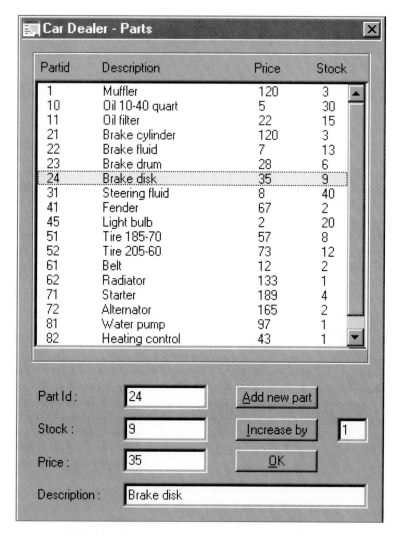

Figure 74. *Parts List Window of OODialog GUI Application*

"This dialog shows all of the part objects available in a list box. If the user selects a particular part, its details are shown in the entry fields at the bottom. The user can increase the *Stock* field by typing in the amount to increase by and clicking on the **Increase by** push button. To add a new part, the user fills in the entry fields and then clicks on the **Add new part** push button," said Curt, exercising these options.

"This looks great, Curt," said Hanna.

"Thanks," said Curt. He closed the Parts List window.

Service Items Dialog

"If the user comes back to the main window of the OODialog GUI application and clicks on the **Services** button, the Service Items window opens," Curt said, on a roll [see Figure 75].

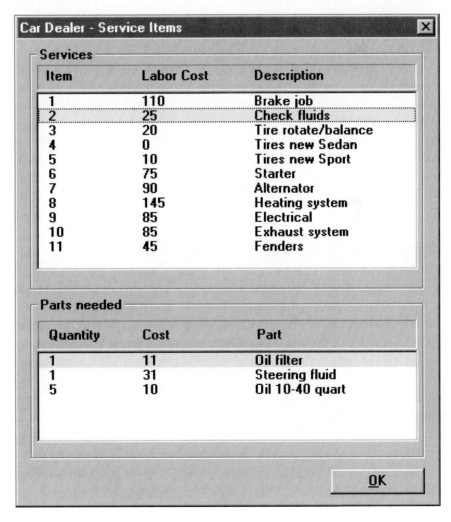

Figure 75. *Service Items Window of OODialog GUI Application*

"This window lists all service items defined, with their associated standard labor cost. When the user clicks on a particular service item, the list of parts needed to carry out a service of this type is retrieved. The parts list is displayed in the lower list box with the quantities required and the cost per part. And that's all the user does with this window" concluded Curt, closing it.

"Good job," said Steve, "you learned to handle OODialog in a short time!"

"Well, it looks wonderful to me," said Hanna. "And it seems pretty robust. I didn't notice any glitches or crashes."

"Of course, we made use of the class libraries we developed for the Trusty Trucks application. We managed to get a high degree of reuse," Steve reasoned.

"That's exactly what we were trying to achieve, and I'm delighted that it's working out so well," said Hanna. "What's the next step, Steve?"

"I'm due at Classy Cars tomorrow morning to review progress on my GUI development," said Steve. "I think the code is in good shape. I'm sure they'll be happy with it. If they are, I can start developing the new classes required to use DB2 for the persistent storage of our objects."

"Good luck, Steve," said Hanna. "We've got to win the business at Classy Cars. We've invested a lot to make this application configurable, and we've got to get a return on that investment."

Steve smiled. "Don't worry, Hanna," he said. "I'm sure they'll sign. They need our system to get better control of their operation."

Source Code for OODialog GUI Interface

The source code for the car dealer OODialog GUI interface is not listed in the appendix; it is available in the car dealer directory on the CD, or on a hard drive after Object REXX has been installed (see Table 27 on page 302).

The source code to start the OODialog GUI program is listed in *Program to Run the Car Dealer Application* on page 527.

How to Structure OODialog Programs

Here are some hints and tips regarding the structure of OODialog programs with multiple windows:

- Use a subdirectory for all source files, for example, OOD.

- Create one main program, for example, car-ood.cmd or car-ood.rex. Put the logic to display the first dialog at the beginning of the main program. Use a *::requires* statement for the source file of the main window:

  ```
  ::requires 'ood\mainmenu.dlg'
  ```

- Create one Object REXX program for each dialog window. Use extension .DLG [dialog], for example, mainmenu.dlg.

- Define the main window as a subclass of a predefined OODialog class and use *::requires* statements for the source files of the subordinate windows. Invoke the subordinate windows through action methods:

  ```
  ::requires 'ood\custvehi.dlg'
  ::requires 'ood\orders.dlg'
     ...
  ::class CardealerMainDialog subclass UserDialog
  ::method init
     ...
  ::method customers
    dlg = .CustomerVehicleDialog~new
     ...
  ::method ok
     ...
  ```

- For the subordinate window dialogs [.dlg], subclass your own dialog windows from an OODialog class, overwrite the initialization methods, and add methods for all actions of the dialog:

  ```
  ::requires 'oodialog.cls'

  ::class CustomerVehicleDialog subclass UserDialog
  ::method init
     ...
  ::method InitDialog
     ...
  ::method myAction
     ...
  ```

- Tokenize all of the dialogs when they have been tested. See *Tokenizing Object REXX Programs* on page 75 for more details. Consider merging all dialog source programs into one file for this purpose. The CARDEAL\OOD\SRC directory contains a sample *BUILD* program. Change the main program to require only the merged file:

  ```
  ::requires 'ood\ood.mrg'
  ```

OODialog Class Files

The OODIALOG.CLS master file is built from the source files of all the OODialog classes:

```
basedlg.cls
userdlg.cls
catdlg.cls
resdlg.cls
stddlg.cls
anibuttn.cls
dialog.cls
```

Use the *::requires* statement for the whole set:

```
::requires 'oodialog.cls'
```

The OODialog source files are available in the OODIALOG\SCRIPTS sub-directory of Object REXX. A *BUILD* program is provided in that directory to create a merged tokenized file of your choice. The merged file cannot be named OODIALOG.CLS, which is the name of the file shipped with the product.

OODialog Sample Programs

OODialog comes with a few, small, sample programs that show many of the aspects of programming with OODialog. Use the samples as models for your own dialogs. See *OODialog Samples* on page 305 for a brief description of the samples.

8

Persistent Objects in DB2

In this chapter, we find out how objects can be made persistent by storing them in a DB2 database. We use DB2 for Windows NT and Windows 95 [Version 2.1.2] for this exercise. Because DB2 is part of the DB2 family and provides connectivity to all other members of the family through DDCS or DB2 Client Application Enabler [CAE], the approach described in this chapter could be used, regardless of the platform on which the DB2 databases are stored. We also restricted the SQL functions used in this chapter to a simple subset of the ANSI SQL standard. Therefore, the code should be portable with more or less effort across any of several other vendors' relational DBMSs. In Chapter 9, *Using Advanced DB2 Facilities,* on page 185, we exploit some of the more advanced functions of DB2 Version 2.

Storing Objects in DB2

"Hi Steve," said Hanna as she walked into the office. "I've just been over to see Trusty Trucks. Our car dealer application is running so smoothly, they're just delighted!"

"That's great," replied Steve. "We spent a lot of time designing that system—it *should* run smoothly! But the real benefits of our approach will surface only when we start building and delivering different versions to meet different customers' needs."

"Right," agreed Hanna. "Speaking of which, how are you doing with the DB2 work for Classy Cars?

"It's been really easy to do, Hanna," replied Steve. "All the trouble we took up front to make sure that we could fit DB2 support into the system later has paid off. Look, here's a picture of the class inheritance I need to build the DB2 support." Steve showed Hanna Figure 76.

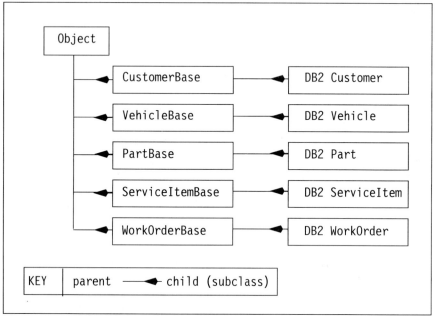

Figure 76. *DB2 Class Inheritance Diagram*
The DB2 classes could also inherit from the Persistent class. This does not provide an advantage, however, because all methods have to be coded in the DB2 class, regardless.

"The base classes contain the methods that are common across DB2 and FAT files, and the DB2 classes contain the DB2-specific methods," Steve explained. "Since the DB2 classes are subclassed from the base classes, they inherit all the methods of the base classes."

"That sounds quite straightforward," said Hanna. "What else do you need to do?"

"Well," said Steve, "I took the data definitions that Curt drew up when we first went through the car dealer requirements." [See Figure 42 on page 83.] "All I had to do was turn his COBOL into DB2 SQL. Oh, and get rid of the repeating groups in the service and work order objects."

"What have you done with them?" asked Hanna.

"I've made them separate tables," said Steve. "Look, here's the table diagram I have drawn up." Steve opened a Freelance picture on his ThinkPad [see Figure 77].

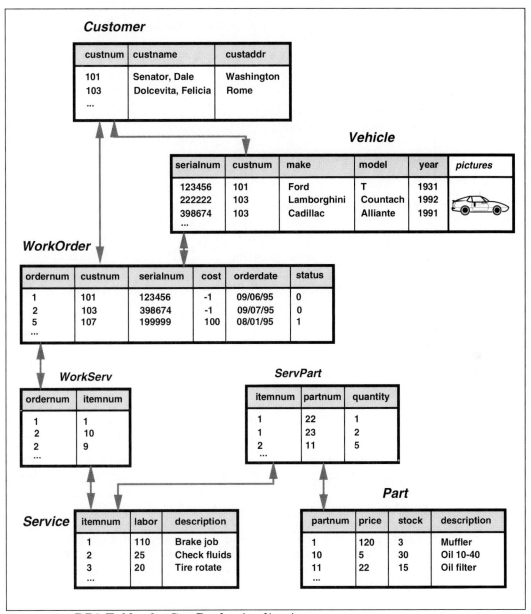

Figure 77. *DB2 Tables for Car Dealer Application.*
The *pictures* column in the vehicle table is discussed in Chapter 9, *Using Advanced DB2 Facilities,* on page 185.

"We need a DB2 table for each class," explained Steve. "I've given them the same names as the classes themselves. And then there are two extras to hold the repeating groups. I've called them *Servpart* and *Workserv. Servpart* will be used to store the relationship between the service objects and all the parts that each one needs. *Workserv* will be used to store the relationship between the work orders and the services that each one specifies."

"And here are the SQL commands I think I'll need." Steve opened a Notepad window on his ThinkPad [Figure 78].

```
DROP    TABLE CARDEAL.CUSTOMER
DROP    TABLE CARDEAL.PART;
...
CREATE TABLE CARDEAL.CUSTOMER
    (CUSTNUM              SMALLINT  NOT NULL,
     CUSTNAME             CHAR(20)  NOT NULL,
     CUSTADDR             CHAR(20)  NOT NULL) ;
CREATE TABLE CARDEAL.PART
    (PARTNUM              SMALLINT  NOT NULL,
     PRICE                SMALLINT  NOT NULL,
     STOCK                SMALLINT  NOT NULL,
     DESCRIPTION          CHAR(15)  NOT NULL) ;
...
CREATE UNIQUE INDEX CUSTOMER_IX ON CARDEAL.CUSTOMER (CUSTNUM);
CREATE UNIQUE INDEX PART_IX   ON CARDEAL.PART (PARTNUM)
...
```

Figure 78. *DB2 Table Definitions*
Extract of SQL DDL statements for table definitions.

Hanna studied the SQL commands. "Have you set up a database for this yet?" she asked.

"Sure," answered Steve [Figure 79].

```
CREATE DATABASE DEALERDB ON d          -- "d" is the disk drive letter
```

Figure 79. *DB2 Database Definition*

"And I've run the SQL. I wrote a little REXX command file called run-sql.rex [see Table 31 on page 304] to read this file and pass it over to the DB2 command line utility, and I've already run these table definitions through it. A couple of times!" he added. "That's why I've got the *DROP TABLE* commands at the top. There were a few errors in my SQL the first time around."

Hanna smiled. "I believe you!" she sympathized.

"I've also coded up the SQL required to insert our test values into the DB2 tables," said Steve, dragging an icon from a folder and dropping it on the editor. A long string of insert commands appeared, and Steve scrolled down through them [Figure 80].

```
delete * from cardeal.customer
  ...
commit
insert into cardeal.customer  (custnum, custname, custaddr)
                   values (101, 'Senator, Dale', 'Washington')
  ...
insert into cardeal.vehicle   (serialnum, custnum, make, model, year)
                   values (123456,   101,    'Ford', 'T', 1931)
  ...
insert into cardeal.workorder (ordernum, custnum, serialnum, cost, orderdate, status)
                   values (1,        101,     123456,    -1,   '09/06/95', 0)
  ...
insert into cardeal.service   (itemnum, labor, description)
                   values (1,        110,   'Brake job')
  ...
insert into cardeal.part      (partnum, price, stock, description)
                   values (21,       120,   3,     'Brake cylinder')
  ...
insert into cardeal.workserv  (ordernum, itemnum)
                   values (1,        1)
  ...
insert into cardeal.servpart  (itemnum, partnum, quantity)
                   values (1,       21,      1)
  ...
commit
```

Figure 80. *DB2 Sample Table Load*
Extract of SQL statements to load sample DB2 tables.

"And this one starts with a whole bunch of delete commands—just in case?" asked Hanna.

"Right!" agreed Steve. "I've already made sure that they work, too. But the test data is loaded, and now I'm working on the definitions of the DB2 classes. We're going to need a whole lot of new methods."

"Oh dear!" said Hanna apprehensively. "I hope this doesn't turn out to be a lot of extra work."

Steve's frustrations boiled over. "Hanna, you and Curt keep challenging me about the DB2 support. But Classy Cars is a much bigger operation than Trusty Trucks. Their turnover was five times bigger last year. They've got branches in twenty cities around the country. Sure, it's going to take work to adapt our application to meet their needs. But we'll get far more revenue out of them than we'll ever see from Trusty Trucks. And once we've adapted our application to fully support a GUI front end and a real database, it will be a far more marketable product than it is today. How many businesses want a clunky character interface when they buy a computer package nowadays?"

"You're 100% right, Steve," she said soothingly. "All of us recognize that Classy Cars is a wonderful business opportunity. But we're a very small operation. I'm worried that we may go bankrupt before we get a chance to show them how good we are. We have to make absolutely sure that the Trusty Trucks implementation completes on the due date with no hitches, so we can get paid on schedule."

"I know that, Hanna," Steve replied. "The best guarantee for a smooth installation is a good design. That's why I keep on insisting that we get the design right, instead of jumping into coding."

Hanna smiled. "You're right, Steve," she said. "We've all been working hard on this project to make sure it's a success. So let's settle down and do some more designing! Have you decided whether you're going to load all the objects from DB2 into storage when the system starts up, or fetch them as you need them?"

Steve relaxed as he turned back to his design. "The people at Classy Cars haven't yet decided whether they want one centralized database or whether each operation will get its own," he mused. "If it's centralized, the volumes will be pretty big, and we'll have to go for a *load-on-demand* approach. But if they decentralize, no single operation is so big that its objects wouldn't fit into storage."

"So what's the answer?" asked Hanna.

Persistent Methods for DB2 Support

"We can't wait for them to make up their minds," Steve answered. "We have to assume the worst case, and make sure we can handle it.

That means loading objects only when required and updating them directly on disk every time they change. Of course, there's only a limited number of part- or service-type objects, no matter how big the operation is. We can carry on loading all those into storage when the application comes up. But customers, vehicles, and work orders will have to stay out on disk."

"Will this mean a lot of extra coding, Steve?" asked Hanna.

"I've worked out that we'll need the following methods," replied Steve, as he showed her Tables 13–17.

Table 13. Methods for Customer Persistent Storage in DB2

Method	Type	Purpose
findName	Class	Find list of customers in DB2 given an abbreviated name
findNumber	Class	Find customer in DB2 given the number; create customer object in memory with cars and work orders
persistentInsert	Instance	Insert a new customer into DB2
persistentUpdate	Instance	Update an old customer in DB2
persistentDelete	Instance	Delete an old customer from DB2
ListCustomerShort	Class	List customers on standard output
ListCustomerLong	Class	List customers and cars on standard output

Table 14. Methods for Part Persistent Storage in DB2

Method	Type	Purpose
persistentLoad	Class	Load all parts from DB2
persistentInsert	Instance	Insert a new part into DB2
persistentUpdate	Instance	Update an old part in DB2

Table 15. Methods for Service Item Persistent Storage in DB2

Method	Type	Purpose
persistentLoad	Class	Load all service items from DB2

Table 16. Methods for Vehicle Persistent Storage in DB2

Method	Type	Purpose
persistentLoadByCust	Class	Load all vehicles of a customer into memory
persistentInsert	Instance	Insert a new vehicle into DB2
persistentUpdate	Instance	Update an old vehicle in DB2
persistentDelete	Instance	Delete an old vehicle from DB2

Table 17. Methods for Work Order Persistent Storage in DB2

Method	Type	Purpose
persistentLoadByCust	Class	Load all work orders of a customer into memory
findNumber	Class	Get work order by number
findStatus	Class	Get all work orders by status
newNumber	Class	Make new work order number
persistentInsert	Instance	Insert a new work order into DB2
persistentUpdate	Instance	Update an old work order in DB2
persistentDelete	Instance	Delete an old work order from DB2
persistentInsertServ	Instance	Add a new service to the work order
persistentDeleteServ	Instance	Remove a service from the work order
ListWorkOrder	Class	List work orders on standard output

"Wow, Steve—that looks like a lot!" said Hanna concerned.

"I've already coded up some of the simpler methods," Steve replied, "and I estimate that the whole job will take about twice as many lines of code as the methods we developed to support persistent storage in ASCII files. That's not bad, when you consider all the extra things that DB2 will give us:

❏ Support for multiple workstations performing updates concurrently

❏ Automatic rollback of programs that fail

❏ Logging of all updates

❏ Recovery of corrupt databases from the log

❏ The ability to handle large volumes of data

❏ The ability to run the database on servers as big as an ES/9000."

"Enough, already!" Hanna interrupted him. "You don't have to sell me on the advantages of DB2, you know that I love using it. Are you including all the SQL we'll have to code in your estimates?"

"For sure," responded Steve.

"OK, Steve," said Hanna. "I've got to get back to Trusty Trucks. Curt has everything there pretty well under control, but I want to make sure one more time that the users are ready for the system. If we need you, I'll call you, but in the meantime it would be fine for you to carry on with the DB2 design. It will get us well ahead of the schedule we agreed to with Classy Cars. There's nothing better than getting off to a flying start."

Steve smiled his appreciation. "I'll be here if you need me," he said. "Good luck with the users!"

Implementation of DB2 Support

The steps to add DB2 support are:

1. Define the DB2 database.

2. Define the tables in the database; an extract is listed in Figure 78 on page 178.

3. Load the tables with sample data; an extract of possible SQL commands is listed in Figure 80 on page 179.

These three steps are part of the car dealer DB2 setup program. Then:

4. Write the Object REXX code for DB2 persistence:

   • No changes are necessary to the base classes. They already have the coding to invoke the persistent methods from the FAT implementation. For example, the *init* method invokes *persistentInsert* for new application objects.

   • Prepare the classes as subclasses of the base classes:

     ```
     ::class Customer public subclass CustomerBase
     ```

   • Write all the additional methods for DB2 persistence.

   • Implement the creation of memory objects at application start for parts and services, and load-on-demand for customers, vehicles, and work orders.

Implementation of Load at Application Start

During initialization of the application, all parts and services are loaded into memory by using the *persistentLoad* methods, similar to the flat file support but with data from the DB2 database.

```
┌──── Loading of parts at application start (abbreviated) ─────────────┐
│ ::class Part                                                          │
│ ::method persistentLoad class                                        │
│    stmt = 'select p.partnum, p.price, p.stock, p.description' ,       │
│           ' from cardeal.part p order by 1'          /* SQL Select */ │
│    call sqlexec 'PREPARE s1 FROM :stmt'                               │
│    call sqlexec 'DECLARE c1 CURSOR FOR s1'                            │
│    call sqlexec 'OPEN c1'                                             │
│    do ipart = 0 by 1 until sqlca.sqlcode \= 0                         │
│        call sqlexec 'FETCH c1 INTO :xpartid, :xprice, :xstock, :xdesc2'│
│        if sqlca.sqlcode = 0 then                                      │
│            partx = self~new(xpartid, xdesc2, xprice, xstock)  /* part object */│
│    end                                                               │
│    call sqlexec 'CLOSE c1'                                            │
│    return ipart                                                       │
└──────────────────────────────────────────────────────────────────────┘
```

Implementation of Load-on-Demand

Customers, vehicles, and work orders are loaded on demand, based on the assumption that there would be too many for all of them to be loaded into memory.

To leave intact the pointer implementation of the base classes between customers, their vehicles and work orders, and the services of a work order, we always load all the data associated with a customer.

Customers are loaded into memory by their number. The *findNumber* method implements the DB2 load of a customer, then invokes the *Vehicle* and *Work Order* classes to load all the data associated with that customer.

```
┌──── Loading of customers on demand (abbreviated) ───────────────────┐
│ ::class Customer                                                      │
│ ::method findNumber class                                            │
│    use arg custnum                         /* input is customer number */│
│    stmt = 'select c.custname, c.custaddr' ,    /* SQL select statement   */│
│           ' from cardeal.customer c where c.custnum =' custnum        │
│    call sqlexec 'PREPARE s1 FROM :stmt'         /* prepare  the SQL    */│
│    call sqlexec 'DECLARE c1 CURSOR FOR s1'      /* define and open a cursor */│
│    call sqlexec 'OPEN c1'                                             │
│    call sqlexec 'FETCH c1 INTO :xcustn, :xcusta'/* fetch the matching row  */│
│    if sqlca.sqlcode = 0 then do                 /* found a customer    */│
│        custx = self~new(custnum, xcustn, xcusta) /* make an OREXX object */│
│        .Vehicle~persistentLoadByCust(custx)     /* load the vehicles ... and*/│
│        .WorkOrder~persistentLoadByCust(custx)   /* work orders of the cust. */│
│        end                                                           │
│    else custx = .nil                            /* customer not found  */│
│    call sqlexec 'CLOSE c1'                       /* close the cursor    */│
│    return custx                                 /* return the customer obj. */│
└──────────────────────────────────────────────────────────────────────┘
```

When accessing work orders directly by number, we retrieve the customer number of the work order from DB2, then all the data of that customer is loaded as shown above, including the requested work order.

Implementation Notes

1. To define the tables and indexes, we wrote the `runsql.rex` program, which reads a file with SQL DDL statements and submits them to the DB2 command processor (`DB2.EXE`).

2. For the sample application, the DB2 tables are loaded from the same files used for the flat file persistent storage. The load program, `load-db2.rex`, reads the files and inserts the data into the DB2 tables.

3. To prepare and set up the DB2 system, we wrote `db2setup.rex` and `db2ddl.rex`, which invokes `runsql.rex` with the proper DDL files to define the tables and indexes, and then `load-db2.rex` to load the sample data into the tables.

4. We did not use DB2 referential integrity to check the relationships between primary and foreign keys in the tables.

5. Customers can also be retrieved by partial name. DB2's *LIKE* facility is used to search the database, and an array of matching customer names, together with their number, is returned. Data is loaded into memory with the *findNumber* method only when a customer from the resulting array is selected.

6. All updates to the data are performed first in memory and then immediately thereafter in DB2 with the *persistentInsert*, *persistentupdate*, and *persistentDelete* methods. The DB2 database is, therefore, always up to date.

Setting Up DB2 on Windows NT and Windows 95

The installation and preparation of the DB2 system on both Windows NT and Windows 95 is covered in *Installation of DB2 Version 2* on page 290.

Source Code for DB2 Class Implementation

The source code for the DB2 classes is described in Table 23 on page 301 and listed in *Persistence in DB2* on page 516.

The source code for the table definitions and the DB2 setup and load programs is not listed in the appendix; it is available in the car dealer directory on the CD, or on a hard drive after Object REXX has been installed (see Table 31 on page 304).

9

Using Advanced DB2 Facilities

In this chapter, we exploit some of the more advanced features of DB2 for Windows NT and Windows 95 delivered in Version 2 of the product. We make use of DB2's BLOBs to store multimedia data.

Multimedia in DB2 BLOBs

"I hope things go well today when you call on Classy Cars, Steve!" called out Hanna. "We need you to bring back a signed contract."

"I'll do my best," replied Steve. "Classy Cars is really keen on our car dealer package. I'm just a bit worried about delivering the multimedia function that we've promised to give them. Time's getting short."

"Is multimedia really necessary, Steve?" Hanna asked. "Wouldn't it be simpler to install the application without it, and then come back to it later if they really want it?"

"They *do* really want it, Hanna," Steve replied. "As I've mentioned, they make more money from selling cars than from servicing them. They want to boost their sales, and they believe that the multimedia facilities I described and demoed to them will be a big help. Where they really hope to score is by exchanging information between different branches about cars they have for sale. So if a customer expresses interest in some type of car that the branch doesn't have, they can quickly search the records of cars for sale at the other branches. If they find the car, they can use multimedia to show it to the customer. If the customer likes it, they will arrange to transfer the car to the most convenient branch for the customer. Classy Cars is convinced that their sales will skyrocket."

"That sounds very ingenious," said Hanna. "But how are they going to capture multimedia images of the cars they have in stock? I know that you can take color pictures and have a print shop scan it and turn it into an image file, but that's slow and quite expensive."

Steve grinned. "Ah! I haven't shown you my latest toy," he said. He zipped open his bag and pulled out a black object that looked a bit like a camera. "Here we have a camera that captures image files directly. The lens focuses the image onto a charge-coupled device array [CCD] instead of conventional film, and the camera copies that into its own RAM storage in compressed format. It can hold up to 48 high-quality images. The camera comes with a cable to plug it into a PC's serial port and software to download the images."

"Wow!" said Curt. "I bet that costs plenty."

"About the same as a conventional camera," Steve replied, "And the really good news is—you never have to buy film for it! That's a saving."

Curt shook his head. "You can see who's the bachelor around here," he said.

"Marry in haste, repent at leisure," said Steve.

"Well, show us what it can do, Steve," said Hanna.

Steve looked around for a suitable subject and then said, "Look, there's Boxie." The cat from the neighboring house often visited for the saucer of milk and tidbits she knew she could wheedle from Hanna. At the moment, Boxie was doing her best to melt into a wooden bench in the morning sunshine. She looked up sleepily as Steve approached her with the camera.

"Got it!" said Steve. He connected the camera to the serial port of his ThinkPad with a thin cable and brought up the camera software. Then he started to download the image. "This will go fast. I've only got one image in the camera," Steve said. A series of small frames was presented on the screen. Only one contained an image, and when Steve double-clicked on it, up came an image of Boxie. Steve zoomed in [see Figure 81].

Figure 81. *Boxie the Cat*
The real picture is in full color!

"Oh, that's lovely!" said Hanna. "I've often wanted a picture of Boxie, but I've never gotten around to bringing in my camera. Could you print that, Steve?"

"Sure thing," said Steve. He selected the print menu, chose the color printer, and clicked on the OK button. A short while later the printer oozed out a picture. They picked it up and inspected it.

"This is pretty good, Steve," said Hanna.

"Yes, and you can do a lot with the image before you print or store it," Steve responded. "You can rotate it and crop it. You can edit the color tones too, very simply. This picture has come out a bit blue. It would be easy to warm it up by emphasizing the red tones. Anyhow, I'm taking this camera out to Classy Cars to show them how they could capture multimedia images. I'm sure they'll be excited. Which brings me back to the question of how we're going to build the code."

"Maybe Curt could look at that while you're busy," said Hanna. "If you swap ThinkPads with him, he can get on with it while you're out visiting Classy Cars' branches."

"Oh—aren't you still busy with Trusty Trucks, Curt?" asked Steve.

"Not unless something breaks," answered Curt. "If you'll let me have your multimedia ThinkPad, I'll give it a whirl. You keep on telling us how easy it is to handle multimedia in REXX. And the BLOB support in DB2 Version 2 should make it easy to store and fetch multimedia data."

"OK," Steve agreed somewhat reluctantly. "I'll have to transfer the files I need this week onto your ThinkPad. I'll upload them onto the server." Steve sat down again, powered on, and plugged his PC into the LAN. Curt, likewise, started uploading files from his PC onto the server.

"Wait a minute," said Steve. "I've built up a whole set of groups with special icons for the Classy Cars project and I don't want to have to rebuild them all on your PC, Curt."

"No problem, Steve," responded Curt. "Just drag them and drop them on the server directory icon. Windows 95 will copy the whole structure for you. Then you can drag the icon off the Server and drop it onto my PC's desktop."

"Of course!" said Steve.

They swapped ThinkPads and downloaded their files from the server. Steve powered off Curt's PC, put it in his bag, and left to accompany the Classy Cars IT Manager on a series of visits to their bigger remote branches.

Curt opened the groups that Steve had defined for the Classy Cars project and tried running the multimedia demo. He was able to display images and play audio and video clips. He opened the settings notebooks of the various icons to find out what REXX commands they used, and opened these commands in the editor. "This does look quite straightforward," he said. "Now I'll need to dig into the DB2 manuals and find out how BLOBs work."

"Let me know when you find out," said Hanna, looking up from her work. "I'd like to understand more about BLOBs too."

Using DB2 BLOBs from Object REXX

Curt spent the next several hours reading the DB2 manuals and building small pieces of code to try out the BLOB features. By mid afternoon he was ready to share with Hanna something of what he had learned.

"The DB2 developers have done a great job with BLOBs," said Curt. "I've managed to get some things working without any trouble at all."

Hanna closed her ThinkPad's lid and came over to see what Curt had built.

"For starters," said Curt, "they have defined three different types of BLOBs. Well, LOBs, actually—large objects, they call them. Binary LOBs are just one of these three types. They have also defined Character LOBs [CLOBs] and Double-Byte Character LOBs [DBCLOBs] too."

"If we're storing images and audio and video clips, we'll need just plain BLOBs, right?" asked Hanna.

"Yes," said Curt. "We can define multiple LOBs in a single row, and each LOB can be up to 2 GB in size."

"That's huge!" gasped Hanna. "How do you go about loading LOB data into a DB2 column?"

"Well, you can assemble the LOB data into a host variable and then put that into a DB2 column with a normal SQL insert or update statement," Curt answered. "Or if the LOB data is in a disk file, you can simply give DB2 a host variable that contains the name of the file that contains the LOB data on disk. That way the application program doesn't need to read the entire LOB into storage. DB2 copies the LOB data straight from its source disk file into a DB2 column."

"That's a nice option," said Hanna.

"Yes," agreed Curt. "I've defined a simple DB2 table and written a load program in Object REXX that loads a BLOB into it. I just pass DB2 the name of the file that contains the BLOB. Look, here it is."

Curt showed Hanna the code [see Figure 82]. "See," he explained, "I need to tell DB2 that my host variable is a locator and contains a file name. I declare it with the *language type blob file* options. If I were coding this in C, COBOL, or Fortran, I would have to build a structure containing information about the file—its name, length, and whether I wanted to read it or write it. The REXX interface is much simpler. My locator host variable is actually the name of a REXX stem variable. I store the name of the file in a compound variable, using the stem with the *name* tail, and store the file read/write options using the *file_options* tail. This is the code I wrote to declare the file locator and the update statement that transfers the media file into the DB2 *picture* column," said Curt.

```
1  call sqlexec 'declare :media language type blob file'
2  media.name = 'd:\cardeal\media\boxie.bmp'
3  media.file_options = 'read'
4  stmt = 'update myTable set myBLOB = cast(:media as blob(4M))'
5  call sqlexec 'prepare s1 from :stmt'
6  call sqlexec 'execute s1'
7  call sqlexec 'clear sql variable declarations'
```

Figure 82. *Using REXX to Update a DB2 BLOB*

"Look," said Curt, "to update the DB2 BLOB:

1 "I declare a file locator variable called *media.*

2 "I put the name of a bitmap image file into the *media.name* variable, and

3 "I put the file options into *media.file_options.*"

"OK so far," responded Hanna. Curt continued, "Then,

4 "I build an SQL statement to update *myBLOB*—the column that contains the BLOB—and next

5 "I prepare it,

6 "I execute it, and

7 "I clear the SQL variable declarations."

"Hold on," said Hanna. "What's the *cast(:media as blob(4M))* in line 4 for?"

"*Cast* is new in Version 2," replied Curt. "I used it here to tell DB2 that my BLOB file locator host variable *media* will be used to store a BLOB no bigger than 4 MB."

"And the *clear SQL variable declarations* in line 7?" asked Hanna.

"BLOB file locator host variables don't get released until the process that created them terminates," said Curt. "Since they're potentially very big, it's good practice to release them as soon as possible. That's what this new *clear* command does."

"Well that took some explaining, but you managed to get the job done with very little code," said Hanna. "Is it just as easy to get the BLOB back out of DB2?"

"It sure is," replied Curt. "This is the code I developed to do the job." [See Figure 83.]

```
1   call sqlexec 'declare :media language type blob file'
2   media.name = 'media.bmp'
3   media.file_options = 'overwrite'
4   stmt = 'select myLOB from myTable'
5   call sqlexec 'prepare s2 from :stmt'
6   call sqlexec 'declare c2 cursor for s2'
7   call sqlexec 'open c2'
8   call sqlexec 'fetch c2 into :media :mediaInd'
9   call sqlexec 'close c2'
10  call sqlexec 'clear sql variable declarations'
```

Figure 83. *Using REXX to Fetch a DB2 BLOB*

"First,

1 "I declare the *media* file locator variable. Then

2 "I put the name of a bitmap image file into the *media.name* variable, and next

3 "I put my *overwrite* file option into *media.file_options*."

"This looks familiar," responded Hanna.

"Yes, I was able to copy some of this code from the update program," Curt agreed.

4 "This is the SQL select statement. Very simple! I have only one BLOB loaded, so I don't even need to specify which row. Of course, the code I develop for Classy Cars would specify a vehicle in this select statement. Next,

5 "I prepare the SQL select statement,

6 "I declare a cursor on it,

7 "I open the cursor and

8 "I fetch the BLOB into the file.

9 "I close the cursor and

10 "I clear the SQL variable declarations."

"And then?" asked Hanna.

"And then it's ready to display," answered Curt. "Like so." He opened the Windows Explorer, found the image file that DB2 had just created, double clicked on it, and a picture of Boxie appeared in a Paintbrush window.

"That's great, Curt!" said Hanna. "And it didn't take you long at all. What more do you have to build?"

"I need to change the Classy Cars database definitions," said Curt. "Apart from adding a new column to the vehicle table, I have to define a separate DB2 table space to store the multimedia data. Then, when I define the new vehicle table, I'll specify that DB2 should perform no logging on the column that holds the multimedia data. Otherwise, it would waste log space." [See Figure 84.]

```
CREATE REGULAR TABLESPACE VEHICLESPACE        -- table space for non multimedia
    MANAGED BY DATABASE                        -- columns of the vehicle table
    USING ( FILE 'vehiclea' 300);             -- 300 blocks of 4K

CREATE LONG TABLESPACE VEHICLESLOB            -- table space for long (BLOB)
    MANAGED BY DATABASE                        -- columns of the vehicle table
    USING ( FILE 'vehicleb' 4000);            -- 4000 blocks of 4K = 16 MB

CREATE TABLE CARDEAL.VEHICLE                   -- Vehicle table
    (SERIALNUM          INTEGER   NOT NULL,
    CUSTNUM             SMALLINT  NOT NULL,
    MAKE                CHAR(12)  NOT NULL,
    MODEL               CHAR(10)  NOT NULL,
    YEAR                SMALLINT  NOT NULL,
    PICTURES            BLOB(4M)  NOT LOGGED )  -- BLOB column, up to 4 MB
    IN VEHICLESPACE                            -- assignment for normal columns
    LONG IN VEHICLESLOB;                       -- assignment for long (BLOB) column
```

Figure 84. *DB2 Definition for the Vehicle Table with Multimedia*

"Then, of course, I have to generalize this code to support multiple media files per vehicle, and also different media types. Currently, I'm handling only images, but audio and video will be almost identical. I guess I should have something working by the end of the week."

"Wonderful!" said Hanna. "Steve will be back in the office on Monday and then we can all look at it together."

Multiple Multimedia Files in BLOBs

"If you're planning to store images and audio clips jumbled together in one BLOB, how on earth will you ever unscramble them?" asked Steve. It was Monday, Steve's first morning back at the office in a week.

"No problem!" said Curt with a smile. "DB2 provides facilities to break BLOBs into pieces and handle one piece at a time. The really neat thing about this is, DB2 doesn't even have to read the whole BLOB into its own buffers to give you access to the part you need. That's very important. The images and audio clips may range from 100 to 500 KB each, but if we include video clips..."

"Are video clips for real, Steve?" interrupted Hanna.

"Sure!" replied Steve. "We can do only limited video on this ThinkPad, but the latest home PCs from IBM include a chip that can display full-screen, full-motion video. And, of course, the IBM PowerPC is so powerful that it can deliver full video without needing any hardware assist. It does the whole job in software."

"Wow!" said Hanna.

"It's true," agreed Curt, "and I've heard that the Intel Pentium Pro processor has the same kind of capability."

"Yes," said Steve, "and it would be silly for us to ignore that kind of capability, since it's almost here now. And our car dealer application is going to be around for a *long time*, isn't it, team?"

"Right!" chorused Hanna and Curt.

"So it won't hurt to make sure that our multimedia design can handle video when our customers ask for it," continued Curt. "Windows 95's multimedia capabilities make it very easy to handle video. It uses the same commands as audio. And it sure makes for a powerful demo when you're trying to close a sale!"

"That sounds great, Curt," said Steve, "but you haven't answered my original question. How are you going to separate out all this multimedia data if you jumble it together in one big BLOB? Wouldn't it be better to store each piece of multimedia data as a separate BLOB? You could add three new columns to the vehicle table—one for the image, one for the audio, and one for the video."

"DB2 would allow us to do that," replied Curt, "although some other database managers wouldn't. But Classy Cars wants to be able to store several pictures of some of their cars—front view, side view, and so forth."

"Oh, yes," said Steve. "Well, it's obviously a repeating group, so why don't you normalize the data? Create a new DB2 table called *VehicleMedia,* key it on the vehicle's serial number and a multimedia sequence number, give it a BLOB column, and put the multimedia descriptive data in there. That way each vehicle could have as many or as few associated multimedia files as you want."

Curt looked thoughtful. "That approach could also work, Steve," he said, "but if you'd just listen for a moment, I'll tell you how I'm handling it."

"OK," said Steve, resolving to be patient [see Figure 85].

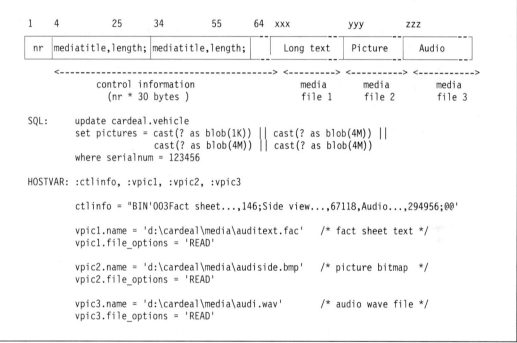

Figure 85. *Layout of Self-Defining BLOB and SQL Statements to Build BLOB*

"I've written code to put all the multimedia data for a given car into one BLOB. I also embed control information in the BLOB. I use the first 3 bytes of each BLOB to store a counter that tells me how many multimedia files it contains. It's in character format, so that allows me up to 999 multimedia files per vehicle."

"OK so far," said Hanna, "tell us more."

"Following the 3-byte counter," Curt continued, "I've got a 30-byte string of control information for each multimedia file in the BLOB. It contains a 20-byte title for the multimedia data, and its length. I strip these out using the DB2 substring function and pass them to the GUI code, which inserts the titles into a list box. This shows the user which multimedia files are available for playing. I use the relative position of the title within the list and the sizes of the multimedia files that come before it to calculate its position within the BLOB. Then I use the DB2 substring function to pull just the bytes we need out of the BLOB. So when the user clicks on a particular title and asks to play it, it's very efficient."

"Does DB2 read the multimedia data into one of your program variables?" asked Hanna.

"It could," answered Curt, "but I'm exploiting DB2's ability to transfer the data directly from the BLOB to a file on disk. My program never even sees the data. Once DB2 has copied it to disk, I issue a multimedia *play* command, and the rest happens automatically."

"How do you load multiple multimedia files into one DB2 BLOB column, Curt?" asked Steve. "Do you read each file into a separate REXX variable, concatenate them together in storage, and then insert that data into the DB2 column?"

"I thought of doing it that way," answered Curt, "but then I found an easier way. This is how I build the SQL that I need." Curt showed them a piece of code [Figure 86].

```
1   hostvar = ':ctlinfo'
2   ctlinfo = right(numpic,3)':'
3   stmt = 'update cardeal.vehicle set pictures = cast(? as blob(1K))'
4   do i=1 to numpic
5       piclength  = stream(picfile.i,'c','query size')
6       ctlinfo = ctlinfo''left(pictitle.i,20)''right(piclength,8)';'
7       call sqlexec 'declare :vpic'i 'language type blob file'
8       hostvar = hostvar', :vpic'i
9       call value 'vpic'i'.name', picfile.i
10      call value 'vpic'i'.file_options', 'READ'
11      stmt = stmt '|| cast(? as blob(4M))'
12  end
13  ctlinfo = "BIN'"ctlinfo"@@'"
14  stmt = stmt 'where  serialnum =' oldserial
15  call sqlexec 'prepare s1 from :stmt'
16  call sqlexec 'execute s1 using' hostvars
```

Figure 86. *Using Object REXX to Build and Store a DB2 BLOB*

Curt explained his logic. "To begin,

1 "I start the list of host variables with the control information variable.

2 "I initialize this variable with the number of media files.

3 "I code the beginning of the SQL update statement.

4 "I loop as many times as there are media files to be inserted into DB2. Each time,

5 "I get the length of the media file, and

6 "I concatenate the title and length to the control information.

7 "I declare a new DB2 locator file host variable and

8 "I concatenate its name to the list of host variables.

9 "I set the locator variable's file name and

10 "I also set its file options.

11 "I concatenate another place-marker to the SQL update statement.

12 "Once out of the loop,

13 "I mark the control information host variable as binary, and

14 "I complete the SQL update statement.

15 "I prepare it, and

16 "I execute it, using the list of host variables that I built up.

"DB2 concatenates all the multimedia files together to form a single BLOB field, and I never even touch them in my Object REXX code. Pretty neat, hey?"

"Wow! I never realized how powerful DB2's BLOB handling capabilities are," said Hanna. "And you're making full use of them, Curt."

Curt smiled. "Thanks, Hanna. Want to hear it play?"

"Yes please," said Hanna.

Multimedia in the Car Dealer Application

Curt started up the application using the OODialog interface that Steve had developed. "I've added the logic for the button called **Media** in the vehicle dialog window," he said [see Figure 69 on page 165].

"Of course, the button is only enabled if there is some media data for the particular customer. You click on the **Media** button and the application opens a new window that lists the cars of the current customer. When you select a car, the multimedia files associated with that car are listed below on the right-hand side." Curt opened the Vehicle Multimedia window as he spoke [see Figure 87].

"Then you just click on the multimedia file you want!" Curt did this. A line of text in large bold letters scrolled smoothly from right to left across the *Facts* area in the Media window. It carried a description of the selected car.

"And since Object REXX supports concurrent processing," continued Curt, "I can kick off something else while the text display is still rolling." He clicked on a multimedia line describing a bit map picture, and a picture of a car appeared in another area of the window. Then Curt selected a sound bite and they heard a recording of his voice describing the car that he had selected.

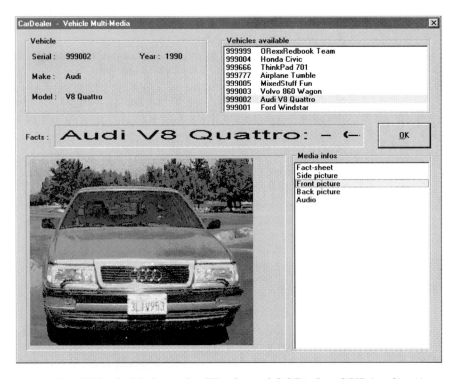

Figure 87. *Vehicle Multimedia Window of OODialog GUI Application*

"Classy Cars will be really impressed when they see what you've developed," said Hanna. "It will give them a wonderful marketing aid. I know they were thinking of using it for their marketing staff, but it's so impressive, I think they could also show it directly to prospective car buyers. What do you think, Steve?"

All this time Steve had been watching Curt's demo silently. "Yes, it is impressive," he answered Hanna.

"But?" prompted Hanna. She could see that Steve wasn't completely happy.

"I'm worried about storing multiple multimedia files and the catalog of multimedia information in the BLOB itself," Steve answered. "We may need to add more control information later on, and this approach is limiting."

"There's no limit," said Curt. "I can easily increase the size of the control field if we need to."

"Well," responded Steve, "if you had created a new vehicle multimedia table and stored one multimedia file per BLOB, we could add new columns to that table any time we needed to by using the DB2 *ALTER*

TABLE command. We wouldn't have to unload the existing data and reformat it, or even change existing applications. They would keep on working, while new applications made use of the new columns."

"What new columns?" asked Curt. "Are you changing the application specs while I'm still writing the code?"

"I was talking with the consultant that Classy Cars has engaged to help them develop an IT architecture," answered Steve. "He isn't happy with our proposal that Classy Cars install a separate database manager in each of their branches."

"Why not?" asked Hanna. "We've priced it out, and it's a good, economic solution. DB2 is inexpensive, and they won't have to get into the complexities and costs that networking their branches into a central database manager would entail. And Classy Cars told us right from the beginning that each branch runs as an autonomous unit. They don't have any need to share data."

"That *is* what they told us," agreed Steve. "Of course, their head office does want sales and service revenue figures on a weekly basis..."

"We agreed with them that their head office would get that data by dialing into the distributed DB2 databases each week," interrupted Curt.

"Right," agreed Steve. "But the consultant has uncovered something that Classy Cars didn't tell us. They deal with several large companies all over the country. Currently, each branch of Classy Cars deals with the branches of these large companies in isolation. Many of these companies are unhappy with this situation. They want a single, consolidated bill from Classy Cars each month, and they want a single national phone number where they can talk to one person about all their dealings with Classy Cars. The consultant says the best way of achieving this would be to have a single central database manager, with all the branches hooked into it."

"That sounds like a big change, Steve," said Hanna. "I don't know if we can support that approach. What are the implications for our design and the code we have already written?"

"No problem!" interjected Curt. "DB2 can support a distributed operation over a Netbios or TCP/IP network, and the program code doesn't have to change a bit. All we have to do is install the DB2 CAE client package on each remote Windows 95 PC and point them to the central Windows NT server."

"That's true," agreed Steve. "DB2 gives us a great deal of flexibility in that area. But I'm worried about the implications of shipping multimedia files over the wide area network every time a dealer wants to display a picture or play a sound clip. It would overload their network and kill their response times."

"Well for Pete's sake!" said Curt, his anger boiling up. "It was *your* idea to add multimedia to this application. Classy Cars never even dreamed of doing it till you talked them into it. And now it turns out to be unaffordable, and they'll probably decide to can the whole car dealer application. When will you learn to be sensible and do what the customer asks for, instead of getting so smart you can't deliver what you promise?"

Steve was about to respond angrily, but Hanna stepped between the two of them. "Hold on there, guys," she said. "Let's make sure that we understand how big a problem this is before we start shouting at each other." She held her ground until Curt and Steve backed off.

"It's clearly late in the day for Classy Cars to decide that they want to run on a centralized database," she said. "They've already signed off our design, and that specified one database per branch. If they want to change their minds, we will have to assess the impact of that change and tell them what it will cost, in terms of network bandwidth, extra coding, or whatever. What would the impact be if we ran the multimedia off ASCII files on the users' PCs instead of using DB2 to store them?" she asked Steve.

"That would work fine," he said, "except there wouldn't be any easy way to distribute new multimedia files when new models come out. If we store all the multimedia files in DB2, it's easy to make sure every user has the most recent multimedia information, whether they're local or remote users."

"You can't have it both ways," said Curt. "You can't plan to use DB2 to distribute multimedia files and then complain that it will use too much bandwidth."

"Maybe we can," said Steve. "Supposing we use DB2 to distribute the multimedia data, but keep copies on the users' PCs and reuse them as long as they're still current."

"How would you know if a user's copy is still current?" Curt asked.

"By putting extra columns into the vehicle table," Steve answered. "If we put the multimedia file's time and date stamp in there, our multimedia playing logic could fetch those columns from DB2 and check whether the user has a current copy of the multimedia file on the PC. If not, we ask DB2 to give us a copy, play it to the user, but also keep it for next time. But the way you're handling the multimedia control information, there's no way to do that."

"I could easily extend my control information to handle file date and time stamps," retorted Curt.

"Sure!" said Steve sarcastically. "But what about the next change that we need?"

"Steve, you're coming up with a whole lot of new requirements and criticizing Curt because his code can't handle them," said Hanna. "Now, let's think this through together. We have already agreed with

Classy Cars that we'll implement our application as a pilot in their San Jose branch next month. That's going to be six PCs on a LAN with a stand-alone database, right?"

"Yes," agreed Steve.

"Fine," said Hanna. "Curt's multimedia code would work perfectly in that environment, wouldn't it?"

"Yes," said Steve again.

"The pilot is due to run for a month," continued Hanna. "That will give Classy Cars time to think through whether they really need a centralized database and us time to think through the implications of making such a change. Right?"

Steve looked relieved. "You're right, Hanna," he said. "I guess I don't have to start panicking yet. There's still a fair amount of time before they go live across multiple branches. And if the pilot is successful, their first payment is due. At least we'll be able to eat while we're working out what to do next."

"Now you're talking, Steve," said Hanna. "Curt has put together some really smart code, and it seems to work well. We've still got time to put it through acceptance testing with the users and implement it as part of the pilot installation. That way, we'll be delivering it before the date we committed to. I'm sure that Classy Cars will be happy."

"I sure hope so," said Curt.

"I'm due back at Classy Cars tomorrow to start working out the implementation plan once the pilot has proved successful," said Steve. "During the pilot, I'll talk to them about the approach we want to take for distributed databases."

"Let us know what happens," said Hanna.

Implementing the DB2 Multimedia Support

Here are the steps required to implement multimedia data in DB2 Version 2:

1. Define two DB2 table spaces for the vehicle table, to separate the normal data from the large multimedia data (BLOBs).

2. Define the vehicle table so that the BLOB column is stored in the special table space for such columns (*long in* keyword).

   These two steps are shown in Figure 84 on page 191.

3. Write a DB2 program, load-mm.rex, to update the vehicle table with the multimedia files in the BLOB column. An extract of the program with the SQL statements is shown in Figure 86 on page 194.

- We described all the multimedia files in a specification file (in media\media.dat):

```
/* serial, title of file    , filename     */
   999001, Fact-sheet        , ford.fac
   999001, Side view         , fordsid.bmp
   999001, Front view        , fordfrt.bmp
   999001, Back view         , fordbck.bmp
   999001, Angle view        , fordang.bmp
   999001, Audio             , ford.wav
   999002, Fact-sheet        , audi.fac
   999002, Side view         , audisid.bmp
   999002, Front view        , audifrt.bmp
   999002, Back view         , audibck.bmp
   999002, Audio             , audi.wav
   ...
   end
```

- The multimedia update program reads this file and updates the vehicle table with multimedia BLOBs.

4. Write three new methods for the vehicle class to retrieve the multimedia data (in db2\src\carvehi.cls):

- Retrieve and return the number of media files of a vehicle:

```
::method getmedianumber
    expose medianumber mediacontrol
    if symbol("medianumber") = 'VAR' then return medianumber
    medianumber = 0
    mediacontrol = ''
    stmt = 'select substr(v.pictures,1,3)' ,
           ' from cardeal.vehicle v  where v.serialnum =' self~serial
    call sqlexec 'PREPARE s2 FROM :stmt'
    if sqlca.sqlcode \= 0 then return 0
    vpicind = -1
    call sqlexec 'DECLARE c2 CURSOR FOR s2'
    call sqlexec 'OPEN c2'
       call sqlexec 'FETCH c2 INTO :vpic :vpicind'
    call sqlexec 'CLOSE c2'
    if vpicind >=0 then medianumber = vpic
    return medianumber
```

- Retrieve the control information of multimedia files for a vehicle:

```
::method getmediacontrol
    expose medianumber mediacontrol
    if symbol("medianumber") = 'LIT' then return ''
    if medianumber <= 0 then return ''
    stmt = 'select substr(v.pictures,5,30*'medianumber')' ,
           ' from cardeal.vehicle v  where v.serialnum =' self~serial
    call sqlexec 'PREPARE s2 FROM :stmt'
    call sqlexec 'DECLARE c2 CURSOR FOR s2'
    call sqlexec 'OPEN c2'
       call sqlexec 'FETCH c2 INTO :vpic :vpicind'
       rcv = sqlca.sqlcode
    call sqlexec 'CLOSE c2'
    if rcv = 0 & vpicind >= 0 then mediacontrol = vpic
    return mediacontrol
```

- Retrieve one multimedia file from the BLOB of a vehicle:

```
::method getmediainfo
    expose medianumber mediacontrol
    if symbol("medianumber") = 'LIT' then return ''
    if mediacontrol = '' then self~getmediacontrol
    arg medianum
    if medianumber = 0 | medianum > medianumber | medianum <= 0 | ,
       mediacontrol = '' then return ''
    mediatitle  = substr(mediacontrol,medianum*30-29,20)
    medialength = substr(mediacontrol,medianum*30- 8, 8)
    mediastart = 7 + 30 * medianumber
    do i=1 to medianum -1
       blg = substr(mediacontrol,i*30-8,8)
       mediastart = mediastart + blg
    end
    call sqlexec 'CLEAR SQL VARIABLE DECLARATIONS'
    call sqlexec 'DECLARE :vpic3 LANGUAGE TYPE BLOB FILE'
    vpic3.file_options = 'OVERWRITE'
    temp = value('TMP',,'ENVIRONMENT')
    if temp = '' then temp = directory()
    tnam = 't'self~serial''medianum
    shorttitle = mediatitle~left(4)
    select
       when shorttitle = 'Fact' then vpic3.name = ''
       when shorttitle = 'Audi' then vpic3.name = temp'\'tnam'.WAV'
       when shorttitle = 'Vide' then vpic3.name = temp'\'tnam'.AVI'
       otherwise                      vpic3.name = temp'\'tnam'.BMP'
    end
    vfacts = vpic3.name
    stmt = 'select substr(v.pictures,'mediastart','medialength')' ,
           ' from cardeal.vehicle v  where v.serialnum =' self~serial
    call sqlexec 'PREPARE s2 FROM :stmt'
    call sqlexec 'DECLARE c2 CURSOR FOR s2'
    call sqlexec 'OPEN c2'
       if vfacts = '' then call sqlexec 'FETCH c2 INTO :vfacts'
                      else call sqlexec 'FETCH c2 INTO :vpic3 :vpicind3'
       if sqlca.sqlcode \= 0 then vfacts = ''
    call sqlexec 'CLOSE c2'
    call sqlexec 'CLEAR SQL VARIABLE DECLARATIONS'
    return mediatitle'::'vfacts
```

The fact sheet is retrieved directly into a variable, whereas pictures (.bmp), audio (.wav), and video (.avi) are retrieved into temporary files (in the Windows *TMP* directory), and the file name is returned to the caller.

5. Write the code to play audio and video multimedia files. Sample code to play an audio file and to display a video (extract from car dealer class in base\src\cardeal.cls):

```
::method playaudio class
    arg filename
    call PlaySoundFile filename, "YES"     /* implemented in OODIALOG.DLL */

::method playvideo class
    arg filename
    "mplayer /PLAY" filename               /* mplay32 in Windows NT */
```

6. Pictures are displayed in bitmap buttons by the OODialog GUI builder, or using the Windows *Paintbrush* program in the ASCII interface.

Implementation Notes

1. The DB2 table spaces and the vehicle table are set up by the car dealer DB2 setup programs db2setup.rex and db2ddl.rex. All tables are loaded as well, including the multimedia data. We have provided the programs load-db2.rex and load-mm.rex to load the sample data into DB2; they are called from db2ddl.rex.

2. We retrofitted multimedia support into the FAT implementation. The FAT vehicle class was enhanced by the same three methods (*getmedianumber*, *getmediacontrol*, *getmediainfo*), and the respective multimedia files are passed to the code directly from the distributed data files.

    This allows the ASCII and GUI applications to be run with FAT persistence support and multimedia data.

3. Multimedia data is available for customers *New and used cars*, *Holder*, *Turton*, and *Wahli*.

Source Code for DB2 Multimedia Implementation

The source code for the DB2 Vehicle class is listed in *DB2 Vehicle Class* on page 518.

The multimedia descriptive file is listed in *Multimedia Data Definition File* on page 492.

Audio and video play methods are part of the car dealer class, which is introduced in *Overall Car Dealer File Structure* on page 222, and the source code is listed in *Cardeal Class* on page 508.

The source code for the multimedia load program load-mm.rex is not listed in the appendix; it is available in the car dealer INSTALL directory on the CD, or on a hard drive after Object REXX has been installed (see Table 31 on page 304).

10

Data Security with Object REXX and DB2

In this chapter we exploit DB2 stored procedures to solve a common security problem when using dynamic SQL.

The Security Problem

The next day, Hanna and Curt were working quietly in the office when the phone rang. Hanna answered it.

"Hello, Hacurs Software Systems," she said. "Oh hello, Steve. We were wondering how your morning went with Classy Cars. What? What's the problem? They don't like our data security? No...wait...hold on, Steve! I think that you're overreacting. Come into the office straight away and tell us what happened. I'm sure we'll be able to sort something out."

"That sounded like trouble," observed Curt.

"Steve's very upset," said Hanna. "He said that the IT consultant that Classy Cars has engaged has persuaded them that there's a major security exposure in our system. Steve said he couldn't talk them out of it; they're saying they can't implement the system as it is."

"We've invested a lot of effort in Classy Cars, and so far we've had nothing but problems with them," said Curt. "I think we should cut our losses. There are lots of other car dealers around. We're sure to sell our system with less time and trouble than we're having."

"We've invested too much time and effort in Classy Cars to just walk away," Hanna responded. "Let's wait and see what the problem is, Curt. I've got a lot of faith in you and Steve. I'm sure you'll be able to handle it."

Curt didn't look convinced. They both tried to keep working at their tasks while waiting for Steve. At last they heard the crunch of his car tires outside the office. He came in moments later, slamming the door.

"That confounded consultant is really making things hard for us," Steve said.

"What is it now, Steve?" asked Hanna.

"Well, he's still going on about the need for a centralized database manager," said Steve. "And he seems to have convinced Classy Cars that that's the way they must go. I explained to them that they have already signed off our design based on a separate database per branch, and that's the way we'll have to install the pilot. It's too late to change without impacting the schedule. They agreed to that. We'll investigate the impact of changing to a distributed system later on."

"What else, Steve?" asked Hanna.

"The consultant has been reviewing our design in detail," Steve responded. "He's come to the conclusion that its security is weak, and that this will be a problem, particularly for their customer data."

"Why does he say that?" asked Hanna.

"Mainly because we're using dynamic SQL in all our applications," answered Steve. "The implication is that we will have to authorize the end users to access the DB2 tables directly. So long as they use our programs, we can control what data they can see. But they could equally well use a package like Lotus 1-2-3 or Excel to access the tables, and then we can't control what they do."

"But isn't access to DB2 password-protected, Steve?" asked Hanna.

"Yes," replied Steve, "but the user is asked to perform the logon when our code first tries to access DB2. So users have to know their own logon ID and password. And once they've logged on to allow our application to run, they can start up other applications and access the database with them."

"Hold on, Steve," said Curt. "What you say is true for a user working on the database server itself. But someone using a client PC to access a DB2 server must issue a *connect* command to DB2, quoting a user ID and password. That *connect* command must be embedded in the application program. And we're not planning to allow users to run applications directly on the DB2 server machine."

"I wish that I'd had you with me this morning, Curt," said Steve. "But if the DB2 connect statement is in a REXX program, anyone can look at the source, and then they'll see the user ID and password, won't they?"

"That used to be true, but not any more," said Hanna. "Object REXX includes a new utility called *REXXC*. You can use this to read REXX source code and produce a new program that does what the original program does, but is unreadable, similar to compiling C or COBOL source, which produces unreadable object text." [See *Tokenizing Object REXX Programs* on page 75 and *The REXXC Utility* on page 467 for more information.]

"That's great," said Steve, "but if a REXX program contains a user ID and password as plain text literals and it gets processed by the *REXXC* command, won't the literals still be there in the output file?"

"Let's find out," said Curt. He typed in a small REXX command file, processed it through *REXXC*, and looked at the output. "Hmm—yes, the literals are stored as plain text in the output file."

"Hey!" said Steve. "Maybe we can write the logon data in an encrypted form in our programs, then include code to decrypt it before we pass it to DB2. The Object REXX *translate* or *bitxor* methods could do the trick. That way, no one could see the logon information in our programs, because it wouldn't be there—in readable form."

"I'm impressed!" said Hanna. "You guys have thought of lots of ways to tackle this security issue, and it didn't take you long at all."

"I'm going straight back to Classy Cars," said Steve. "I think we can overcome their concerns about security."

"Let us know how it goes," called out Hanna as Steve strode for the door.

Hanna and Curt settled down to their work again. It was mid-afternoon before they heard from Steve. He strode into the office with a troubled look on his face.

"Hi, Steve," said Curt. "How did Classy Cars like our approach to ensuring the security of their data?"

"They were impressed," Steve answered. "So was their IT consultant, except on one issue. They definitely want to move toward a single, centralized database. They accept that this wasn't in the original spec that they signed off, so they're prepared to implement using separate databases in each branch and then to centralize over time. I'm sure we can work out an approach that will satisfy them."

"What's the IT consultant's concern?" asked Curt.

"He's been helping Classy Cars plan how they will run in the future," Steve answered. "They want central control over their customer accounts. It turns out that lots of their customers have run up substantial debts, and some simply switched their business to another branch when the first branch refused to extend them any more credit. Their branches don't exchange customer information. They really want to fix that. But they're pretty worried, because the accounting data they want to store will be very sensitive. They want a guarantee that unauthorized personnel can't read it—and, even more important, alter it."

"I don't understand the problem, Steve," said Hanna. "DB2 has very good built-in facilities to restrict the people who can access a specific table."

"Yes," agreed Steve, "but every branch must have users authorized to capture and view accounting data for their own branch only, but not to update or delete it. I was trying to work out a way we could do this with the *check* option of the DB2 view facility, but their requirements as to who can see what and who can update what may be too complicated to handle this way. The consultant says that the best way to implement really tight security is to have the application code running on the server in a locked room, and not on a hundred-plus PCs all around the country. He says if you can't even keep games and viruses off users' PCs, how can you hope to keep fraudulent code off?"

"So what's wrong with the security schemes we came up with this morning?" asked Curt.

"Well, our schemes all depend upon the remote user having an access user ID and password," said Steve. "We can do a lot to keep those hidden, but if there's collusion and somehow an ID and password pass into the wrong hands, the security of their accounts data will be lost, and they won't even know about it."

"Is this for real?" asked Curt. "Aren't they being a bit paranoid?"

"I'm afraid not," answered Steve. "Last year they had to write off more than a quarter of a million dollars in bad debt. They suspect that there may have been some collusion between some customers and some of their staff. But there's no way they can prove anything. They just don't have the right controls in place. Our computer system could help them, but its security will have to be watertight."

"Ouch!" said Curt. "It's a tough world out there."

"I've got an idea that some of the new DB2 features may provide a solution in this area," said Hanna, "but I'm not sure if we can use them from Object REXX. I'll take the manuals home tonight and check it out."

"Good hunting, Hanna," said Steve. "If you can come up with a really watertight solution to their problems, it would be worth a lot to them—and to us!"

Coding Stored Procedures with Object REXX

The next morning, Hanna came in clutching the DB2 manuals and smiling. "I think I've got the answer, guys!" she said.

"Cut the suspense, Hanna!" said Steve. "Tell us what your approach is, please."

"The consultant suggested that the code dealing with the most sensitive data should run on the central server only," said Hanna. "Historically, that's the way transaction programs have been handled on mainframes. Normally we build our REXX programs to run directly on the client PCs. Our challenge is to find a way to get some of the REXX code to run on the secure server and still to be able to access it from the client PCs. The answer I thought of is to use DB2's stored procedures facility. It's often used to reduce network traffic and to improve server performance by moving code that accesses the database heavily onto the database machine. But it can also be used to improve security. It would allow us to move key code off the client's PCs and to access secure DB2 tables by using a special logon ID and password in code that runs on the server only."

"Hanna," said Curt, "I hate to puncture a great idea, but a client program must be connected to a DB2 database before it can invoke a DB2 stored procedure. Which means that it has already supplied a logon ID and password. The DB2 stored procedure isn't allowed to issue another *connect* command, so it has to operate under the client's ID and password. Anything that the stored procedure can do in DB2, the client can do, too. And since the client's ID and password are embedded in code on the client PC, your proposal doesn't sound any more secure than do the approaches Classy Cars has already turned down."

Hanna just smiled. Curt and Steve were really intrigued. What did she have up her sleeve? She moved to the whiteboard and picked up the pen.

"What you say is true, Curt," she said. "I thought of that, too. But I also thought, Is there anything new in Object REXX that could help us in this situation? I did some reading about DB2 and Object REXX last night, and I came up with an idea. I wrote some code to check it out, and it looks like it will work. But I had only one ThinkPad to test it on. We'll have to try it out on a couple of PCs connected over our LAN."

"Come on, Hanna, you're driving us crazy!" exclaimed Steve. "What's your idea?"

"It's quite simple, really," said Hanna. And for once, she actually drew something on the whiteboard. "This is the way that DB2 stored procedures are normally put together," she said [see Figure 88].

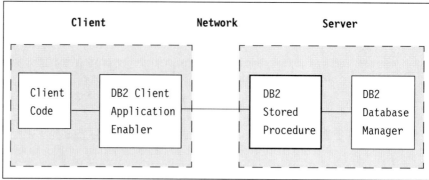

Figure 88. *DB2 Stored Procedure*

"The client code tells DB2 to call a stored procedure," explained Hanna. "The Client Application Enabler [CAE] on the client PC relays the request to the DB2 database manager on its server. DB2 schedules the stored procedure code, passing it the arguments on the original call command. The stored procedure runs, accessing DB2, and passes results back to DB2, which relays them back to the client code."

Hanna continued. "We can write both the client code and the stored procedure in Object REXX. But as you pointed out, Curt, the stored procedure has to use the DB2 connect that the client code has already issued, and, therefore, has no more authority than does the client. Now for the magic!" Hanna changed the figure on the whiteboard [Figure 89].

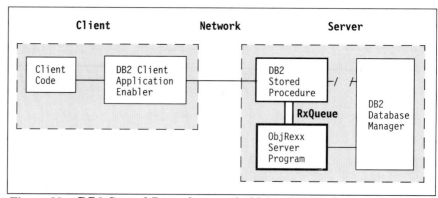

Figure 89. *DB2 Stored Procedure with Object REXX Server*

"The key thing here is that although the DB2 stored procedure has access to DB2 by virtue of the connect that the client PC issued, *it doesn't use it*," Hanna explained. "At least, not for accessing the really sensitive data, because the client doesn't have authority to do that. Instead, we automatically start up a disconnected process each time the server boots up, running an Object REXX server command. This command issues its own connect to DB2 using a secure ID and password, and creates a REXX queue using *RxQueue*. This queue can be used by any Object REXX command running on the server. In particular, DB2 stored procedures written in Object REXX can use it to relay requests to the Object REXX server command that created the queue. The server command waits for requests, handles them, and sends responses back to the requester through another REXX queue, passed to the server as an argument."

"This is brilliant, Hanna!" said Steve. "Show us your code."

"This is the Object REXX server code," said Hanna, bringing up the code on the screen [Figure 90].

"Now this isn't production-strength code. There isn't any error-checking in it," explained Hanna. "I just did enough to make sure that it would work the way I thought it should. Let me step you through the main points:

1 "This is the file that would run when the server boots up. It contains definitions for the DB2 server class and methods. I create an input queue for the client requests.

2 "I create a server object to process the requests.

3 "I connect to DB2 with the special ID and password. This gives me the authority to anything the special ID can do.

4 "I go into a loop, sending the *Request* message to the server object. Each time, it waits for a client request, then processes it. I make this loop quit if the client sends an exclamation mark [!] character, just to ease debugging.

5 "Here's where I define the DB2 server class and its methods.

6 "The *Request* method activates the input queue and waits for a request. The incoming request is parsed to extract the client's result queue and the input parameter.

7 "The *Request* method then invokes the *Respond* method to process the request.

8 "I return the server's response to the client's result queue, reset the queue, and return to the server procedure.

9 "There's only token logic in the *Respond* method. If the input transaction is a *CONNECT* request, I tell DB2 to select the special SQL value *User*, which is my DB2 connection ID, and return this to the client. That's just enough logic to verify that I can access DB2 data and to make sure that I'm using the right DB2 connection.

```
/****** server.rex ******/
q = RXQUEUE('create','DB2IN')              /* define the input queue   */   1
server = .DB2server~new                    /* make a DB2 server object */   2
if RxFuncQuery('SQLEXEC') then             /* register SQL functions   */
call RxFuncAdd 'SQLEXEC', 'DB2AR', 'SQLEXEC'
call sqlexec "connect to dealerdb user special using secret"  /*******/    3
say "The OREXX server is active..."        /* server is ready          */
do until input = '!'                       /* loop                     */   4
   input = server~Request                  /* process a client request */
end
call sqlexec "connect reset"|
call SysSleep 3                            /* let gateway/client end   */
q = RXQUEUE('delete','DB2IN')              /* delete the input queue   */
say "The OREXX server is ending."

::class DB2server                          /* DB2 SERVER CLASS         */   5

::method Request                           /* invoked by server loop   */   6
   expose input output
   originalq = RXQUEUE('set','DB2IN')      /* set queue to input       */
   input = linein('queue:')                /* wait for a line in queue */
   say 'Server: waiting...'
   parse var input '(' outqueue ')' input  /* parse the request        */
   say 'Server: input:' input
   self~Respond                            /* server db2 process       */   7
   say 'Server: reply:' output '('outqueue')'
   oldq = RXQUEUE('set',outqueue)          /* set queue for result     */   8
   queue output                            /*   and place result       */
   oldq = RXQUEUE('set',originalq)         /* set queue to original    */
   return input                            /* return to loop           */

::method Respond                           /* invoked from Request      */   9
   expose input output
   select
      when input~translate = 'CONNECT' then do     /*** CONNECT *****/
         stmt = "select user from sysibm.systables",
                "where name = 'SYSTABLES'"          /* return userid */
         call sqlexec "prepare s1 from :stmt"
         call sqlexec "declare c1 cursor for s1"
         call sqlexec "open c1"
         call sqlexec "fetch c1 into :output"
         call sqlexec "close c1"
         end
      when input~translate~word(1) = 'CUST' then do  /*** CUST xxx ****/   10
         custno = input~word(2)
         stmt = 'select * from cardeal.customer where custnum =' custno
         call sqlexec "prepare s2 from :stmt"        /* return the    */
         call sqlexec "declare c2 cursor for s2"     /* customer info */
         call sqlexec "open c2"
         call sqlexec "fetch c2 into :custnx, :custname, :custaddr"
         if sqlca.sqlcode = 0 then
             output = 'Cust' custnx':' strip(custname) 'in' strip(custaddr)
         else output = 'Cust' custno':'  not found'
         call sqlexec "close c2"
         end
      otherwise output = input~reverse     /* just to show we're here  */   11
   end
```

Figure 90. *DB2 Stored Procedure with RxQueues: Server*

10 "If the input is a *CUST* request, I retrieve the customer from the database and return its information.

11 "Otherwise, I simply reverse the input, just so I can see that something happened.

"And here's the DB2 stored procedure code," said Hanna [Figure 91].

```
/****** gateway.cmd ******/

newq = RXQUEUE('create')            /* define the result queue      */  1

originalq = RXQUEUE('set','DB2IN')  /* make input queue active      */  2
sqlroda.1.sqldata = 'anything'      /* touch arg to make DB2 happy  */
say 'Gateway: queue:' sqlrida.1.sqldata '('newq')'
queue '('newq')'sqlrida.1.sqldata   /* queue parameters for server  */

oldq = RXQUEUE('set',newq)          /* make result queue active     */  3
sqlroda.2.sqldata = linein('queue:')/* get result from queue/server */  4
sqlca.sqlcode = 0                   /* set return code for client   */

oldq = RXQUEUE('set',originalq)     /* set queue to original        */  5
q = RXQUEUE('delete',newq)          /* delete the result queue      */
```

Figure 91. *DB2 Stored Procedure with RxQueues: Gateway*
Note that a stored procedure coded in REXX must have extension .CMD.

"You'll see that there really isn't much to it. It acts as a gateway between the remote client and the Object REXX server code.

1 "I create a new REXX queue to retrieve the result from the server, and capture its name.

2 "I make the server's input queue the active queue and add the client request, *sqlrida.1.sqldata*, to the queue, prefixed with the name of my result queue.

3 "I make the result queue the active queue and wait for the server to post the result line.

4 "I store the result in *sqlroda.2.sqldata* and set the *sqlcode* to zero to indicate that the call worked correctly. DB2 will pass the result back to the remote client that called my procedure.

5 "After resetting the queue, I delete the result queue."

"The gateway is tiny, Hanna," said Curt, "there are only ten lines of code. Is this what they call *middleware*?"

"I guess so," Hanna replied.

"Where's the client code?" asked Curt.

"Here it is," said Hanna, bringing up the code [Figure 92]. "I wrote this as a stand-alone command that I can invoke from the command line. You'll see that there really isn't much to the client code either."

```
/****** client.rex ******/
call sqlexec "connect to dealerdb user humble using humbly"        1
reply = " "~left(60)                    /* prime reply so DB2 knows */   2
proc = "gateway.cmd"                    /* gateway code on DB2server*/   3
say "Client : Active.... I'm going to use the DB2 server..."

do until reply = "!"                    /* ask for input         */    4
    say "Give me an argument (any, connect, cust xxx, ! to end)"
    parse pull argument
    call sqlexec "call :proc (:argument, :reply)"  /***** call proc ***/ 5
    if sqlca.sqlcode = 0 then
        say "Client : reply:" strip(reply)
    else say "Client : Error:" sqlca.sqlcode", msg="sqlca.sqlerrmc
end
call sqlexec "connect reset"
say "Client : The DB2 client is terminating."
```

Figure 92. *DB2 Stored Procedure with RxQueues: Client*

"Let me step you through this code," Hanna said.

1 "I connect to DB2 using a low-security ID and password.

2 "I'm going to use the SQL *CALL* command. I have to prepare the field in which the reply will come by assigning a representative value to it.

3 "My DB2 stored procedure is called gateway.cmd.

4 "The client loops, asking the user for input until the user keys in an exclamation mark [!].

5 "This is the real meat of the code. The client calls the DB2 stored procedure, passing it the user's input string in argument and the *reply* field for the reply. I check the SQL return code, and if it's good I give the reply back to the user. Otherwise, I display the SQL code and error message."

To show them how it worked, Hanna opened a DOS command line window and entered the rexx server command. The server code displayed a message saying it was active and waiting for customers. Then she opened a second DOS command line window, and entered the rexx client command. The client code also notified them that it was active, and asked for some input. Hanna typed in Hello! and back came !olleH. She did it again, and the same response came back instantly. Then she typed in connect, and back came the answer SPECIAL.

"That's the server process's logon ID, not the client's," observed Hanna. Then she typed CUST 106, and the response was the name and address of the customer *Helvetia*. Finally, she typed ! into the client command line. Both the server and the client commands terminated in their respective windows.

"Hanna, this is brilliant," said Curt, "but the client, gateway, and server code are all running on the same PC. How does this scale up?"

"DB2 stored procedures can be called by remote client PCs," Hanna answered. "The clients can be running under a variety of operating systems, including Windows 95, Windows 3.1, OS/2, DOS, and AIX. DB2 supports connections over both LANs and WANs and can handle SNA, TCP/IP, NetBIOS, and IPX/SPX communications protocols. It's very flexible."

"Hanna, you're a genius!" said Steve. "This approach will allow us to implement really tight control over Classy Cars' sensitive data. I'm due to visit them later today, and I'd really like to take the code that you've developed and to review your ideas and code with them. If they're happy with it—and I'm sure they will be—we can start implementing their pilot branch while we build secure code to handle their accounts data."

"I'm glad you like it, Steve," Hanna replied. "This new version of REXX is so powerful, we're all going to end up looking like heroes!"

"I love it," said Steve, "and I'm sure that Classy Cars will, too, once I explain it to them. Let me copy the code you developed, and I'll go there right away."

Later that day, Hanna and Curt were in the office, waiting to hear from Steve about how his visit to Classy Cars had gone. They had expected him to phone after his visit, but he hadn't. There was an edge of nervousness in the office as Hanna and Curt tried to keep busy with things that needed doing. But the Classy Cars deal was so important to the future of their company that they found it hard to concentrate on anything else. Suddenly, they heard Steve's footsteps outside the door, and moments later he walked in with his ThinkPad slung over his shoulder and a large brown paper packet in his hands. As he put the bag down, it made a clinking sound.

"How did it go?" asked Hanna. She had a suspicion that the bag contained the answer to her question. Steve didn't answer immediately. He took a bottle of sparkling wine from the bag and placed it on the desk, followed by three glasses.

"Cut the suspense, Steve," said Curt. "Tell us what happened."

"They signed."

"Congratulations," said Hanna, hugging him. Curt got up and shook his hand vigorously, as if he had just announced his engagement.

"Thanks, Hanna. Thanks, Curt," said Steve. "This has really been a team effort. We did it together. And Hanna, I want to thank you especially for helping us work as a team whenever Curt and I got bogged down in silly arguments." Having said this, Steve reached once more into the brown paper bag and, somewhat shamefacedly, pulled out a beautiful, if slightly smashed, bunch of red roses, which he handed to Hanna. This gift was so unexpected that she blushed.

"Thanks, Steve," said Hanna, "these are really lovely." She put them into a vase and added water while Curt tried to get some more information out of Steve.

"What did they sign for?" asked Curt. "What do they want us to deliver? And when?"

"They want us to install the application we've already built and demonstrated to them," Steve answered. "They want the OODialog GUI front end. Oh, and they want the application to run against multiple distributed copies of DB2, one per branch, for the initial implementation. They want us to quote on extending the application to run off a single centralized copy of DB2 on a Windows NT server in about three months' time. And, most importantly, they wrote a check to cover our development effort to date. Here it is!"

Steve pulled out the check and showed it to the others. Hanna took it and said, "Well done, Steve! I'll deposit that in our bank account later today. Our bank manager will be very happy to see it."

"All this talking," said Curt, "and you haven't even offered us a drink."

"You're right," Steve responded, "what am I thinking of?" He loosened the cork, filled the three glasses, and passed them around. "I propose a toast to Hacurs—may it prosper and grow."

"To Hacurs," said Hanna and Curt in agreement.

Demonstration notes

- ❑ The code for the three commands is in the `StorProc` subdirectory of the car dealer application.
- ❑ Make sure DB2 is started.
- ❑ Open two DOS windows and make the `StorProc` subdirectory the current directory in both windows.
- ❑ Type `rexx server` in one window, and wait for the *ready* message.
- ❑ Type `rexx client` in the other window, and then enter any text, or the special keywords `CONNECT` or `CUST xxx`.
- ❑ The response of the *SPECIAL* user ID when entering `CONNECT` is proof that the code on the server runs under the user ID of the server.
- ❑ Type ! to end both client and server.
- ❑ You can also run the server on Windows NT and the client on Windows 95. Change the client *connect* statement to use the local alias name of the server database. See *DB2 Setup for Remote Database Access* on page 295 for instructions. The two user IDs, *SPECIAL* as local administrator with password *SECRET*, and *HUMBLE* as regular user with password *HUMBLY,* must be defined on the NT server and authorized to DB2.

11

Configuration Management with Object REXX

In this chapter, we discuss ways of managing an Object REXX application that is large and has different versions, all of which must be supported concurrently. We shall see how to use Object REXX classes with inheritance and polymorphism to help us achieve these goals. The grouping of related files into subdirectory structures can also help.

Most REXX programmers know that writing small, one-off applications is fun. It's quick to do, and the users are often grateful to get a fast response to their needs. But, of course, there is always the risk that, after a while, the application might become very popular with many users. Suddenly, the code must run in environments never contemplated and, therefore, turns into a maintenance burden.

This is the kind of problem that a software company like Hacurs loves to have. One-off applications yield revenue once only. The real money-spinners are those applications that can be sold to a number of different customers. Inevitably, the operating environment will be different in each location. There may be different database managers to interface with and possibly different GUI packages, as well.

When classic REXX was first designed, no one could have guessed how widely used it would become or how big some REXX applications would grow. The base language has some facilities for managing large applications by separating called subroutines into separate files, but Object REXX brings a lot more to the table.

We've spoken about the benefits of classes, polymorphism, and inheritance. We've claimed that these make it easier to substitute parts without impact to the rest of the system. Now it's time to deliver. We must show practical ways to make these promises come true. In this chapter, we talk about the problems that confront "successful" applications and show how the features of Object REXX can be used to ease the creation, distribution, implementation, and maintenance of such applications.

Breaking an Application into Multiple Files

Hanna was working alone in the Hacurs offices. Curt and Steve were out at Classy Cars, training more staff to use the pilot car dealer application that was now installed and running. Hanna was working through the various pieces of the car dealer application on the server. Although it had been Hacurs' goal to work off a common and shared set of class libraries, things had gotten a little out of control while Curt was struggling to meet deadlines at Trusty Trucks and Steve working to satisfy Classy Cars. The time had now come to reconcile any differences there might be and to consolidate both versions of the application into a single library.

Hanna knew that once a source file grows bigger than about 400 lines, it becomes hard to read and understand. It was time to break the source into a number of separate files. Each component file should deal with a separate part of the overall system, and, ideally, each part of the system should be dealt with in only one place. The Hacurs team had tried to follow this approach with classic REXX, with limited success. While classic REXX enables the programmer to split procedures off into separate source files, the code in a separate file can see the data passed only as call arguments. This is good in terms of hiding data that the called code should not see or change, but bad when the amount of data that must be shared with the called routine is large. The number of arguments needed on the call statement can become unmanageable, and getting the callers and callee's parameter lists to agree can be difficult.

With Object REXX, sets of related data can and should be grouped together into objects. When a procedure or routine in another file is called, only a short list of objects must be passed. When an object is passed to a subroutine, only a reference, not the object's data, is actually passed. Hanna was trying to work out the best way of applying Object REXX's new capabilities to segmenting the car dealer application code.

Curt and Steve came tramping into the office with a take-out lunch they had bought on the way. They offered Hanna a share.

"Thanks," said Hanna. "How did the training go?"

"No problems," answered Steve. "We agreed to do three more training sessions with them, and that should be all they need from us. How does the converged version of our application look?"

"Just a little chaotic," Hanna answered. "I'm surprised at how many differences you and Curt managed to sneak into your code without consulting anyone. I've drawn up a list of them and have shown what I think the converged version should look like. I'd like you two to go through this list and tell me if you agree or disagree."

Steve and Curt groaned but settled down at their desks and powered up their ThinkPads to review the list that Hanna had stored on the server. About half an hour later, they had completed this task.

"Your suggestions all look good to me, Hanna," said Curt.

"Me, too," agreed Steve. "It's mainly a question of making sure that each class definition includes all the methods and features that we need for both Trusty Trucks and Classy Cars. I think you've got it all sorted out."

"Thanks, guys," said Hanna. "I've also come up with an idea of how we can split the source code into separate files. I'd like to review that with you. We've already moved the major class definitions into separate files. We had to write *::requires* directives in our source files so that the code in each file could see the other classes and methods that it needs." [See *The Requires Directive* on page 116.]

Hanna produced a sketch from her files. "The *Work Order* class requires the *Vehicle* class because it references the vehicle's serial number," she said, "and the *Vehicle* class requires the *Customer* class because it references its owner's ID. The *Work Order* class also requires the *Service* class, since each work order contains one or more services; and the *Service* class references the parts required for a particular service." [See Figure 93.]

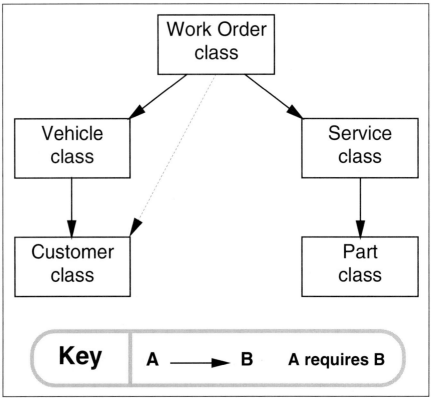

Figure 93. *Car Dealer Data Class Relationships*

"The *Work Order* class also references the *Customer* class," chimed in Steve.

"That's right," agreed Hanna. "I'll show that with a dotted line. The work order file doesn't have to contain a *::requires* directive because *Work Order* requires *Vehicle* which in turn requires *Customer*, so the *Customer* class is visible to *Work Order*. Strictly speaking, we don't need the customer's ID in the work order object, since we can get it from the vehicle object. But, in theory, a vehicle can change ownership while it's undergoing service, and there could be arguments about who's liable for the costs of the service."

"In practice, the dealer owns the database," said Steve, "and they would register a change in vehicle ownership only after they had made sure that the new owner would accept the service charges. But Trusty Trucks was worried about this part of the data model, and our zealous salesman bent over backward to meet their needs, as usual."

"Some of the biggest sales in the history of our industry have been made by salesmen who showed they were keen to meet their customers' needs," responded Curt.

Using Multiple Subdirectories

"The way it works out, a lot of the class and method definitions are (or should be) the same across both versions of our application," she continued. "But some of the method definitions are different, depending on whether it's the FAT or DB2 version. I wanted to get some uniformity in the file-naming conventions, so I've used the same file name for the common or base class definitions, the FAT ones, and the DB2 ones. All *Customer* class definitions are stored in files called `carcust.cls`, for example."

"Now hold on, Hanna," said Curt. "If the base, FAT, and DB2 class definition files all have the same name, they'll wipe each other out when you copy them into the common directory."

"I thought of that, Curt," said Hanna, "and decided that the cleanest approach is to create separate subdirectories for the common base class definitions, and likewise for the FAT and DB2 ones. I store the class definitions each in its own subdirectory, so there are no name conflicts. It could look something like this," said Hanna, pulling another sketch from her file [Figure 94].

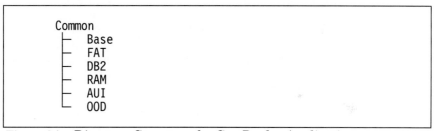

Figure 94. *Directory Structure for Car Dealer Application*

"Why so many subdirectories?" asked Steve.

"I've got a list here," Hanna replied, producing yet another piece of paper:

Common	files common to all configurations
Base	base object management classes
FAT	persistent storage in disk files
DB2	persistent storage in DB2 tables
RAM	initialization of objects in memory
AUI	ASCII user interface
OOD	OODialog GUI builder

"What's the RAM subdirectory for?" asked Curt.

"We did our initial development without any persistent storage—remember? I think we can keep that version alive with almost no effort, using the same techniques that we need to separate the FAT version from the DB2 version. I plan to put that code into the RAM subdirectory."

Configuration Files

"This all looks wonderfully neat and tidy, Hanna," said Steve, "but how on earth will Object REXX know where to find the files that you've hidden in those subdirectories when it runs the application? It will never see them, unless all the subdirectories are in the *PATH* environment variable. And if they are, it will always pick the files it needs from the first subdirectory that appears in the *PATH* variable."

"I thought of that too, Steve," said Hanna with a smile, "and I built a sample configuration file to try out an idea." Hanna opened an editor window to reveal the sample code [Figure 95].

```
::requires 'DB2\carcust.cls'
::requires 'DB2\carvehi.cls'
::requires 'DB2\carpart.cls'
::requires 'DB2\carserv.cls'
::requires 'DB2\carwork.cls'

::requires 'Base\cardeal.cls'
```

Figure 95. *DB2 Configuration Command File*

"As you can see, I included the relative subdirectory name as part of each *::requires* command," said Hanna, "and Object REXX was able to find all of the files with no trouble, so long as the common directory was the current directory when I invoked the configuration command file that contains all these statements."

"That's pretty neat," said Steve, "but what happens if the common directory *isn't* the current directory when you issue the configuration command?"

"It works fine, provided that the common directory is in the *PATH* variable," Hanna responded. "Which is what we would need, even if all our files were merged into a single subdirectory."

"That sounds great," chimed in Curt, "but you've got the relative subdirectory hard-coded into the configuration command file. What will you do when you need to include the class definition files from the FAT subdirectory instead of DB2?"

"I guess we'll have to have a different configuration file for each different configuration of files we need to use," Hanna answered. "It's sort of like the *make* file you build to tell the C compiler where all the source files are for a particular project, except the *make* file gets used at compile and link times, while my configuration would be used by Object REXX at run time. In fact, I started out by thinking of all the configurations that we may have to support, and that's what got me to develop a tidy way of handling them all. This is the sketch I made," said Hanna, scratching through her papers. She produced a sketch [see Figure 96].

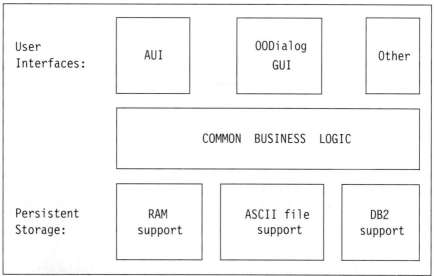

Figure 96. *Car Dealer Application Configurations*

"I've included the storage-based version we started out with for completeness," said Hanna. "I called it the *RAM version*. So, we currently have two different front ends and three different persistent storage systems. In theory, we could support 6 different configurations. And if we succeed in selling our application to other customers, the list of persistent storage systems could grow. We need a way of managing this complexity."

"This is very ingenious," said Steve. "But wouldn't it be simpler just to give every class definition file a different name and put them all into a single, common subdirectory? Suppose you give all the FAT class definitions a file extension of .FAT and all the DB2 definitions a file extension of .DB2. That would resolve the conflict."

"Yes, that would do the trick," said Hanna. "But would it also work when we have to merge the subdirectories that contain the AUI and OODialog GUI projects? And when we come to write the car dealer installation program, I'm sure that it would be easier if all the files we need for DB2 support are in one subdirectory, all the files for FAT in another, and so on. Then the installation program won't need to know which files are required for each type of support; it will just copy complete subdirectories."

"All this comes from having an obsessively tidy mind," said Curt, "but I can see that it would lead to a tightly controlled system and reduce the number of surprises when we need to implement major new versions of the application. For example, I was talking to an outfit called *Value Vans* the other day, and they are very interested in our application. But they already have several Oracle-based packages running, and we would have to port our code to Oracle before they would even look at it. With this approach, we would create a new subdirectory called *Oracle* and develop the new code we needed in there."

"It also allows us to put fences around portions of the code," said Hanna. "If we get contractors in to develop the Oracle code, for example, we could direct the server to give them read/write access to the Oracle subdirectory and read-only access to the others. That way, they couldn't accidentally break the FAT or DB2 code while they were building the Oracle code."

"That's a good idea," said Steve, "and maybe not just for contractors! I accidentally saved one of my DB2 class definition files on top of Curt's FAT version the other day, and I had to recover his code from the backup tape. I might make fewer mistakes if my default server profile gave me read-only access to the FAT subdirectory. I could always request the server to give me read/write access if I needed it."

"Thanks for your help, guys," said Hanna. "I still need to think this problem through some more. I'll take it home with me. Maybe we can look at it together again tomorrow."

"That's fine by me," said Steve, and Curt grunted agreement, too.

Overall Car Dealer File Structure

The next morning, Hanna was already in when Curt and Steve reached the office.

"Hi, Hanna," they called out as they entered.

"I've got a question," said Steve. "I copied the files you were working with yesterday from the server. When I looked at the end of your configuration file [see Figure 95 on page 220], I noticed a new class file named cardeal.cls. What is it?"

"I found that we need a place to put initialization code for all the other classes," Hanna explained. "Every class needs to fetch its initial objects, for example. There didn't seem to be a good place to put it, so I made the car dealer class. It will be responsible for initializing the application and terminating it properly, as well—for example, to disconnect from DB2."

Hanna dug a sketch from her bag. "I was working on the overall structure of our application last night, and it looks like this," she said [see Figure 97].

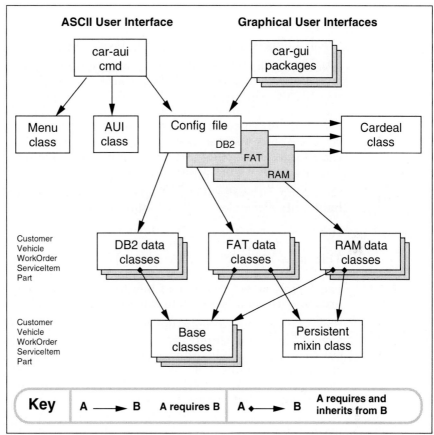

Figure 97. *Car Dealer Application Overall Class Relationships*

"This shows all the files we need for the various configurations we have to support," Hanna explained. "Each file is shown as a box in the sketch. There were so many, I've simplified it by showing boxes stacked on one another. There are *Customer*, *Vehicle*, *Work Order*, *Service*, and *Part* classes all hiding behind the box I labeled *Base classes*, for example, and likewise for the boxes labeled *FAT*, *DB2*, and *RAM data classes*. Each different configuration we need to support will have its own configuration file. I've shown them as a stack labeled *Config file*."

"This looks complicated," exclaimed Steve. "Do we really need all these files?"

"I think so, Steve," answered Hanna. "Most of them already exist today for the systems that we've developed for Trusty Trucks and Classy Cars. We just haven't put all of them together on one piece of paper before. For example, the car-aui.rex, caraui.cls, and car-menu.cls files are all used to drive the AUI interface for the Trusty Trucks version of our application. And the OODialog GUI package that we used to build the front end for the system, and potentially other GUI builders in the future, are hiding under the label *car-gui packages*, like spiders under a rock."

"Yeah—I guess you're right," said Steve as he stared at the sketch.

"I've shown that there's more than one configuration file," said Hanna. "When a user installs our application onto a PC, the install program will list the various options available, then copy in the configuration file that implements the options chosen. This file will contain *::requires* directives for either the FAT or the DB2 data handling classes. When we need to switch between different configurations, we can edit our own configuration file or copy one of a set of standard configurations into our working directory."

"Now that I can see it all mapped out like this, I realize that we've built quite a complex system," said Steve.

"Have we?" asked Curt. "Or have we built two simple systems and made life difficult for ourselves by trying to share code between them? This looks like a lot of work to me. We aren't a research lab, we're a small software development company. We have to meet customer needs fast, or we'll go out of business. We don't have time to mess around with complicated schemes like this one."

Steve squared up to reply, but before he did so, Hanna intervened by saying "You're absolutely right, Curt. We need to be able to respond to our customers quickly. And we all know that we can't do that with our old invoicing application. We've installed five—no, six different versions of it for different customers. They all started out the same, but today they're all different. Maintaining that code is chewing up a lot of our time. Yet, all of the different versions do much the same thing. We need to be smarter with the car dealer application. You're doing a great job finding prospects for the product. We need to make sure that we can deliver all they need without creating a monster maintenance problem."

Turning back to her sketch, Hanna said "As I said before, most of the files shown in this sketch already exist. We just need to tidy them up so they can reside in the subdirectory structure we looked at yesterday. What do you think, Curt?"

Communication Among Classes

Curt pondered for a while, then said, "Well, for starters, we'll have a problem that one class will not know about other classes. How can a method in the *Customer* class access a method in the *Vehicle* class?" he asked. "Shouldn't every application class have access to all the other application classes, in case we decide to enhance the system?"

Steve had a concerned look on his face, but then he lightened up and shouted, "We could use the Object REXX local directory for this!" He continued, "If every class puts itself into the local directory, all classes will have access to each other."

The Local Directory

Steve brought up two editor windows with the *Vehicle* and *Customer* classes and changed the source code to make use of the local directory [see Figure 98].

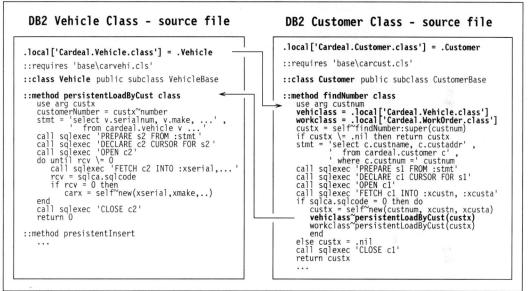

```
DB2 Vehicle Class - source file

.local['Cardeal.Vehicle.class'] = .Vehicle
::requires 'base\carvehi.cls'
::class Vehicle public subclass VehicleBase
::method persistentLoadByCust class
   use arg custx
   customerNumber = custx~number
   stmt = 'select v.serialnum, v.make, ...' ,
          ' from cardeal.vehicle v ...'
   call sqlexec 'PREPARE s2 FROM :stmt '
   call sqlexec 'DECLARE c2 CURSOR FOR s2 '
   call sqlexec 'OPEN c2'
   do until rcv \= 0
      call sqlexec 'FETCH c2 INTO :xserial,... '
      rcv = sqlca.sqlcode
      if rcv = 0 then
         carx = self~new(xserial,xmake,..)
   end
   call sqlexec 'CLOSE c2'
   return 0

::method presistentInsert
   ...
```

```
DB2 Customer Class - source file

.local['Cardeal.Customer.class'] = .Customer
::requires 'base\carcust.cls'
::class Customer public subclass CustomerBase
::method findNumber class
   use arg custnum
   vehiclass = .local['Cardeal.Vehicle.class']
   workclass = .local['Cardeal.WorkOrder.class']
   custx = self~findNumber:super(custnum)
   if custx \= .nil then return custx
   stmt = 'select c.custname, c.custaddr' ,
          ' from cardeal.customer c' ,
          ' where c.custnum =' custnum
   call sqlexec 'PREPARE s1 FROM :stmt'
   call sqlexec 'DECLARE c1 CURSOR FOR s1'
   call sqlexec 'OPEN c1'
   call sqlexec 'FETCH c1 INTO :xcustn, :xcusta'
   if sqlca.sqlcode = 0 then do
      custx = self~new(custnum, xcustn, xcusta)
      vehiclass~persistentLoadByCust(custx)
      workclass~persistentLoadByCust(custx)
   end
   else custx = .nil
   call sqlexec 'CLOSE c1'
   return custx
   ...
```

Figure 98. *Using the Local Directory*

"That's cool," said Curt, "I can use the same technique between the *Menu* and the *AUI* class. When the *aui* object is created, I store it in the local directory. This way I don't need to pass the *aui* object to the *menu* methods."

Curt thought a few seconds, then said, "Let's keep our copies of the code that's currently running at Trusty Trucks and Classy Cars untouched in their respective directories on our server. We can start restructuring the code along these lines, but I would like to be able to show Value Vans that we can meet their requirements as soon as possible. So we can't afford to get bogged down for weeks in a big restructuring exercise that prevents us from building and running demos."

"That's reasonable," said Hanna. "The question is, how long will it take us to restructure the code along these lines?"

"If we all work at it, I think we could have it done in two or three days," replied Steve. "Then we'll have to test it out, of course."

"Sounds good to me," said Hanna. "Let's do it!"

> **Using the local directory**
>
> The local directory object (*.local*) is available to all Object REXX programs running in one process.
>
> For the car dealer application we used the local directory to record:
>
> ❏ Each class as *.local['Cardeal.**classname**.class']*
>
> ❏ The relationship between work orders and service items as *.local['Cardeal.WorkServRel']*
>
> ❏ The ASCII window interface object (*aui*) as *.local['Cardeal.aui.object']*
>
> ❏ The active persistent storage as *.local['Cardeal.Data.Type']*, either FAT, DB2, or RAM
>
> ❏ The directory of the FAT data files as *.local['Cardeal.Data.dir']*
>
> ❏ The directory of the multimedia files (pictures, audio, video) as *.local['Cardeal.Media.dir']*

Installation Program Considerations

Three days later the Hacurs team met to review progress.

"I've got my AUI front end working with the new class structure," said Curt.

"I've got my OODialog front end working with it, too," said Steve.

"Sounds like it's time for a shoot-out," said Hanna with a smile.

The threesome put their ThinkPads side by side and went through their standard demo process in parallel. Everything seemed to work perfectly.

"Great work, team!" said Hanna. "The class conversion work wasn't hard at all. Are you running against FAT files or DB2, by the way?"

"FAT files," said Curt.

"DB2," said Steve simultaneously.

The two looked at each other. "There's actually no easy way to tell, short of looking to see which configuration file is currently active," said Steve.

"I guess that proves something," said Hanna. "How easy is it to switch from DB2 to FAT?"

"We'll have to develop an installation program," said Steve.

"No, it's simpler than that," said Curt. He clicked on the directory structure to open the DB2 subdirectory, and drag-copied the configuration file within it back into its parent directory. After confirming the overwrite, he restarted his application. It ran as before, this time using the DB2 configuration file.

"Well that's a handy way for programmers to do it," said Steve. "But our users will still need an installation program. Come on, it won't take long to build. The way Hanna parcelled everything out into separate directories, it should be a snap."

"Count me out," said Curt. "I've got an appointment to see Value Vans, and I don't want to be late. See you later." Curt left with a wave.

"OK," said Hanna, "I'll work with you. Should we use a GUI builder tool?"

"Absolutely!" answered Steve. "We want everything about this application to look professional. There, I've created a new resource file for OODialog; let's open it and edit it ... right, I've got an empty form. What should I put in it?"

"The target disk and path for our installation," Hanna answered.

"OK," said Steve. "I'll provide an entry field for that."

"Fine," said Hanna. "Now we need to offer the user a choice of persistent storage techniques—ASCII disk files or DB2 database."

"Hmm," said Steve, "I'll build a group box labeled *Persistent storage option* and put some radio buttons into it with the two storage options available. I'll add the RAM option too—let's call it *Objects in memory*."

"Now we need to offer the user a choice of user interfaces—the ASCII character, or the OODialog GUI," said Hanna.

"OK," said Steve, "I'll copy the storage options group box to make the *User interface option* box. I need two radio buttons, and I must change the text to show the interface options that we have available."

"And then we need an **OK** button," said Hanna, as Steve finished this task.

"I'll put in an **OK** button and a **Cancel** button," said Steve. "Some folks get a little nervous if they can't see a **Cancel** button. There, that does it. Now, let's just neaten this up a bit." Steve standardized the alignments and sizes of the controls he had built.

"That looks really professional, Steve," commented Hanna on Steve's design [see Figure 99].

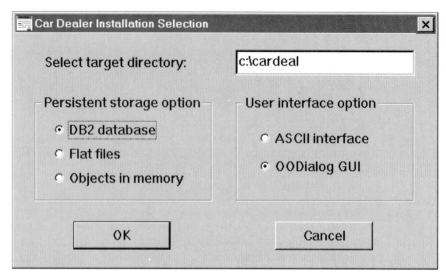

Figure 99. *Simple Car Dealer Installation Program*

"Now I've got to add the logic," said Steve. "But that really shouldn't be hard, thanks to the directory structure you set up."

"OK, I'll leave you to it," said Hanna, getting up.

"Just a moment, Hanna," said Steve, rising, too. "There's something I need to tell you." Steve suddenly looked serious, and rather strained. "I've been thinking about this for a while; maybe it's time I settled down and sorted out my life. We've been so busy getting our company going, I haven't had time to think about myself. But now that we've got our first big application installed with two customers and the money is starting to come in..." Steve's voice trailed off.

Hanna felt uneasiness, almost panic. Did Steve want to leave? Their little company had only just started to find its feet, and every member of the team was vital to its continued existence. If Steve left at this stage, Hacurs would never survive. And what did he mean by "settle down and sort out his life?" Was there a woman in his life? Where had he found time? They had all been so busy getting the company going. Hanna's heart started to pound.

"So...what I mean is," Steve struggled on. "Do you want to see the ball game on Saturday?"

A flood of relief swept through Hanna. She laughed involuntarily, and Steve was startled. He might have taken offense, but Hanna's broad smile and shining eyes reassured him that she would very much like to see the ball game on Saturday.

Implementation of Configuration Files

All configuration files are named `carmodel.cfg`. There is one for FAT persistence, one for DB2 persistence, and one for objects in memory (RAM). Each file is in the subdirectory of its respective implementation.

Object REXX executes any REXX code placed at the beginning of a file required by other programs that use the *::requires* directive. This feature allowed us to place entries in the local directory, load REXX function packages, and then connect to DB2.

Figure 100 shows the configuration file for FAT; Figure 101 shows the configuration file for DB2.

```
Parse source . . me .
maindir = me~left(me~lastpos('\')-1)      /* main cardeal directory */

.local['Cardeal.Data.type'] = 'FAT'               /* Data in Files   */
.local['Cardeal.Data.dir']  = maindir'\FAT\Data'/* Data directory   */
.local['Cardeal.Media.dir'] = maindir'\Media'    /* Media directory */

::requires 'base\cardeal.cls'
::requires 'fat\carcust.cls'
::requires 'fat\carvehi.cls'
::requires 'fat\carpart.cls'
::requires 'fat\carserv.cls'
::requires 'fat\carwork.cls'
```

Figure 100. *Configuration File for FAT Persistence*

```
if RxFuncQuery('SQLDBS') then
    call RxFuncAdd 'SQLDBS', 'DB2AR', 'SQLDBS'
if RxFuncQuery('SQLEXEC') then
    call RxFuncAdd 'SQLEXEC', 'DB2AR', 'SQLEXEC'

call sqlexec "CONNECT RESET"
call sqlexec "CONNECT TO DEALERDB USER userid USING password"
if sqlca.sqlcode \= 0 then do; say 'Cannot connect to DEALERDB'
                            exit 16;  end

.local['Cardeal.Data.type'] = 'DB2'                /* Data in DB2   */
.local['Cardeal.Data.dir']  = '-none-'             /* Data in DB2   */
.local['Cardeal.Media.dir'] = '-none-'             /* Media in DB2  */

::requires 'base\cardeal.cls'
::requires 'db2\carcust.cls'
::requires 'db2\carvehi.cls'
::requires 'db2\carpart.cls'
::requires 'db2\carserv.cls'
::requires 'db2\carwork.cls'
```

Figure 101. *Configuration File for DB2 Persistence*
Placing the SQL *CONNECT* call into the configuration file relieves the ASCII and GUI interface from dealing with DB2.

Using the Configuration File

There are two ways of using the configuration file:

❑ Put a *::requires* directive at the end of the source program to embed the configuration file:

```
::requires "carmodel.cfg"
```

❑ Alternatively, *call* the configuration file at the start of the program:

```
call 'carmodel.cfg'
```

The configuration file must either be located in the current directory or be found through the *PATH* variable. In our application, we copy one of the three configuration files into the main car dealer directory to make it *active*. Object REXX finds the currently active configuration file—DB2, FAT, or RAM. The application has no knowledge of which persistent storage method was selected. This technique is valid for both the window application (AUI) and the OODialog GUI application. The *::requires* statements are placed at the end of car-aui.rex for the ASCII application and at the end of car-ood.rex for the OODialog GUI application.

Configuration File for List Routines

We use an additional configuration file, carlist.cfg, to select the correct routines to list customers and work orders for the ASCII user interface according to file or DB2 persistence.

This configuration file is copied from FAT or DB2 subdirectories to the AUI subdirectory automatically, according to the configuration set for persistence.

Implementation of the Car Dealer Class

The *Car Dealer* class is responsible for initialization and termination of the environment. It is also a good place to hold the methods for multimedia—that is, *playaudio* and *playvideo*.

An extract of the class is shown in Figure 102.

```
.local['Cardeal.Cardeal.class'] = .Cardeal

::class Cardeal public

::method initialize class
    self~mciRxInit                                    /* initialize multimedia */
    .local['Cardeal.Part.class']~initialize          /* let each class         */
    .local['Cardeal.ServiceItem.class']~initialize /* initialize itself      */
    .local['Cardeal.Customer.class']~initialize      /* and load objects       */
    .local['Cardeal.Vehicle.class']~initialize
    .local['Cardeal.WorkOrder.class']~initialize
    return 0

::method terminate class
    if .local['Cardeal.Data.type'] = 'DB2' then      /* disconnect from DB2    */
        call sqlexec "CONNECT RESET"

::method playaudio class
    arg filename
    call PlaySoundFile filename, "YES"

::method playvideo class
    arg filename
    "mplayer /PLAY" filename     /* Windows 95 */

::method mciRxInit class private  /* load multimedia function package */
    call RXFUNCADD 'PlaySoundFile','OODIALOG','PlaySoundFile'
```

Figure 102. *The Car Dealer Class (Extract)*

Using the Car Dealer Class

Each version of the car dealer application has to make one call, *.Cardeal~initialize*, at the beginning of the program to initialize the application, and one call, *.Cardeal~terminate*, at the end of the program to terminate the application.

Source Code for Configuration Management

The source code for the configuration files is listed in *Configuration for File Storage* on page 509 for persistence in files and in *Configuration for DB2 Storage* on page 516 for persistence in DB2.

The source code for the *Car Dealer* class is described in Table 21 on page 301 and listed in *Cardeal Class* on page 508.

12

Object REXX and the World Wide Web

The World Wide Web (Web) on the Internet is fast becoming the platform of choice for advertising applications. Therefore, in this chapter, let's rewrite the car dealer application to run on a Web server and use any Web browser as the GUI.

With minimal effort, we can port the car dealer application to run under the control of a Web server, using DB2 as the database. We can redesign the user interface, using the Hypertext Markup Language (HTML). The car dealer application creates most of the HTML documents from the data stored in DB2, using Common Gateway Interface (CGI) programs written in Object REXX.

Hacurs Connects to the Internet

It was after the long Labor Day weekend when Steve walked into the office with an unhappy expression on his face, seemingly carrying the weight of the world on his shoulders.

"What's going on with you?" asked Hanna, concerned.

"Now that we've implemented the application for both Classy Cars and Value Vans, we are simply not busy enough" Steve replied. "We need to advertise our skills and our beautiful application, so that we get more companies interested in our services. I just have not figured out a good way of doing it."

Curt, who had listened half-hearted to the conversation, suddenly got up from his chair and shouted "The Internet!"

"The Internet?" asked Steve.

"Yes, the Internet," reiterated Curt. "I visited the Computer Software Exposition at the Convention Center over the weekend, and lots of companies advertised their services and applications using one of those Web browsers connecting to their main home site."

Hanna was silent for a moment, reflecting on what she had just heard. Then she said, "I think that's a great idea, Curt. I have read so many articles lately about the Internet and the World Wide Web; we need to get our act together and become part of this exciting new technology."

"What does it all take, Curt?" Steve asked, a little shyly. He felt badly that he did not really know much about the Web.

"Let's sit down and make a list," suggested Hanna. "Curt, you lead the discussion; of the three of us, you know most about the Web."

Hacurs Makes a Plan for the Web

Curt got up from his chair, grabbed a marker pen, and marched to the flipchart stand. "Let's see," he began. "There are several things we have to do.

[1] "First, we must physically connect our server to the Internet. That's usually done through a high-speed leased phone line provided by the phone company. Then we need a modem at our end of line. We connect TCP/IP to the modem and line, using the Serial Line Internet Protocol (SLIP) or Point-to-Point Protocol (PPP)."

"Our line traffic will not be very big, I guess?" asked Hanna.

"True," replied Curt. "We can get by with a medium-speed phone line for quite a while."

"Luckily, we've already configured our LAN with TCP/IP," said Steve. "It should be a breeze to connect our desktop machines and the ThinkPads to the Internet through our LAN server."

"There you go, Steve," laughed Curt.

[2] "Second, we have to install an Internet server program on our LAN server. Many server products are on the market, but for our Windows NT system, I think one of the best servers is the IBM Internet Connection Server. I saw a demonstration at the exposition in the IBM booth. IBM currently has a promotion, and it takes only a few minutes to download the server for free from an IBM site."

"Doesn't Microsoft provide an Internet server as well?" asked Hanna.

"Yes, they do," replied Curt, "But it only runs on an NT server and we are running an NT workstation for our small office."

"Is the IBM server hard to install?" asked Steve.

"It looks very easy," replied Curt. "There is only one configuration file to be updated with our installation-specific information, and the product even provides a Web browser dialog to do most of the tailoring."

"I guess we have to install one of those Web browsers," added Hanna.

[3] "You're right, Hanna" responded Curt. "That is the third point: a Web browser on every machine. For our Windows 95 systems, we can either install Netscape Navigator or Microsoft Internet Explorer. Both companies just recently brought out new versions of their products.

"Great," intervened Steve. "We'll try out both. What else do we need, Curt?"

"What does a user see when he connects to our server?" asked Hanna.

[4] "That's item number four: a home page," Curt said. "The home page is the first thing you see when you point your browser to a Web server. Our home page must make a statement about our company that entices people to want more information about us. It has to be attractive and lure users into our net—the car dealer application."

"I'll help you design the home page," said Hanna. "We can use our logo, add some information about ourselves, and then go directly into advertising the car dealer application."

"That sounds wonderful, Hanna," Curt agreed.

"By the way, how is a home page designed?" asked Steve.

Curt explained: "All Web pages are written as a file with the Hypertext Markup Language, or HTML for short. It's a tag language, similar to some word processors. There are many tools on the market to design Web pages interactively in WYSIWYG mode, then generate the HTML file. Our home page is probably simple enough to just code directly in HTML."

"Don't we have to create the Web pages for the car dealer application from the data stored in DB2?" asked Steve. He was now very interested in understanding and learning more about Web technology.

[5] "Yes," said Curt. "And this leads directly to the fifth item—the car dealer application. We have to design the flow of how a user can look at the car dealer data. Then we design each of the pages individually and write an Object REXX program to generate the page."

"How are these programs invoked?" asked Steve.

"Most Web servers support the Common Gateway Interface, or CGI for short," replied Curt. "In the configuration file, you specify which requests should be handled by a program, as opposed to just returning a predefined HTML file. The program can create the HTML file on disk and tell the server about it or, for better performance, it can pass the lines of the generated HTML page directly to the server. Most servers pick up the output by rerouting standard output, so we just use the Object REXX *say* instruction to prepare the pages."

"That sounds easy enough for me," Steve added. "I'll work on that because I understand the DB2 database the most. The hard part will be to learn the syntax of HTML. I had better go to the bookstore to buy a manual."

"I bet you will find a great way to generate those pages from DB2," Hanna joked. "Maybe, you'll even define an Object REXX class to handle the HTML easily!"

"Hmm, not a bad idea from a young kid like you!" Steve replied, and he started to leave.

[6] "Don't run away yet!" said Curt, holding Steve back by the arm. "We have to decide on an Internet name for our server and register it with the gods of the Internet."

"What does an Internet name look like?" Hanna asked.

"Well, it's something like 'www.ibm.com,' so I suggest we name our Internet server 'www.hacurs.com,' and our machines could then have the names 'steve@hacurs.com' and so forth."

"I like it!" Steve exclaimed, and Hanna agreed as well, after deeply pondering her new name.

"OK Curt, you and I can install the Internet server and Web browsers this afternoon," she said. "We can work with them on our existing LAN without the leased line for now. Then we'll meet tomorrow morning to work on the home page. Steve, you can go to the bookstore and get us some manuals about HTML and the CGI way of invoking programs. I think we're on a roll!"

Hanna was happy to see that Steve was excited about the World Wide Web. He had been morose for quite some time, but now his face was lit up, and he was ready to tackle any problems that might arise. Indeed, everything looked bright again.

Hacurs Designs a Home Page

The next morning, Hanna and Curt worked together to design the home page. Both were eager to get it done quickly.

"We don't have to design the *ultimate* home page," Hanna reasoned. "It should be simple, not too long, and provide the essential information about our company. What information do we need on it?"

"Let's make a list," suggested Curt.

They brainstormed for 15 minutes and came up with the following topics.

❑ Company logo

❑ People (Hanna, Curt, Steve), with some personal details

❑ Services offered

❑ Introduction to the car dealer application

"The company logo we can enter as is, because Web browsers handle all kind of graphic files," Curt explained. "For the people, we use a table with our names and personal details. Then we list our services in boldface, and for the car dealer application we could design some cute little icons. One of these icons will start the application."

"We could make the table a little more interesting by adding a picture of our car to each row. I mean, we do have that neat camera to take electronic pictures!" Hanna suggested.

"That's a good start; let's go to work," said Curt, who was getting eager as well, and the HTML manuals Steve bought from the bookstore were all ready to get dirty.

The Home Page

Within a few hours, Hanna and Curt managed to get the home page coded in HTML. The table of the people was a little tricky, but after some trials, the home page [Figures 103 and 104] saw the light of the day on Curt's ThinkPad.

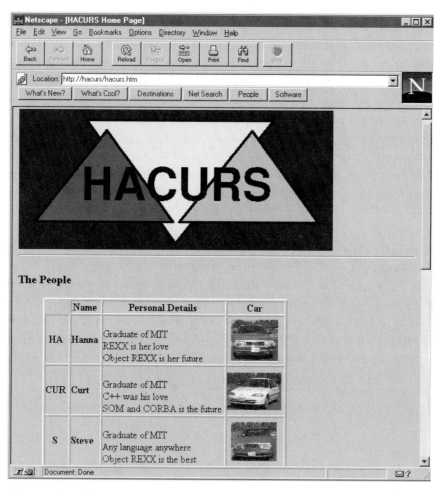

Figure 103. *Hacurs Home Page: Top Half*

Notes:

To connect to the home page of the Hacurs company with a Web browser, you would enter:

```
http://www.hacurs.com/
  or
http://www.hacurs.com/Hacurs.htm
```

We used the TCP/IP *HOSTS* file to make a shorthand entry, *hacurs*, to point to the Windows machine with the Internet Connection Server.

```
129.33.160.207  www.hacurs.com  hacurs
```

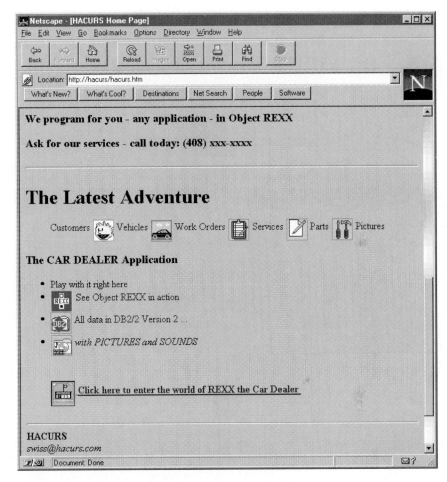

Figure 104. *Hacurs Home Page: Bottom Half*

Those readers who want to know what the Hacurs' home page looks like in HTML can see the actual coding in Figure 105. The home page is usually stored in the HTML directory of the Web server.

```
<!------------------------------------------------------------------->
<! WWW\Hacurs.htm        CarDealer - Web - Hacurs Home Page  ITSO-SJC ->
<!------------------------------------------------------------------->
<html> <head> <title> HACURS Home Page </title> </head>
<body>
<img align=top src="hacurs.gif">
<hr>
<h3> The People </h3>
<dir>
```

Figure 105. *(Part 1 of 2) Hacurs Home Page HTML Code*

```
<table border=2 cellpadding=0>
<tr>
<th> </th> <th> Name </th> <th> Personal Details </th> <th> Car </th>
<tr>
<td align=center> <b> HA </b> </td> <td align=left  > <b> Hanna </b> </td>
<td align=left  > <br> Graduate of MIT      <br> REXX is her love
                  <br> Object REXX is her future              </td>
<td align=center> <img align=middle src="carhanna.gif"> </td>
<tr>
<td align=center> <b> CUR </b> </td> <td align=left  > <b> Curt </b> </td>
<td align=left  > <br> Graduate of MIT      <br> C++ was his love
                  <br> SOM and CORBA is the future            </td>
<td align=center> <img align=middle src="carcurt.gif"> </td>
<tr>
<td align=center> <b> S </b> </td> <td align=left  > <b> Steve </b> </td>
<td align=left  > <br> Graduate of MIT      <br> Any language anywhere
                  <br> Object REXX is the best                </td>
<td align=center> <img align=middle src="carsteve.gif"> </td>
<tr>
</table>
</dir>
<p>
<hr> <h3> We program for you - any application - in Object REXX </h3>
     <h3> Ask for our services - call today:  (408) xxx-xxxx    </h3>
<hr>
<h1> The Latest Adventure </h1>
<dir>  <p> Customers    <img align=middle src="customer.gif">
           Vehicles     <img align=middle src="vehicle.gif">
           Work Orders  <img align=middle src="workordr.gif">
           Services     <img align=middle src="service.gif">
           Parts        <img align=middle src="parts.gif">
           Pictures                                           <p>
</dir>
<h3> The CAR DEALER Application </h3>
<ul>
  <li> Play with it right here
  <li> <img align=middle src="myorexx.gif"> See Object REXX in action
  <li> <img align=middle src="db2.gif">     All data in DB2/2 Version 2 ...
  <li> <img align=middle src="media.gif">   <em> with PICTURES and SOUNDS </em>
</ul>
<dir>
  <table border=4 cellpadding=0> <br>
  <a href="/cardeal/cardeal.htm">
     <img align=middle src="cardeal.gif">
     <strong> Click here to enter the world of REXX the Car Dealer </strong> <
/a>
  </table>
</dir>
<hr> <b> HACURS </b>
     <address> swiss@hacurs.com    <br> (408) xxx-xxxx </address>
     <p>
     <b> Ulrich (Ueli) Wahli - IBM ITSO San Jose </b>
     <address> wahli@vnet.im.com </address>
<hr>
</body></html>
```

Figure 105. *(Part 2 of 2) Hacurs Home Page HTML Code*

Note: Web browsers compress multiple blanks to single blanks, and lines are concatenated unless a tag forces a new line.

Web Car Dealer Application

In the meantime, Steve had designed the car dealer application for the Internet. On a few sheets of paper, he sketched out the different formats for presenting the car dealer data in Web browser pages. He called Curt and Hanna over to his desk and showed them his initial design [see Figure 106].

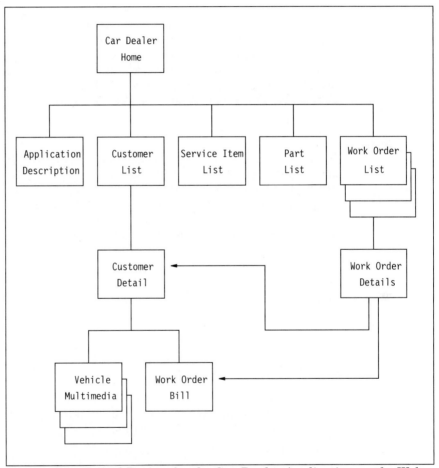

Figure 106. *Initial Design for the Car Dealer Application on the Web*

Steve explained: "I start with a home page, from where we can invoke the different paths. The path most used will be the customer list. We provide a customer search facility by partial name, as we did in the GUI applications." [See Figure 68 on page 163.]

"Customer search presents a list of matching customers, from where we can invoke the details of one customer. The details will include all the cars of the customer, the work orders for each car, including the list of services and parts of the work order," Steve continued.

"Then you can invoke the bill for a selected work order," said Hanna.

"That's right," Steve responded. "And for our multimedia *New and used cars* customer, we can display the pictures or play the sounds and videos. I represented that with the three stacked boxes. The other paths are to list all service items, parts, or work orders, and I think we should also have a short application description."

"Why do you show three stacked boxes for *Work Order List*?" asked Curt.

"Ah, yes, I forgot to mention that," said Steve. "I designed it so that we can list incomplete work orders, complete work orders, or all work orders. Remember, we have that search facility implemented in the *Work Order* class. When a work order is selected, I will show the details, including the service items with parts, and the customer and vehicle. From there, the user can get the customer details or the bill."

"That all looks very good," said Curt. "When can we see it running?" he asked, smirking.

"I will start coding a simple page first, such as the *Part List*. Once I get familiar with the CGI technique of invoking an Object REXX program, it should be a breeze to get the other pages done. Remember, the object model is working and stable. Retrieving the data from DB2 is simple; we already have all the methods. It is just a matter of accepting the parameters from the Web browser and creating the HTML output."

"Show us your first page tomorrow—I have lots of confidence in you," said Hanna, smiling and she left. Steve just stood there, but what Hanna had said filled him with pride. He would have something running by the morning.

Web Common Gateway Interface

Steve studied the documentation of the Internet Connection Server carefully. He found that the way to invoke a CGI program was by entering the Web browser request as:

```
http://hacurs/cgi-bin/progname?parms
```

This would invoke the program *progname* in the CGI-BIN subdirectory of the server (d:\WWW\CGI-BIN). The program could be either a .EXE or .BAT file. Using a small .BAT file we can also invoke a REXX program. [See *Customizing the File Organization on the Web Server* on page 251 for details.]

The parameters would not be passed directly to the program. They would be stored as environment variables, together with other useful information about the request [Figure 107].

REMOTE_ADDR	TCP/IP address of the requester (xxx.xxx.xxx.xxx)
SCRIPT_NAME	Request string before the ? (/cgi-bin/progname)
QUERY_STRING	Parameters following the ? in the request (parms)
	(blanks are replaced by + signs)
...	

Figure 107. *CGI Environment Variables (Extract)*

Steve proceeded to write the first program to list all parts in the database. All he had to do was to initialize the application, output the top part of the HTML file, iterate through all the parts and output each part in HTML, conclude the HTML file, and close the application. He decided to use an HTML table to display the part list [Figure 108].

```
/*--------------------------------------------------------------*/
/* WWW\partall1.cmd      CarDealer - Web - Part list 1     ITSO-SJC */
/*--------------------------------------------------------------*/
   .Cardeal~initialize
   partclass = .local['Cardeal.Part.class']
   say 'Content-Type: text/html'
   say ''
   say '<html>'
   say '<head><title>Object REXX Car Dealer Application</title></head>'
   say '<body>'
   say '<H2>Part List</H2>'
   say '<table border=2 cellpadding=0>'
   say '<tr>'
   say '<th>Number</th> <th>Description</th> <th>Price</th> <th>Stock</th>'
   say '<tr>'
   do part over partclass~extent
      say '<td>' part~number '</td>'
      say '<td>' part~description '</td>'
      say '<td align=right>' part~price '</td>'
      say '<td align=right>' part~stock '</td>'
      say '<tr>'
   end
   say '</table>'
   say '</body>'
   say '</html>'
   .Cardeal~terminate
   return
::requires carmodel.cfg          /* include the configuration file */
```

Figure 108. *CGI Program to List All Parts*

Steve ran the program and was pleased with the output. He called Hanna and Curt and showed them how simple the program was.

"This looks really easy!" Curt said in astonishment. "But what are those first two *say* instructions?" he asked.

Steve explained: "A CGI program must first tell the server what kind of output is produced. The string *Content-Type: text/html* tells the server that a regular HTML file will be generated, and the second *say* instruction must be blank."

"I thought you were going to write an HTML class to simplify the coding of the generated HTML lines," Hanna interjected.

"That's true," said Steve. "But first I wanted to have a simple working example. Now I can design the HTML class to provide the functions that are used most."

"Show us the output in the browser," demanded Curt, who was excited and wanted to see the program in action.

"Here we go," said Steve as he started the Web browser and entered http://hacurs/cgi-bin/partall1. It took a while, but eventually the screen filled with the Part List [Figure 109].

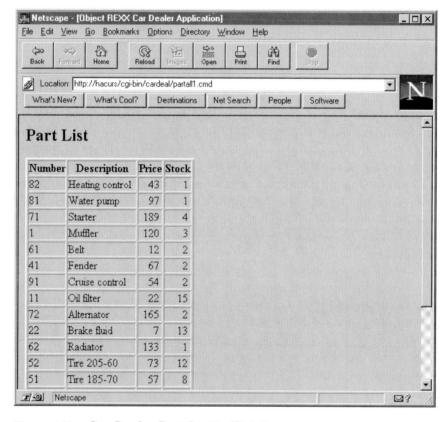

Figure 109. *Car Dealer Part List in Web Browser*

HTML Class

After a nice lunch at the nearby Mexican cantina, Steve proceeded to rewrite the code using a new HTML class. He thought of the functions that are used most often and designed those as methods of the class.

He also decided that each car dealer output page should have a reference to the car dealer home page and a common signature area at the bottom. The redesigned code looked definitively more object-oriented [Figure 110].

```
/*-------------------------------------------------------------------*/
/* WWW\partall2.cmd      CarDealer - Web - Part list 2      ITSO-SJC */
/*-------------------------------------------------------------------*/
   .Cardeal~initialize
   partclass = .local['Cardeal.Part.class']
   html = .HTML~new
   html~title('Object REXX Car Dealer Application')
   html~carhome                 /* reference to car dealer home page */
   html~h2('Part List')
   html~table('border=2 cellpadding=0')
   html~tr
   html~~~th('Number')~~~th('Description')~~~th('Price')~~~th('Stock')
   html~tr
   do part over partclass~extent
     html~~~td(part~number)~~~td(part~description)
     html~~~td(part~price,'align=right')~~~td(part~stock,'align=right')
     html~tr
   end
   html~etable
   html~~~p~carhome             /* reference to car dealer home page */
   html~sign                    /* common signature at bottom        */
   html~send                    /* output all the accumulated lines  */
   .Cardeal~terminate
   return
::requires html.frm             /* HTML class */
::requires carmodel.cfg         /* car dealer configuration file */
```

Figure 110. *Object-Oriented CGI Program to List All Parts*

The HTML class allocates an array of lines. Each method basically adds a line to the array in the proper HTML format. Some of the methods produce matching start-and-end tags, with the argument passed as the text between the tags. For example:

```
html~h2('Part List')  ==> <H2>Part List</H2>
```

Other HTML tags are produced by individual start-and-end methods:

```
html~table('border=2 cellpadding=0') ==> <table border=2 cellpadding=0>
html~etable                          ==> </etable>
```

The *title* method produces all of the required HTML tags at the start of the document:

```
html~title('xxxxxx')  ==> <html> <head> <title>xxxxxx </head> <body>
```

The *carhome* method produces the reference to the car dealer home page, the *sign* method produces the common ending, and the *send* method outputs the whole array as REXX *say* instructions. Not every HTML tag has a matching method. Tags without a method can be generated with generic methods, where the name of the tag is passed, as well. [See Figure 111 for an extract of the HTML class.]

```
/* WWW\html.frm        CarDealer - Web - HTML Framework    ITSO-SJC */

::class HTML public subclass array

::method init                          /* initialize an html object    */
  expose array_index type              /* index into the array, docu type */
  array_index = 1                      /* start at the first item       */
  type = 'text/html'                   /* default document type         */
  forward class (super)                /* do superclass initialization  */
                                       /* Start the html array off      */
::method put                           /* over ride of the put method   */
  expose array_index                   /* get the current index         */
  parse arg text
  self~put:super(text, array_index)
  array_index = array_index + 1
::method title                         /* title tag                     */
  parse arg text
  self~put('<html><head><title>'text'</title></head><body>')
::method h1                            /* header 1 tag                  */
  parse arg text
  self~put('<H1>'text'</H1>')
::method tag      1                    /* generate any tag              */
  parse arg name, text
  self~put('<'name'>'text)
::method text                          /* add raw text to the stream    */
  parse arg text
  self~put(text)
::method p                             /* paragraph tag                 */
  parse arg text
  self~put('<p>'text)
::method ul                            /* ul tag                        */
  self~put('<ul>')
::method li                            /* li tag                        */
  parse arg text
  self~put('<li>'text)
::method table                         /* table tag                     */
  parse arg options
  self~put('<table' options'>')
::method td                            /* td tag                        */
  parse arg text, options
  if text = '' then self~put('<td' options'>')
  else            self~put('<td' options'>'text'</td>')
::method sign                          /* signature/end                 */
  self~~hr~b('Hacurs - Car Dealer Application')
  self~br('Ulrich (Ueli) Wahli - IBM ITSO San Jose')
  self~address('wahli@vnet.im.com')
  self~~hr~~etag('body')~~etag('html')
::method send                          /* send the HTML from the array  */
  expose type
  crlf = '0d0a'x
  say 'Content-Type:' type
  say ''
  say '<!doctype html public "html2.0">'
  do line over self                    /* loop over the array           */
    say line                           /* send out the next line        */
  end
```

Figure 111. *HTML Class for CGI Programs (Extract)*

Customer Search Form

The next morning, Steve showed the HTML class to Hanna and Curt. "This will make future coding much easier," he explained.

"That's true," said Hanna. "But how are you going to implement the customer search facility? Can you put a push button into an HTML page?"

"I already investigated that last night," Steve said. "HTML provides the form facility with entry fields, radio buttons, and check boxes, and a **Submit** button to pass the values of the form to the next CGI program. The extract of the customer home page for customer search looks like this." [Figure 112.]

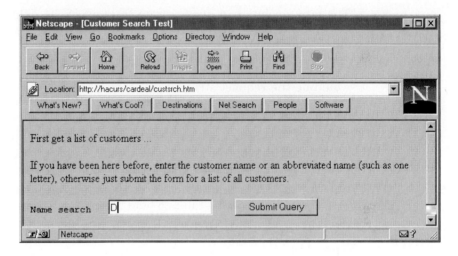

Figure 112. *Customer Search Form*

"Explain this one to me, please," said Curt.

"Sure, I can do that," Steve answered. "Just look at the HTML code that creates this form." [Figure 113.]

```
<html> <head> <title> Customer Search Test </title> </head> <body>
<form method="GET" action="/cgi-bin/CustList">
 <p> First get a list of customers ...
 <p> If you have been here before, enter the customer name or
     an abbreviated name (such as one letter),
     otherwise just submit the form for a list of all customers.
 <p> <pre>Name search   <input name="name" type="text" size="20">    <input type="submit">
     </pre>
</form>
</body> </html>
```

Figure 113. *HTML for Customer Search Form*

"The *form* tag defines the method of passing data and the program, *CustList*, that is invoked. The *GET* method passes all data in the request string, whereas the *POST* method tells the program to retrieve the data from the browser once it has been invoked. I specified the *GET* method because the amount of data is small.

"The input tags specify the different fields and buttons of the form. Here I used only one input field *name* of 20 bytes, and one **Submit** button. The *<pre>* tag specifies that this line is preformatted, with blanks between the text label, the input field, and the **Submit** button. Normally, Web browsers reduce all blanks to a single blank," Steve concluded.

"What does the program get passed when I click on the **Submit** button?" asked Hanna.

"The browser builds a query string from all of the fields of the form. Each field is passed in the format *fieldname=value*, separated by an ampersand. In our simple form with one field,

```
http://hacurs/cgi-bin/CustList?name=D
```

"would be the request string if you enter *D* in the search field. If the form had a name and an address field, the request string would include both fields, separated by an ampersand."

"Come see me after lunch, and I'll show you the customer search in action," said Steve, who was confident that it would be fairly easy to write the second program, using the form and his new HTML class.

After lunch, Steve showed the customer list output to Hanna and Curt. He had designed a table to hold the customer data. He made the customer names active so that clicking on a name would invoke the next program, *CustDetail*, to generate the customer detail page. [See Figure 114.]

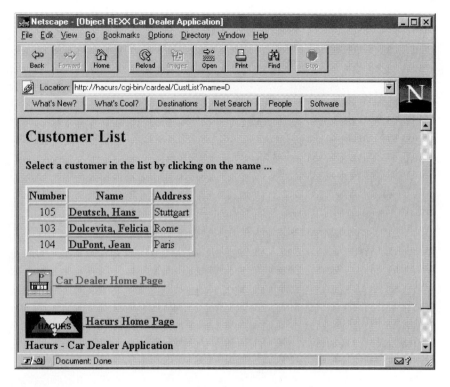

Figure 114. *Customer List in Web Browser*

"Wow, you really did a lot of work!" exclaimed Hanna, who was very pleased with the progress Steve had made. The other pages would be fairly easy to add. The work on the object model and the configuration paid off with every new application based on that model.

"Have you tried to run the application with persistent storage in files?" asked Curt.

"No problem," replied Steve. "I am doing most of the test with the file system because it is faster than the DB2-based application. I just switch the configuration file [carmodel.cfg], using our car-run program. But when we make the Web application available to outside users, it is better for advertising if it runs on DB2."

Steve had another ace up his sleeve. He clicked on a customer name in the list, and the details of the customer showed up in the Web browser [see Figure 115].

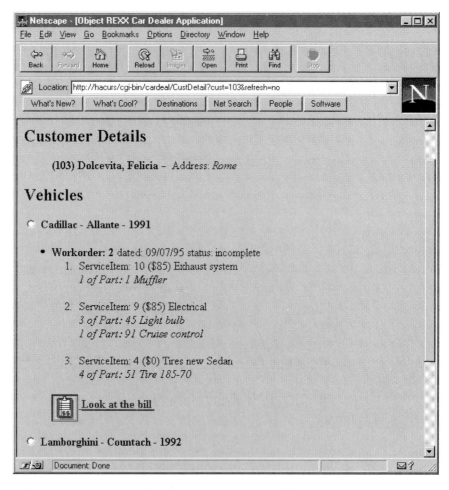

Figure 115. *Customer Details in Web Browser*

"What else is there to do?" asked Curt. "Just a few more programs generating the other Web pages."

"I think there are a few more items on my list," Steve replied.

Program Organization

"The car dealer is just the first application we put on the Internet. In the future, we might add other applications. I have to organize my files better, so that future applications do not interfere with the car dealer," Steve continued.

"Steve, that's good thinking ahead," said Hanna. "The Internet could be useful for many things we do over the next few months. We had better start organizing all the programs and HTML files we produce for the car dealer application."

Customizing the File Organization on the Web Server

Steve decided to put all the car dealer HTML files and programs into a separate subdirectory. At first, he considered using a subdirectory within the Internet Connection Server directory structure but, after studying the documentation on server administration, he decided to use a subdirectory within the existing car dealer directory:

```
d:\CARDEAL\WWW
```

He then tailored the server administration file to point to the new directory. The `httpd.cnf` administration file is stored in the main Windows directory.

Figure 116 shows an extract of the tailored administration file.

"Why are you making these changes, Steve?" asked Hanna, glancing over Steve's shoulder. She had just returned with coffee from the machine and wondered why Steve was so engrossed in his work.

It was as if Steve had just awakened. He had not realized that Hanna was standing right behind him. He started to apologize for not noticing her, but then he just shrugged and explained:

1 "The first *Welcome* line directs the server to display the Hacurs home page:

```
http://www.hacurs.com                ==>  d:\WWW\HTML\Hacurs.htm
http://www.hacurs.com/Hacurs.htm     ==>  same
```

2 "The second *Welcome* line directs the server to display the car dealer home page if the car dealer directory is selected:

```
http://www.hacurs.com/cardeal              ==>  d:\CARDEAL\WWW\cardeal.htm
http://www.hacurs.com/cardeal/cardeal.htm  ==>  same
```

[**Note:** Point **5** directs any requests beginning with */cardeal* to the `d:\CARDEAL\WWW` subdirectory.]

```
      # Sample configuration file for IBM Internet Connection Server
      #
      ......
      ......
      # added for car dealer application (next 2 lines)
[1]   Welcome    Hacurs.htm
[2]   Welcome    cardeal.htm
      Welcome    Welcome.html
      Welcome    welcome.html
      Welcome    index.html
      Welcome    Frntpage.html
      ......
      ......
      # added for car dealer application (next 4 lines)
[3]   Exec    /cgi-bin/cardeal/*        D:\CARDEAL\WWW\CGI.BAT
[4]   Pass    /cardeal/media/*          D:\CARDEAL\Media\*
[5]   Pass    /cardeal/*                D:\CARDEAL\WWW\*
[6]   Pass    /tmp/*                    C:\temp\*

      Exec    /admin-bin/*  C:\WWW\ADMIN\*
      Exec    /cgi-bin/*  C:\WWW\CGI-BIN\*
      Pass    /Docs/*    C:\WWW\DOCS\*
      Pass    /httpd-internal-icons/*  C:\WWW\ICONS\*
      Pass    /icons/*  C:\WWW\ICONS\*
      Pass    /Admin/*    C:\WWW\ADMIN\*
      Pass    /*    C:\WWW\HTML\*
      ......
```

Figure 116. *Tailored Web Server Administration File*
Extract of the HTTPD.CNF file in the Windows directory.

[3] "The *Exec* line invokes a small batch program, CGI.BAT, for every CGI request starting with */cgi-bin/cardeal:*

```
/cgi-bin/cardeal/progname?parms
```

"The small batch program contains only one line to invoke my common REXX gateway program, CGIREXX.CMD:

```
@rexx cgirexx.cmd
```

"I plan to write one interface program that handles the environment variables and some housekeeping before invoking the individual function programs."

"I guess that putting common code into one CGI program will make the individual programs a little simpler," remarked Hanna.

Steve nodded and continued:

[4] "The first *Pass* line directs the server to the Media subdirectory for any */cardeal/media* requests. We will need that to display the car pictures if we run with file persistence.

[5] "The second *Pass* line directs any car dealer request to the WWW subdirectory.

6 "The last *Pass* line directs any requests for */tmp* to the temporary directory of the Windows system. That's where the pictures are extracted to when we run with DB2." [Examples are c:\temp or c:\Windows\temp.]

"I am impressed!" gasped Hanna. "You have thought of everything. This keeps all the car dealer files nicely separated from the normal Web server files.

Have you thought about performance yet?" she added. "How can you keep all of the class objects in memory?"

Car Dealer Common Interface Program

Next, Steve attacked the common interface program, *CGIREXX*. He had to implement a number of common functions:

❑ Pick up the environment variables holding the request and the parameters from the Web server.

❑ Start the car dealer application. Steve decided to *Call* the configuration file, carmodel.cfg, and then initialize the application.

❑ Connect to the DB2 database if the application was running with DB2.

❑ Invoke the individual program to handle the request. He decided to pass the same Web server environment variables to all programs, even if they were not needed.

The task was not too difficult, and soon Steve tested the new interface program shown in Figure 117.

```
/* WWW\cgirexx.cmd      CarDealer - Web - CGI Rexx Interface      */

parse source env . me .
envir = 'ENVIRONMENT'
sourcedir = me~left(me~lastpos('\')-1
maindir   = me~left(me~lastpos('\WWW\')-1))
script = value('SCRIPT_NAME',,envir)        /* Web server variables */
who    = value('REMOTE_ADDR',,envir)
list   = value('QUERY_STRING',,envir)
parse var script '/cgi-bin/' type           /* extract request type */
list=translate(list, ' ', '+'||'090a0d'x)   /* Whitespace, etc.     */
ddir   = sourcedir                          /* CARDEAL\WWW directory */
sqlca.sqlcode = 0                           /* init DB2 return code  */
c = directory(maindir)
call 'carnodel.cfg'                         /* configuration file    */
x = directory(sourcedir)
.Cardeal~initialize                         /* initialize car dealer */
if .local['Cardeal.Data.type'] = 'DB2' then do
   call sqlexec "CONNECT RESET"             /* just to be sure       */
   call sqlexec "CONNECT TO DEALERDB"       /* connect to database   */
end
```

Figure 117. *(Part 1 of 2) Car Dealer Common Interface Program*

```
                                              /* analyze the request    */
select
   when .local['Cardeal.Data.type'] = .nil then
       call returnfile ddir'\cardealN.htm' /* CAR DEALER NOT RUNNING */
   when sqlca.sqlcode \= 0 then
       call returnfile ddir'\cardealN.htm' /* DB2 DB CONNECT FAILED  */
   when type='cardeal/cardeal' then
       call returnfile ddir'\cardeal.htm'  /* cardeal home page      */
   when type='cardeal/CustList' then
       call 'custlist.www' file, type, list, who
   when type='cardeal/CustDetail' then
       call 'custdeta.www' file, type, list, who

   /* others similar ...... */

   otherwise
       call error                          /* returns an HTML error page */
end
.Cardeal~terminate                         /* terminate car dealer  */
return

/*--------------- return a precoded HTML file ---------------------*/
RETURNFILE:
    parse arg resultfile
    say 'Location:' ,
        '/cardeal'translate(substr(resultfile,length(ddir)+1),'/','\')
    say ''
    return
/*--------------- return an error HTML file ---------------------*/
ERROR:
    say 'Content-Type: text/html'
    say ''
    say '<p><b>Invalid request of type:' type '<br>with parms:' list '</b>'
    say '<br>Who   :' who
    say '<br>Script:' script
    say '<br>Type  :' type
    say '<br>List  :' list
    say '<br>Dir   :' ddir
    say '<br>'
    return
```

Figure 117. *(Part 2 of 2) Car Dealer Common Interface Program*

Multimedia on the Web

Working late that day, Steve implemented a few more of the individual CGI programs. The next morning, he called Hanna and Curt over to his desk and showed them the latest additions.

"Look," he said. "When you display the multimedia customer [*New and used cars*], you get the list of pictures, audio sounds, and videos." [See Figure 118.]

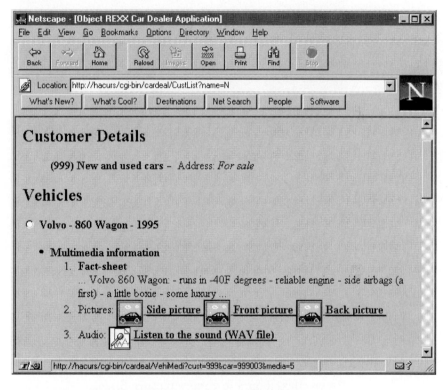

Figure 118. *New and Used Car List in Web Browser*

"Can you click on one of these to see the picture?" asked Curt.

"Yes, these are active links, and when you click on one of them, you get a new page that includes the picture of the car. Most Web browsers handle many picture formats, including BMP, GIF, and JPEG.

"When I click on the Volvo, the picture is displayed." [See Figure 119.]

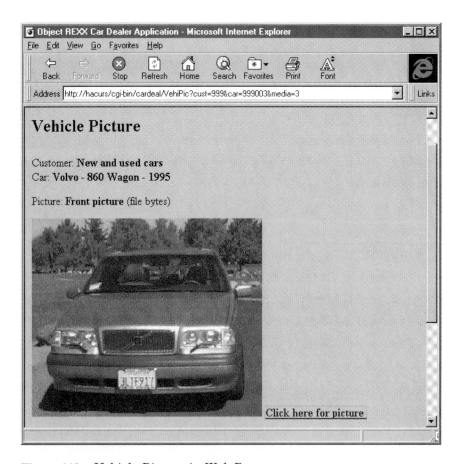

Figure 119. *Vehicle Picture in Web Browser*
For a change, we show the Microsoft Internet Explorer.

"I am surprised at how fast the pictures appear," said Curt, after Steve clicked on a few more picture lines.

"Remember, we are on a local network," replied Steve. "For users on the real Internet, the pictures will appear more slowly because our BMPs are not compressed. Pictures in GIF or JPEG format are smaller than BMP, but the GUI builders do not display those formats in the GUI applications.

"Try out one of the audio sounds now," he commanded Curt.

Curt clicked on an audio sound, and soon a familiar voice advertised the features of the Volvo wagon. Clicking on the simple demonstration video played the movie nicely in the multimedia TV window.

"Does every Web browser support audio and video files?" asked Hanna.

"Most browsers can be configured to invoke the operating system's multimedia function," Curt answered, before Steve even had a chance to explain how he managed to play the multimedia files on his Think-Pad.

Interacting with Web Users

One morning, Hanna arrived at the office with a new idea. She immediately called Curt and Steve over to explain her idea.

"I had a dream last night," she said. "We must involve the Web user in the application. What I want is thus: The user enters his or her name and address and information about a car. We enter this new customer and vehicle data into the database and then we let the user create a work order, select the services to be performed, and, finally, look at the bill for the job."

"That's an amazing idea," Curt shouted. "The user will come back to our home page several times to check whether the information is still there. That will prove how reliable the DB2 database is."

"What about security?" asked Steve. "The user could pretend to be somebody else when visiting our home page and create many new customers and add work orders to any of our demonstration customers. We need some control, so that each Web user can add only one car and not modify any of our own customers in the database."

"That's a real concern, Steve, you are right," said Hanna. "Maybe we can use the address field of the customer and store the Web user's TCP/IP address as a reference. Remember, the Web server passes the address in an environment variable to the CGI program," she added.

"That's a neat solution," said Steve. "Nobody will be able to touch our existing customers. But we have to extend the DB2 object model to include a method to search the customer table by address. That would enable us to check whether a customer already exists for a given TCP/IP address."

"And since we generate the resulting HTML file by the CGI program, we can include the active link to create a work order only for the customer entry of the current Web user." Curt was thinking quickly, as well.

"There is just one problem," he added. "Clever Web users can fake TCP/IP addresses and change customer records of other Web users. It's only a small problem, however, because our existing customer records cannot be touched."

"I think that's good enough for a start," said Hanna. "Our prospects are hardly of the hacker kind. Let's go to work. I will design the layout of the interactive form so that a Web user can add a customer and a vehicle. It will be a static HTML file, and I can do that!"

"Curt, you work on the program to create a new work order. You have to know how to code a CGI program; we cannot depend on Steve alone," she said, turning to Steve and smiling.

"And you, Steve, modify the existing customer display program to add an active link to create a new work order if the customer matches the TCP/IP address. And while we are at it, we can also allow Web users to delete the work order and the customer if they so choose," she concluded.

Hanna felt good, she was in charge. It had been *her* dream, and nobody could take away *her* idea.

Adding a Web Customer

Hanna quickly designed the form for a new customer and car. She deliberately added a field for the TCP/IP address, which could then be compared with the address passed by the Web server, thus eliminating a few cases of users trying to fool the system. [See Figure 120.]

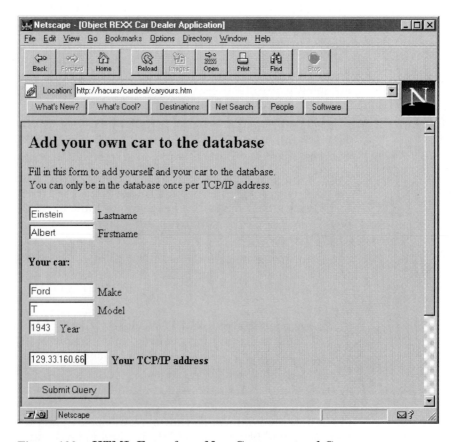

Figure 120. *HTML Form for a New Customer and Car*

In the meantime, Steve added a *findAddress* method to the *Customer* class for both file and DB2 persistence. The new code could be tested with the file system first before running on the DB2 database. Implementing the method for both types of persistence also kept the object model in sync.

Steve then modified the customer detail page to show an active link to delete the customer and create a new work order if the address matched the TCP/IP address passed by the Web server. The additional code was simple:

```
parse arg file, type, list, who
parse var list 'cust=' custnum '?'
...
customer = custclass~findNumber(custnum)
...
if customer~address = who then
    html~~~br~href('CDDelete?cust='customer~number, '==> Click here to delete the customer')
...
if customer~address = who then
    html~~~li~href('NewWork?cust='custnum'&car='car~serial, ,
                    '==> Click here for new workorder')
```

He could always replace the active text link with a nice, small picture icon later. For now, it was important to get his code working before Curt was ready with the *customer delete* and the *create new work order* routines.

Curt implemented the delete routine with a little pain. It was his first attempt at CGI programming, and it took a few trials to get the parameters right, delete the information in the object model, and generate a suitable HTML reply.

He then tackled the new work order program. Creating a work order was simple, it just needed a customer and a vehicle; all other attributes were generated by the model. The hard part was designing the addition of service items to the work order. He decided to use an HTML form, display all the service items as check boxes, and let the user select any number of them before sending the form by using the **Submit** button. [See Figure 121.]

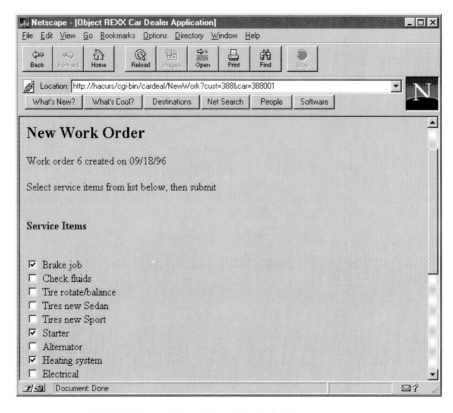

Figure 121. *HTML Form for a New Work Order*
There is a **Submit** button at the bottom of the form.

Curt decided that after processing the form the resulting Web page would be the existing customer detail display that Steve had done previously. [See Figure 115 on page 250.]

The design of the car dealer application on the Web was now complete. [Figure 122 shows the final application flow diagram.]

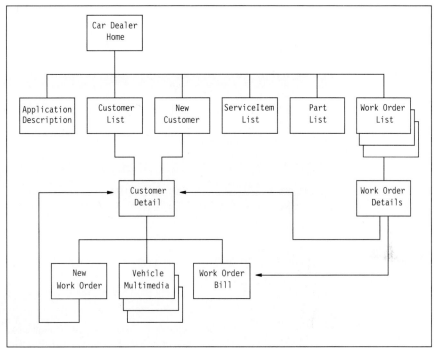

Figure 122. *Final Design for Car Dealer Application on the Web*

Car Dealer Home Page

Hanna thought about a few other pages that would enhance the function of the application, but time was running out. The leased phone line was installed, and they had to get the application out to the market.

There would be another day to make further changes. The Web was an active place, and enhancements could be added any time. Their object model and Steve's CGI program design would make it easy to maintain the attractiveness of the application and its currentness in the face of the ever-changing Web technology.

Hanna completed the car dealer home page with the new function of user interaction and tested it herself. Then she called Steve and Curt over and proudly presented the Hacurs car dealer home page [see Figure 123].

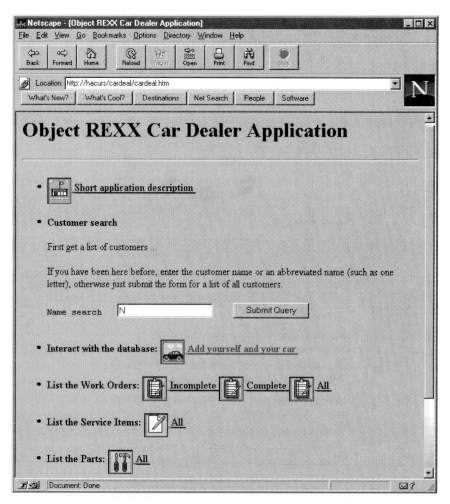

Figure 123. *Web Car Dealer Application Home Page*

"I think that's a start," said Curt, and Steve added, "You cleverly used our icons as active links to the different programs. Let's put it out on the external Internet Connection Server."

"Let the world enjoy Object REXX and the car dealer on the Web!" Hanna exclaimed, as she pushed the button to activate the external connection to their server.

Implementation Notes

When installing the IBM Internet Connection Server on a Windows NT system you can choose to have the server installed as a service. Alternatively the server is installed as a normal program with an icon in a folder.

The IBM Internet Connection Server can also be installed on a Windows 95 system. You have to manually add the program library d:\WWW\BIN to the *PATH* variable.

You have to configure your browser to handle bitmaps (.BMP), audio files (.WAV), and video files (.AVI).

Source Code

The source code for the car dealer on the World Wide Web is not listed in the appendix; it is available in the car dealer directory on the CD, or on a hard drive after Object REXX has been installed (see Table 29 on page 303).

Part 3

Object REXX and Concurrency

13

Object REXX and Concurrency

In this chapter, we experiment with the concurrency facilities of Object REXX. Object REXX provides both inter- and intraobject concurrency.

Interobject concurrency enables us to run a method against each of several different objects concurrently. Intraobject concurrency enables us to run multiple methods concurrently against a single object.

There is a detailed description of Object REXX concurrency in the Object REXX Reference manual.

Object-Based Concurrency

Every Object REXX object contains its own encapsulated method variables. It is given the processing power needed to run its methods and to exchange messages with other objects. Each object is a totally self-contained entity, and any number of objects can be active at the same time. This is defined as *interobject concurrency*. There is no danger of multiple updates to the same object variable because each object variable is owned by only one object, and each object runs only one method at a time.

Object REXX also supports another type of concurrency, where more than one method can run against the same object at the same time. This is defined as *intraobject concurrency*. Careful planning and synchronization are needed to ensure that the variables shared between methods are updated by only one method at a time. Object REXX provides facilities to manage these aspects.

The Object REXX Concurrency Facilities

The facilities provided by Object REXX to manage concurrency are: *early reply*, *message objects*, *unguarded methods*, and the *guard* instruction.

Early Reply

A method can send an early reply to its caller using the *reply* statement, then continue running. The calling routine will be able to resume its own work while the called method continues to execute (Figure 124).

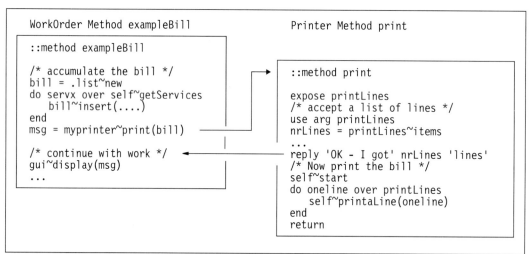

```
WorkOrder Method exampleBill                    Printer Method print

  ::method exampleBill

  /* accumulate the bill */                        ::method print
  bill = .list~new
  do servx over self~getServices                   expose printLines
      bill~insert(....)                            /* accept a list of lines */
  end                                              use arg printLines
  msg = myprinter~print(bill)                      nrLines = printLines~items

  /* continue with work */                         ...
  gui~display(msg)                                 reply 'OK - I got' nrLines 'lines'
  ...                                              /* Now print the bill */
                                                   self~start
                                                   do oneline over printLines
                                                       self~printaLine(oneline)
                                                   end
                                                   return
```

Figure 124. *Concurrency with Early Reply*

Message Objects

Message objects enable an Object REXX program to *start* a method executing in parallel with itself. The caller continues executing and can later ask the intermediate message object for the results of the call (see Figure 125).

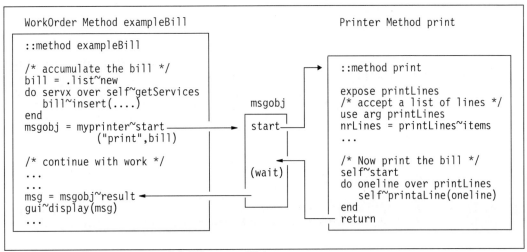

Figure 125. *Concurrency with Message Objects*

> **Note:** When the caller asks the message object for the results, Object REXX makes it wait if the invoked method has not yet completed.

Unguarded Methods

A method can be declared *unguarded*:

```
::method getnumber unguarded
```

An unguarded method will run even if another method is already active for the same object. This enables intraobject concurrency. It is usually quite safe to make read-only methods unguarded because they do not modify the shared variable pool. It is, however, possible that some of the variables in the pool will be inconsistent with others in the same pool. Suppose, for example, that an object's methods maintain a list of numbers and the sum of all the numbers in this list within the object's variable pool. If an unguarded method reads the numbers in this list and compares their sum to the sum maintained by the other methods, the sums may differ if another method happens to be updating the list at the time it is read.

Unguarded methods are needed in recursive situations. For example, the *init* method for a vehicle invokes the *addVehicle* method of the customer, which, in turn, invokes the *getOwner* method of the vehicle to check whether the vehicle is already owned. The *getOwner* method must be declared as unguarded so that it can run in parallel with the *init* method that is already active for the vehicle in question.

The Guard Instruction

The *guard* instruction acquires or releases exclusive control of an object's variable pool. This allows a method to alternate between exclusive access to all variables and parallel execution with other methods (Figure 126).

```
/* method code */
...
guard on                        /* acquire exclusive control */
                                /* wait if another method has exclusive control */
...
x = x + 1                       /* process variables */
...
guard off                       /* release exclusive control, allow others */
...
guard on when z > 0             /* acquire exclusive control when
                                      variable z is greater than zero */
...                             /* ===> wait until z changes to positive */
```

Figure 126. *Concurrency with Guard*

For an examples of the use of *guard on when* see the fork class of the philosophers' forks (Figure 131 on page 275).

Examples of Early Reply with Unguarded and Guarded Methods

The example that follows shows what happens when early reply is used to achieve intraobject concurrency. We start with completely unguarded methods, which utilize full intraobject concurrency (see Figure 127).

The program contains a main routine that creates an object and sends a *repeat1* message to it. The expected result (a string) is displayed with *say*. The main routine sleeps for one second, and then displays the variable *cvar*.

If we look at the object class *example* and the three methods *repeat1*, *repeat2*, and *repeat3*, we see they are all unguarded. Thus, all three can run concurrently on the same object. The object's variables *reps* and *cvar* are concurrently available to all three methods.

The first method, *repeat1*, initializes the variable subpool with the arguments from the main routine. It immediately calls the *repeat2* method for the same object and waits.

```
/* Xamples\xmpreply.rex          Early reply example - DOS window    */

   repetitions = 3                                  /* may change      */
   call RxFuncAdd 'SysSleep', 'RexxUtil', 'SysSleep'
   lvar = '(Main)'                                  /* init variables  */
   cvar = 'Main'
   cobj = .example~new                              /* allocate object */
   say lvar cobj~repeat1(repetitions, cvar)         /* - invoke repeat1 */
   call SysSleep 1
   say lvar 'Var =' cvar
   return


   ::class example

   ::method repeat1 unguarded                       /* repeat1 method  */
     expose reps cvar
     use arg reps, cvar
     lvar = '(R1)'
     say lvar self~repeat2                           /* - invoke repeat2 */
     reply 'Reply from' lvar                         /* - early reply    */
     do reps                                         /* - loop           */
        say lvar '- Var =' cvar
        cvar = 'R1'
     end

   ::method repeat2 unguarded                       /* repeat2 method  */
     expose reps cvar
     lvar = '(R2)'
     say lvar self~repeat3                           /* - invoke repeat3 */
     reply 'Reply from' lvar                         /* - early reply    */
     do reps                                         /* - loop           */
        say lvar '- Var =' cvar
        cvar = 'R2'
     end

   ::method repeat3 unguarded                       /* repeat3 method  */
     expose reps cvar
     lvar = '(R3)'
     reply 'Reply from' lvar                         /* - early reply    */
     do reps                                         /* - loop           */
        say lvar '- Var =' cvar
        cvar = 'R3'
     end
```

Figure 127. *Example of Early Reply with Unguarded and Guarded Methods*

The *repeat2* method calls the *repeat3* method for the same object and waits. We now have four invocations stacked on the activity chain (the main routine, *repeat1*, *repeat2*, and *repeat3*). When the *repeat3* method issues a *reply command*, a new activity chain (thread) is started for the *repeat3* method, and control goes back to the next instruction in method, *repeat2* (the one following the invocation of method *repeat3*). Similarly, *repeat2* uses an early reply to *repeat1*, and *repeat1* uses an early reply to the main routine.

Running the program produces the kind of output shown in Figure 128. In the left column (first run) we leave all methods unguarded; in the middle column, all methods are guarded (remove the keyword *unguarded* from the source code); and in the right column, we use a mix of guarded and unguarded methods.

```
Methods:          UNGUARDED              GUARDED                MIXED

repeat1:          unguarded              guarded                unguarded
repeat2:          unguarded              guarded                guarded
repeat3:          unguarded              guarded                guarded

output:     (R2) Reply from (R3)   (R2) Reply from (R3)   (R2) Reply from (R3)
            (R3) - Var = Main      (R1) Reply from (R2)   (R1) Reply from (R2)
            (R1) Reply from (R2)   (Main) Reply from (R1) (R2) - Var = Main
            (R3) - Var = R3        (R1) - Var = Main      (Main) Reply from (R1)
            (R2) - Var = R3        (R1) - Var = R1        (R2) - Var = R2
            (Main) Reply from (R1) (R1) - Var = R1        (R1) - Var = R2
            (R3) - Var = R3        (R3) - Var = R1        (R2) - Var = R2
            (R1) - Var = R3        (R3) - Var = R3        (R1) - Var = R1
            (R2) - Var = R2        (R3) - Var = R3        (R3) - Var = R2
            (R1) - Var = R1        (R2) - Var = R3        (R1) - Var = R1
            (R2) - Var = R2        (R2) - Var = R2        (R3) - Var = R3
            (R1) - Var = R1        (R2) - Var = R2        (R3) - Var = R3
            (Main) Var = Main      (Main) Var = Main      (Main) Var = Main

Notes:            (1)                    (2)                    (3)
```

Figure 128. *Sample Output of Early Reply with Unguarded and Guarded Methods*

Notes:

1. Unguarded: The sequence in which this output appears will change each time the program is run. The three methods run in parallel and compete for processor time. Which method runs when is up to the system scheduler.

2. Guarded: Once a method gets control, it will run to completion. Only after this can another one continue. Method *repeat1* gets control first from the reply of *repeat2*, and finishes its work.

3. Mixed: Because method *repeat1* is unguarded, it can run in parallel with *repeat2*, whereas *repeat3* must wait until *repeat2* is finished.

Other combinations of guarded and unguarded methods can be tried. You can find the program in xamples\xmpreply.rex.

Philosophers' Forks

Let's join our Hacurs team again to see a visual demonstration of Object REXX's concurrency capabilities.

On the Monday morning after a rainy weekend in October, Hanna came into the office beaming.

"Hi, Hanna, why the big smile?" called out Steve. "Are you up to something?"

"I spent the weekend playing with Object REXX's concurrency facilities. Let me show you what I built. Do you know the philosophers' forks problem?" she asked.

"Hmm," said Curt, "isn't that the one with five philosophers sitting around a table trying to grab forks and eat in turn?"

"Yes, that's the one," replied Hanna with a smile.

The philosophers' forks

❏ Five philosophers sit around a table. Each one goes through a cycle of sleeping and eating.

❏ There is a fork between each two philosophers, so there are five forks on the table, as well.

❏ To eat, a philosopher has to grab the forks on both sides. If a fork has already been taken by the philosopher on the other side of the fork, the philosopher must wait until that fork is free.

❏ The philosophers reach for forks in no particular order, but once they reach out for a fork and have to wait, they don't change their mind, even if the other fork is available.

❏ When they have finished eating, the philosophers put down both forks and go back to sleep.

❏ The times that they sleep and eat vary randomly around given values.

Philosophers' Forks in an DOS Window

"I wasted my weekend watching the fifth game of the World Series," said Steve. "It didn't produce a winner, and I missed the final game because I had to go to a cousin's wedding. So how did you implement the philosopher's forks, Hanna?" he asked.

"I developed a main program to control the operation and two classes—one for philosophers and one for forks," said Hanna. She opened her ThinkPad and fired it up. Steve and Curt gathered around her desk.

"The main program sets the parameters, creates the forks and philosophers, then runs all philosophers concurrently, using the *start* method," Hanna explained [see Figure 129]. "Then it just waits for everything to finish."

```
/* oodialog\samples\philfork.rex     Philosophers' Forks - Main */

arg parms                                /* parameters default values: */
if parms = '' then parms = '8 6 any 2'   /* - sleep = 8 sec, eat = 6    */
parse var parms psleep peat pside prepeats /* - grab forks from ANY side */
T.eat = peat                             /* - run 2 cycles              */
T.sleep = psleep
T.veat = trunc(peat / 2)                 /* random variations           */
T.vsleep = trunc(psleep / 2)             /* - for eat and sleep times   */
if      pside = 'L' then T.side = 100    /* grab left  fork first       */
else if pside = 'R' then T.side = 0      /* grab right fork first       */
                    else T.side = 50     /* grab in random order        */
T.repeats =prepeats

f1 = .fork~new(1)                        /* allocate 5 forks            */
f2 = .fork~new(2)
f3 = .fork~new(3)
f4 = .fork~new(4)
f5 = .fork~new(5)

p1 = .phil~new(1,f5,f1)                  /* allocate 5 philosophers     */
p2 = .phil~new(2,f1,f2)
p3 = .phil~new(3,f2,f3)                  /* tell them which forks       */
p4 = .phil~new(4,f3,f4)                  /* they must use               */
p5 = .phil~new(5,f4,f5)

m1 = p1~start("run",T.)                  /* start the 5 philosophers    */
m2 = p2~start("run",T.)                  /* concurrently                */
m3 = p3~start("run",T.)
m4 = p4~start("run",T.)
m5 = p5~start("run",T.)

m1~result                                /* wait for the 5 message      */
m2~result                                /* objects to complete         */
m3~result
m4~result
m5~result
return 0
```

Figure 129. *Philosophers' Forks: Main Program*

"I'm surprised at how straightforward it looks, Hanna," said Steve.

"The philosopher class is also quite simple," said Hanna [see Figure 130].

"The *init* method stores references to the fork objects and prepares an output string for indentation. The *run* method loops through sleeping and eating, picking up the forks, and laying them down again."

"It may look simple to you, Hanna," said Curt, "but that's because you wrote it. Still, it is pretty short. Where's the magic?"

```
::class phil            /* Philosopher Class */

::method init                              /* initialization          */
   expose num rfork lfork out              /* store fork objects       */
   use arg num, rfork, lfork
   out = ' '~copies(15*num-14)             /* prepare output indentation */

::method run                               /* run through the cycle    */
   expose num rfork lfork out
   use arg T.
   x =  random(1,100,time('S')*num)
   say out 'Philosopher-'num               /* announce who you are     */
   do i=1 to T.repeats
      stime = random(T.sleep-T.vsleep,T.sleep+T.vsleep)
      say out 'Sleep-'stime                /* announce you are sleeping */
      rc=SysSleep(stime)                   /* sleep some random seconds */
      say out 'Wait'                       /* announce wait for forks  */
      if random(1,100) < T.side then do    /* which fork first ?       */
         lfork~pickup(1,'left',num)        /*  - pick up left fork     */
         rfork~pickup(2,'right',num)       /*     then    right        */
         end
      else do
         rfork~pickup(1,'right',num)       /*  - pick up right fork    */
         lfork~pickup(2,'left',num)        /*     then    left         */
         end
      etime = random(T.eat-T.veat,T.eat+T.veat)
      say out 'Eat-'etime                  /* announce you are eating  */
      rc=SysSleep(etime)                   /* eat some random seconds  */
      lfork~laydown(num)                   /* lay down both forks      */
      rfork~laydown(num)
   end
   say out 'Done'                          /* announce you are done    */
   return 1
```

Figure 130. *Philosophers' Forks: Philosopher Class*

"My secrets are hidden in the fork class," said Hanna. "That's where the concurrency and synchronization are managed, but Object REXX makes it pretty easy to do." [See Figure 131.]

```
::class fork            /* Fork Class */

::method init                              /* initialization          */
   expose used
   used = 0                                /* initialize "used" flag   */

::method pickup                            /* pick up the fork        */
   expose used
   guard on when used = 0                  /* WAIT until "used" flag = 0 */
   used = 1                                /* set "used" flag "occupied" */

::method laydown unguarded                 /* pay down the fork       */
   expose used
   used = 0                                /* set "used" flag to "free" */
```

Figure 131. *Philosophers' Forks: Fork Class*

"Ah," said Steve, "now it starts to get interesting. Walk us through this code, Hanna."

"The fork's *used* variable is the key," Hanna explained. "It's initially set to zero, indicating that the fork is free. The *pickup* method changes it to 1, but it contains a *guard* instruction that forces it to wait until the fork is free, which happens in the *laydown* method."

"Sounds good," said Curt, "but let's see it in action!"

Hanna started the program, and soon the window was filled with announcements of the philosophers' activities [see Figure 132].

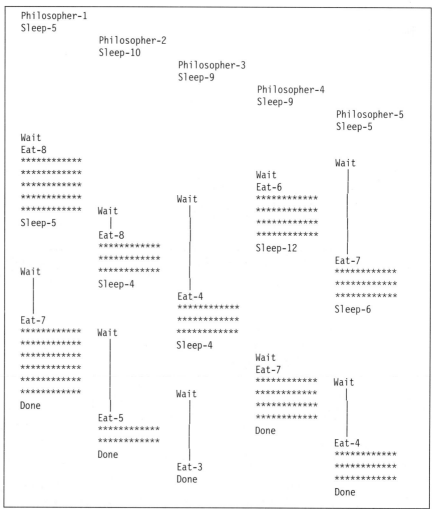

Figure 132. *Philosophers' Forks: Sample Output*
The output has been enhanced with blocks of asterisks (*) to indicate eating and vertical lines to indicate waiting. No more than two philosophers can eat at the same time because of the shared forks.

"Cool!" said Steve. "I wonder if we could OODialog to make this look a bit more snazzy."

"Sounds like a great idea, Steve," said Hanna. "Why don't you try? You've got Classy Cars running so smoothly, you probably don't have anything better to do this week."

"Me and my big mouth!" said Steve with a rueful smile. "I guess I walked straight into that one. You knew that I would, didn't you? You were just waiting for me to make that suggestion," he accused Hanna. Her smile broadened, but she said nothing.

Visualizing Philosophers' Forks with OODialog

The next day, Steve came to the office late but looking rather smug. He called Hanna and Curt over to his desk to show off the graphical GUI version of the philosophers' forks. He started his ThinkPad and clicked on an icon to launch the application. A window opened and displayed Steve's inventive representation of the classical philosophers' forks problem [see Figure 133].

Figure 133. *Philosophers' Forks GUI: OODialog Layout*

"I implemented philosophers and forks as bitmap buttons, and, what you can't see yet, the philosophers have hands to grab the forks," said Steve.

"That looks great, but what happens when you run it?" asked Hanna.

Steve clicked on the **Start** button, and suddenly the philosophers' faces changed while they were sleeping, waiting, or eating. A hand appeared when a philosopher was waiting for a fork, and then the hand held the fork for eating. Hanna and Curt watched the unfolding story in admiration [see Figure 134].

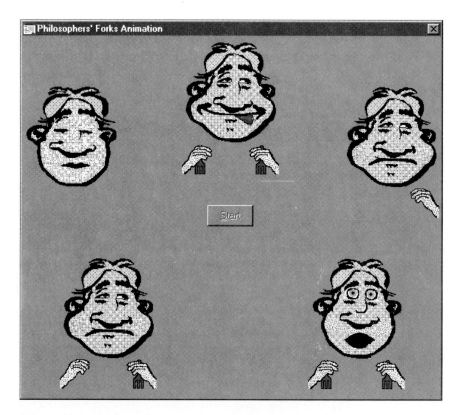

Figure 134. *Philosophers' Forks GUI: Animation Run*

"The philosophers look boring while sleeping," Steve explained.

"They turn into angry faces while waiting for a fork," said Hanna.

"And they lick their mouths while eating," remarked Curt. "The food must be very spicy!"

"The forks kind of move around," added Steve. "They are between the philosophers when not in use and appear in the hands when the philosophers are eating."

As the philosophers completed their specified number of sleeping and eating cycles, they disappeared from the screen one by one. When all had finished, the window disappeared.

"Marvelous," exclaimed Hanna, "that looks much better than my DOS window version."

"Can it run any faster?" asked Curt.

"No problem," replied Steve, "I'll set the sleep and eat times to 1 second each and set it going again. For now I have to make the change in the code but I might add a setup window later."

Steve did so. Now the philosophers faces changed much faster than before, and the three cycles completed in less than 15 seconds.

"Now let's really soup this up," said Steve. He set the times to 0 seconds and started again. Faces, hands, and forks flashed rapidly across the window, and in just about 5 seconds it was all over.

Steve then set the number of cycles to 30 and restarted the application. Nothing happened. Steve turned white; he was as angry as the five philosophers who were all waiting for a fork.

"What's happening?" asked Curt.

"It's a deadlock!" exclaimed Hanna. "Look, all the philosophers happened to grab their left forks at the same time, and now they're all waiting for their right forks. How do you get out of this mess, Steve?"

Steve closed the window while he searched for a solution. "I'll have to add an interrupt button to take away the forks from the philosophers and end the deadlock," he said.

"That should do the trick," said Hanna, "and it will also allow you to interrupt the program while it's running."

"That won't take long to do," said Steve.

The three members of the Hacurs team enjoyed a hot, spicy lunch at a little Mexican restaurant near their office. Shortly after returning to his desk, Steve called Hanna and Curt over and showed them the upgraded application.

"How do you interrupt the application?" asked Hanna.

Steve just smiled and clicked on the **Start** button. It disappeared, and an **Interrupt** button appeared in its place as the application started running.

"Sneaky!" said Hanna.

"When I click on the **Interrupt** button, the philosophers quit their cycle at the end of their loop, and that makes the application stop," Steve explained, demonstrating this function as he spoke.

"Let's see if you can break a deadlock," said Curt. "Can you force one?"

"Sure," Steve responded. "I'll change the logic so that all philosophers grab the left fork first, and we'll get a deadlock."

Steve followed this procedure and was able to create a deadlock, then break it by using the **Interrupt** button.

GUI Design of the Philosophers' Forks with OODialog

"Were you able to reuse the logic I developed for the DOS window?" asked Hanna.

"Oh yes, almost all of it," replied Steve. "I needed a class for the dialog with methods to change the bitmaps of the philosophers, hands, and forks. I decided to use a resource dialog [of class *ResDialog*] with all the bitmaps stored in a DLL for fast access. I basically kept your philosopher and fork classes, and just added an instance variable for the dialog window and the calls to the dialog methods to change the bitmaps.

Steve opened an editor window and showed the code to Hanna and Curt [see Figure 135].

```
::class phil

::method init
  expose num rfork lfork dlg
  use arg num, rfork, lfork, dlg
  ...
::method sleep
  expose num dlg
  use arg ds
  dlg~setphil(num, 'sleep')
  if ds > 0 then call sleepms(ds*100)
...

::class fork

::method init
  expose used num dlg
  use arg num, dlg
  used = 0

::method pickup
  expose used num dlg
  guard on when used = 0
  dlg~setfork(num, 'blank')
  used = 1
...
```

Figure 135. *Philosophers' Forks GUI: Model Logic*

Steve continued, "The *setphil* and *setfork* methods change the bitmap which is displayed on the bitmap button. They are implemented as methods of the dialog. In the main program, I store the IDs of all the dialog items and bitmaps in a stem and pass it to the new method of the dialog. This technique enables all the dialog methods to address the bitmap buttons symbolically." [See Figure 136.]

```
/*oodialog\samples\oophil.rex      Philosophers' Forks - Dialog */

v.oophildll = 'oophil.dll'

v.anidialog = 100        /* animation dialog graphical  */
v.bmpwait   = 1001       /* phil wait                   */
v.bmpeat    = 1002       /*      eat                    */
v.bmpsleep  = 1003       /*      sleep                  */
v.bmpfork   = 1004       /* fork                        */
...
v.idp       = 100        /* phil    101-105             */
v.idf       = 105        /* fork    106-110             */
v.idhr      = 111        /* hand-r  121,131,141,151,161 */
v.idhl      = 112        /* hand-l  122,132,142,152,162 */
...

dlg = .phildlg~new(v.)
dlg~~startit~~tothetop~show("SHOWTOP")
dlg~myexecute(parms.)
...

::class phildlg subclass ResDialog

::method init
  expose v.
  use arg v.
  self~init:super(v.oophildll, v.anidialog, empty.)
...

::method setphil unguarded
  expose v.
  use arg num, bmp
  self~ChangeBitmapButton(v.idp + num, value('v.bmp'bmp) )

::method setfork unguarded
  expose v.
  use arg num, bmp
  self~ChangeBitmapButton(v.idf + num, value('v.bmp'bmp) )
...
```

Figure 136. *Philosophers' Forks GUI: Dialog Class*

Your main program logic, where the instances of the philosophers and forks are created and started asynchronously, ended up in the *InitDialog* and *MyExecute* method of the dialog." [See Figure 137.]

```
::class phildlg subclass ResDialog

::method InitDialog
  expose f1 f2 f3 f4 f5 p1 p2 p3 p4 p5 v.
  self~InitDialog:super
  self~3Doff
  do i = 1 to 5
     ret = self~ConnectBitmapButton("", v.idp + i, v.bmpblank)
     ret = self~ConnectBitmapButton("", v.idf + i, v.bmpfork)
     ret = self~ConnectBitmapButton("", v.idhl + 10*i, 0)
     ret = self~ConnectBitmapButton("", v.idhr + 10*i, 0)
  end
```

Figure 137. *(Part 1 of 2) Philosophers' Forks GUI: Dialog Setup and Run*

```
f1 = .fork~new(1, self)                          /* create 5 forks   */
f2 = .fork~new(2, self)
f3 = .fork~new(3, self)
f4 = .fork~new(4, self)
f5 = .fork~new(5, self)
p1 = .phil~new(1,f5,f1, self)                    /* create 5 philos. */
p2 = .phil~new(2,f1,f2, self)
p3 = .phil~new(3,f2,f3, self)
p4 = .phil~new(4,f3,f4, self)
p5 = .phil~new(5,f4,f5, self)

::method MyExecute
expose f1 f2 f3 f4 f5 p1 p2 p3 p4 p5
use arg parms.
T.sleep = parms.101
T.eat = parms.102
T.veat = trunc(T.eat / 2)
T.vsleep = trunc(T.sleep / 2)
if parms.104 = 1 then T.side = 100               /* left fork first  */
else if parms.105 = 1 then T.side = 0            /* right            */
                  else T.side = 50               /* random           */
T.repeats = parms.103
m1 = p1~start("run",T.)                          /* run 5 philsophers*/
m2 = p2~start("run",T.)
m3 = p3~start("run",T.)
m4 = p4~start("run",T.)
m5 = p5~start("run",T.)
do while(m1~completed+m2~completed+m3~completed+m4~completed ,
        +m5~completed < 5) & (self~finished \= 1)
    self~HandleMessages
end
m1~result          /* finish dialog */
m1~result
m2~result
m3~result
m4~result
m5~result
self~stopit
```

Figure 137. *(Part 2 of 2) Philosophers' Forks GUI: Dialog Setup and Run*

"How did you implement the **Interrupt** button?" asked Curt.

"I am using a little trick, making the **Interrupt** button actually the **OK** button, which just frees all the forks in the associated *OK* method," Steve concluded [see Figure 138.]

```
::method OK
expose f1 f2 f3 f4 f5 p1 p2 p3 p4 p5 v.
self~ok:super
f1~laydown
f2~laydown
f3~laydown
f4~laydown
f5~laydown
```

Figure 138. *Philosophers' Forks GUI: Interrupt Logic*

"That's a smart design, Steve," said Hanna. She admired Steve's work, but then a new idea crept into her always busy mind. "Isn't it sad that the philosophers have nothing to eat?

Curt laughed. "I can see where you are going! You want Steve to enhance the application and make it even more appealing."

Hanna just smiled and said: "No, no, Curt. I was actually thinking that you could contribute some features too. I did the original application and Steve did the fancy GUI; now it's your turn to add the cake!"

"The cake?" Curt asked.

"You got it!" Hanna answered. "Put a nice big cake in the middle, and every time a philosopher eats, take away one piece. Maybe you could even change the philosopher's face while he is eating."

"And while you are at it, add some audio sounds," Steve added. "Let your imagination run wild and present us with the best multimedia application. A demonstration tomorrow morning would be just fine with me."

Curt's face turned red. "Are you challenging me?" he asked. "I know that I can do this; a piece of cake actually. Tomorrow, you better bring a real cake to the office, because I will present you the ultimate multimedia philosophers' forks application."

"Stop fighting, boys," Hanna interjected.

"OK," Steve said. "I'm sorry. It wasn't meant like that. I will bring a cake tomorrow to celebrate another glorious Hacurs demonstration application."

The next morning, Steve came in early. He had brought a white table cloth and covered one of the desks with it. He put the triple chocolate cake from the neighborhood bakery in the middle, and went to prepare a special Brazilian coffee for his partners. He even put an orange rose for Hanna into a small vase.

Hanna gleamed when she saw the setup half an hour later. "Wow!" was all she managed to say. She was a bit embarrassed and was happy that Curt showed up right at this moment.

Curt fired up his ThinkPad to demonstrate the wonderful application [see Figure 139]. A great looking lemon-chocolate cake appeared in the middle of the philosophers' table and the they changed faces while eating the cake. When the cake was gone, one philosopher even asked for a new cake.

The Hacurs trio celebrated the day with Steve's cake and sipped the imported coffee. Life was good after all!

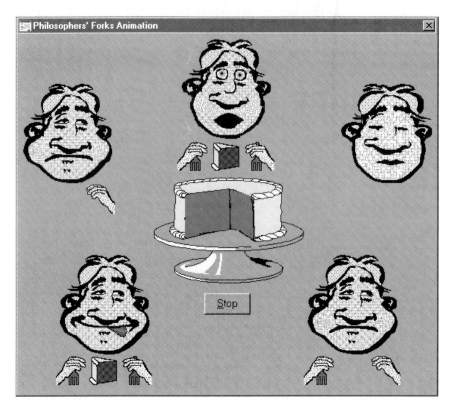

Figure 139. *Philosophers' Forks GUI: The Cake and the Icing*

Implementation Notes

The philosophers' forks application is part of the sample applications shipped with OODialog. It consists of a REXX program, oophil.rex, two resource files—oophil.rc and oophil2.rc—containing the dialog definitions, and many bitmaps. The bitmaps are loaded into memory for fast execution. The files are stored in the Object REXX subdirectory OODIALOG\Samples and its subdirectories RC and BMP.

The final application consists of a data entry dialog and the animation dialog [see Figure 139]. The data entry dialog contains the parameters of the application, such as the sleeping and eating times, the sequence in which the forks are picked up (left, right, or random), and the number of repetitions.

Part 4

Installing Object REXX, DB2, and the Sample Applications

14

Installing Object REXX, DB2, and the Sample Applications

In this chapter, we discuss the installation of Object REXX and DB2 for Windows NT and Windows 95, and how to install and run the sample applications of this redbook.

Object REXX for Windows NT and Windows 95 contains the REXX interpreter, OODialog to build and run GUI applications, and the IBM Resource Workshop to layout dialog windows and build resource files.

Content of the CD

The CD distributed with this redbook contains the products listed below for installation on your machine:

❑ Object REXX for Windows NT and Windows 95

❑ OODialog and IBM Resource Workshop

❑ The car dealer application

❑ DB2 Version 2.1.2 for Windows NT and Windows 95

The CD also contains ready-to-run versions of Object REXX, OODialog, IBM Resource Workshop, and the car dealer application

Installation and Run from the CD

The CD contains two programs to run the sample applications directly from the CD:

CDStart.bat Batch file to start the Installation and Run dialog. CDStart.bat sets the *PATH* to run Object REXX from the CD and invokes CDStart.rex.

CDStart.rex Dialog to install products and run samples from the CD (see Figure 140).

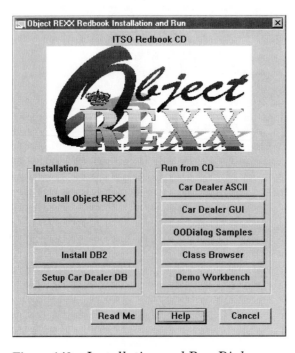

Figure 140. *Installation and Run Dialog*

You can install the products from the dialog, and you can execute the sample applications before installing Object REXX on your hard drive. Note, however, that running from the CD is slower than running from the hard drive.

Installation of Object REXX

Although you may execute the sample applications directly from the CD, we suggest that you install Object REXX on your machine. Run the *SETUP* program in the INSTALL directory of the CD and follow the instructions of the installation program.

Select the *typical* or *custom* install check box and be sure to mark the OODialog GUI builder and the redbook car dealer application for installation.

OODialog and IBM Resource Workshop

The OODialog GUI builder is installed in the OODIALOG subdirectory of Object REXX. OODialog class definitions are stored in the OODIALOG\SCRIPTS subdirectory. The tokenized version, OODIALOG.CLS, is stored in the OODIALOG subdirectory.

The Resource Workshop is installed in the main Object REXX directory and has its own icon in the Object REXX program group.

Running the Car Dealer Application from the CD

The CD directory CARDEAL contains an executable version of the car dealer application that can be run after Object REXX has been installed.

Use the *CAR-RUN* command in the CARDEAL directory to start any of the car dealer programs:

```
rexx car-run a          (ASCII window version)
rexx car-run g          (OODialog GUI version)
```

Play with the sample applications as described in *Running the Car Dealer Application* on page 298.

Note: You can run the car dealer application from the CD only with FAT persistence. We strongly recommend installing the sample applications on your machine and experiment with the DB2 version of the car dealer application.

Installation of DB2 Version 2

The CD contains a 60-day "try-and-buy" copy of DB2 Version 2.1.2. This version can be installed on a Windows 95 machine as a single-user DB2 system, and on a Windows NT machine as a single-user or server DB2 system.

Start the installation program by running *SETUP* in the INSTDB2\DISK1 subdirectory. Two groups are created by the installation program; *DB2 for Windows 95* (or *DB2 for Windows NT*) and *DB2 Information* (documentation).

DB2 Installation on Windows 95

Select the single-user version for installation. This version also enables you to connect to a DB2 system on a Windows NT or OS/2 server.

For the sample applications, you do not need Distributed Database Connection Services (DDCS) or the DB2 Software Developer's Kit (SDK). Select the *try-and-buy* check box for a 60-day evaluation license. Select custom installation to limit the amount of code being installed. Select the administrator's toolkit and the documentation; the other components are optional. In the details of the administrator's toolkit you may remove visual explain and the performance monitor.

Reboot the system after installation. Start DB2 using the *DB2START* program in SQLLIB\BIN.

DB2 Installation on Windows NT

Select the single-user version for a stand-alone NT workstation. For a Windows NT server with Windows 95 clients, select the server version.

Select the same components as described above in *DB2 Installation on Windows 95*.

DB2 is started as a service on Windows NT. You will find two DB2 services in the **Services** windows (from Control Panel); DB2 - DB2, and DB2 Security Server. You can start both services manually, or add them to the Startup list.

Installing the Car Dealer Application

The car dealer application is included with Object REXX. Select the application when installing Object REXX.

Prerequisites for the Car Dealer Application

The car dealer application requires the following:

- ☐ Object REXX must be installed.
- ☐ OODialog of Object REXX must be installed to run or modify the car dealer GUI application.
- ☐ Windows multimedia support must be installed for audio and video play; without it, only the color pictures of the cars can be seen.
- ☐ DB2 Version 2.1.2 (or 2.1.1) must be installed to run the application with the database using BLOBs for multimedia data.

Object REXX Redbook Program Group

During installation a program group is created for the sample applications of the redbook. It contains icons to set up the DB2 database, configure the car dealer application to run with files or DB2, and to run the ASCII and GUI versions of the application.

Additional icons start the philosophers' forks in a window or as a GUI, the samples delivered with OODialog, and the class browser.

Figure 141 shows the *Object REXX Redbook* group after installation.

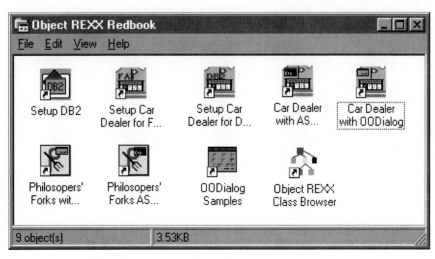

Figure 141. *Object REXX Redbook Group*

Table 18 shows icons that are available in the program group.

Table 18. Icons of the Object REXX Redbook Group

Icon	Description
Setup DB2	Car Dealer DB2 Setup program to define the DB2 database and tables, and to load the sample data (db2setup.rex).
Setup Car Dealer for FAT	Set up Car Dealer to run with FAT persistence (car-run.rex f).
Setup Car Dealer for DB2 database	Set up Car Dealer to run with DB2 (car-run.rex d).
Car Dealer with ASCII interface	Car Dealer Run ASCII Window Program (`car-run.rex a`). Start the ASCII version in an DOS window (car-aui.rex).
Car Dealer with OODialog	Run Car Dealer OODialog program (car-run.rex g). Start the GUI version using OODialog (car-ood.rex).
Philosopers' Forks with OODialog	Run Philosophers' Forks using OODialog (oophil.rex).
Philosopers Forks ASCII interface	Run Philosophers' Forks in a DOS window (philfork.rex).
OODialog Samples	Start the sample programs delivered with OODialog (sample.rex).
Object REXX Class Browser	Start the experimental Object REXX GUI Browser (browser.rex).

DB2 Setup for Car Dealer Application

This optional step prepares the DB2 system for the car dealer application. The car dealer application can run purely with file persistent storage, but running with a real database is much more exciting.

Double-click on the **DB2 Setup** icon in the Object REXX Redbook group or run the DB2SETUP command in a *DB2 Command* window in the CARDEAL\INSTALL directory:

```
cd cardeal\install
rexx db2setup
```

Note: DB2 commands must run in a DB2 command window, which can be started from the DB2 program group or by typing DB2CMD in a DOS window. DB2SETUP invokes DB2DDL in a DB2 command window:

```
db2cmd rexx d:\cardeal\install\db2ddl
```

The DB2DDL command defines the DB2 database, the tables and indexes, and loads the sample data.

Make sure that the TMP environment variable is set up; it is used in the application to extract multimedia data from DB2 BLOBs:

```
SET TMP=C:\temp              (Windows NT example)
SET TMP=C:\Windows\temp      (Windows 95 example)
```

Define the DB2 Database

The DB2 database has the name *DEALERDB*. The setup program asks for the disk drive of the new database. Be patient while DB2 performs this lengthy step. The command to create the database manually is:

```
DB2 CREATE DATABASE DEALERDB ON C
```

Define the DB2 Tables

The data is stored in seven tables, one for each of the five classes and two for the m:m relationships between the classes.

The vehicle table contains the BLOB column for multimedia data, and two table spaces are defined to separate the basic vehicle data from the BLOB data.

The DDL statements are shown in the window while they are executed (see Figure 142).

```
-- Create car dealer tables (install\createtb.ddl)

CREATE TABLE CARDEAL.CUSTOMER
    (CUSTNUM            SMALLINT  NOT NULL,
     CUSTNAME           CHAR(20)  NOT NULL,
     CUSTADDR           CHAR(20)  NOT NULL)

CREATE TABLE CARDEAL.PART
    (PARTNUM            SMALLINT  NOT NULL,
     ...
           )
...

CREATE REGULAR TABLESPACE VEHICLESPACE
    MANAGED BY DATABASE
    USING ( FILE 'vehiclea' 300)

CREATE LONG TABLESPACE VEHICLESLOB
    MANAGED BY DATABASE
    USING ( FILE 'vehicleb' 4000)

CREATE TABLE CARDEAL.VEHICLE
    (SERIALNUM          INTEGER   NOT NULL,
     CUSTNUM            SMALLINT  NOT NULL,
     MAKE               CHAR(12)  NOT NULL,
     MODEL              CHAR(10)  NOT NULL,
     YEAR               SMALLINT  NOT NULL,
     PICTURES           BLOB(4M)  NOT LOGGED )
   IN VEHICLESPACE  LONG IN VEHICLESLOB

CREATE UNIQUE INDEX CUSTOMER_IX
    ON CARDEAL.CUSTOMER (CUSTNUM)
...
```

Figure 142. *DB2 Table and Index Definition*

This step can be rerun at any time to redefine the tables and indexes—for example, when the space for the multimedia data must be increased.

The car dealer database can be removed completely by issuing the command:

```
DB2 DROP DATABASE DEALERDB
```

Load the DB2 Tables

The tables are loaded using two load programs. The first program, LOAD-DB2, reads the sample data provided in the SampData subdirectory and loads the basic information about customers, vehicles, parts, services, and work orders. The second program, LOAD-MM, reads the multimedia data provided in the MEDIA subdirectory and loads the BLOB column in the vehicle table. A progress window is shown while loading the tables (see Figure 143).

```
Loading customers...
Execute: 0 : INSERT INTO CARDEAL.CUSTOMER values (101, 'Senator, Dale', 'Washington')
Execute: 0 : INSERT INTO CARDEAL.CUSTOMER values (102, 'Akropolis, Ida', 'Athens')
...
Loading vehicles...
Execute: 0 : INSERT INTO CARDEAL.VEHICLE (SERIALNUM, CUSTNUM, MAKE, MODEL, YEAR)
                      values (123456, 101, 'Ford', 'T', 1931)
Execute: 0 : INSERT INTO CARDEAL.VEHICLE (SERIALNUM, CUSTNUM, MAKE, MODEL, YEAR)
                      values (297465, 102, 'Volkswagen', 'Camper', 1971)
...
Loading parts...
Execute: 0 : INSERT INTO CARDEAL.PART values (1, 120, 3, 'Muffler')
...
Loading services...
Execute: 0 : INSERT INTO CARDEAL.SERVICE values(1, 110, 'Brake job')
...
Execute: 0 : INSERT INTO CARDEAL.SERVPART values(1, 21, 1)
...
Loading workorders...
Execute: 0 : INSERT INTO CARDEAL.WORKORDER values (1, 101, 123456, -1, '09/06/95', 0)
...
Execute: 0 : INSERT INTO CARDEAL.WORKSERV values(1, 1)
...


Now run Multimedia load next (load-mm.rex)

Updating serial 999001
- Fact-sheet            length   112 in ..\media\ford.fac
- Side picture          length  64050 in ..\media\fordsid.bmp
- Front picture         length  90190 in ..\media\fordfrt.bmp
- Back picture          length  79462 in ..\media\fordbck.bmp
- Angle picture         length  94678 in ..\media\fordang.bmp
- Audio                 length 180268 in ..\media\ford.wav
Ctlinfo=BIN' 6:Fact-sheet         ,     112;Side picture      ,   64050;
              Front picture        ,   90190;Back picture      ,   79462;
              Angle picture        ,   94678;Audio             ,  180268;@@'
BLOB length=508946
SQL=update cardeal.vehicle   set pictures = CAST(? AS BLOB(1K)) || CAST(? AS BLOB(4M)) ||
        CAST(? AS BLOB(4M)) || CAST(? AS BLOB(4M)) || CAST(? AS BLOB(4M)) ||
        CAST(? AS BLOB(4M)) || CAST(? AS BLOB(4M)) where serialnum = 999001
VAR=:ctlinfo, :vpic1, :vpic2, :vpic3, :vpic4, :vpic5, :vpic6
prepare=0 SQLMSG
execute=0 SQLMSG
...
```

Figure 143. *DB2 Table Load*

This step can be rerun at any time to reinitialize the tables with the original data.

DB2 Setup for Remote Database Access

If you have a Windows NT server and Windows 95 clients you can set up the DB2 database on the Windows NT machine, and access the database from the car dealer application running on the Windows 95 clients. DB2 must be installed on all machines.

Server Setup for Remote Database Access

Remote database access supports multiple protocols, such as TCP/IP and NETBIOS. These protocols must be installed on server and client machines before setting up DB2 remote access. The server setup for DB2 involves several steps:

❑ First you set up system environment variables for communication using the **System** icon in the *Control Panel*:

```
SET DB2COMM=TCPIP,NETBIOS      (==> DB2 communications protocols)
SET TZ=PST8PDT                 (==> time zone for TCP/IP)
```

❑ For TCP/IP you set up two ports in the *services* file (winnt\system32\drivers\etc\services) by inserting new lines:

```
#    DB2 connection
db2fundy       3702/tcp      # choose a name and unused number
db2fundy1      3703/tcp      # any name and next higher number
```

Update the database manager configuration by issuing (in a DB2 command window):

```
DB2 UPDATE DBM CFG USING SVCENAME db2fundy
```

The name *db2fundy* must match the first name given in the TCP/IP *services* file.

❑ For NETBIOS you must update the database manager configuration by issuing:

```
DB2 UPDATE DBM CFG USING NNAME myntname
```

The name *myntname* is a unique workstation name within the NETBIOS network; it is stored in upper-case.

If you have more than one network adapter card, check that the environment variable *DB2NBADAPTERS* points to the LAN number of the proper network adapter card:

```
SET DB2NBADAPTERS=0
```

Open the *Network* dialog in the *Control Panel*. Find the *NETBIOS* interface under *Services* and open its properties. Assign the *Lana* number 0 to the network route starting with *Nbf->*; assign higher numbers to *NetBT->*, and so forth.

❑ Check the configuration for *svcename* and *nname* before rebooting the server:

```
DB2 GET DBM CFG
```

Client Setup for Remote Database Access

The client setup for DB2 involves several steps as well:

❑ For TCP/IP you set up a port in the *services* file (windows\services):

```
#    DB2 connection
db2fundy       3702/tcp        # same name and number as server
```

❑ For NETBIOS you must update the database manager configuration by issuing:

```
DB2 UPDATE DBM CFG USING NNAME my95name
```

The name *my95name* is a unique workstation name within the NETBIOS network; it is stored in upper-case. The value can also be viewed or changed using the **DB2 Client Setup** icon in the DB2 program group (select *Client* menu, *Configure...*, *Communications* tab).

Cataloging the Remote Database

A remote database must be cataloged in the DB2 system of the client machine. This task involves cataloging the server node and the database:

❑ For TCP/IP you issue the commands:

```
DB2 CATALOG TCPIP NODE mynttcp REMOTE nthost SERVER db2fundy
DB2 CATALOG DATABASE DEALERDB AS dealerft AT NODE mynttcp
```

The name *mynttcp* is any unique node name on the client machine, *nthost* is the TCP/IP host name of the server, *db2fundy* is the service name defined in the services file, and *dealerft* is the unique local alias name defined for the DEALERDB database on the server.

❑ For NETBIOS you issue the commands:

```
DB2 CATALOG NETBIOS NODE myntnb REMOTE myntname ADAPTER 0
DB2 CATALOG DATABASE DEALERDB AS dealerfn AT NODE myntnb
```

The name *myntnb* is any unique node name on the client machine, *myntname* is the NETBIOS workstation name of the server, and *dealerfn* is the unique local alias name defined for the DEALERDB database on the server.

❑ Cataloging of the nodes and the remote databases can also be done using the **DB2 Client Setup** icon in the DB2 program group:

• Define the node using the *New...* selection in the *Node* pull-down.

• Define the database by opening the node and using the *New...* selection in the *Database* pull-down.

Authorizing Remote Users on the Server

Remote users have to connect to a database with a *userid* and *password*. Define users on the server with the *User Manager* in the *Administrative Tools* group. Grant users access to the car dealer database by issuing the DB2 commands:

```
DB2                                        (==> cmd-line processor)
CONNECT TO DEALERDB
GRANT DBADM ON DATABASE TO userid1         (==> full authorization)
GRANT SELECT ON cardeal.customer TO userid2  (==> partial)
```

Testing the Remote Database

To test the remote access after setting up communications and cataloging the database, open a DB2 command window, then type:

```
DB2                                        (==> command line processor)
CONNECT TO dealerft USER userid USING password
SELECT * FROM cardeal.customer
QUIT
```

Note: You connect to the alias name *dealerft* defined for the remote database. Use a valid *userid* and *password* defined on the NT server. The *userid* must be authorized to access the database.

Rebinding REXX Programs to a Database

If you reinstall DB2 and recatalog the car dealer database, REXX programs may terminate with an SQL code of -805. You have to rebind REXX to the database in a DB2 command window:

```
db2                            (==> command line processor)
connect to dealerdb            (==> connect to car dealer database)
bind \sqllib\bnd\@db2ubind.lst grant public    (==> bind programs)
connect reset
```

The BIND.REX program provided in the CARDEAL\INSTALL subdirectory executes these commands.

Running the Car Dealer Application

The car dealer application runs with either file persistence or DB2 persistence, and can be started as an ASCII window or OODialog GUI application. Icons to run the application are provided in the Object REXX Redbook group (see Figure 141 on page 291).

A command file, car-run.rex, is provided in the main CARDEAL directory to set up the persistent storage option and to start the application:

```
rexx car-run f                    (set up file persistence)
rexx car-run d                    (set up DB2 persistence)

rexx car-run a                    (run ASCII window version)
rexx car-run g                    (run OODialog GUI version)

rexx car-run d g                  (set up and run)
```

Refer to *Appearance of ASCII User Interface* on page 105 for more information on the ASCII application, and to *The Car Dealer GUI* on page 162 for more information on the OODialog application.

Running the Car Dealer with a Remote Database

The application uses a small control file, `database.def`, to connect to a local or remote car dealer database. The first record in the file specifies the database or database alias name, and the userid and password used to connect to the remote database:

```
DEALERDB                        <=== local database
DEALERFT userid password        <=== remote database
DEALERFN userid password
```

Running the Car Dealer Application on the World Wide Web

To run the car dealer application on the Web:

❑ Install the IBM Internet Connection Server (Version 4.1).

❑ Tailor the configuration file (`httpd.cnf`) as described in *Customizing the File Organization on the Web Server* on page 251. The configuration must point to the `CARDEAL\WWW` subdirectory for HTML files and CGI programs.

❑ Start the Internet Connection Server and make sure that DB2 is started if the car dealer configuration file is set up for DB2.

❑ Use a Web browser, for example Netscape Navigator or Microsoft Internet Explorer, and point to the server:

```
http://hostname/cardeal/hacurs.htm
```

❑ Use the hot links to invoke different pieces of the application.

Installed Sample Applications

The distributed code of the car dealer application is installed in the CARDEAL directory, or in the directory selected during installation of Object REXX.

Note: The REXX programs in most car dealer directories have been tokenized. The REXX source code of each directory is stored in a subdirectory named *SRC*. Run the *TOKEN* program to tokenize the car dealer source after modifications:

```
rexx token cardeal
```

OODialog sample programs are installed in the OODIALOG\Samples subdirectory of Object REXX. (See *OODialog Samples* on page 305.)

Car Dealer Directory

Within the *CARDEAL* directory the code is structured into many subdirectories, as shown in Tables 19–31.

Table 19. Files of the Master CARDEAL Directory.

Filename	Description
car-run.rex	Program to run car dealer with FAT, DB2, or RAM
carood.bat	Starts the car dealer OODialog GUI application
rxfctsql.rex	Program to load REXX-DB2 functions
carerror.rex	Program to check for proper directory
carmodel.cfg	Active configuration (copy of FAT, DB2, or RAM)
database.def	Contains the name of the car dealer database and the userid and password for remote database connection
rxdb2con.rex	Program to connect to a local or remote car dealer database
token.rex	Program to tokenize all car dealer source programs
token1.rex	Program to tokenize files of a given file mask
*.ico	Icon files for redbook program group
SRC	Subdirectory with REXX source programs

Table 20. Files of the Sampdata Subdirectory.
Master files with sample data. Used as initial state for FAT persistent storage and to load the sample data into DB2 tables.

Filename	Description
customer.dat	Master file with sample customer data
vehicle.dat	Master file with sample vehicle data
workord.dat	Master file with sample work order data
service.dat	Master file with sample service item data
part.dat	Master file with sample part data

Table 21. Files of the Base Subdirectory.
Base class definitions for objects in storage.

Filename	Description
carcust.cls	Base class definition for customers
carvehi.cls	Base class definition for vehicles
carwork.cls	Base class definition for work orders
carserv.cls	Base class definition for service items
carpart.cls	Base class definition for parts
cardeal.cls	Car dealer class for initialization and termination
persist.cls	Class for definition of persistent methods

Table 22. Files of the FAT Subdirectory.
Class definitions for persistent objects in files.

Filename	Description
carcust.cls	FAT class definition for customers
carvehi.cls	FAT class definition for vehicles
carwork.cls	FAT class definition for work orders
carserv.cls	FAT class definition for service items
carpart.cls	FAT class definition for parts
carmodel.cfg	Configuration file for persistence in files
carlist.cfg	Configuration file for carlist.rtn (file persistence)
carlist.rtn	Additional routines for list on standard output
Data	Subdirectory with persistent file storage. Initially, this is a copy of the SampData subdirectory (see Table 20). Running the car dealer application updates the files in this directory. The original state can be restored by copying the files from the SampData directory.

Table 23. Files of the DB2 Subdirectory.
Class definitions for persistent objects in DB2. Initially, DB2 is loaded with data from the SampData subdirectory.

Filename	Description
carcust.cls	DB2 class definition for customers
carvehi.cls	DB2 class definition for vehicles
carwork.cls	DB2 class definition for work orders
carserv.cls	DB2 class definition for service items
carpart.cls	DB2 class definition for parts
carmodel.cfg	Configuration file for persistence in DB2
carlist.cfg	Configuration file for carlist.rtn (DB2 persistence)
carlist.rtn	Additional routines for list on standard output (DB2)

Table 24. Files of the RAM Subdirectory.
Class definitions for objects in RAM. Sample data is loaded into memory using REXX statements.

Filename	Description
carcust.cls	RAM class definition for customers
carvehi.cls	RAM class definition for vehicles
carwork.cls	RAM class definition for work orders
carserv.cls	RAM class definition for service items
carpart.cls	RAM class definition for parts
carmodel.cfg	Configuration file for persistence in RAM
carlist.cfg	Configuration file for `carlist.rtn` (RAM, same as FAT)

Table 25. Files of the AUI Subdirectory.
Class definitions for ASCII interface and menus, and basic list routines for displaying the class contents on standard output.

Filename	Description
caraui.cls	AUI class with methods for window interactions
carmenu.cls	Menu class for menu display and run
menu.dat	Menu definition file
carlist.cfg	Configuration file for list on standard output; copy of same-named file from either FAT or DB2
carlist.rtn	Basic list routines
car-aui.rex	Program to run car dealer in ASCII window

Table 26. Files of the Media Subdirectory.
Media files (pictures, audio, video).

Filename	Description
media.dat	List of all multimedia files by vehicle
*.fac	Fact sheets
*.bmp	Pictures
*.wav	Audio files
*.avi	Video files

Table 27. (Part 1 of 2) Files of the OOD Subdirectory.
GUI definitions and programs for OODialog.

Filename	Description
car-ood.rex	Car dealer GUI program using OODialog
ood.mrg	Merged dialog source files (:::requires file for GUI program)
build.rex	Program to merge all dialog source files (.dlg)

Table 27. (Part 2 of 2) Files of the OOD Subdirectory.
GUI definitions and programs for OODialog.

Filename	Description
SRC*.dlg	Subprograms, one per dialog window
BMP	Subdirectory with bitmaps
RC	Subdirectory with resource definitions

Table 28. Files of the StorProc Subdirectory.
Sample commands to use stored procedures in a client/server
environment for DB2 security purposes.

Filename	Description
server.rex	Command file to start server for stored procedures
gateway.cmd	Command file for gateway between client and stored procedures
client.rex	Command file for client (user of stored procedure)
read.me	A description and instructions

Table 29. Files of the WWW Subdirectory.
Car Dealer on the World Wide Web (Internet)

Filename	Description
Hacurs.htm	Hacurs home page
cardeal.htm	Car dealer main page
*.htm	Other car dealer pages
html.frm	HTML class definition
cgi.bat	Common Gateway Interface batch file to invoke cgirexx.cmd
cgirexx.cmd	Common Gateway Interface REXX program
partall*.cmd	Part list test programs 1 and 2
*.www	Individual CGI programs for car dealer application
hacurs.gif	Hacurs logo
car*.gif	Car pictures (Hanna, Curt, Steve)
*.gif	Small icon pictures for active links
http.cnf	Tailored Web server administration file (sample)

Table 30. (Part 1 of 2) Files of the Xamples Subdirectory.
Additional small examples of the redbook.

Filename	Description
rexxcx.cmd	Command file to invoke the REXXC utility
browser.rex	GUI class browser— start program
browser.lst	GUI class browser— list of included classes
browser.bld	GUI class browser—build program for merged class file

Table 30. (Part 2 of 2) Files of the Xamples Subdirectory.
Additional small examples of the redbook.

Filename	Description
browser.cls	GUI class browser— OODialog class definition
browscls.rex	Experimental Object REXX class browser in a DOS window
xmpreply.rex	Early reply example with guarded/unguarded methods

Table 31. Files of the Install Subdirectory.
DB2 setup and load programs and DDL for table definitions.

Filename	Description
db2setup.rex	Program to set up and load DB2 tables for car dealer application
db2ddl.rex	Define DB2 database, tables, and indexes
load-db2.rex	Load program for DB2 tables, uses SampData directory
load-mm.rex	Load program for multimedia data, uses media.dat (see Table 26)
runsql.rex	Program to run SQL DDL through DB2 command line processor
bind.rex	Rebind REXX programs to the car dealer database
createdb.ddl	DDL to create database DEALERDB
createtb.ddl	DDL to create tables for DB2 Version 2
createt1.ddl	DDL to create tables without multimedia data
createix.ddl	DDL to create indexes on tables
droptb.ddl	DDL to drop tables
dropt1.ddl	DDL to drop tables (if created without multimedia)

Source Code for Running the Car Dealer Application

The source code of the car dealer run program is listed in *Running the Car Dealer Application* on page 527.

Removing Object REXX and the Sample Applications

To remove Object REXX and the sample applications from your system:

❏ Select the *Deinstall* program in the Object REXX group or select Object REXX in the *Add/Remove* panel of the system settings.

❏ To remove the CARDEAL database from the DB2 system, start the DB2 Command Line Processor and enter:

```
DROP DATABASE CARDEAL
```

❏ To remove the car dealer application from your system, but keep Object REXX, delete the CARDEAL directory and the Object REXX Redbook group.

OODialog Samples

The easiest way to get acquainted with OODialog features is to run the OODialog samples provided in the \OODIALOG\SAMPLES directory. Simply type rexx sample to start the samples.

The SAMPLES directory contains a set of Object REXX programs that use bitmaps, sounds, and resources from the BMP, WAV, and RC subdirectories.

In an effort to avoid creating a dry and boring application, our application looks sort of funny, but it enables us to introduce you to such features as scrolling messages and animated buttons. So come along and play!

The main samples dialog provides eight push buttons, which demonstrate different ways to create a dialog [see Figure 144].

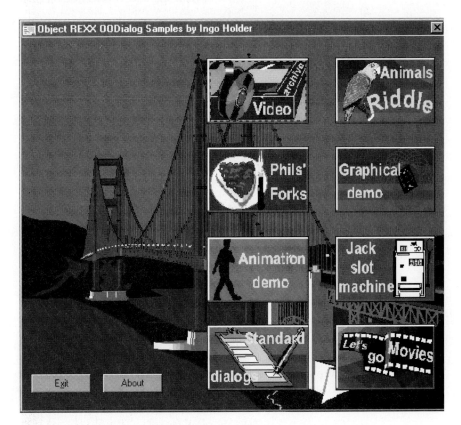

Figure 144. *OODialog Samples*

In SAMPLE.REX you can find how easy it is to load a dialog from a Resource Workshop file, place a bitmap over a push button, or play a sound.

Video Archive

The video archive dialog demonstrates the use of different types of entry fields and of loading values from a stem variable into a dialog [see Figure 145].

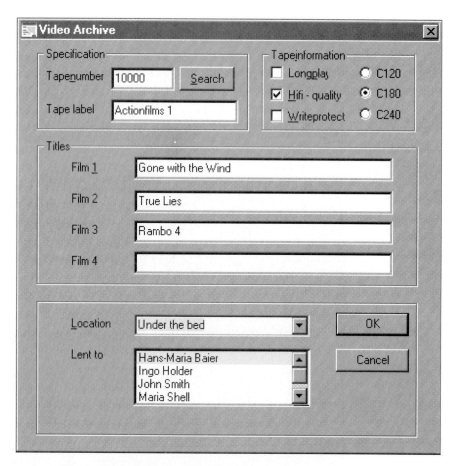

Figure 145. *Video Archive Sample*

You can change the values in the entry fields, select an entry in the *Location* combo box and in the *Lent to* list. In the *Tapeinformation* group you can select multiple check box entries, but only a single radio button. The **Search** button does nothing, except for displaying a message window.

If you click on the **OK** push button, all values you changed or selected are saved in the file called *test.log* and listed in the originating DOS window. If you click on **Cancel**, you are prompted with a *Yes/No* dialog box for confirmation.

The code for this dialog can be found in the oovideo.rex file.

Animals Riddle

The animals riddle dialog features eight push buttons with animal pictures. When you click on a button, an information message is displayed or you might hear the particular voice of the animal—that is, if you have a sound card installed on your machine. Your task is to replace all of the *unknown animal* entry fields with the correct animal names [see Figure 146].

Figure 146. *Animals Riddle Sample*

Use lower case letters to enter the names. When you are finished, click on the **OK** button. An error message will show your mistakes. The **Cancel** button can save you the embarrassment and let you go back to the main dialog.

If you have a hard time recognizing the animals, just push the **Help** button, and the correct names are displayed for you.

The code for this dialog can be found in the `oopet.rex` file. A second file, `oopet1.rex`, uses bitmaps from a DLL.

Philosophers' Forks

This dialog runs the philosophers' forks sample which is discussed in detail in *Philosophers' Forks* on page 273.

In the first dialog you can set up the parameters for sleeping and eating times and for the number of repetitions. You can enter the values directly or use the spin buttons. The radio buttons let you select which hand the philosophers will use first to pick up a fork.

The second dialog presents the animation of philosophers fighting for the forks and eating a cake. It demonstrates the strength of Object REXX in dealing with multiple threads.

The code for this dialog can be found in the oophil.rex file. Note that the bitmaps are all preloaded into memory for fast display.

Graphical Demonstration

The first dialog of the graphical demonstration presents different scrolling messages and buttons [see Figure 147].

Figure 147. *Graphical Demonstration Sample: Scrolling*

The code for this dialog can be found in the oograph.rex file.

By clicking on the **Bitmap-Viewer** button, you get the bitmap viewer dialog. Here the combo list has a number of bitmap files. Just select one and it is displayed [see Figure 148].

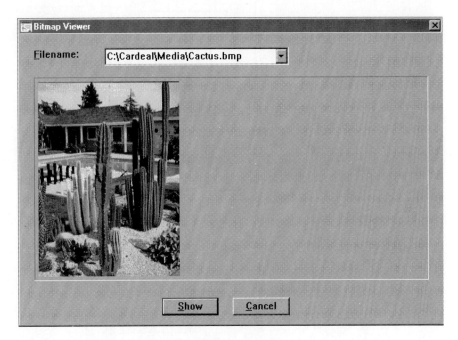

Figure 148. *Graphical Demonstration Sample: Bitmap Viewer*

You can also type in the full file name of any bitmap (.BMP) file in your system and display it by clicking on the **Show** button.

If you select "…" in the combo box instead of a file name, you get the system *Open a File* window, where you can search for bitmaps in the system directories and select one.

You can find the code for the bitmap viewer in the `oobmpvu.rex` file.

By clicking on the **Draw-Color-Demo** button in the main dialog (Figure 147) you start a demonstration of the color and drawing facilities of OODialog. A dialog is presented filled with concentric rectangles. At the bottom you can choose among seven push buttons to invoke different graphical animations (see Figure 149).

Figure 149. *Graphical Demonstration Sample: Color Drawing*

The graphical animations include the drawing of colored rectangles, squares of varying pens, individual colored pixels (not shown in Figure 149), lines arranged as a star, random lines of varying thickness, randomly colored squares on a black background, and circles, ellipses and pie shapes of varying sizes.

Each of the seven color drawing demonstrations is a long running time animation. Use the **Interrupt** button to stop each animation.

The code for the color drawing demonstration can be found in the oodraw.rex file.

Note: All three graphical dialogs (scrolling, bitmap viewer, and color drawing) are created dynamically.

Animation Demonstration

The animation demonstration dialog demonstrates the use of animated buttons. You can change the horizontal and vertical movements
of the walker dynamically without disrupting the walker's pace. He
can even go backward if you enter a negative number in the *MoveX*
entry field. Every time the walker hits the walls of his corridor, a
sound is played [see Figure 150].

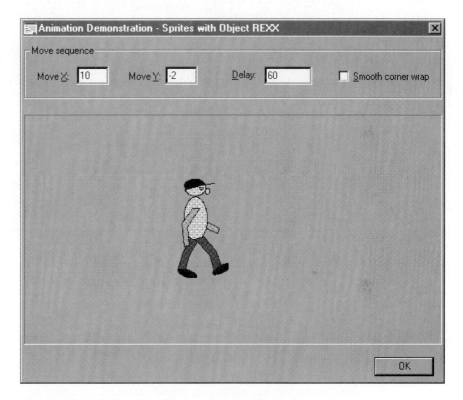

Figure 150. *Animation Demonstration Sample*

By clicking on the *Smooth corner wrap* check box, the walker will go
smoothly through the walls.

Be aware of the danger zone marked with flashing !!! signs. If the
walker goes through the danger zone with the upper body, the animation ends with a surprise. The danger zone is steady at first but starts
moving around over time.

The code for this dialog can be found in the oowalker.rex file. A second
version, oowalk2.rex, uses a binary resource for the bitmaps.

Note that the *WalkButton* class is a subclass of the *AnimatedButton*
class.

Jack Slot Machine

You can play the jack slot machine game in much the same way as you would use a real slot machine. Watch for three pictures of the same kind and click on the **Stop** button [see Figure 151].

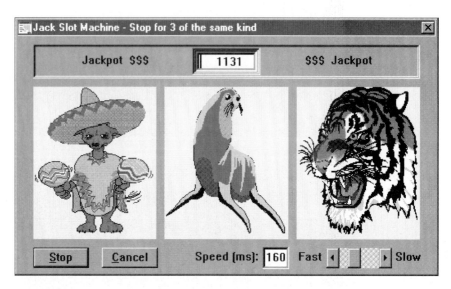

Figure 151. *Jack Slot Machine Sample*

If the slot machine displays three identical pictures after stopping, you have hit the jackpot! You can adjust the speed of the slot machine using the scroll bar; the faster it runs, the higher the jackpot. The jackpot is decreasing over time, and every time you stop and miss, the jackpot is reduced by 25% (two equal pictures) or 50% (three different pictures).

The code for this dialog can be found in the oobandit.rex file. The whole dialog, including the three bitmap buttons, is created dynamically using the *DefineDialog* method, which overwrites the default method of the *UserDialog* class.

Standard Dialogs

This demonstration runs through all the standard dialogs, starting with a *TimedMessage*, followed by *InputBox, ListChoice, MultiInputBox, CheckList, SingleSelection, IntegerBox, PasswordBox*, and *MultiListChoice* dialogs. All of the dialogs are typical for a real application.

The code for this dialog can be found in the `oostddlg.rex` file. This dialog introduces the most important classes provided for simple user input. All of these small dialogs are created dynamically. The data entered or selected is displayed in the originating DOS window. An alternative file, `oostdfct.rex`, uses the OODialog callable functions.

Let's Go to the Movies

Imagine that you want to go to movies but are not sure about which film to see or the particular cinema to attend. The only thing you know is *when* you want to go. The sample dialog is not fully implemented; it just gives you a flavor of the real one. It demonstrates the use of *categorized dialogs*.

On the first page, *Movies*, you can select one or more of the films currently playing [see Figure 152].

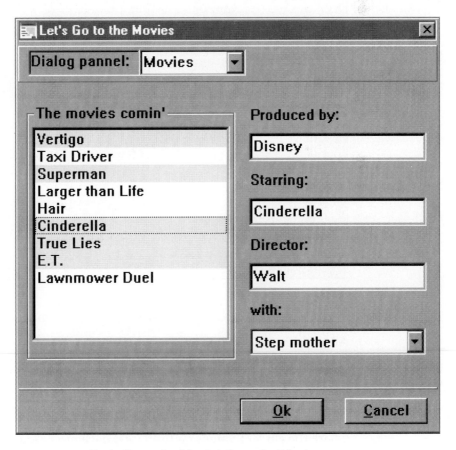

Figure 152. *Let's Go to the Movies Sample: Movies*
This page show the *drop-down* style using a combo box.

Then you go through the pages of the dialog using the selections at the top or the **OK** button. On the *Cinemas* page, check one or more cinemas in the region. On the *Days* page, click on the radio button for the day of your choice. Finally, on the *Ticket* page [see Figure 153], the application lists all films that match the day and cinemas you selected in the combo list.

Figure 153. *Let's Go to the Movies Sample: Ticket*
This page shows the *topline* style using radio buttons.

All you have to do is click on the **Get the Ticket** button. Nothing really happens in the current application, but imagine that you would be asked for your credit card number and then the ticket be printed.

The code for this dialog can be found in the ooticket.rex file. Note that you can switch many times between the different pages of the dialog. Every switch calls the *PageHasChange*d method, and that is where the current values on the *Ticket* page are produced.

Part 5

Reference Information

15

OODialog Method Reference

This chapter is designed to serve as a reference manual for OODialog. The use of the classes is described in Chapter 7, *Graphical User Interfaces with OODialog,* on page 121, which serves as a user's guide.

The sequence and flow of the main methods of a dialog is shown in Figure 55 on page 145.

Syntax diagrams are used extensively to describe the detailed parameters of the OODialog methods. The structure of the syntax diagrams is explained in Appendix C, "Definition for Syntax Diagram Structure," on page 529.

OODialog Samples

To learn more about GUI programming with OODialog, check out the sample programs delivered with OODialog. For brief descriptions of the sample programs, see *OODialog Samples* on page 305.

OODialog Classes

The classes provided by OODialog form a hierarchy as shown in Figure 154.

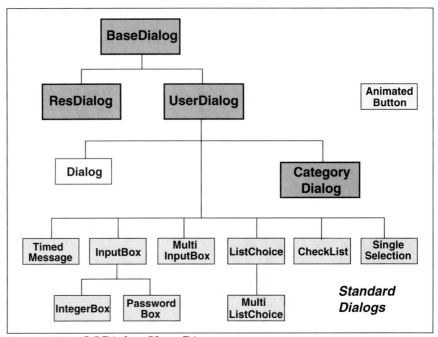

Figure 154. *OODialog Class Diagram*

BaseDialog	Base methods regardless of whether the dialog is implemented as a binary resource, a script, or dynamically.
UserDialog	Subclass of *BaseDialog* to create a dialog with all of its control elements, such as push buttons, check boxes, radio buttons, entry lines, and list boxes.
ResDialog	Subclass of *BaseDialog* for dialogs with a binary (compiled) resource file (.DLL).
CategoryDialog	Subclass of *UserDialog* to create a dialog with multiple pages that overlay each other on the same part of the window.
TimedMessage	Class to show a message window for a defined duration.
InputBox	Class to dynamically define a dialog with a message, one entry line, and two push buttons (**OK, Cancel**).

IntegerBox	Similar to *InputBox*, but only numeric data can be entered in the entry line.
PasswordBox	Similar to *InputBox*, but keystrokes in the entry line are shown as asterisks (*).
MultiInputBox	Similar to *InputBox*, but with multiple entry lines.
ListChoice	Class to dynamically define a dialog with a list box, where one line can be selected and returned to the caller.
MultiListChoice	Similar to *ListChoice*, but more than one line can be selected and returned to the caller.
CheckList	Class to dynamically define a dialog with a group of check boxes, which can be selected and returned to the caller.
SingleSelection	Class to dynamically define a dialog with a group of radio buttons, where one can be selected and returned.
Dialog	Subclass of *UserDialog* for your simple dialogs. You can change the default dialog style from *UserDialog* to *ResDialog*.
AnimatedButton	Class to implement an animated button within a dialog.

OODialog Standard Dialog Functions

The standard dialog classes can also be executed as callable functions. These functions are described with their respective classes in *Standard Dialog Classes and Functions* on page 436.

OODialog External Functions

OODialog provides a number of callable functions that can be used in your Object REXX programs.

InfoMessage Display an information message window:

```
call InfoMessage "some message text"
ret = InfoMessage("another text")
```

ErrorMessage Display an error message window:

```
call ErrorMessage "some error message text"
ret = ErrorMessage("another error message")
```

YesNoMessage Display a message and ask the user for a YES or NO answer:

```
ret = YesNoMessage("press Yes or No")
if ret = 1 then /* this is yes */
```

GetScreenSize Query the monitor size in dialog units and pixels:

```
val = GetScreenSize()
parse var val dlgunitx dlgunity pixelx pixely
```

PlaySoundFile Play a sound file (.WAV):

```
call PlaySoundFile "d:\wav\sound.wav"
ret = PlaySoundFile("d:\wav\sound.wav", "YES")
```

The optional second parameter *YES* plays the file asynchronously, that is the program continues execution. See also the routine *Play* on page 390.

PlaySoundFileInLoop Play a sound file (.WAV) continuously and asynchronously:

```
call PlaySoundFileInLoop "d:\wav\sound.wav"
```

StopSoundFile Stop play of an asynchronous sound file (.WAV):

```
call StopSoundFile
```

GetFileNameWindow Display an **Open File** window:

```
file = GetFileNameWindow(filename, handle, filter)
```

Parameters are optional; *filename* is a preselected name; *handle* is the parent window handle; and *filter* is a file mask specification, for example:

```
"Text files (*.txt)"||'0'x||"*.TXT"||'0'x|| ,
"All files (*.*)"||'0'x||"*.*"
```

SleepMS Sleep for a given time interval (milliseconds):

```
call SleepMS(3000)     /* 3 seconds */
```

WinTimer Start, stop, and wait for a windows timer:

```
tid = WinTimer("START",300)  /* 0,3 seconds */
call  WinTimer("WAIT,tid)    /* wait... */
ret = WinTimer("STOP",tid)   /* stop premature */
```

Registering OODialog Functions

OODialog functions are registered automatically when the first dialog is initialized. If no dialog has been created, register individual or all functions with:

```
call RxFuncAdd fct-name, "OODialog", fct-name       /* one function */

call RxFuncAdd "InstMMFuncs", "OODialog", "InstMMFuncs"
call InstMMFuncs                                    /* all functions */
```

Definition of Terms

id
Identification number of a dialog or a dialog item. An ID is assigned by the user when the dialog item is created using the Resource Workshop or dynamically. IDs 1, 2, and 9 are reserved for the **OK**, **Cancel**, and **Help** push buttons; IDs 10 to 9999 are available.

handle
A handle is a unique reference to a Windows object and is assigned by the system. It can be a reference to a dialog window, a particular dialog item, or a graphic object (pen, brush, font). Handles are required for certain methods; they can be retrieved from the system when needed.

device context
A device context stores information about the graphic objects (bitmaps, lines, pixels, etc.) that are displayed and the tools (pen, brush, font) that are used to display them. A device context can be acquired for a dialog window or a button; it must be explicitly freed when the text or graphic operations are completed.

pixel
Individual addressable point within a window. VGA screens support 640 by 480 pixels; SVGA screens support higher resolutions, such as 800 by 600, 1024 by 768, 1280 by 1024, and 1600 by 1200. Pixel values in a dialog window start at the top left corner and include the window title and border.

dialog unit
Dialog units are used within dialog box templates to define the size and position of the dialog box and its control items. There is a horizontal and a vertical dialog base unit to convert width and height of dialog boxes and controls from dialog units to pixels and vice versa. The value of these base unit depends on the screen resolution and the active system font; they are stored in attributes *FactorX* and *FactorY* of the *UserDialog* class.

```
xPixels = xDialogUnits * self~FactorX
```

color
Each color supported by the Windows operating system is assigned a number. The color indexes are 0 (black), 1 (dark red), 2 (dark green), 3 (dark yellow), 4 (dark blue), 5 (purple), 6 (blue grey), 7 (light grey), 8 (pale green), 9 (light blue), 10 (white), 11 (grey), 12 (dark grey), 13 (red), 14 (light green), 15 (yellow), 16 (blue), 17 (pink), and 18 (turquoise).

BaseDialog Class

The *BaseDialog* class implements base methods for all dialogs regardless of whether the dialog is implemented as a binary resource, a resource script, or created dynamically. Binary (compiled) resources are stored in a DLL. A dialog is created dynamically by using *Add...* methods. Dialogs that are implemented using a *resource script* (.RC) are semi-dynamically generated dialogs.

See the subclasses *UserDialog Class* on page 391 and *ResDialog Class* on page 419 for additional information.

Requires: Basedlg.cls is the source file of this class. Use the tokenized version of OODialog, oodialog.cls, to shorten the dialog startup time.

    ::requires 'oodialog.cls'

Attributes: Instances of the *BaseDialog* class have the following attributes:

AutoDetect	Automatic data field detection on (=1, default) or off (=0). For the *UserDialog* subclass the default is off and *Connect...* methods, *Add...* methods, or a resource script are usually used.
AutomaticMethods	A queue containing the methods that are started concurrently before the execution of the dialog.
BkgBitmap	A handle to a bitmap that is displayed in the dialog's background.
BkgBrushBmp	A handle to a bitmap that is used to draw the dialog's background.
DataConnection	Protected attribute to store connections between dialog items and the attributes of the dialog instance.
DlgHandle	A handle to the dialog.
Finished	0 if dialog is executing, 1 if terminated with OK, and 2 if canceled.
InitCode	Result of the *init* method; in case *init* failed, its value is 1.
IsExtended	Protected attribute that is true (=1) if graphics extension is installed.
UseStem	Protected attribute that is true (=1) if a stem variable was passed to *init*.

Routines: See *Public Routines* on page 390 for a description of the audio *Play* routine.

Methods: Instances of the *BaseDialog* class implement the methods listed in Table 32.

Table 32. (Part 1 of 5) BaseDialog Instance Methods

Method...	...on page
AddAttribute	341
AddAutoStartMethod	386
AddComboEntry	349
AddListEntry	353
AddUserMsg	339
AutoDetection	334
BackgroundBitmap	366
Cancel	389
Center	386
ChangeBitmapButton	364
ChangeComboEntry	352
ChangeListEntry	355
ClearButtonRect	363
ClearMessages	333
ClearRect	363
ClearWindowRect	363
CombineELwithSB	359
ComboAddDirectory	352
ComboDrop	353
ConnectAnimatedButton	387
ConnectBitmapButton	335
ConnectButton	334
ConnectCheckBox	338
ConnectComboBox	338
ConnectControl	336
ConnectEntryLine	337
ConnectList	337
ConnectListBox	338
ConnectMultiListBox	339
ConnectRadioButton	338

Table 32. (Part 2 of 5) BaseDialog Instance Methods

Method...	...on page
ConnectScrollBar	358
CreateBrush	376
CreateFont	373
CreatePen	376
DeInstall	390
DeleteComboEntry	350
DeleteFont	374
DeleteListEntry	354
DeleteObject	377
DisableItem	382
DisplaceBitmap	367
Draw	361
DrawAngleArc	382
DrawArc	379
DrawBitmap	365
DrawButton	361
DrawLine	378
DrawPie	381
DrawPixel	379
EnableItem	382
EndAsyncExecution	331
Execute	329
ExecuteAsync	330
FillDrawing	381
FindComboEntry	350
FindListEntry	354
FontColor	375
FontToDC	374
FreeButtonDC	369
FreeDC	368
FreeWindowDC	368
Get	360
GetArcDirection	380
GetAttrib	348

Table 32. (Part 3 of 5) BaseDialog Instance Methods

Method...	...on page
GetBitmapSizeX	365
GetBitmapSizeY	365
GetBmpDisplacement	367
GetButtonDC	368
GetButtonRect	361
GetCheckBox	346
GetComboItems	351
GetComboLine	346
GetCurrentComboIndex	351
GetCurrentListIndex	354
GetData	342
GetDataStem	349
GetDC	368
GetEntryLine	344
GetItem	360
GetListItems	354
GetListLine	344
GetMultiList	345
GetPixel	379
GetPos	360
GetRadioButton	346
GetSBPos	358
GetSBRange	357
GetSize	360
GetTextSize	375
GetValue	347
GetWindowDC	368
GetWindowRect	361
GraphicExtension	375
HandleMessages	332
Help	389
HideItem	383
HideItemFast	383
HideWindow	383

Table 32. (Part 4 of 5) BaseDialog Instance Methods

Method...	...on page
HideWindowFast	384
Init	328
InitAutoDetection	388
InitDialog	329
InsertComboEntry	350
InsertListEntry	353
IsDialogActive	331
ItemTitle	343
ListAddDirectory	356
ListDrop	356
LoadBitmap	364
MakeArray	346
Move	385
MoveItem	385
NoAutoDetection	334
ObjectToDC	377
OK	388
OpaqueText	370
Rectangle	378
RedrawButton	362
RedrawRect	362
RedrawWindowRect	362
RemoveBitmap	364
Resize	385
ResizeItem	384
Run	329
ScrollBitmapFromTo	366
ScrollButton	373
ScrollInButton	373
ScrollText	372
SendMessageToItem	333
SetArcDirection	380
SetAttrib	348
SetCheckBox	348

Table 32. (Part 5 of 5) BaseDialog Instance Methods

Method...	...on page
SetComboLine	346
SetCurrentComboIndex	351
SetCurrentListIndex	355
SetData	342
SetDataStem	348
SetEntryLine	344
SetListLine	345
SetListTabulators	356
SetMultiList	345
SetRadioButton	346
SetSBPos	358
SetSBRange	357
SetStaticText	343
SetTitle	343
SetValue	348
SetWindowTitle	343
Show	331
ShowItem	383
ShowItemFast	383
ShowWindow	384
ShowWindowFast	384
StartMessageHandling	332
StopIt	331
TiledBackgroundBitmap	366
Title	360
ToTheTop	332
TransparentText	369
Update	386
Validate	389
Write	371
WriteDirect	369
WriteToButton	371
WriteToWindow	370

Instance Methods of BaseDialog

The methods of the *BaseDialog* class are grouped by their usage in this section (an alphabetical list was in Table 32).

Preparing and Running the Dialog

This section presents the methods used to prepare (initialize) a dialog, show it, run it, and stop it.

Init

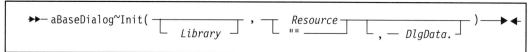

The constructor of the class installs the necessary C functions for the Object REXX API manager and prepares the dialog management for a new dialog.

Protected:	This method is protected. You cannot create an instance of *BaseDialog*. You can only create instances of its subclasses.
Arguments:	The arguments are:

	Library	This is the file name of a .DLL file. Pass an empty string if you are not using binary resources.
	Resource	The ID of the dialog within the resource file.
	DlgData.	A stem variable (do not forget the period) that contains initialization data for the dialog. For example, if you assign the string "Hello world" to *DlgData.103*, where 103 is the ID of an entry field, it is initialized with this string. If the dialog is terminated with OK, the data of the dialog is copied into this stem variable.

Example:	This example shows how the subclass *ResDialog* (see *ResDialog Class* on page 419) is implemented, overwriting the *init* method. If your subclass overwrites the *init* method, ensure that it calls the *init* method of its superclass:

```
::class ResDialog subclass BaseDialog
::method Init
   expose Library Resource DlgData.
   use arg Library, Resource, DlgData.
   return self~init:super(Library, Resource, DlgData.)
```

InitDialog

```
aBaseDialog~InitDialog
```

The *InitDialog* method is called after the Windows dialog has been created. It is useful for setting attributes of dialog items, and initializing combo and list boxes. Do not use *Set...* methods because the *Set-Data* method [page 342] is executed automatically afterwards and sets the values of all dialog items from the attributes.

Protected: The method is designed to be overwritten in subclasses; it cannot be called from outside the class.

Example: This sample shows how to use *InitDialog* to initialize dialog items; in this case a list box:

```
::class MyDialog subclass Userdialog
::method InitDialog
  self~InitDialog:super
  AddListEntry(501, "this is the first line")
  AddListEntry(501, "and this one the second")
```

Run

```
aBaseDialog~Run
```

The *Run* method dispatches messages from the Windows dialog until the user terminates the dialog by one of the following actions:

- ❏ Push the **OK** button (that is the push button with ID 1)
- ❏ Push the **Cancel** button (that is the push button with ID 2)
- ❏ Press the Enter key (if **OK** or **Cancel** is the default button)
- ❏ Press the Esc key (same as Cancel)

Protected: *Run* is a protected method. You cannot call this method directly; it is called by the *Execute* method [page 329].

Execute

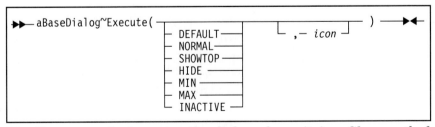

```
aBaseDialog~Execute( ┬─────────┬ ──┬──────────┬ )
                     ├ DEFAULT ┤   └ ,─ icon ─┘
                     ├ NORMAL ─┤
                     ├ SHOWTOP ┤
                     ├ HIDE ───┤
                     ├ MIN ────┤
                     ├ MAX ────┤
                     └ INACTIVE┘
```

The *Execute* method creates the dialog, shows it (see *Show* method [page 331]), starts automatic methods, and destroys the dialog. The data is passed to the Windows dialog before execution and received from it after the dialog is terminated.

Return code: The return code is 0 if the dialog was not executed, 1 if terminated using the **OK** button, and 2 if terminated using the **Cancel** button.

Arguments: The arguments are:

show See *Show* method [page 331].

icon The resource ID of the application's icon.

Example: Instantiate a new dialog object (remember that it is not possible to instantiate an object of the *BaseDialog* class), create a dialog template, and run the dialog as the topmost window:

```
MyDialog = .UserDialog~new(...)
MyDialog~Create(...)
MyDialog~Execute("SHOWTOP")
```

ExecuteAsync

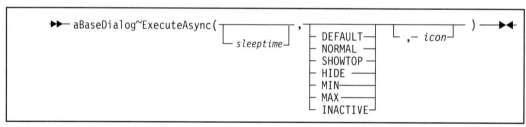

The *ExecuteAsync* method does the same as the *Execute* method [page 329], except that it dispatches messages asynchronously. Therefore, the *ExecuteAsync* method returns immediately after the dialog has been started.

Return code: The return code is 0 if the dialog started, 1 if error (do not call *EndAsyncExecution* in this case).

Arguments: The arguments are:

sleeptime This argument defines the time slice in milliseconds after which the next message is processed.

show See *Show* method [page 331].

icon The resource ID of the application's icon.

Example: This example starts a dialog and runs the statements between *ExecuteAsync* and *EndAsyncExecution* asynchronously to the dialog:

```
ret = MyDialog~ExecuteAsync(1000, "SHOWTOP")
if ret = 0 then do
    /* statements to run while dialog is executing */
    MyDialog~EndAsyncExecution
    end
else call ErrorMessage("Could not start dialog")
```

EndAsyncExecution

The *EndAsyncExecution* method is used to complete the asynchronous execution of a dialog. It does not terminate the dialog but waits until the user terminates it. Do not call *EndAsyncExecution* if *ExecuteAsync* failed.

Return code: The return code is 1 if terminated using the **OK** button, and 2 if terminated using the **Cancel** button.

Example: See example in the *ExecuteAsync* method [page 330].

IsDialogActive

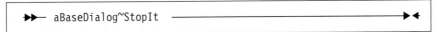

The *IsDialogActive* method returns 1 if the Windows dialog still exists.

Example: This example tests whether the dialog is active:

```
if MyDialog~IsDialogActive then ...
```

StopIt

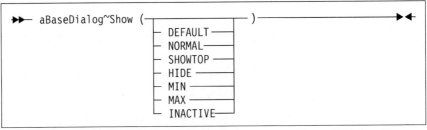

The *StopIt* method removes the Windows dialog from memory. It is called by the *Execute* method [page 329], after the user terminates the dialog.

Protected: This method is protected and for internal use only.

Show

```
►►─ aBaseDialog~Show (─┬──────────┬─) ─────────────►◄
                       ├─ DEFAULT ─┤
                       ├─ NORMAL ──┤
                       ├─ SHOWTOP ─┤
                       ├─ HIDE ────┤
                       ├─ MIN ─────┤
                       ├─ MAX ─────┤
                       └─ INACTIVE ┘
```

The *Show* method shows the dialog; it is usually called by *Execute* [page 329] or *ExecuteAsync* [page 330].

Argument: The argument must be one of:

DEFAULT	Default, same as NORMAL.
NORMAL	Displays dialog in the given size.
SHOWTOP	Makes the dialog the topmost dialog.
HIDE	Makes the dialog invisible.

MIN	Minimizes the dialog.
MAX	Maximizes the dialog.
INACTIVE	Deactivates the dialog.

Example: The following statement hides the dialog:

```
MyDialog~Show("HIDE")
```

ToTheTop

```
aBaseDialog~ToTheTop
```

Use the *ToTheTop* method to make the dialog the topmost dialog.

Example: This sample uses the *ToTheTop* method to make the user aware of an *alarm* event:

```
aDialog = .MyDialog~new
msg = .Message~new(aDialog, 'Remind')
a = .Alarm~new('17:30:00', msg)

::class MyDialog subclass UserDialog
  ...
::method Remind
  self~SetStaticText(102, "Don't forget to go home!")
  self~ToTheTop
```

Note: *Message* and *Alarm* are built-in classes of Object REXX. See the online Object REXX Reference for further information.

StartMessageHandling

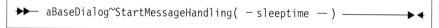

```
aBaseDialog~StartMessageHandling( - sleeptime - )
```

The *StartMessageHandling* method starts the asynchronous handling of dialog messages. It is invoked automatically by the *ExecuteAsync* method [page 330]. A message in this context is the name of an object method that will be processed. You can set the messages that should be sent by using connect methods (see *Connect Methods* on page 333).

Protected: This method is protected and for internal use only.

Arguments: The only argument is:

sleeptime   The time slice in milliseconds after which the next message is processed.

HandleMessages

```
aBaseDialog~HandleMessages
```

The *HandleMessages* method handles dialog messages synchronously. It is called by the *Execute* method [page 329].

ClearMessages

```
►►─  aBaseDialog~ClearMessages  ─────────────────────────────────  ►◄
```

The *ClearMessages* method clears all pending dialog messages.

SendMessageToItem

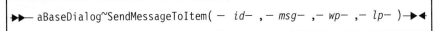

The *SendMessageToItem* method sends a Windows message to a dialog item. It is used to influence the behavior of dialog elements. See also *AddUserMsg* [page 339] for more information about Windows messages.

Arguments: The arguments are:

    id   The ID of the dialog item.

    msg   The Windows message (you need a Windows SDK to look up these numbers).

    wp   The first message parameter (wParam).

    lp   The second message parameter (lParam).

Example: This example sets the marker to radio button 9001:

```
MyDialog~SendMessageToItem(9001, "0x000000F1", 1, 0)
```

Connect Methods

The methods listed below create a connection between a dialog item (dialog control) and an Object REXX attribute or method. The behaviors of the connections differ according to the dialog item.

❏ For push buttons you connect a method to the button. The connected method is called whenever the button is clicked.

❏ For data items, such as an entry line, list box, or combo box, an attribute is created and added to the dialog object. The attribute is used as an interface to the data of the entry line, list box, or combo box.

❏ Check boxes and radio buttons are data items as well, and they are therefore connected to an attribute. The only valid values for these attributes are 1 for selected and 0 for not selected.

❏ For a list box, multiple list box, and combo box, you can also connect a method that is called whenever a line in the box is selected.

In a *UserDialog*, the *Connect...* methods are called automatically from the *Add...* methods. The proper place for *Connect...* methods is the *InitDialog* method [page 329].

InitAutoDetection

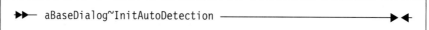

```
aBaseDialog~InitAutoDetection
```

The *InitAutoDetection* method is called by the *Init* method to change the default setting for the automatic data field detection.

Automatic data field detection means that for every dialog data item a corresponding Object REXX attribute is created automatically. If you disable automatic detection, you have to use the *Connect...* methods to assign a dialog item to an Object REXX attribute.

Protected: This method is protected. You can overwrite this method within your subclass to change the standard behavior.

Example: This example overwrites the method to switch off auto detection:

```
::class MyDialog subclass UserDialog
::method InitAutoDetection
   self~NoAutoDetection
```

NoAutoDetection

```
aBaseDialog~NoAutoDetection
```

The *NoAutoDetection* method switches off auto detection.

AutoDetection

```
aBaseDialog~AutoDetection
```

The *AutoDetection* method switches on auto detection.

ConnectButton

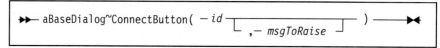

```
aBaseDialog~ConnectButton( – id
                              ,– msgToRaise
                                             )
```

The *ConnectButton* method connects a push button with a method.

Arguments: The arguments are:

    id   The ID of the dialog element.

    msgToRaise   The message that is sent whenever the button is clicked. You should provide a method with the matching name.

Example: Connections are usually placed in the *Init* method [page 328] or *InitDialog* method [page 329]. If both methods are defined, use *Init* as the place for the connections—but not before *Init:super* has been called:

```
::class MyDlgClass subclass UserDialog
::method Init
  self~init:super(...)
  self~ConnectButton(203, "SayHello")
::method SayHello
  say "Hello"
```

ConnectBitmapButton

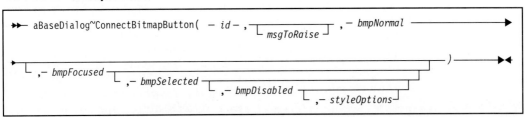

The *ConnectBitmapButton* method connects a bitmap and a method with a push button. The given bitmaps are displayed instead of a Windows push button.

Arguments: The arguments are:

id The ID of the button.

msgToRaise The message that is sent to this object when the button is clicked.

bmpNormal The name (alphanumeric), resource ID (numeric), or handle (*INMEMORY* option) of a bitmap file. This bitmap is displayed when the button is not selected, not focused, and not disabled. It is used for the other button states in case the other arguments are omitted.

bmpFocused This bitmap is displayed when the button is focused. The focused button is activated when the enter key is pressed.

bmpSelected This bitmap is displayed while the button is clicked and held.

bmpDisabled This bitmap is displayed when the button is disabled.

styleOptions There are four possible keywords:

FRAME Draws a frame around the button. When using this option, the bitmap button behaves just like a normal Windows button, except that a bitmap is shown instead of a text.

USEPAL Takes the colors of the bitmap file and stores them as the system color palette. This option is needed when the bitmap was created with a palette other than the default Windows color palette. Use it for only one button, because only one color palette can be active at any time. *USEPAL* is invalid for a bitmap loaded through a DLL.

INMEMORY This option must be used if the named bitmaps are already loaded into memory by using the *LoadBitmap* method [page 364]. In this case, *bmpNormal, bmpFocused, bmpSelected,* and *bmpDisabled* specify a bitmap handle instead of a file.

STRETCH If this option is specified and the extent of the bitmap is smaller then the extent of the button rectangle, the bitmap is adapted to match the extent of the button. *STRETCH* has no effect for bitmaps loaded through a DLL.

Example: This example connects a button with four bitmaps and a method.

```
::method InitDialog
  self~ConnectBitmapButton(204, "BmpButtonClicked", ,
                 "AddBut_n.bmp", "AddBut_f.bmp", ,
                 "AddBut_s.bmp", "AddBut_d.bmp", "FRAME")
  ...
::method BmpButtonClicked
  ...
```

See also *ChangeBitmapButton* method [page 364].

ConnectControl

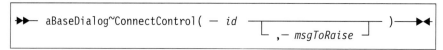

```
aBaseDialog~ConnectControl( — id
                              ,— msgToRaise        )
```

The *ConnectControl* method connects dialog controls (buttons, bitmap buttons, list box, etc.) with a method.

Arguments: The arguments are:

id The ID of the dialog element.

msgToRaise The message that is sent whenever the button is clicked. You should provide a method with the matching name.

ConnectList

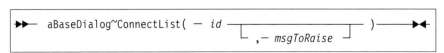

The *ConnectList* method connects a list box, multiple list box, or combo box with a method. The method is called whenever the user selects a new item within the list.

Arguments: The arguments are:

id The ID of the dialog element.

msgToRaise The message that is sent whenever a list item is selected. You should provide a method with the matching name.

ConnectEntryLine

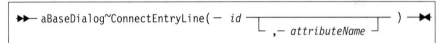

The *ConnectEntryLine* method creates a new attribute and connects it to the entry line *id*. The attribute has to be synchronized with the entry line manually. This can be done globally with the methods *SetData* [page 342] and *GetData* [page 342], or for just one item with the methods *SetEntryLine* [page 344] and *GetEntryLine* [page 344]. It is done automatically by the *Execute* method [page 329] when the dialog starts and after it terminates. If *AutoDetection* is enabled, or if the dialog is created dynamically (manually or based on a resource script), you do not have to use this method (or the other *Connect...* methods that deal with dialog items).

Arguments: The arguments are:

id The ID of the entry field you want to connect.

attributeName
This should be an unused valid REXX symbol, because an attribute with exactly this name is added to the dialog object by this method. Blank spaces, ampersands (&), and colons (:) are removed from *attributeName*. If the second argument is omitted, is invalid, or already exists, an attribute with the name *DATAid* is used (where *id* is the value of the first argument).

Example: The entry line with ID 202 is associated with the attribute *Name*. Then "Put your name here!" is assigned to the newly created attribute. Next the dialog is executed. That action copies the value from the attribute *Name* to the entry line and then executes the dialog. After the dialog has been terminated, the data of the entry line (which the user may have changed) is copied back to the attribute *Name*.

```
MyDialog~ConnectEntryLine(202, "Name")
MyDialog~Name="Put your name here!"
MyDialog~Execute("SHOWTOP")
say MyDialog~Name
```

ConnectComboBox

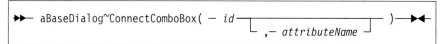

The *ConnectComboBox* method creates an attribute and connects it to a combo box. The value of the combo box, that is, the text in the entry line or the selected list item, is associated with this attribute. See *ConnectEntryLine* [page 337] for a more detailed description.

ConnectCheckBox

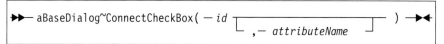

The *ConnectCheckBox* method connects a check box control to a newly created attribute. A check box attribute has only two valid values: 1 if the box has a check mark, and 0 if it doesn't. See *ConnectEntryLine* [page 337] for a more detailed description.

ConnectRadioButton

The *ConnectRadioButton* method connects a radio button control to a newly created attribute. A radio button attribute has only two valid values: 1 if the radio button is marked and 0 if it is not. See *ConnectEntryLine* method [page 337] for a more detailed description.

ConnectListBox

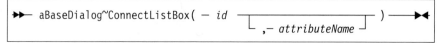

The *ConnectListBox* method connects a list box to a newly created attribute. The value of the attribute is the number of the selected line. Therefore, if the attribute value is 3, the third line is currently selected or will be selected, depending on whether you set data to the dialog or receive it. See *ConnectEntryLine* method [page 337] for a more detailed description.

ConnectMultiListBox

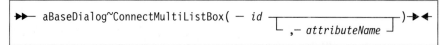

```
►►─ aBaseDialog~ConnectMultiListBox( ─ id ─┬─────────────────────┬─)─►◄
                                           └ ,─ attributeName ┘
```

The *ConnectMultiListBox* method connects a list box to a newly created attribute. The list box has the multiple selection style enabled; that is, you can select more than one item at the same time. The value of the attribute is a string containing the numbers of the selected lines. The numbers are separated by blank spaces. Therefore, if the attribute value is "3 5 6", the third, fifth, and sixth item are currently selected, or will be selected if *the SetData* method [page 342] is executed. See *ConnectEntryLine* [page 337] for a more detailed description.

Example: This example defines a list box with the names of the four seasons. It then preselects the items *Summer* and *Winter*. After execution of the dialog, it parses the value of the attribute.

```
MyDialog = .ResDialog~new(...)
MyDialog~noAutoDetection
MyDialog~ConnectMultiListBox(205, "ListBox")
seasons.1="Spring"
seasons.2="Summer"
seasons.3="Autumn"
seasons.4="Winter"
do season over seasons
    MyDialog~AddListEntry(205, season)
end
MyDialog~ListBox="2 4"
MyDialog~Execute("SHOWTOP")
selItems = MyDialog~ListBox
do until anItem =""
    parse var selItems anItem selItems
    say "You selected: "seasons.anItem
end
```

You must have set the *MULTI* option when adding the list box to enable the multiple choice feature.

AddUserMsg

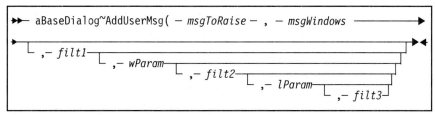

```
►►─ aBaseDialog~AddUserMsg( ─ msgToRaise ─ , ─ msgWindows ─────────────►

►─┬──────────────────────────────────────────────────────────┬─►◄
  └ ,─ filt1 ─┬──────────────────────────────────────────────┘
              └ ,─ wParam ─┬────────────────────────────────┐
                           └ ,─ filt2 ─┬────────────────────┐
                                       └ ,─ lParam ─┬────────┐
                                                    └ ,─ filt3 ┘
```

The *AddUserMsg* method connects any Windows message with an Object REXX method. This message is designed to be used by Windows programmers who are familiar with the Windows API.

You have to pass the Windows message ID and the two message parameters (*wParam* and *lParam*) to specify the exact event you want to catch. In addition you can specify filters for each parameter. Filters are useful for catching more than one message or one parameter with one method.

Protected: This method is protected. You can use it only within the scope of the *BaseDialog* class or its subclasses.

Arguments: The arguments are:

msgToRaise	The message that is sent to the Object REXX dialog object whenever the specified Windows message is caught. You must provide a method with the same name.
msgWindows	Message in the Windows environment that should be caught.
filt1	This filter is used to *binary AND* the incoming Windows message.
wParam	This is the first parameter that must be passed along with the Windows message.
filt2	This filter is used to *binary AND* the *wParam* argument.
lParam	This is the second message parameter.
filt3	This is the filter for *lParam*.

Example: This example shows an implementation of the *ConnectList* method:

```
::class BaseDialog
  ...
::method ConnectList
  use arg msgToRaise, id
  self~AddUserMsg(msgToRaise, '0x00000111', '0xFFFFFFFF', ,
                  '0x0001'||id~d2x(4), '0xFFFFFFFF', 0, 0)
```

Assume this method is called with id=254 and msgToRaise="ListChanged". After the *ConnectList* method [page 337] is executed, the *ListChanged* message is sent to the Object REXX dialog object if the following conditions are true:

- The message "0x00000111" (WM_COMMAND) is generated by Windows in answer to an event (for example, a button is clicked or a list has changed). The filter "0xFFFFFFFF" ensures that only that message is caught; if the filter were "0xFFFFEFFF", the message "0x00001111" would be caught as well.

- The first message parameter is "0x000100FF". The first part, "0x0001", specifies the event, and the second part, "0x00FE" (equals decimal 254), specifies the dialog item where the event occurred. Again, by using another filter it is possible to make more than one event a trigger for the *ListChanged* method; for example, filter "0xFFFFFFFE" would ignore the last bit of the *id*, and this the same event for dialog item 255 would call *ListChanged* as well.

- The second message parameter and its filter are ignored.

This example invokes a user defined method *Double-Click* whenever the left mouse button is double-clicked:

```
self~AddUserMsg('DoubleClick','0x00000203','0xFFFFFFFF', ,
                0,0,0,0)
```

AddAttribute

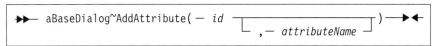

```
▶▶── aBaseDialog~AddAttribute( ─ id ─┬──────────────────┬─ ) ──▶◀
                                      └─ , ─ attributeName ─┘
```

The *AddAttribute* method adds an attribute to the dialog object. The attribute is associated with the given Windows dialog item (*id*).

Protected: This method is for internal use only.

Arguments: The arguments are:

    id   The ID of the dialog item.

    attributeName
        The name you want to give to the attribute. This name must comply with the conventions of Object REXX for valid symbols. *Add-Attribute* checks whether the argument is valid. In case of an invalid argument, an attribute of the name DATA concatenated with the *id* is created. This method automatically removes blanks, ampersands, and colons.

Example: The first and second lines generate attributes *ADD* and *LISTALLITEMS*. The third line generates assembled attribute *DATA34* because *ListAllItems* already exists. The fourth line creates attribute *DATA35* because *Update+Refresh* is not a valid symbol name.

```
self~AddAttribute(32, "&Add")
self~AddAttribute(33, "List all items")
self~AddAttribute(34, "ListALLitems:")
self~AddAttribute(35, "Update+Refresh")
```

Get and Set Methods

Get methods are used to retrieve the data from all or individual dialog elements of the Windows dialog. Set methods are used to set the values of all or individual dialog elements, without changing the associated Object REXX attributes.

GetData

```
▶▶─ aBaseDialog~GetData ──────────────────────────▶◀
```

The *GetData* method receives data from the Windows dialog and copies it to the associated object attributes.

Example: This example shows how *GetData* is used at the end of the dialog to retrieve the user data:

```
MyDialog~ConnectEntryLine(102, "ENTRYLINE_1")
MyDialog~ConnectCheckBox(201, )
MyDialog~ConnectListbox(203, "LISTBOX_DAYS")
...
    /* process the dialog */
...
MyDialog~GetData        /* retrieve dialog item value */
say MyDialog~ENTRYLINE_1
say MyDialog~DATA201
say MyDialog~LISTBOX_DAYS
```

SetData

```
▶▶─ aBaseDialog~SetData ──────────────────────────▶◀
```

The *SetData* method transfers data from the Object REXX attributes to the Windows dialog.

Example: Dialog items with IDs 102, 201 and 203 are connected to attributes *ENTRYLINE_1, DATA201* and *LISTBOX_DAYS*. Attribute *DATA201* is generated by the *ConnectCheckBox* method. Next, the attributes are initialized with some values. This will not change the dialog window, unless you run the *SetData* method.

```
MyDialog~ConnectEntryLine(102, "ENTRYLINE_1")
MyDialog~ConnectCheckBox(201,)
MyDialog~ConnectListbox(203, "LISTBOX_DAYS")
...
MyDialog~ENTRYLINE_1="Memorial Day"
MyDialog~DATA201=1
MyDialog~LISTBOX_DAYS="Monday"
MyDialog~SetData
```

Title

The T*itle* method returns the dialog title.

SetTitle

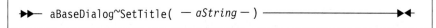

The *SetTitle* method changes the title of the current dialog window.

Arguments: The only argument is:

          aString   The new title text.

SetWindowTitle

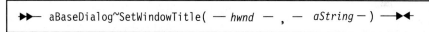

The *SetWindowTitle* method changes the title of a window.

Arguments: The arguments are:

          hwnd   The handle of the window whose title you want to change. See *Get* [page 360] on how to get the window handle.

          aString   The new title text.

ItemTitle

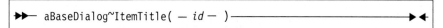

The *ItemTitle* method returns the title of the given dialog item.

Arguments: The only argument is:

          id   The ID of the dialog item.

SetStaticText

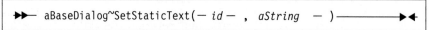

The *SetStaticText* method changes the text of a static text control.

Arguments: The arguments are:

          id   The ID of the static text control you want to set.

          aString   The text that will be put to the static text control.

GetEntryLine

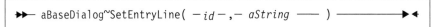

```
aBaseDialog~GetEntryLine( - id - )
```

The *GetEntryLine* method returns the value of the given entry line.

Arguments: The only argument is:

    id   The ID of the entry line.

SetEntryLine

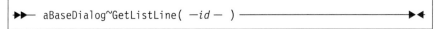

```
aBaseDialog~SetEntryLine( - id -,- aString - )
```

The *SetEntryLine* method puts the value of a string into an entry line.

Arguments: The arguments are:

    id   The ID of the entry line.

    aString   The value that will be assigned to the entry line.

Example: Imagine that three methods are related to a push button. The *SetToDefault* method overwrites the value in the Windows dialog entry line 234 with the value 256 but does not change its associated attribute. Using *SetEntryLine* has the same effect as a change to the entry line made by the user. The associated attribute in the Object REXX object (*DATA234*) still has the original value. Thus it is possible to undo the changes or confirm them.

```
::method SetToDefault
   self~SetEntryLine(234, "256")
::method AcceptValues
   self~GetAttrib(DATA234)
::method UndoChanges
   self~SetAttrib(DATA234)
```

GetListLine

```
aBaseDialog~GetListLine( -id- )
```

The *GetListLine* method returns the value of the currently selected list item. If you need the index of the item, use the *GetCurrentListIndex* method [page 355]. If no item is selected a null string is returned.

Arguments: The only argument is:

    id   The ID of the list box.

SetListLine

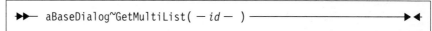

```
►►─ aBaseDialog~SetListLine( ─ id─ ,─ aString ── ) ───────►◄
```

The *SetListLine* method assigns the value of a string to the list box. Thus the item with the value of the given string becomes selected. The first item is selected if the string is not found. This method does not work for a multiple selection list box (see *SetMultiList* [page 345]).

Arguments: The arguments are:

    id   The ID of the list box.

    aString   The value of the item that will be selected.

Example: This example selects item "New York" in list box 232:

```
MyBaseDialog~SetListLine(232, "New York")
```

GetMultiList

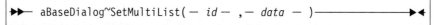

```
►►─ aBaseDialog~GetMultiList( ─ id ─ ) ───────────────►◄
```

The *GetMultiList* method can be applied to a multiple choice list box. It returns a string containing the indexes of all selected items. The numbers are separated by blanks.

Arguments: The only argument is:

    id   The ID of the multiple choice list box.

Example: This example shows how to handle a multiple choice list box. It parses the returned string as long as it contains an index.

```
selLines = MyDialog~GetMultiList(555)
do until selLines = ""
  parse var selLines aLine selLines
  say 'selected line' aLine
end
```

SetMultiList

```
►►─ aBaseDialog~SetMultiList( ─ id ─ ,─ data ─ )───────────►◄
```

Use the *SetMultiList* method to select one or more lines in a multiple choice list box. Provide the indexes of all lines you want to select (separated by blanks) in the second argument.

Arguments: The arguments are:

    id   The ID of the multiple choice list box.

    data   The indexes of the lines to be selected.

Example: This example selects lines 2, 5, and 6 of the list box:

```
MyDialog~SetMultiList(345, "2 5 6")
```

GetComboLine

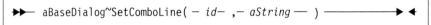

The *GetComboLine* method returns the value of the currently selected list item of a combo box. If you need the index of the item, use the *GetCurrentComboIndex* method [page 351]. If no item is selected a null string is returned.

Arguments: The only argument is:

id   The ID of the combo box.

SetComboLine

The *SetComboLine* method assigns a string to the given combo box. Thus the item with the value of the given string becomes selected. The first item is selected if the string is not found in the combo box.

Arguments: The arguments are:

id   The ID of the combo box.

aString   The value of the item that will be selected.

GetRadioButton

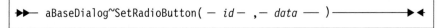

The *GetRadioButton* method returns 1 if the radio button is selected, 0 if it is not selected.

Arguments: The only argument is:

id   The ID of the radio button.

SetRadioButton

```
►►─ aBaseDialog~SetRadioButton( ─ id─ ,─ data ─ )───────►◄
```

The *SetRadioButton* method marks the radio button if the given data value is 1, and removes the mark if the value is 0.

Arguments: The arguments are:

id   The ID of the radio button.

data   The value 1 to select the button, 0 to deselect.

GetCheckBox

```
►►─ aBaseDialog~GetCheckBox( ─ id─ )───────►◄
```

The *GetCheckBox* method returns the value of a check box; 1 if the check box is selected (has a check mark), 0 if it is not selected.

Arguments: The only argument is:

    id   The ID of the check box.

SetCheckBox

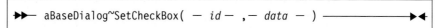

The *SetCheckBox* method puts a check mark in the check box if the given data value is 1, and removes the check mark if the value is 0.

Arguments: The arguments are:

    id   The ID of the check box.

    data   The value 1 to check the box or 0 to remove the check mark.

GetValue

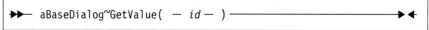

The *GetValue* method returns the value of a dialog item, regardless of its type. The item must have been connected before.

Arguments: The only argument is:

    id   The ID of the dialog item.

SetValue

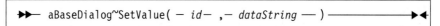

The *SetValue* method sets the value of a dialog item. You do not have to know the type of the dialog item, but it must have been connected before.

Arguments: The arguments are:

    id   The ID of the dialog item.

    dataString   The value that is assigned to the item. It should be a valid value.

Example: This example sets dialog item 111 to (string) value "1 2 3". This is meaningful if 111 is an entry field, or if it is a list box that contains the line "1 2 3". However, it is an error to apply this against a check box. If the list box has the multiple select style enabled, the *SetValue* method will not look for an item with "1 2 3" as a value but will highlight the first, second, and third line

```
MyDialog~SetValue(111, "1 2 3")
```

GetAttrib

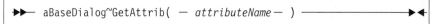

```
►►── aBaseDialog~GetAttrib( ─ attributeName ─ ) ─────────────►◄
```

The *GetAttrib* method assigns the value of the a dialog item to the associated Object REXX attribute. It does not return a value. You do not have to know the ID or the type of the dialog item.

Arguments: The only argument is:

attributeName The name of the attribute.

Example: This example shows how to get the data value of a dialog item without knowing its ID:

```
MyDialog~GetAttrib("FirstName")
if MyDialog~FirstName \= '' then ...
```

SetAttrib

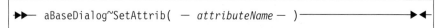

```
►►── aBaseDialog~SetAttrib( ─ attributeName ─ ) ────────────►◄
```

The *SetAttrib* method copies the value of an attribute to the associated dialog item. You do not have to know the ID or the type of the dialog item.

Arguments: The only argument is:

attributeName The name of the attribute.

Example: This example copies the value of the attribute *DATA101* to the associated dialog item:

```
MyBaseDialog~SetAttrib("DATA101")
```

MakeArray

```
►►── aBaseDialog~MakeArray ──────────────────────────►◄
```

The *MakeArray* method returns an array that is filled with the data of all dialog items.

MakeArray is an Object REXX base method that is internally called in the loop construct "do *anItem* over *aCollectionObject*."

SetDataStem

```
►►── aBaseDialog~SetDataStem( ─ dataStem. ─ ) ───────────►◄
```

The *SetDataStem* method sets all Windows dialog items to the values within the given stem; the suffixes of the stem variable are the dialog IDs.

Protected: This method is protected.

Arguments: The only argument is:

> **dataStem.** A stem variable containing initialization data. Do not forget the trailing period.

Example: This example initializes the dialog items with IDs 21, 22, and 23.

```
dlgStem.21="Windows 95"
dlgStem.22="0"
dlgStem.23="1 2 3"
self~SetDataStem(dlgStem.)
```

GetDataStem

```
►►─ aBaseDialog~GetDataStem( − dataStem. − ) ─────────────────►◄
```

The *GetDataStem* method gets the values of all dialog items and copies them into the given stem.

Protected: This method is protected.

Arguments: The only argument is:

> **dataStem.** The name of a stem variable into which the data is returned. Do not forget the trailing period.

Combo Box Methods

These methods deal with combo boxes.

AddComboEntry

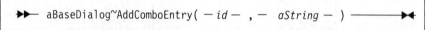

```
►►─ aBaseDialog~AddComboEntry( − id − , − aString − ) ────────►◄
```

The *AddComboEntry* method adds a string to the list of a combo box. The new item becomes the very last one, if the list does not have the *SORT* flag set. In the case of a sorted list, the new item is inserted at the proper position.

Arguments: The arguments are:

> **id** The ID of a combo box.
>
> **aString** The data that will be inserted as a new line.

Example: This example adds the new line, *Another item*, to the list of combo box 103:

```
MyDialog~AddComboEntry(103, "Another item")
```

InsertComboEntry

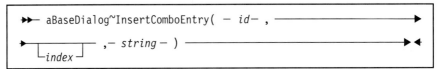

```
►►── aBaseDialog~InsertComboEntry( ─ id─ , ──────────────►

►──────────── ,─ string ─ ) ──────────────────────►◄
      └─index ─┘
```

The *InsertComboEntry* method inserts a string into the list of a combo box.

Arguments: The arguments are:

    id   The ID of the combo box.

    index   The index (line number) in the list where you want to insert the new item. If this argument is omitted, the new item is inserted after the currently selected item.

    string   The data string that will be inserted.

Example: This statement inserts *The new third line* after the second line into the list of combo box 103:

```
MyDialog~InsertComboEntry(103, 2, "The new third line")
```

DeleteComboEntry

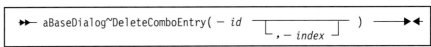

```
►►── aBaseDialog~DeleteComboEntry( ─ id ─┬──────────┬─ ) ──►◄
                                          └─, ─ index ─┘
```

The *DeleteComboEntry* method deletes a string from the combo box.

Arguments: The arguments are:

    id   The ID of the combo box.

    index   The line number of the item that will be deleted. If omitted, the currently selected item is deleted.

Example: This example shows a method that deletes the item that is passed to the method in the form of a text string from combo box 203:

```
::method DeleteFromCombo
   use arg delStr
   idx = self~FindComboEntry(203, delStr)
   self~DeleteComboEntry(203, idx)
```

FindComboEntry

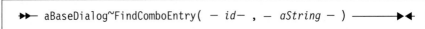

```
►►── aBaseDialog~FindComboEntry( ─ id─ , ─ aString ─ ) ──────►◄
```

The *FindComboEntry* method returns the index corresponding to a given text string in the combo box.

Arguments: The arguments are:

> **id** The ID of the combo box.
>
> **aString** The search string whose index in the combo box you are looking for.

Example: See *DeleteComboEntry* [page 350] for an example.

GetComboItems

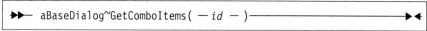

```
aBaseDialog~GetComboItems( — id — )
```

The *GetComboItems* method returns the number of items in the combo box.

Arguments: The only argument is:

> **id** The ID of the combo box.

GetCurrentComboIndex

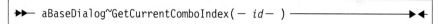

```
aBaseDialog~GetCurrentComboIndex( — id— )
```

The *GetCurrentComboIndex* method returns the index of the currently selected item within the list. See *GetComboLine* [page 346] on how to retrieve the value of the selected combo box item.

Arguments: The only argument is:

> **id** The ID of the combo box.

Example: This sample method displays the line number of the currently selected combo box item within entry line 240:

```
::class MyListDialog subclass UserDialog
  ...
::method Init
   self~Init:super
   self~ConnectList(230, "ListSelected")
  ...
::method ListSelected
   line = self~GetCurrentComboIndex(230)
   SetEntryLine(240, line)
```

Method *ListSelected* is called whenever the selected item within the combo box changes.

SetCurrentComboIndex

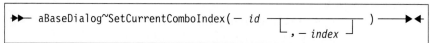

```
aBaseDialog~SetCurrentComboIndex( — id           )
                                      └ , — index ┘
```

The *SetCurrentComboIndex* method selects the item with the given index within the list. If called without an index, all items are deselected. See *SetComboLine* [page 346] on how to select a combo box item using a data value.

Arguments: The arguments are:

id The ID of the combo box.

index The index within the combo box.

ChangeComboEntry

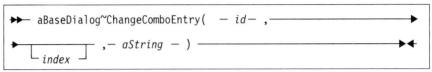

The *ChangeComboEntry* method changes the value of a given entry of a combo box to a new string.

Arguments: The arguments are:

id The ID of the combo box.

index The index number of the item you want to replace (if omitted, the currently selected item is changed). Use *FindComboEntry* [page 350] or *GetCurrentComboIndex* [page 351] to find the index.

aString The new text.

Example: The sample method *ChangeButtonPressed* changes the currently selected line of combo box 230 to the value in entry line 250:

```
::method ChangeButtonPressed
    idx = self~GetCurrentComboIndex(230)
    str = self~GetEntryLine(250)
    self~ChangeComboEntry(230, idx, str)
```

ComboAddDirectory

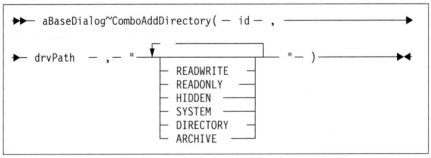

The *ComboAddDirectory* method adds all or selected file names within the given directory to the combo box.

Arguments: The arguments are:

id The ID of the combo box.

drvpath The drive, path, and name pattern.

fileAttributes Use this argument to specify the file attributes the files must possess in order to be added:

READWRITE Fetches normal file, same as none.
READONLY Fetches files with the read-only bit.
HIDDEN Fetches files with the hidden bit.
SYSTEM Fetches files with the system bit.
DIRECTORY Fetches subdirectories.
ARCHIVE Fetches files with the archive bit.

Example: This example fills the combo box list with the names of all read/write files with extension .REX in the given directory:

```
MyDialog~ComboAddDirectory(203,drive":\"path"\*.rex", ,
                            "READWRITE")
```

ComboDrop

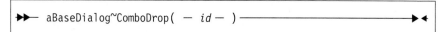

```
aBaseDialog~ComboDrop( — id — )
```

The *ComboDrop* method deletes all items from the list of the given combo box.

List Box Methods

These methods deal with list boxes.

AddListEntry

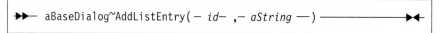

```
aBaseDialog~AddListEntry( — id— , — aString —)
```

The *AddListEntry* method adds a string to the given list box. See also *AddComboEntry* [page 349]. The line is added at the end by default, or in sorted order if the list box was defined with the sorted flag.

Arguments: The arguments are:

id The ID of the list box.

astring The data inserted as a new line.

InsertListEntry

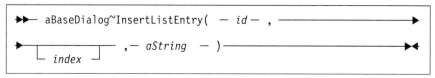

```
aBaseDialog~InsertListEntry( — id — ,

          index         , — aString — )
```

The *InsertListEntry* method inserts a string into the given list box. See also *InsertComboEntry* [page 350].

Arguments: The arguments are:

id The ID of the list box.

item The index (line number starting with 1) of the item after which the new item is inserted. If this argument is omitted, the new item is inserted after the currently selected item.

aString The text string that will be inserted.

DeleteListEntry

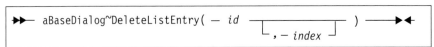

The *DeleteListEntry* method deletes an item from a list box. See also *DeleteComboEntry* [page 350].

Arguments: The arguments are:

id The ID of the list box.

index The line number of the item that is deleted (if omitted, the currently selected item is deleted). Use the *FindListEntry* method [page 354] to retrieve the index of an item.

FindListEntry

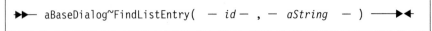

The *FindListEntry* method returns the index of the given string within the given list box. The first item has index 1; the second, index 2; and so forth. If the list box does not contain the string, 0 is returned.

Arguments: The arguments are:

id The ID of the list box.

aString The item text you are looking for.

Example: This example shows a method that adds the contents of an entry line (214) to the list box (215) if no item with the same value is already in it:

```
::method PutEntryInList
    str = self~GetEntryLine(214)
    if self~FindListEntry(215, str) = 0 then
        self~AddListEntry(215, str)
```

GetListItems

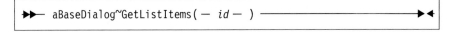

The *GetListItems* method returns the number of items in the list box.

Arguments: The only argument is:

id   The ID of the list box.

GetCurrentListIndex

The *GetCurrentListIndex* method returns the index of the currently selected list box item, or 0 if no item is selected. See *GetListLine* [page 344] on how to retrieve the selected list box item.

Arguments: The only argument is:

id   The ID of the list box.

SetCurrentListIndex

The *SetCurrentListIndex* method selects the item with the given index within the list. If called without an index, all items in the list are deselected. See *SetListLine* [page 345] on how to select a list box item using a data value.

Arguments: The arguments are:

id   The ID of the list box.

index   The index within the list box.

ChangeListEntry

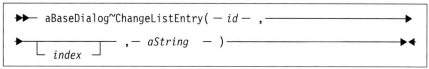

The *ChangeListEntry* method changes the contents of a line in a list box.

Arguments: The arguments are:

id   The ID of the list box.

index   The index of the item that you want to replace. If this argument is omitted, the currently selected item is changed.

aString   The new text of the item.

SetListTabulators

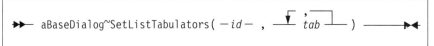

The *SetListTabulators* method sets the tabulators for a list box. Thus you can use items containing tab characters ('09'x), which is useful for formatting the list in more than one column.

Arguments: The arguments are:

  id   The ID of the list box.

  tab The positions of the tabs relative to the left edge of the list box in dialog units.

Example: This example creates a four-column list and adds a tab-formatted row to the list. The tabulator positions are 10, 20, and 30.

```
MyDialog~SetListTabulators(102, 10, 20, 30)
MyDialog~AddListEntry(102, var1 || '09'x || ,
                var2 || '09'x || var3 || '09'x || var4)
```

ListAddDirectory

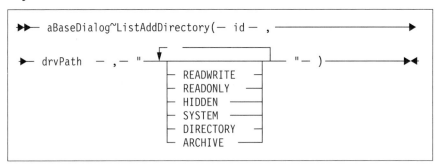

The *ListAddDirectory* method adds all or selected file names of a given directory to the list box. See *ComboAddDirectory* [page 352] for more information.

ListDrop

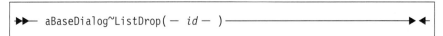

The *ListDrop* method removes all items from the list box.

Arguments: The only argument is:

  id   The ID of the list box.

Scroll Bar Methods

The methods listed below are for setting or getting the behavior of a scroll bar. You can connect scroll bars to numerical entry fields to edit the value with the mouse.

GetSBRange

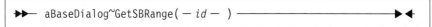

```
▶▶─── aBaseDialog~GetSBRange( ─ id ─ ) ──────────────────▶◀
```

The *GetSBRange* method returns the range of a scroll bar control. It returns the two values (minimum and maximum) in one string separated by a blank.

Protected: This method is protected.

Arguments: The only arguments is:

   id   The ID of the scroll bar.

Example: This example demonstrates how to get the minimum and the maximum values of the scroll bar:

```
::method DumpSBRange
    SBrange = self~GetSBRange(234)
    parse var SBrange SBmin SBmax
    say SBmin " - " SBmax
```

SetSBRange

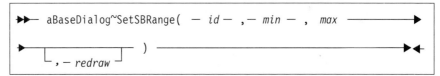

```
▶▶─── aBaseDialog~SetSBRange(  ─ id ─ , ─ min ─ , max ────────▶

▶──────┬───────────┬── ) ───────────────────────▶◀
       └ , ─ redraw ┘
```

The *SetSBRange* method sets the range of a scroll bar control. It sets the minimum and maximum values.

Protected: This method is not intended to be used outside of the *BaseDialog* class.

Arguments: The arguments are:

   id   The ID of a scroll bar control.

   min   The minimum value.

   max   The maximum value.

   redraw   A flag indicating whether (=1, default) or not (=0) the scroll bar should be redrawn.

Example: This example allows the scroll bar to take values between 1 and 10:

```
MyDialog~SetSBRange(234, 1, 10, 1)
```

GetSBPos

The *GetSBPos* method returns the current value of a scroll bar control.

Arguments: The only argument is:

      id   The ID of the scroll bar.

SetSBPos

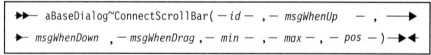

The *SetSBPos* method sets the current value of a scroll bar control.

Protected: This method is protected.

Arguments: The arguments are:

      id   The ID of the scroll bar.

      pos   The value to which you want to set the scroll bar. It must be within the defined range.

      redraw   A flag indicating whether (=1, default) or not (=0) the scroll bar should be redrawn.

ConnectScrollBar

```
▶▶─ aBaseDialog~ConnectScrollBar( ─ id ─ , ─ msgWhenUp ─ , ──▶
▶─ msgWhenDown , ─ msgWhenDrag , ─ min ─ , ─ max ─ , ─ pos ─)─▶◀
```

The *ConnectScrollBar* method initializes and connects a scroll bar to an Object REXX object. Use this method in the *InitDialog* method [page 329].

Protected: This method is protected.

Arguments: The arguments are:

      id   The ID of the scroll bar.

      msgWhenUp   The method that is called whenever the scroll bar is incremented.

      msgWhenDown   The method that is called whenever the scroll bar is decremented.

      msgWhenDrag   The method that is called whenever the scroll bar is dragged with the mouse.

      min, max   The minimum and maximum values for the scroll bar.

pos   The current or preselected value.

Example: In this example, scroll bar 255 is connected to three methods and initialized with 1 as the minimum, 20 as the maximum, and 6 as the current value:

```
::class MyDialog subclass UserDialog
  ...
::method InitDialog
  self~ConnectScrollBar(255, "Increase", "Decrease", "Drag", ,
                        1, 20, 6)
  ...
::method Increase
  ...
::method Decrease
  ...
::method Drag
  ...
/* see CombineElWithSB below for continuation */
```

CombineELwithSB

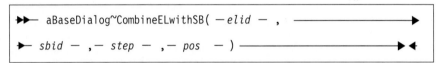

The *CombineELwithSB* method connects an entry line with a scroll bar such that whenever the slider of the scroll bar is moved, the value of the entry field is changed. This method must be used in a method registered with *ConnectScrollBar* [page 358].

Arguments: The arguments are:

elid   The ID of the entry line.

sbid   The ID of the scroll bar.

step   The size of one step. If, for example, *step* is 3 and the current position is 4, the next position will be 7.

pos   If the *step* value is zero, this sets the position of the scroll bar and entry line. Use it in the method registered for *drag*.

Example: This example continues the example of *ConnectScrollBar*. In the registered methods an entry line [251] is combined with the scroll bar [255]:

```
::method Increase
  self~combineElwithSB(251,255,+20)
::method Decrease
  self~combineElwithSB(251,255,-20)
::method Drag
  use arg wparam, lparam              /* wparam=position */
  self~combineElwithSB(251,255,0,wparam)
```

Methods for Window Handles, Sizes, and Positions

The methods listed below return information about the dialog or a single dialog control.

Get

```
►►── aBaseDialog~Get ───────────────────────────► ◄
```

The *Get* method returns the handle of the current Windows dialog. A handle is a unique reference to a particular Windows object. Handles are used within some of the methods to work on a particular Windows object.

GetItem

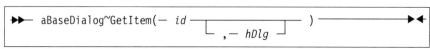

```
►►── aBaseDialog~GetItem(── id ──┬──────────┬── ) ──────────►◄
                                 └ ,── hDlg ┘
```

The *GetItem* method returns the handle of a particular dialog item.

Arguments: The arguments are:

     id   The ID of the dialog element.

     hDlg   The handle of the dialog. If it is omitted, the main dialog handle is used.

Example: This example returns the handle of a push button:

```
hndPushButton = MyDialog~GetItem(101)
```

GetSize

```
►►── aBaseDialog~GetSize──────────────────────────► ◄
```

The *GetSize* method returns the dialog window's size in pixels. The values are returned in a string separated by blanks for parsing.

Example: This example moves the Window to the center of the screen, similar to the *Center* method [page 386]. *GetScreenSize* is an external function of OODialog.

```
parse value self~GetSize with wx wy
parse value GetScreenSize() with . . sx sy
self~Move( (sx-wx)%2%self~FactorX, ,
           (sy-wy)%2%self~FactorY, "SHOWWINDOW")
```

GetPos

```
►►── aBaseDialog~GetPos ──────────────────────────► ◄
```

The *GetPos* method returns the dialog window's position in pixels. The values are returned in a string separated by blanks for parsing.

Example: This example moves the Window towards the left top of the screen.

```
parse value self~GetPos with px py
self~Move( px%self~FactorX-10, py%self~FactorY-10)
```

GetButtonRect

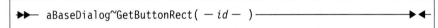

```
aBaseDialog~GetButtonRect( — id — )
```

The *GetButtonRect* method returns the size and position of the given button in pixels. The four values (left, top, right, bottom) are returned in one string separated by blanks.

Arguments: The only argument is:

id   The ID of the button.

GetWindowRect

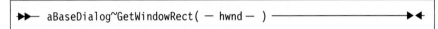

```
aBaseDialog~GetWindowRect( — hwnd — )
```

The *GetWindowRect* method returns the size and position of the given window in pixels. The four values (left, top, right, bottom) are returned in one string separated by blanks.

Arguments: The only argument is:

hwnd   The handle of the window. Use the *Get* method [page 360] to retrieve the window handle.

Window Draw Methods

The methods listed below are used to draw, redraw, and clear window areas.

Draw

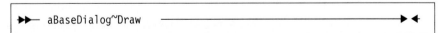

```
aBaseDialog~Draw
```

The *Draw* method draws the dialog.

DrawButton

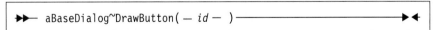

```
aBaseDialog~DrawButton( — id — )
```

The *DrawButton* method draws the given button.

Arguments: The only argument is:

id   The ID of the button.

RedrawRect

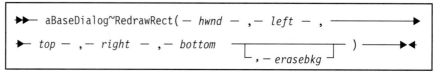

The *RedrawRect* method redraws the given rectangle. The values are in pixels.

Arguments: The arguments are:

hwnd The handle of the window. See *Get* [page 360] on how to get a window handle.

left The horizontal value of the left side of the rectangle.

top The vertical value of the rectangle's top.

right The horizontal value of the right side.

bottom The vertical value of the bottom.

erasebkg If true (1), the method deletes the background before redrawing (default is 0).

RedrawButton

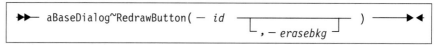

The *RedrawButton* method redraws the given button.

Arguments: The arguments are:

id The ID of the button.

erasebkg Determines whether (=1) or not (=0, default) the background of the drawing area should be erased before redrawing.

RedrawWindowRect

The *RedrawWindowRect* method redraws the given window rectangle.

Arguments: The arguments are:

hwnd The handle to the window. See *Get* [page 360] on how to get a window handle.

erasebkg If this argument equals 1, the background is deleted before redrawing (default is 0).

ClearRect

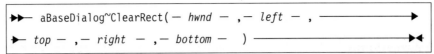

```
▶▶── aBaseDialog~ClearRect( ─ hwnd ─ ,─ left ─ , ──────────▶
▶─ top ─ ,─ right ─ ,─ bottom ─ ) ──────────────▶◀
```

The *ClearRect* method clears the given rectangle of a window. The values are in pixels.

Arguments: The arguments are:

hwnd   The handle of the window. See *Get* [page 360] on how to get a window handle.

left   The horizontal value of the left side of the rectangle.

top   The vertical value of the rectangle's top.

right   The horizontal value of the right side.

bottom   The vertical value of the bottom.

Example: This example clears a rectangle of the size 20 by 20:

```
hwnd=MyDialog~Get
MyDialog~ClearRect(hwnd, 2, 4, 22, 24)
```

ClearButtonRect

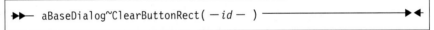

```
▶▶── aBaseDialog~ClearButtonRect( ─ id ─ ) ──────────▶◀
```

The *ClearButtonRect* method erases the draw area of the given button.

Arguments: The only argument is:

id   The ID of the push button.

ClearWindowRect

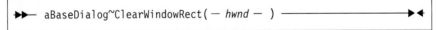

```
▶▶── aBaseDialog~ClearWindowRect( ─ hwnd ─ ) ──────────▶◀
```

The *ClearWindowRect* method erases the draw area of the given window.

Arguments: The only argument is:

hwnd   The handle of the window. See *Get* [page 360] on how to get a window handle.

Example: This example gets the window handle and then clears the window:

```
hwnd = MyDialog~Get
MyDialog~ClearWindowRect(hwnd)
```

Bitmap Methods

The methods listed below deal with bitmaps.

LoadBitmap

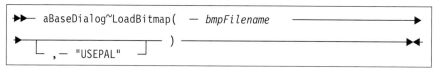

```
▶▶──  aBaseDialog~LoadBitmap(   ─ bmpFilename ──────────────────▶
▶──────────────┬────────────────── )  ─────────────────────────▶◀
       └ ,─ "USEPAL" ─┘
```

The *LoadBitmap* method loads a bitmap from a file into memory and returns a handle to the bitmap.

Arguments: The arguments are:

        bmpFilename The name of a bitmap file. The name can include a relative or absolute path.

        option   You can set the last argument to:

                USEPAL This sets the color palette of the bitmap as the system color palette.

Example: This example loads the bitmap file `Walker.bmp` from the BMP subdirectory into memory. *hBmp* is a handle to this in-memory bitmap.

        `hBmp = MyDialog~LoadBitmap("bmp\Walker.bmp", "USEPAL")`

Do not forget to call the *RemoveBitmap* method [page 364] to free the memory when the bitmap is no longer in use. You have to specify the *INMEMORY* option when using the *ConnectBitmapButton* method [page 335] or *ChangeBitmapButton* method [page 364].

RemoveBitmap

```
▶▶──  aBaseDialog~RemoveBitmap( ─ hBitmap  ─ )  ──────────────▶◀
```

The *RemoveBitmap* method frees an in-memory bitmap that was loaded by *LoadBitmap* method [page 364].

Arguments: The only argument is:

        hBitmap The bitmap handle.

ChangeBitmapButton

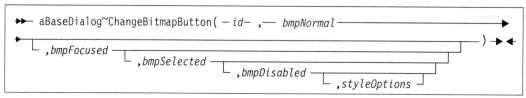

```
▶▶── aBaseDialog~ChangeBitmapButton( ─ id─ ,─ bmpNormal ──────────▶
▶────────────────────────────────────────────────────── )▶◀
    └ ,bmpFocused ─┬─────────────────────────────────────┘
            └ ,bmpSelected ─┬───────────────────────┘
                    └ ,bmpDisabled ─┬──────────┘
                            └ ,styleOptions ─┘
```

The *ChangeBitmapButton* method changes the bitmaps of a bitmap button.

Arguments: The arguments are the same as for *ConnectBitmap-Button* [page 335], except for the second argument (*MsgToRaise*), which is skipped in this method.

Example: This example replaces the current bitmap with a new bitmap:

```
MyDialog~ChangeBitmapButton(501, "NewBB.bmp")
```

GetBitmapSizeX

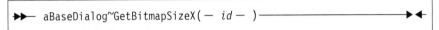

The *GetBitmapSizeX* method returns the horizontal bitmap extension.

Arguments: The only argument is:

    id   The ID of the bitmap button.

GetBitmapSizeY

The *GetBitmapSizeY* method returns the vertical bitmap extension.

Arguments: The only argument is:

    id   The ID of the bitmap button.

DrawBitmap

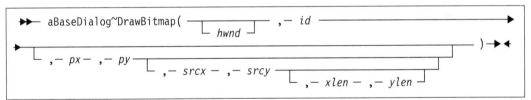

The *DrawBitmap* method draws the bitmap of a button. You can also use this method to move a bitmap or draw a part of it.

Arguments: The arguments are:

    hwnd   The handle of the button. If this argument is omitted the handle of the button is used automatically.

    id   The ID of the button.

    px, py   The upper-left corner of the target space within the button (default is 0).

    srcx, srcy   The upper-left corner within the bitmap (default is 0).

    xlen, yLen   The extension of the bitmap or a part of it (default is the whole bitmap).

ScrollBitmapFromTo

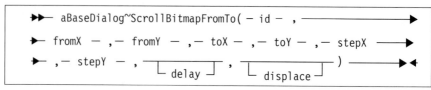

The *ScrollBitmapFromTo* method scrolls a bitmap from one position to another within a button. Values are in pixels.

Arguments: The arguments are:

id	The ID of the button.
fromX, fromY	The starting position.
toX, toY	The target position.
stepX, stepY	The width of one step.
delay	The time in milliseconds this method waits after each move. This determines the speed at which the bitmap moves (default is 0).
displace	If set to 1, the internal position of the bitmap (bitmap displacement) is updated after each move, *DisplaceBitmap* [page 367] is called after each step to adjust the bitmap position. If the dialog is redrawn, the bitmap is shown at the correct position, but the drawing is slower (default is 0).

TiledBackgroundBitmap

The *TiledBackgroundBitmap* method sets a bitmap as the background brush (Windows NT only). If the bitmap size is less than the size of the background, the bitmap is drawn repetitively.

Arguments: The only argument is:

bmpFilename The name of a bitmap file.

BackgroundBitmap

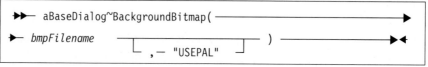

The *BackgroundBitmap* method sets a bitmap as the dialog's background picture.

Arguments: The arguments are:

bmpFilename The name of a bitmap file.

option Set the last argument to *USEPAL* if you want to use the color palette of the bitmap. See *ConnectBitmapButton* [page 335] for more information.

DisplaceBitmap

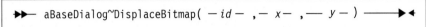

The *DisplaceBitmap* method sets the position of a bitmap within a button.

Arguments: The arguments are:

id The ID of a button.

x The horizontal displacement in screen pixels. A negative value can be used.

y The vertical displacement (negative allowed).

Example: This example moves the bitmap within a button four screen pixels to the right and three to the top:

```
MyBaseDialog~DisplaceBitmap(244, 4, -3)
```

GetBmpDisplacement

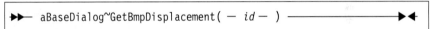

The *GetBmpDisplacement* method gets the position of a bitmap within a button in pixels.

Arguments: The only argument is:

id The ID of the button.

Example: This example shows how to use the *GetButtonRect* [page 361] and *GetBmpDisplacement* methods:

```
bRect = MyBaseDialog~GetButtonRect(244)
parse var bRect left top right bottom
bmpPos = MyBaseDialog~GetBmpDisplacement(244)
parse var bmpPos x y
```

Device Context Methods

The methods listed below are used to retrieve and release a device context. A device context is associated with a window, a dialog, or a push button, and is a drawing area managed by a window. A device context stores information about the graphic objects (bitmaps, lines, pixels, etc.) that are displayed and the tools (pen, brush, font, etc.) that are used to display them.

GetWindowDC

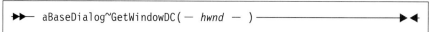
`aBaseDialog~GetWindowDC( — hwnd — )`

The *GetWindowDC* method returns the device context of a window. Do not forget to free the device context after you have completed the operations (see *FreeWindowDC* [page 368]).

Arguments: The only argument is:

hwnd The handle of the window.

GetDC

`aBaseDialog~GetDC`

The *GetDC* method returns the device context of the dialog window. Do not forget to free the device context after you have completed the operations (see *FreeDC* [page 368]).

GetButtonDC

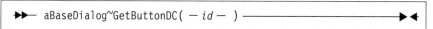
`aBaseDialog~GetButtonDC( — id — )`

The *GetButtonDC* method returns the device context of a button. Do not forget to free the device context after you have completed the operations (see *FreeButtonDC* [page 369]).

Arguments: The only argument is:

id The ID of the button.

FreeWindowDC

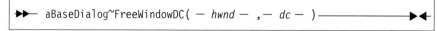
`aBaseDialog~FreeWindowDC( — hwnd — ,— dc — )`

The *FreeWindowDC* method frees the device context of a window.

Arguments: The arguments are:

hwnd The window handle.

dc The device context previously received by the *GetWindowDC* method [page 368].

FreeDC

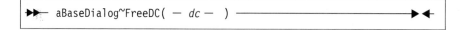
`aBaseDialog~FreeDC( — dc — )`

The *FreeDC* method frees the device context of the dialog window.

Arguments: The only argument is:

> **dc** The device context previously received by the *GetDC* method [page 368].

FreeButtonDC

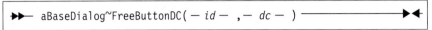

```
▶▶─ aBaseDialog~FreeButtonDC( ─ id ─ ,─ dc ─ ) ──────────────▶◀
```

The *FreeButtonDC* method releases the device context of a button.

Arguments: The arguments are:

> **id** The ID of the button.
>
> **dc** The device context previously received by the *GetButtonDC* method [page 368].

Text Methods

The methods listed below are used to display text dynamically in a window area and to modify the state of a device context. See *GetWindowDC* [page 368], *GetDC* [page 368], and *GetButtonDC* [page 368] on how to retrieve a device context.

WriteDirect

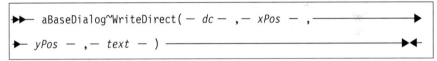

```
▶▶─ aBaseDialog~WriteDirect( ─ dc ─ ,─ xPos ─ ,──────────────▶
▶─ yPos ─ ,─ text ─ ) ───────────────────────────────────▶◀
```

The *WriteDirect* method enables you to write text to a device context at a given position.

Arguments: The arguments are:

> **dc** A device context.
>
> **xPos, yPos** The position (in pixels) where the text is placed.
>
> **text** The string you want to write to the window.

TransparentText

```
▶▶─ aBaseDialog~TransparentText ──────────────────────────▶◀
```

The *TransparentText* method enables you to write text to a device context using *WriteDirect* [page 369] in transparent mode, that is, without a white background behind the text. Restore the default mode using *OpaqueText*.

OpaqueText

The *OpaqueText* method restores the default text mode, that is, writing text with a white background overlaying whatever is at that position in the window. Use *OpaqueText* after transparent mode was set using *TransparentText*.

WriteToWindow

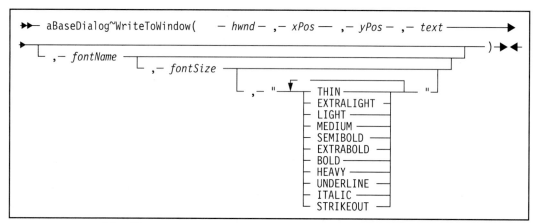

The *WriteToWindow* method enables you to write text to a window in the given font and size to the given position. The text is temporary, if the window is hidden and redisplayed, the text is gone.

Arguments: The arguments are:

hwnd The handle of the window. See *Get* [page 360] on how to get a valid handle.

xPos, yPos The starting position of the text in pixels.

text The string you want to write to the window.

fontName The name of a font. If omitted, the *System* font is used.

fontSize The size of the font. If omitted, the standard size (10) is used.

fontStyle The last argument can be one or more of the keywords listed below. If you use more than one keyword, put all keywords in one string separated by blanks.

THIN EXTRALIGHT LIGHT MEDIUM SEMIBOLD EXTRABOLD BOLD HEAVY UNDERLINE ITALIC STRIKEOUT

Example: This example writes the string "Hello world!" to the dialog window using a 24-point Arial font in bold and italic style:

```
hwnd=MyDialog~Get
MyDialog~WriteToWindow(hwnd, 23, 15, "Hello world!", ,
                            "Arial", 24, "BOLD ITALIC")
```

WriteToButton

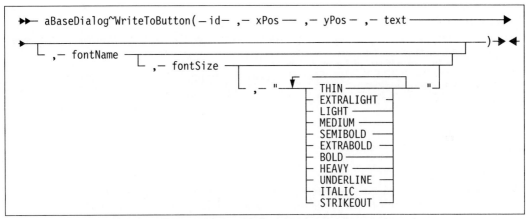

The *WriteToButton* method enables you to write text to a button in the given font and size to the given position.

Arguments: The arguments are:

id   The ID of a button.

See *WriteToWindow* [page 370] for a description of the other arguments.

Write

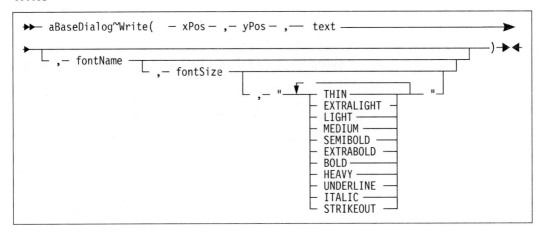

The *Write* method enables you to write text to the dialog in the given font and size, to the given position. This method does not take a handle or an ID; it always writes to the dialog window.

Arguments: See *WriteToWindow* [page 370] for a description of the other arguments.

ScrollText

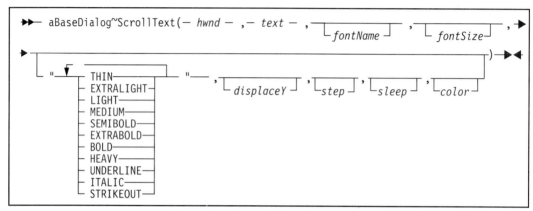

The *ScrollText* method scrolls text in a window with the given size, font, and color. The text is scrolled from right to left. If the method is started concurrently, call it a second time to stop scrolling.

Arguments: The arguments are:

    hwnd The handle of the window in which the text is scrolled.

    text A text string that is scrolled.

    displaceY The vertical displacement of the text relative to the top of the window's client area (default 0).

    step The size of one step in screen pixels (default 4).

    sleep The time in milliseconds that the program waits after each movement (default 10). This determines the speed.

    color The color of the text (default 0, black).

See *WriteToWindow* [page 370] for a description of the other arguments.

Example: This example scrolls the string "Hello world!" from left to right within the given window. The text is located 2 pixels below the top of the client area, one move is 3 screen pixels, and the delay time after each movement is 15 ms.

```
MyDialog~ScrollText(hwnd, "Hello world!", , , , 2, 3, 15, )
```

ScrollInButton

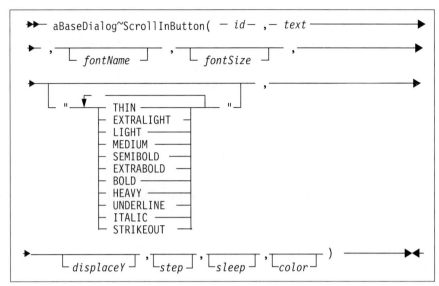

The *ScrollInButton* method scrolls text within a button. It is similar to the *ScrollText* method [page 372], except that you have to pass an ID instead of a window handle.

ScrollButton

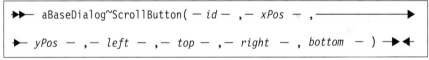

The *ScrollButton* method moves the rectangle within a button. It is used to move bitmaps within buttons.

Arguments: The arguments are:

id	The ID of the button.
xPos, yPos	The new position of the rectangle (in pixels).
left, top, right, bottom	The extension of the rectangle.

CreateFont

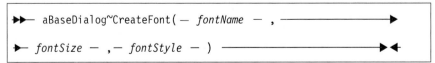

Use the *CreateFont* method to create a font. It returns a handle that you can use in the *FontToDC* method [page 374] to activate the font in a device context.

Arguments: The arguments are:

fontName The name of a font. You can look for valid fonts in the *Fonts* folder of your Windows Control Panel.

fontSize The size of the font.

fontStyle The last argument can be one or more of the keywords listed below. Use one string for multiple keywords separated by blanks.

THIN EXTRALIGHT LIGHT MEDIUM SEMIBOLD EXTRABOLD BOLD HEAVY UNDERLINE ITALIC STRIKEOUT

Example: This example creates a 16-point, italic, Arial font:

```
hfnt = MyDialog~CreateFont("Arial", 16, "ITALIC")
```

FontToDC

```
▶▶── aBaseDialog~FontToDC( ─ dc ─ , ─ hFont ─ ) ──────────▶◀
```

The *FontToDC* method loads a font into the device context of a window and returns the handle of the previous font. Use the *GetWindowDC* [page 368], *GetDC* [page 368], or *GetButtonDC* [page 368] methods to retrieve a window device context, and the *CreateFont* method [page 373] to get a font handle. To reset the original state use another *Font-ToDC* call with the handle of the previous font, and to free the device context use *FreeWindowDC* [page 368], *FreeDC* [page 368], or *FreeButtonDC* [page 369].

Arguments: The arguments are:

dc The device context of a window or button.

hFont The handle of a font.

Example: This example loads an Arial font into the current window:

```
hfnt = MyDialog~CreateFont("Arial", 16, "ITALIC")
dc   = MyDialog~GetDC
oldf = MyDialog~FontToDC(dc,hfnt)    /* activate font */
...
MyDialog~FontToDC(dc,oldf)          /* restore previous */
MyDialog~FreeDC(dc)
```

DeleteFont

```
▶▶── aBaseDialog~DeleteFont( ─ hFont ─ ) ──────────────▶◀
```

The *DeleteFont* method deletes a font. This method should be used to remove a font that was created using the *CreateFont* method [page 373]. Restore the previous font or activate another font using *FontToDC* [page 374] before deleting a font.

Arguments: The only argument is:

hFont The handle of a font.

FontColor

```
aBaseDialog~FontColor( − color − ,− dc −)
```

The *FontColor* method sets the font color for a device context.

Arguments: The arguments are:

color The color index of a color in the system's color palette.

dc The device context.

GetTextSize

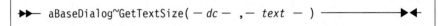

```
aBaseDialog~GetTextSize( − dc − ,− text − )
```

The *GetTextSize* method returns the pixels needed to display the given text in the specified device context. This method is especially useful if you use a proportional font.

Arguments: The arguments are:

dc The device context.

text A text string.

Example: This example uses the *GetTextSize* method to center the text:

```
aString = "A simple text string"
dc = MyDialog~GetDC
tSize = MyDialog~GetTextSize(dc, aString)
parse var tSize tHeight tWidth
MyDialog~Write(300-tWidth%2, 200-tHeight%2, aString)
```

Graphics Methods

These methods deal with drawing graphics within the device context of a window. See *GetWindowDC* [page 368], *GetDC* [page 368], and *GetButtonDC* [page 368] on how to retrieve a device context.

GraphicExtension

```
aBaseDialog~GraphicExtension
```

The *GraphicExtension* method installs API functions necessary for some graphical methods. It is called automatically.

Protected: This method is protected and for internal use only.

CreateBrush

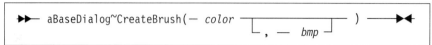

The *CreateBrush* method creates a color brush or a bitmap brush. It returns a handle to a brush object. To remove the brush, use the *DeleteObject* method [page 377]. The brush is used to fill rectangles (see *Rectangle* [page 378]), pies (see *DrawPie* [page 381]), and other outlines (see *FillDrawing* [page 381]).

Arguments: The arguments are:

    color   The color number.

    bmp   The name of a bitmap file; if omitted a solid color is used.

CreatePen

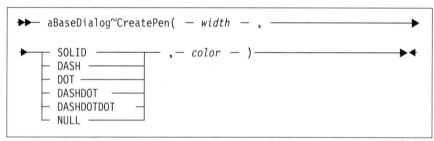

The *CreatePen* method creates a pen in the given color and style. It returns a handle to a pen object. To remove the pen, use the *DeleteObject* method [page 377]. The pen is used to draw lines and outlines of rectangles.

Arguments: The arguments are:

    width   The width of the lines the pen will draw.

    style   The second argument can be one of:

        SOLID DASH DOT DASHDOT DASHDOTDOT NULL

        Values other than *SOLID* or *NULL* have no effect on pens of width greater than 1.

    color   The color number of the pen.

Example: This example creates a dotted red pen object with width 1:

```
hPen = MyDialog~CreatePen(1, "DOT", 13)
```

ObjectToDC

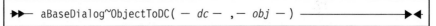

The *ObjectToDC* method loads a graphic object (a pen or a brush) into a device context. Subsequent lines, rectangles, and arcs are drawn using the pen and brush.

Return code: The function returns the handle of the previous active pen or brush. This handle can be used to restore the previous environment.

Arguments: The arguments are:

dc The device context.

obj The object, a pen or a brush.

Example: This example activates a pen for drawing:

```
dc = MyDialog~GetDC
hPen = MyDialog~CreatePen(2, "SOLID", 4)
MyDialog~ObjectToDC(dc,hpen)
... /* do lines, rectangles, ... */
MyDialog~DeleteObject(hpen)
```

DeleteObject

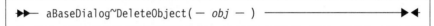

The *DeleteObject* method deletes a graphic object (a pen or a brush). See *CreatePen* [page 376] and *CreateBrush* [page 376] on how to get the handle of a pen or brush.

Arguments: The only argument is:

obj The handle of a pen or a brush.

Graphic Drawing Methods

The methods listed below are used to draw rectangles, lines, pixels, and arcs in a device context. See *GetWindowDC* [page 368], *GetDC* [page 368], and *GetButtonDC* [page 368] on how to retrieve a device context. A pen and a brush can be activated using *ObjectToDC* [page 377] before invoking the drawing methods.

Note: Because the pixel values include the title bar in a dialog window it is easier to define a button filling the window, and then draw to the button.

Rectangle

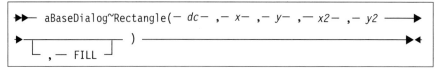

The *Rectangle* method draws a rectangle to the given device context. The appearance is determined by the graphics objects currently active in the device context. The active pen draws the outline and, optionally, the active brush fills the inside area. The default pen is thin black, and the default brush is white.

Arguments: The arguments are:

> **dc**   The device context (window or button).
>
> **x, y**   The position of the upper left corner of the rectangle (in pixels).
>
> **x2, y2**   The position of the lower right corner.
>
> **option**   Specify *FILL* to have the rectangle filled with the active brush.

Example: This example draws a red rectangle filled in yellow, surrounded by a black rectangle:

```
dc = self~getButtonDC(100)
brush = self~createBrush(15)           /* yellow */
pen = self~createPen(10,'solid',13)    /* thick-red */
oldb = self~objectToDC(dc,brush)
oldp = self~objectToDC(dc,pen)
self~rectangle(dc,50,50,200,150,"FILL")
self~objectToDC(dc,oldp); self~deleteObject(pen)
self~objectToDC(dc,oldb); self~deleteObject(brush)
self~rectangle(dc,40,40,210,160)       /* default */
```

DrawLine

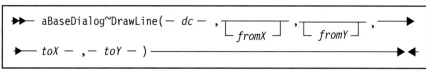

The *DrawLine* method draws a line within the device context. The active pen is used to draw the line.

Arguments: The arguments are:

> **dc**   The device context (window or button).
>
> **fromX, fromY** The starting position (in pixels); if omitted the previous end point of a line or arc is used.
>
> **toX, toY**   The target position.

DrawPixel

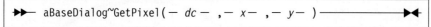

```
►►─ aBaseDialog~DrawPixel(─ dc ─ ,─ x─ ,─ y─ ,─ color ─)─►◄
```

The *DrawPixel* method draws a pixel within the device context.

Arguments: The arguments are:

    dc   The device context (window or button).

    x, y   The position (in pixels).

    color   The color number for the single pixel.

GetPixel

```
►►─ aBaseDialog~GetPixel(─ dc ─ ,─ x─ ,─ y─ )──────────►◄
```

The *GetPixel* method returns the color index of a pixel within the device context.

Arguments: The arguments are:

    dc   The device context (window or button).

    x, y   The position (in pixels).

DrawArc

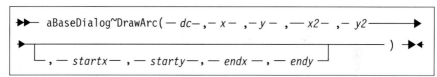

```
►►─ aBaseDialog~DrawArc(─ dc─,─ x─ ,─ y ─ ,─ x2─ ,─ y2────►
►────────────────────────────────────) ─►◄
   └─,─ startx─ ,─ starty─,─ endx ─, ─ endy ─┘
```

The *DrawArc* method draws a circle or ellipse to the given device context using the active pen for the outline. The circle or ellipse is drawn within the boundaries of an imaginary rectangle whose coordinates are given. A partial figure can be drawn by giving the end points of two radials. By default the figure is drawn counterclockwise, but the direction can be modified using the *SetArcDirection* method [page 380].

Arguments: The arguments are:

    dc   The device context (window or button).

    x, y   The position of the upper left corner of the imaginary rectangle (in pixels).

    x2, y2   The position of the lower right corner of the imaginary rectangle.

startx, starty, endx, endy
    The end points of two radials for drawing the figure (see below). A full circle or ellipse is drawn if no start and end are given. Omitted values default to 0.

Example: This example draws a full ellipse and a quarter circle:

```
dc = self~getButtonDC(100)
pen = self~createPen(4,'solid',13)   /* red */
oldp = self~objectToDC(dc,pen)
self~drawArc(dc,50,50,200,150)   /* full ellipse */
self~drawArc(dc,100,100,150,150, 200,50,75,75)
self~objectToDC(dc,oldp); self~deleteObject(pen)
```

Imaginary radials are drawn from the center to the start and end points. The circle or ellipse is then drawn between the intersection of these lines with the full figure as illustrated in Figure 155.

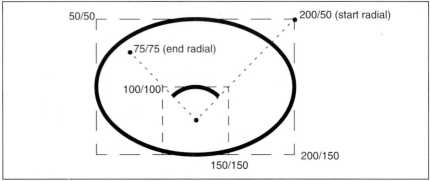

Figure 155. *Circle and Ellipse Drawing*

GetArcDirection

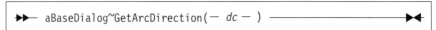

The *GetArcDirection* method returns the current drawing direction for the *DrawArc* method. The value is either *COUNTERCLOCKWISE* (default) or *CLOCKWISE*.

Arguments: The only argument is:

    dc The device context (window or button).

SetArcDirection

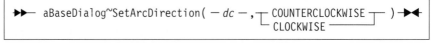

The *SetArcDirection* method changes the drawing direction for the *DrawArc* and *DrawPie* method.

Arguments: The arguments are:

    dc The device context (window or button).

    direction The new drawing direction.

DrawPie

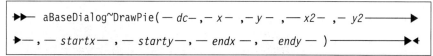

```
►►── aBaseDialog~DrawPie( ─ dc─ ,─ x─ ,─ y ─ ,─ x2─ ,─ y2 ───────►
►─ , ─ startx─ , ─ starty─, ─ endx ─ , ─ endy ─ ) ───────────►◄
```

The *DrawPie* method draws a pie of a circle or ellipse to the given device context using the active pen for the outline and the active brush to fill the pie. The circle or ellipse is drawn within the boundaries of an imaginary rectangle whose coordinates are given. The arc is drawn between start and end radials in the direction specified by *SetArcDirection* [page 380].

Arguments: The arguments are:

    dc   The device context (window or button).

    x, y   The position of the upper left corner of the imaginary rectangle (in pixels).

    x2, y2   The position of the lower right corner of the imaginary rectangle.

    startx, starty, endx, endy
                The end points of the two radials (same as for *DrawArc* [page 379]).

FillDrawing

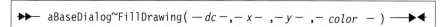

```
►►── aBaseDialog~FillDrawing( ─dc─,─ x─ ,─ y ─ ,─ color ─ ) ──►◄
```

The *FillDrawing* method fills an outline figure in the given device context using the active brush.

Arguments: The arguments are:

    dc   The device context (window or button).

    x, y   The inside starting position for filling the outlined figure with the color of the brush (in pixels).

    color   The color number of the figure outline that will be filled.

Example: This example fills a red ellipse with yellow:

```
pen = self~createPen(4,'solid',13)   /* red */
brush = self~createBrush(15)          /* yellow */
oldp = self~objectToDC(dc,pen)
oldb = self~objectToDC(dc,brush)
self~drawArc(dc,50,50,200,150)  /* full ellipse */
self~fillDrawing(dc,100,100,13)
```

DrawAngleArc

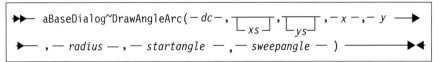

The *DrawAngleArc* method draws a partial circle (arc) and a line connecting the start drawing point with the start of the arc to the given device context using the active pen for the outline. The circle is drawn counterclockwise with the given radius between the given angles.

Arguments: The arguments are:

dc   The device context (window or button).

xs, ys   The start position (in pixels); if omitted the previous end point of a line or arc is used.

x, y   The center of the circle (in pixels).

radius   The radius of the circle (in pixels).

startangle, sweepangle
The starting and ending angles for the partial circle in degrees (0 is the x axis).

Enable/Disable and Show/Hide Methods

The methods listed below are used to enable or disable and show or hide dialog items.

Some of the methods come in two flavors, normal (for example, *Show-Window*) and fast (for example, *ShowWindowFast*). The *fast* extension indicates that the method does not redraw the item or window immediately. After modifying several items, invoke the *Update* method [page 386] to redraw the dialog.

EnableItem

The *EnableItem* method enables the given dialog item.

Arguments: The only argument is:

id   The ID of the item.

DisableItem

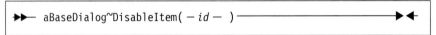

The *DisableItem* method disables the given dialog item. A disabled dialog item is usually indicated by a gray instead of a black title or text; it cannot be changed by the user.

Arguments: The only argument is:

id The ID of the item.

HideItem

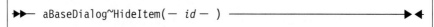

The *HideItem* method makes the given item disappear from the screen and thus unavailable to the user. In fact, the item is still in the dialog and you can transfer its data.

Arguments: The only argument is:

id The ID of the item.

HideItemFast

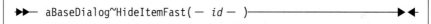

The *HideItemFast* method hides an item without redrawing its area. It is similar to the *HideItem* method [page 383], but it is faster because the item's area is not redrawn. The *HideItemFast* method is used when more than one item state is modified. After the operations, you can manually redraw the dialog window, using the *Update* method [page 386].

Arguments: The only argument is:

id The ID of the item.

ShowItem

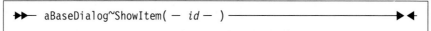

The *ShowItem* method makes the given dialog item reappear on the screen.

Arguments: The only argument is:

id The ID of the item.

ShowItemFast

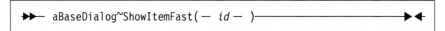

The *ShowItemFast* method shows an item without redrawing its area. It is the counterpart to the *HideItemFast* method [page 383].

HideWindow

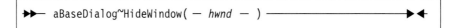

The *HideWindow* method hides a whole dialog window or a dialog item.

Arguments: The only argument is:

hwnd A handle to the window or dialog item. Use *Get* [page 360] to get a handle.

Example: This example hides the whole dialog:

```
hwnd = MyDialog~Get
MyDialog~HideWindow(hwnd)
```

HideWindowFast

```
►►─ aBaseDialog~HideWindowFast( ─ hwnd ─ ) ───────────►◄
```

The *HideWindowFast* method is similar to the *HideWindow* method [page 383], but it is faster because the window's or item's area is not redrawn. The *HideWindowFast* method is used when more than one state is modified. After the operations, you can manually redraw the dialog window, using the *Update* method [page 386].

Arguments: The only argument is:

hwnd A handle to the window or dialog item.

ShowWindow

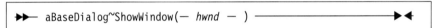

```
►►─ aBaseDialog~ShowWindow(─ hwnd ─ ) ────────────►◄
```

The *ShowWindow* method shows the window or item again.

Arguments: The only argument is:

hwnd The handle of a window or an item.

ShowWindowFast

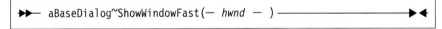

```
►►─ aBaseDialog~ShowWindowFast(─ hwnd ─ ) ───────────►◄
```

The *ShowWindowFast* method is the counterpart to the *HideWindow-Fast* method [page 384].

ResizeItem

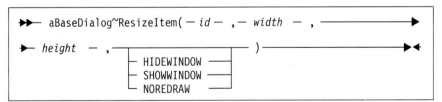

```
►►─ aBaseDialog~ResizeItem( ─ id ─ , ─ width ─ , ────────►

►─ height ─ , ─┬──────────────┬─ ) ──────────────►◄
               ├─ HIDEWINDOW ─┤
               ├─ SHOWWINDOW ─┤
               └─ NOREDRAW ───┘
```

The *ResizeItem* method changes the size of a dialog item.

Arguments: The arguments are:

id The ID of the dialog item.

width, height The new size in dialog units.

showOptions The last argument can be one of:

HIDEWINDOW	Hides the item.
SHOWWINDOW	Shows the item.
NOREDRAW	Resizes the item without updating the display. Use the *Update* method [page 386] to manually update the display.

Example: This example resizes a dialog item:

```
MyDialog~ResizeItem(123, 40, 30, "SHOWWINDOW")
```

Resize

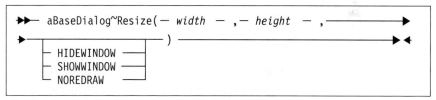

The *Resize* method resizes the dialog window.

Arguments: See *ResizeItem* [page 384] for a description of the arguments.

MoveItem

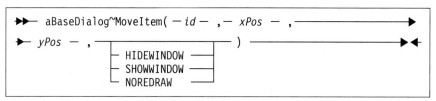

The *MoveItem* method moves a dialog item to another position within the dialog window.

Arguments: The arguments are:

id The ID of the dialog item you want to move.

xPos, yPos The new position in dialog units relative to the dialog window.

showOptions See *ResizeItem* [page 384] for a description of the options.

Move

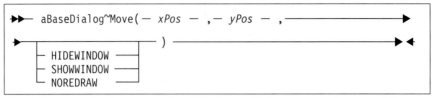

The *Move* method moves the Windows dialog to another position on the screen.

Arguments: See *MoveItem* [page 385] for a description of the arguments.

Center

The *Center* method moves the dialog to the screen center.

Arguments: The only argument can be one of:

HIDEWINDOW   Hides the dialog.

SHOWWINDOW   Shows the dialog.

NOREDRAW   Center the dialog without updating the display. Use the *Update* method [page 386] to manually update the display.

Update

The *Update* method redraws the dialog. It is usually invoked after several of the *fast* methods or methods using the *NOREDRAW* option have been completed.

Animated Buttons

The methods listed below work with animated buttons.

AddAutoStartMethod

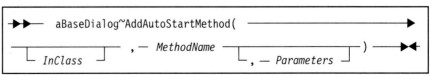

The *AddAutoStartMethod* method adds a method name and parameters to a special internal queue. All methods in this queue will be started automatically and run concurrently when the dialog is executed. The given method (*MethodName*) in the given class (*InClass*) is started concurrently with the dialog when the dialog is activated using the *Execute* [page 329] or *ExecuteAsync* [page 330] methods. This is useful for processing animated buttons.

Arguments: The arguments are:

        InClass   The class where the method is defined. If this argument is omitted, the method is assumed to be defined in the dialog class.

        MethodName   The name of the method.

        Parameters   All parameters that are passed to this method.

Example: This example installs the *ExecuteB* method of the *MyAnimatedButton* class so that it is processed concurrently with the dialog execution:

```
MyDialog~AddAutoStartMethod("MyAnimatedButton", ,
                            "ExecuteB")
::class MyAnimatedButton
::method ExecuteB
   ...
```

ConnectAnimatedButton

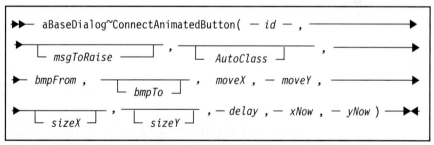

The *ConnectAnimatedButton* method installs an animated button and runs it concurrently with the main activity.

Arguments: The arguments are:

        id   The ID of the button.

        msgToRaise   The name of a method within the same class. This method is called whenever the button is clicked.

        AutoClass   The name of the class that controls the animation (default is *AnimatedButton*).

	bmpFrom	The ID of the first bitmap in the animation sequence within a binary resource. It can also be an array containing handles of bitmaps to be animated, and *bmpTo* is omitted. See *LoadBitmap* [page 364] on how to get bitmap handles. The array starts at index 1.
	bmpTo	The ID of the last bitmap in the animation sequence within a binary resource. If omitted, *bmpFrom* is expected to be an array of bitmap handles.
	moveX, moveY	Size of one move (in pixels).
	sizeX, sizeY	Size of the bitmaps (if omitted, the size of the bitmap is retrieved).
	delay	The time in milliseconds the method waits after each move.
	xnow, ynow	The start position of the bitmap.
Example:		This example defines and runs an animated button:

```
MyDialog~ConnectAnimatedButton(100,"STOP",,1001,,5,0, ,
                                         ,,20,140,70)
```

Standard Event Methods

The methods listed below are abstract methods that are called whenever a push button with ID 1, 2, or 9 is clicked.

OK

```
►►─ aBaseDialog~OK ──────────────────────────► ◄
```

The *OK* method is called in response to a clicked **OK** button. The *OK* method calls the *Validate* method [page 389] to get its return code. The default return code is the *finished* attribute value, which is usually 1, and the dialog is terminated. The *InitCode* attribute is set to 1 if the dialog is terminated.

Protected:	This method is protected. You might want to overwrite it in your subclass. If you do, forward the OK message to the parent class after your processing is finished. Set the *finished* attribute to 1 or 0 and return it. The dialog continues if *finished* is set to 0. See also *Validate* [page 389].
Example:	This example shows how to overwrite the *OK* method:

```
::method OK
   ...  /* own processing */
   self~ok:super()
   self~finished = 1
   return self~finished
```

Cancel

The *Cancel* method is called in response to a clicked **Cancel** button. The default return code is the *finished* attribute value, which is usually 1 and the dialog is terminated. The *InitCode* attribute is set to 2 if the dialog is terminated.

Protected: This method is protected. You might want to overwrite it in your subclass. If you do, forward the Cancel message to the parent class after your processing is finished. Set the *finished* attribute to 1 or 0 and return it. The dialog continues if *finished* is set to 0.

Help

The *Help* method is called in response to a clicked **Help** button.

Protected: This method is protected. You might want to overwrite it in your subclass.

Validate

The *Validate* method is an abstract method that is called to determine whether or not the dialog can be closed. This method is called by the *OK* method. The standard implementation is that *Validate* returns 1 and the dialog is closed. The dialog is not closed if *Validate* returns 0.

Protected: The method is designed to be defined in a subclass.

Example: In this example *Validate* checks whether entry line 203 is empty. If it is empty *Validate* returns 0, which indicates that the dialog cannot be closed.

```
::class MyDialog subclass UserDialog
::method Validate
   if self~GetEntryLine(203) = "" then return 0
   else return 1
```

DeInstall

```
►►── aBaseDialog~DeInstall ──────────────────────────────────►◄
```

The *DeInstall* method removes the external functions from the Object REXX API manager. *DeInstall* should be called at the end of each dialog. The installed functions are freed when all dialogs are finished.

Public Routines

The routine listed below is used to play audio sounds.

Play

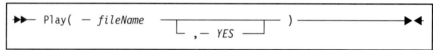

```
►►── Play( ── fileName ─┬──────────┬─ ) ──────────────►◄
                        └─ ,── YES ─┘
```

The *Play* routine can be used to play an audio file using the Windows multimedia capabilities. See also the *PlaySoundFile* function in *OODialog External Functions* on page 319.

Arguments: The arguments are:

fileName   The file name of an audio (.WAV) file. The file name is looked up in the directories of the *SOUNDPATH* environment variable.

option   You can set the last argument to:

YES   This plays the audio file asynchronously.

Example: This example plays a welcoming message:

```
rc = play('Welcome.wav')
```

UserDialog Class

The *UserDialog* class extends the *BaseDialog* class. (See *BaseDialog Class* on page 322). It provides methods to create a dialog with these control elements:

❏ Entry lines
❏ Push buttons
❏ Check boxes
❏ Radio buttons
❏ List boxes and combo boxes
❏ Frames and rectangles

There are two ways of creating a dialog:

❏ Load the dialog from a resource script (.RC file) using the *Load* method. A resource script can be created with a graphical resource editor such as the Resource Workshop.

❏ Invoke *Add...* methods to an instance of this class or a subclass and create the dialog step by step, one method for one dialog item. The best place to invoke these *Add...* methods is to overwrite the *DefineDialog* method. The *DefineDialog* method is called automatically when the instance is created.

There are also methods that enable you to define a group of the same dialog elements together. The names of these methods end with *Group* or *Stem*.

You can also combine loading a dialog from a resource script and adding elements dynamically.

Requires: Userdlg.cls is the source file of this class. Use the tokenized version of OODialog, `oodialog.cls`, to shorten your dialog's startup time:

```
::requires 'odialog.cls'
```

Subclass: The *UserDialog* class is a subclass of *BaseDialog* (see page 322).

Attributes: Instances of the *UserDialog* class have the following attributes:

AktPtr   An attribute for internal use.

BasePtr   An attribute for internal use.

DialogItemCount
An attribute for internal use.

FactorX   Horizontal size of one dialog unit (in pixels).

FactorY   Vertical size of one dialog unit (in pixels).

SizeX   Width of the dialog in dialog units.

SizeY   Height of the dialog in dialog units.

Methods: Instances of the *UserDialog* class implement the methods listed in Table 33.

Table 33. (Part 1 of 2) UserDialog Instance Methods

Methods...	...on page
AddBitmapButton	400
AddBlackFrame	416
AddBlackRect	416
AddButton	399
AddButtonGroup	413
AddCheckBox	404
AddCheckBoxStem	411
AddCheckGroup	407
AddComboBox	404
AddComboInput	410
AddEntryLine	402
AddGrayFrame	415
AddGrayRect	415
AddGroupBox	402
AddInput	407
AddInputGroup	409
AddInputStem	410
AddListBox	403
AddOkCancelLeftBottom	416
AddOkCancelLeftTop	417
AddOkCancelRightBottom	416
AddOkCancelRightTop	417
AddPasswordLine	403
AddRadioButton	405
AddRadioGroup	405
AddRadioStem	412
AddScrollBar	412
AddText	401
AddWhiteFrame	415
AddWhiteRect	415
CheckFile	395
CheckID	395

Table 33. (Part 2 of 2) UserDialog Instance Methods

Methods...	...on page
Create	394
CreateCenter	395
DefineDialog	396
ErrorFile	396
GetDefaultOpts	417
GetStaticID	417
Init	393
InitAutoDetection	394
Load	396
LoadFrame	397
LoadItems	398
StartIt	417
StopIt	418

Instance Methods of Class UserDialog

The methods of the *UserDialog* class are grouped by their usage in this section (an alphabetical list was in Table 33).

Note: The class also inherits the methods of its parent class (see *Base-Dialog Class* on page 322).

Init

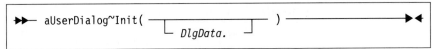

```
►►── aUserDialog~Init( ─────────────── ) ─────────────►◄
                    └─ DlgData. ─┘
```

The *Init* method initializes a new dialog object.

Arguments: The only argument is:

DlgData. A stem variable that is used to initialize the data fields of the dialog. If the dialog is terminated by means of the **OK** button, the values of the dialog's data fields are copied to this variable. The ID of the dialog items is used to name the entry within the stem.

Example: This example creates a new dialog object:

```
MyDialog=.UserDialog~new(aStem.)
```

InitAutoDetection

```
►►── aUserDialog~InitAutoDetection ──────────────────────►◄
```

The *InitAutoDetection* method is called by the *Init* to determine whether or not automatic data field detection should be used. For a *UserDialog*, autodetection is disabled.

Protected: This method is protected. It is called by the class itself and can be overwritten.

Example: This example overwrites the method to switch off auto detection:

```
::class MyClass subclass UserDialog
::method InitAutoDetection
   self~NoAutoDetection
```

Create

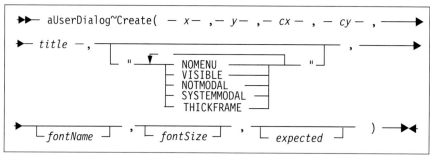

The *Create* method creates a Windows dialog. You can set the size, title, and style of the dialog. Create calls *DefineDialog* [page 396] where you can use *Add...* methods to place dialog items.

Arguments: The arguments are:

x, y The position of the upper-left edge of the dialog in dialog units.

cx, cy The extent (width and height) of the dialog in dialog units.

title The dialog's title that is displayed in the title bar.

options Possible values are:

NOMENU	Creates a dialog without a menu.
VISIBLE	Creates a visible dialog.
NOTMODAL	Creates a dialog with a normal window frame.
SYSTEMMODAL	Creates a dialog that blocks all other windows.
THICKFRAME	Creates a dialog with a thick frame.

fontName The name of a font used by the dialog for all text. The default font is *System*.

fontSize The size of the font used by the dialog. The default value is 8.

expected This argument determines the maximum number of dialog elements (entry lines, list boxes, and the like) the dialog can handle. The default value is 200. If your dialog has more than 200 elements, you must set this value; otherwise, the dialog fails.

Example: This example creates a dialog with a size of 300 by 200 dialog units. The dialog has no system menu in its upper-left corner. It has a thick frame and a 12-point font. The dialog has capabilities for up to 100 elements.

```
MyDialog~Create(20, 20, 300, 200, "My first Dialog",,
                "THICKFRAME NOMENU", "Courier", 12, 100)
```

CreateCenter

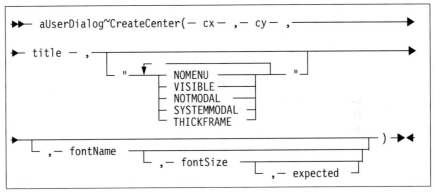

The *CreateCenter* method creates a dialog and centers its position. See *Create* [page 394] for a description of all arguments and an example.

CheckFile

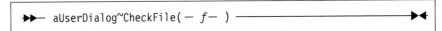

The *CheckFile* method is private and for internal use only.

CheckID

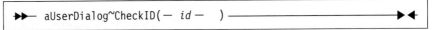

The *CheckID* method is private and for internal use only. It is used to check if the control item ID is valid.

ErrorFile

```
▶▶─ aUserDialog~ErrorFile(─ f ─ ,─ s─ ) ──────────────▶◀
```

The *ErrorFile* method is private and for internal use only.

DefineDialog

```
▶▶─ aUserDialog~DefineDialog ──────────────────▶◀
```

The *DefineDialog* method is called by *Create* [page 394]. It is designed to be overwritten in a subclass of *UserDialog*. You should do all or additional dialog definitions, such as adding dialog items to the dialog, within this method.

Protected: This method is protected. There is no need to call this method from anywhere else than *Create*.

Example: When the dialog is created, a push button and an entry line are added to its client area:

```
::method DefineDialog
    self~AddButton(401, 20, 100, 40, 15, "&More...")
    self~AddEntryLine(402, "INPUT", 20, 30, 150)
```

Load

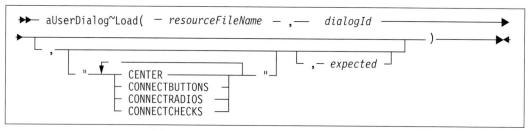

```
▶▶─ aUserDialog~Load( ─ resourceFileName ─ ,─ dialogId ──────────▶
▶─────────────────────────────────────────) ────────▶◀
   └─ , ──────────────────────┐  └─,─ expected ─┘
      └─ "─┬─ CENTER ──────────┬─ "─┘
           ├─ CONNECTBUTTONS ──┤
           ├─ CONNECTRADIOS ───┤
           └─ CONNECTCHECKS ───┘
```

The *Load* method creates the dialog based on the data of a given resource script (a file with the extension .RC). It calls the *LoadFrame* [page 397] and *LoadItems* [page 398] methods to retrieve the dialog data from the file.

Return code: The return code is 0 for a successful load and 1 otherwise.

Arguments: The arguments are:

resourceFileName
The name of the resource script.

dialogId The ID (number) of the dialog. Note that each dialog has a unique ID assigned to it. There can be more than one dialog definition in one resource file. If there is only one dialog resource in the resource file, you do not have to indicate the ID.

options The third argument can be one or more of:

CENTER
The dialog is positioned in the center.

CONNECTBUTTONS
For each button a connection to an object method is established automatically. See *ConnectButton* [page 334] for a description of connecting buttons to a method.

CONNECTRADIOS
Similar to *CONNECTBUTTONS,* this option enforces the method to connect the radio buttons.

CONNECTCHECKS
This option connects the check box controls.

expected This is the maximum number of dialog elements the dialog object can handle. See *Create* [page 394].

Example: This example creates a dialog based on the values for dialog 100 in Dialog1.rc. It also connects the push and radio buttons to a message named after the buttons' title.

```
MyDlg = .UserDialog~new()
MyDlg~Load("Dialog1.rc", 100, ,
          "CONNECTBUTTONS CONNECTRADIOS")
```

LoadFrame

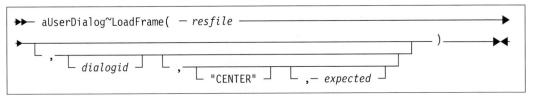

The *LoadFrame* method creates the window frame using the data of the given dialog resource with *dialogid* in file *resfile*. It is usually called by the *Load* method [page 396].

Protected: This method is protected. It can only be used internally within a class method.

Arguments: The arguments are:

resfile The name of the resource file.

dialogid The ID of the dialog. It can be omitted if there is just one dialog; otherwise it must be specified.

expected The number of expected dialog items.

Example: This example overwrites the *Load* method, so it loads the dialog window (just the frame) but not its contents:

```
::class WindowOnlyDialog subclass UserDialog
   ...
::method Load
   self~LoadFrame("Dialog2.rc", 100, "CENTER", 20)
```

LoadItems

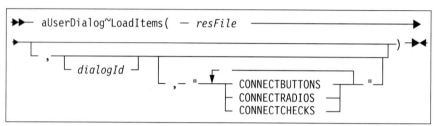

The *LoadItems* method creates the dialog items, using the data of the given resource script. It is either called by the *Load* method, or it can be used in the context of a category dialog.

Protected: This method cannot be called from outside the class.

Arguments: See *Load* [page 396] for a description.

Example: In this example, the dialog is created either with the items of dialog 200 or 300:

```
::class MyDialog subclass UserDialog
   ...
::method Load
   use arg view
   self~LoadFrame("Dialog2.rc", 200, "CENTER", 200)
   if view="special" then
       self~LoadItems("Dialog2.rc",300,"CONNECTBUTTONS")
   else
       self~LoadItems("Dialog2.rc",200,"CONNECTBUTTONS")
```

Add... Methods

The methods listed below (all starting with *Add*) can be used to create a dialog dynamically without any resource script (.RC file). They can also be used in addition to a *loaded* dialog.

The recommended way to create a dialog is to subclass from *UserDialog* and put all *Add...* statements into the *DefineDialog* method [page 396], which is executed when the dialog is about to be created. *Add...* methods call the matching *Connect...* methods to create the associated Object REXX attribute. *Add...* methods cannot be used after *Execute* has started.

Note: The coordinates are usually set in dialog units, if not mentioned explicitly.

AddButton

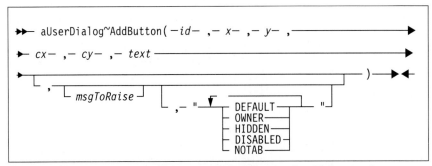

The *AddButton* method adds a push button to the dialog and connects it with a method that is processed whenever the button is clicked.

Arguments: The arguments are:

id   A unique number you have to assign to the button. You need the ID to refer to this control in other methods.

x, y   The position of the button's upper-left corner relative to the dialog measured in dialog units.

cx, cy   The size of the button in dialog units.

text   The button's title which is displayed on the button.

msgToRaise   The name of a method that is invoked whenever the button is clicked.

options   The last argument can be one or more of:

    DEFAULT   The button becomes the default button in the dialog.

    OWNER   The button is *owner drawn*. This option is used for bitmap buttons.

    HIDDEN   The button is not visible at startup time.

    DISABLED   The button is disabled at startup time.

    NOTAB   There is no tab stop at the button, so you cannot get to the button by using just the keyboard (tab key).

Example: This example creates a push button entitled *Get new Info* at position x=100, y=80 and size width=40, height=15. The button's ID is 555, and if the button is clicked, the *getInfo* message is sent to the dialog object.

```
MyDialog~AddButton(555, 100, 80, 40, 15, "&Get new Info", ,
                   "getInfo", "NOTAB")
```

AddBitmapButton

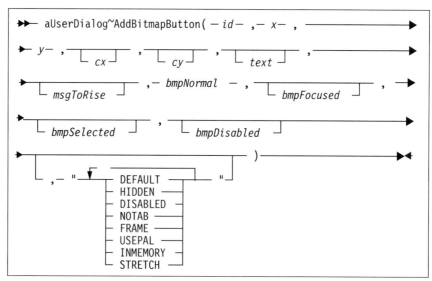

The *AddBitmapButton* method adds a push button with a bitmap (instead of plain text) to the dialog. You can provide four different bitmaps representing the four states of a button.

The bitmaps can be specified by either a file name or a bitmap handle. You can retrieve a bitmap handle by loading a bitmap stored in a file into memory, using the *LoadBitmap* method [page 364]. If you pass a bitmap handle to the method, you must use the *INMEMORY* option.

Arguments: The arguments are the same as for *AddButton*, with the changes listed below:

bmpNormal A bitmap that is displayed.

bmpFocused A bitmap that is displayed if the button is focused. The tab key is used to change the focus between buttons (and dialog items). Normally the focused button is surrounded by a dashed frame.

bmpSelected A bitmap that is displayed while the button is clicked and held.

bmpDisabled A bitmap that is displayed if the button is disabled.

options In addition to *AddButton*, there are four more options:

FRAME The button has a 3D frame. This gives your bitmap the same behavior as a standard Windows button.

USEPAL The color palette of the bitmap is loaded and used. This argument should be specified for just one of the dialog buttons, because only one color palette can be active at any time.

INMEMORY Specifies that the bitmap was loaded into memory before. If you switch often between different bitmaps within one button, the loading of all bitmaps into memory will increase performance.

STRETCH If this option is specified and the extent of the bitmap is smaller then the extent of the button rectangle, the bitmap is adapted to match the extent of the button.

Example: This example defines a button with ID 601. The bitmap in the button1.bmp file is displayed for the push button instead of a black text on a grey background. If the button is disabled (by using the *DisableItem* method [page 382], the bitmap is exchanged and button1D.bmp is shown instead. If the button is clicked, the *BmpPushed* message is sent.

```
MyDialog~AddBitmapButton(601, 20, 317, 80, 30, , ,
        "BmpPushed","button1.bmp",,,"button1D.bmp",,
        "FRAME USEPAL")
```

AddText

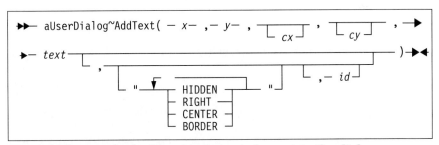

The *AddText* method adds a static text element to the dialog.

Arguments: The arguments are the same as for *AddButton* [page 399], with the changes listed below:

text The text string to be displayed.

options This argument can be one or more of:

HIDDEN The text is not visible at startup time.
RIGHT The text is aligned to the right.
CENTER The text is centered. If neither *RIGHT* or *CENTER* is specified, the text is aligned to the left.

BORDER A rectangle is drawn around the text.

id The ID of the item, -1 is used if omitted.

AddGroupBox

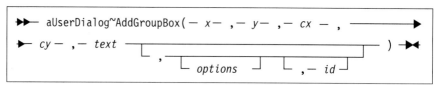

The *AddGroupBox* method adds a group box to the dialog. A group box has a frame and a title.

Arguments: The arguments are the same as for *AddButton* [page 399], with the changes listed below:

text The title of the group box.

options There are currently no options for a group box.

AddEntryLine

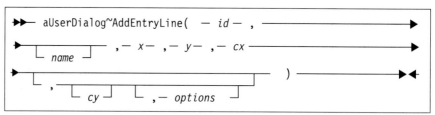

The *AddEntryLine* method adds an entry line to the dialog.

Arguments: The arguments are:

id The unique ID of the entry line.

name This is the name of the entry line. An attribute with exactly this name is added to the object and provides data for the dialog item automatically. See *ConnectEntryLine* [page 337].

x, y The position of the upper-left corner relative to the dialog's client area, measured in dialog units.

cx The length of the entry line in dialog units.

cy The height of the entry line. If this argument is omitted or equal to 0, the height is calculated to fit the font's height.

options There are currently no options for an entry line.

Example: This example puts the entry line with ID 201 and length of 150 dialog units close to the upper-left corner of the dialog's client area. The *FIRSTNAME* attribute is created and connected to the dialog item.

```
MyDialog~AddEntryLine(201, "FIRSTNAME", 12, 14, 150)
```

AddPasswordLine

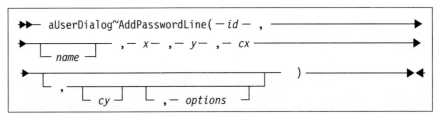

The *AddPasswordLine* method adds a password entry line that does not echo the characters entered but displays asterisks (*) instead.

Arguments: See *AddEntryLine* [page 402] for a description of the arguments.

AddListBox

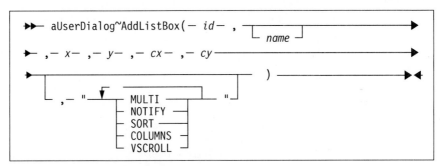

Adds a list box to the dialog.

Arguments: The arguments are the same as for *AddEntryLine* [page 402], with the changes listed below:

options The last argument can be one or more of:

MULTI Makes the list box a multiple choice list box, that is you can select more than one line.

NOTIFY A message is posted whenever the user selects an item of the list box. To use this feature you have to the connect the list to a method using *ConnectList* [page 337].

SORT The items in the dialog are listed in the noted order.

COLUMNS The list box can handle tab characters ('09'x). Use this option together with the *SetListTabulators* method [page 356] to have more than one column in a list.

VSCROLL Adds a vertical scroll bar to the list box. Scroll bars appear only if the list contains more lines than can fit in the available space.

AddComboBox

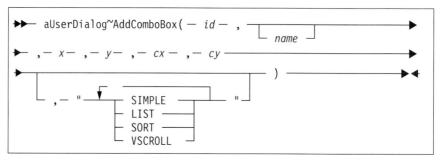

The *AddComboBox* method adds a combo box to the dialog. A combo box is a combination of an entry line and a list box.

Arguments: The arguments are the same as for *AddEntryLine* [page 402], with the changes listed below:

options The last argument can be one or more of:

SIMPLE Displays the list box all the time

LIST No free text can be entered in the entry line; the list contains selectable items only.

SORT The items in the list are sorted by the combo box itself.

VSCROLL Adds a vertical scroll bar to the combo box.

A drop-down list is displayed if neither *SIMPLE* nor *LIST* is specified.

AddCheckBox

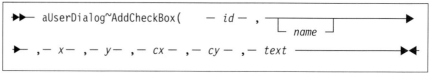

The *AddCheckBox* method adds a check box to the dialog.

Arguments: The arguments are the same as for *AddEntryLine* [page 402], with the changes listed below:

name	The name of the check box. If omitted, *text* is used.
text	The text displayed next to the check box.

AddRadioButton

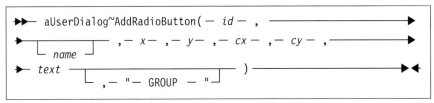

```
▶▶─── aUserDialog~AddRadioButton( ─ id ─ , ────────────────────▶

▶──────────────── ,─ x─ ,─ y─ ,─ cx ─ ,─ cy ─ , ───────────▶
        └─ name ─┘

▶── text ──────────────────────────── ) ──────────────▶◀
            └─ ,─ "─ GROUP ─ "─┘
```

The *AddRadioButton* method adds a radio button to the dialog. There are also methods that create a whole group of buttons automatically; see *AddRadioGroup* [page 405] and *AddRadioStem* [page 412].

Arguments: The arguments are the same as for *AddEntryLine* [page 402], with the changes listed below:

name	The name of the radio button.
text	The text that is displayed next to the radio button.
options	The valid value for the last argument is:

GROUP Makes the radio button the beginning of a new group. In each group if you select a radio button, the previously selected button is automatically deselected.

Example: This example defines seven radio buttons with IDs 501 through 507:

```
RText.1="Monday"   ; RText.2="Tuesday"
RText.3="Wednesday"; RText.4="Thursday"
RText.5="Friday"   ; RText.6="Saturday"
RText.7="Sunday"
do i=1 to 7
    MyDialog~AddRadioButton(500+i, , 20, i*15+13, 40, ,
                            14, RText.i)
end
```

AddRadioGroup

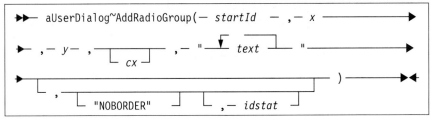

```
▶▶─── aUserDialog~AddRadioGroup( ─ startId  ─ ,─ x ──────────▶

▶── ,─ y─ , ──────────── ,─ "─┬─ text ─┬─ " ──────────▶
            └─ cx ─┘              └──────┘

▶──────────────────────────────── ) ──────────▶◀
    └─ , ─┬─ "NOBORDER" ─┬─ └─ ,─ idstat ─┘
```

The *AddRadioGroup* method creates a group of radio buttons.

Arguments: The arguments are:

startId The ID of the first radio button. The *startId* is increased by 1 for each additional radio button and then assigned to the dialog item.

x, y The position of the first radio button control. The other radio buttons are positioned automatically.

cx The length of the radio buttons plus text. If omitted, the space needed is calculated.

text The text string for each radio button. Single strings have to be separated by blank spaces. This argument determines the number of radio buttons in total. See *AddRadioStem* [page 412] on how to add a group of radio buttons with blanks in the labels.

options The only option is *NOBORDER,* which prevents the method from placing a group box around the group.

idstat This argument is used to set the static frame ID.

Example: This example adds a group of three radio buttons with ids 301, 302, and 303 to the dialog (see Figure 156):

```
MyDialog = .UserDialog~new
MyDialog~Create(100,100,80,60,"Radio Button Group")
MyDialog~AddRadioGroup(301, 10, 5, ,"Fast Medium Slow")
MyDialog~fast = 1
MyDialog~Execute
```

Figure 156. *Sample Radio Button Group*

AddCheckGroup

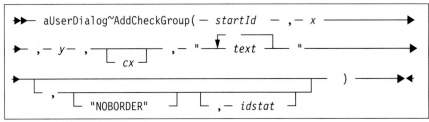

The *AddCheckGroup* method creates a group of check boxes. See
AddRadioGroup [page 405] for a description of the arguments. See
AddCheckBoxStem [page 411] on how to add a group of check boxes
with blanks in the labels.

Example: This example adds a group with four check boxes to
the dialog; two check boxes are preselected (see Figure
157):

```
MyDialog~AddCheckGroup(401, 23, 18, , ,
                    "Smalltalk C++ ObjectREXX OO-COBOL")
MyDialog~smalltalk = 1
MyDialog~objectrexx = 1
```

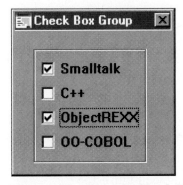

Figure 157. *Sample Check Box Group*

AddInput

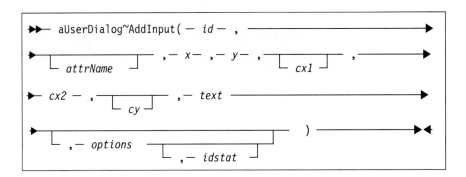

The *AddInput* method adds an entry line with a label (a static text) to the dialog.

Arguments: The arguments are:

id The unique ID of the entry line.

attrName The name used to create an attribute in the dialog object that reflects the contents of the entry line (see *AddEntryLine* [page 402]). If it is skipped, the *text* label is used as the attribute name.

x, y The position of the upper-left edge of the label. The entry line is aligned automatically.

cx1 The length of the label. If omitted, the length is calculated.

cx2 The length of the entry field.

cy The height of the entry field. If omitted, the height is calculated.

text The label displayed in front of the entry field.

options Possible options are:

HIDDEN Makes the input field invisible.

PASSWORD Displays asterisks instead of the typed-in characters.

idstat An ID for the label.

Example: This example creates an entry field and the label *Your e-mail address* (placed on the entry field's left side). It also creates an attribute with the same name (*YOUREMAILADDRESS*). The height of the elements is calculated (see Figure 158).

```
MyUserDialog~AddInput(402, , 20, 30, , 150, , ,
                      "Your e-mail address")
```

Figure 158. *Sample Input Field*

AddInputGroup

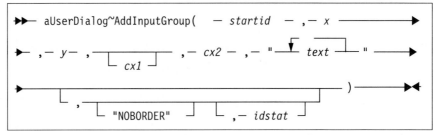

The *AddInputGroup* method creates a group of one or more entry lines.

Arguments: The arguments are:

startid   An ID that is assigned to the first entry line. Consecutive numbers are assigned to the other entry fields.

x, y   Position of the input group's upper-left corner.

cx1   Length of the entry field labels. If omitted, the length is calculated.

cx2   Length of the entry fields in dialog units.

text   The text strings used for each entry field's label. The single strings are to be separated by blank spaces. This argument determines the number of entry fields in total.

options   The only option is *NOBORDER,* which prevents the method from placing a group box around the group.

idstat   The ID of the first label. Usually you do not have to specify this value because labels are static controls.

Example: This example creates a four-line input group. The single entry lines are accessible by IDs 301 through 304.

```
MyDialog~AddInputGroup(301, 20, 20, ,130, ,
                       "Name FirstName Street City")
```

Note: If you want to use labels that include blanks (for example, "First Name" instead of "FirstName"), use the *AddInputStem* method [page 410].

AddComboInput

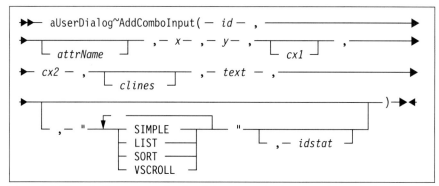

The *AddComboInput* method adds a combo box and a label string to the dialog.

Arguments: The arguments are:

id The ID of the combo box.

attrName The name of the combo box. This name is used as an object attribute name.

x, y Position of the text string of the combo box.

cx1 Length of the text string.

cx2 Width of the combo box.

clines Vertical length of the combo box in number of lines.

text Label being displayed on the left-hand side of the combo box.

options See *AddComboBox* [page 404].

idstat The ID of the label. Usually you do not have to specify this value because labels are static controls.

AddInputStem

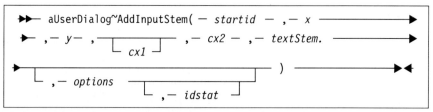

The *AddInputStem* method adds a group of input fields to the dialog. The difference between this method and the *AddInputGroup* method [page 409] is that the titles (and names) of the single lines are passed to the method in a stem variable. Thus, it is possible to use strings containing blank spaces.

Arguments: The arguments are:

startid The ID of the first entry line.

x, y The position of the whole group (upper-left corner).

cx1 The length of the text strings. If omitted, the size is calculated.

cx2 The width of the entry fields.

textStem. A stem variable containing all labels for the entry fields. The object attribute for each field is created on the basis of this string.

options In addition to the options of the *AddInput* method [page 407], *NOBORDER* can be used to prevent the method from placing a group box around the group.

idstat The ID of the first label. Usually you do not have to specify this value because labels are static controls.

Example: This example shows how to use *AddInputStem*. It creates a four-line input group. For each entry line (with IDs 401 through 404) an object attribute is provided. The names might be different from the title because not all characters can be used for Object REXX symbols. In this example the *NAME, FIRSTNAME, STREETNUMBER,* and *CITYZIP* attributes are added to the object.

```
FNames.1="Narme"
FNames.2="Fist Name"
FNames.3="Street & Number"
FNames.4="City & ZIP"
MyDialog~AddInputStem(401, 20, 20, , 150, FNames.)
```

AddCheckBoxStem

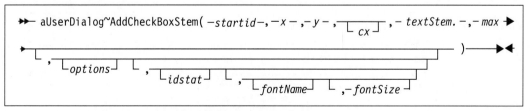

The *AddCheckBoxStem* method creates a group of check box controls. Unlike the *AddCheckGroup* method [page 407] you pass the titles of the check boxes in a stem variable instead of using a string. Thus you can use labels including blanks.

Arguments: See *AddCheckGroup* [page 407] for a description of the arguments. The new arguments are:

textStem. A stem variable containing all labels for the check boxes. The object attribute for each check box is created on the basis of this string.

max The maximum number of check box items in one column. If *textStem* has more items than *max*, a second column is created.

fontName The name of the font used within the dialog.

fontSize The size of the font used within the dialog

Example: This example creates a three-column check box group:

```
CBNames.1="C"
CBNames.2="Pascal"
CBNames.3="Cobol"
CBNames.4="REXX"
CBNames.5="Basic"
CBNames.6="Fortran"
MyDialog~AddCheckBoxStem(501, 20, 20, ,CBNames, 2, ,
                        "NOBORDER", 551, "Courier New", 12)
```

AddRadioStem

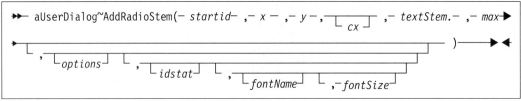

The *AddRadioStem* method adds a group of radio button controls to the dialog.

See *AddCheckBoxStem* [page 411] for a description of the arguments and an example.

AddScrollBar

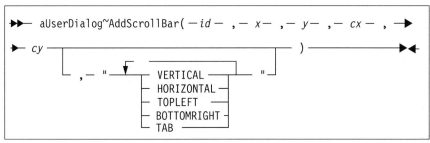

The *Add*ScrollBar method adds a scroll bar to the dialog.

Arguments: The arguments are:

    id   This must be a unique number.

    x, y   The position of the upper-left corner relative to the dialog's client area, measured in dialog units.

    cx   The length of the scroll bar in dialog units.

    cy   The height of the scroll bar.

    options   The last argument can be one or more of:

      VERTICAL
           The scroll bar is positioned vertically.
      HORIZONTAL
           The scroll bar is positioned horizontally.
      TOPLEFT
           The scroll bar is aligned to the top left of the given rectangle and has a predetermined width (if vertical) or height (if horizontal).
      BOTTOMRIGHT
           The scroll bar is aligned to the bottom right of the given rectangle and has a predetermined width (if vertical) or height (if horizontal).
      TAB   The scroll bar is assigned a tab stop.

AddButtonGroup

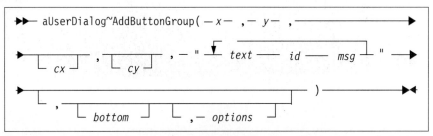

Use the *AddButtonGroup* method to add more than one push button at once to the dialog. The buttons are arranged in a row or in a column.

Arguments: The arguments are:

    x, y   The position of the entire button group.

    cx, cy   The size of a single button. One or both arguments can be skipped. If so, the default values (cx=40, cy=12) are taken.

	text ID msg	These arguments are interpreted as *one* string containing *three* words (separated by blanks) for each button. The first word is the text that is displayed on the button, the second is the ID of the button, and the third is the name of a message that is sent to the object whenever the button is clicked. The fourth to sixth words are for the next button, and so forth.
	bottom	This is a flag to switch between a vertical (=0, default) or horizontal (=1) placement of the buttons.
	options	If *DEFAULT* is used, the first button becomes the default button. For the other options, see *AddButton* [page 399].
Example:		This example creates three buttons (**Add**, **Delete**, and **Update**):

```
MyDialog~AddButtonGroup(20, 235, , , "&Add 301 AddItem" || ,
                                      "&Delete 302 DeleteItem" || ,
                                      "&Update 303 UpdateItem")
```

Frames and Rectangles

The methods listed below add simple graphical elements to the dialog. They are useful for giving the dialog a nice finish. Use Figure 159 to help you find the right element.

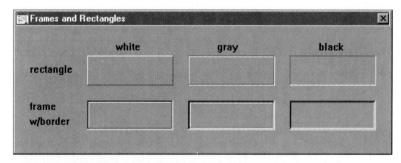

Figure 159. *Frames and Rectangles in 3D Style*

Note: There is currently no difference between rectangles and frames.

AddWhiteRect

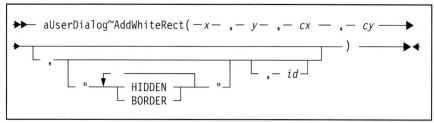

The *AddWhiteRect* method adds a white rectangle to the dialog.

Arguments: The arguments are:

x, y   The position of the rectangle's upper-left corner relative to the dialog, measured in dialog units.

cx, cy   The size of the rectangle in dialog units.

options   The options can be:

HIDDEN   The frame or rectangle is not visible at startup time.

BORDER   A border is drawn around the rectangle or frame.

id   The ID of the item, -1 is used by default.

AddWhiteFrame

The *AddWhiteFrame* method is currently identical to the *AddWhiteRect* method.

AddGrayRect

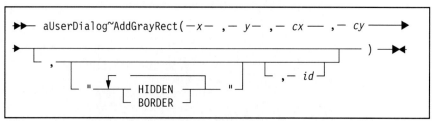

The *AddGrayRect* method adds a gray rectangle to the dialog.

Arguments: See *AddWhiteRect* method [page 415] for a description of the arguments.

AddGrayFrame

The *AddGrayFrame* method is currently identical to the *AddGrayRect* method.

AddBlackRect

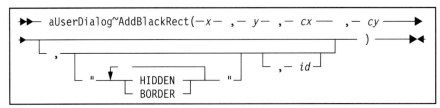

The *AddBlackRect* method adds a black rectangle to the dialog.

Arguments: See *AddWhiteRect* method [page 415] for a description of the arguments.

AddBlackFrame

The *AddBlackFrame* method is currently identical to the *AddBlack-Rect* method.

OK and Cancel Push Buttons

The four methods described in this section add **OK** and **Cancel** push buttons to the dialog. The standard IDs (1 for OK and 2 for Cancel) are assigned to the buttons.

AddOkCancelRightBottom

The *AddOkCancelRightBottom* method adds an **OK** and a **Cancel** push button to the lower-right edge of the dialog.

Example: This example adds the two push buttons to the bottom of the dialog. It further overwrites the standard *OK* and *Cancel* methods.

```
::class MyClass subclass UserDialog
::method DefineDialog

   ...
   self~AddOkCancelRightBottom
::method OK
   ret = YesNoMessage("Are you sure?")
   if ret=1 then self~ok:super
::method Cancel
   ret = YesNoMessage("Do you really want to quit?")
   if ret=1 then self~cancel:super
```

AddOkCancelLeftBottom

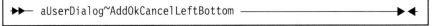

The *AddOkCancelLeftBottom* method adds an **OK** and a **Cancel** push button to the lower-left edge of the dialog.

AddOkCancelRightTop

The *AddOkCancelRightTop* method adds an **OK** and a **Cancel** push button vertically to the upper-right edge of the dialog.

AddOkCancelLeftTop

The *AddOkCancelLeftTop* method adds an **OK** and a **Cancel** push button vertically to the upper-left edge of the dialog.

Dialog Control Methods

The methods described in this section control the execution of the dialog; they are for internal use only.

GetDefaultOpts

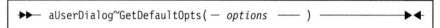

The *GetDefaultOpts* method is for internal use only.

Protected: This method is protected.

GetStaticID

The *GetStaticID* method is for internal use only.

Protected: The method can only be used within the same object.

StartIt

The *StartIt* method is called from *Execute* [page 329] and is for internal use only. It creates a real Windows object based on the dialog template.

Protected: This method is protected and cannot be called from outside the instance. It can be overwritten, although that is not recommended.

Arguments: There is only one argument:

        icon   This argument has no impact at this time.

StopIt

```
►►── aUserDialog~StopIt ──────────────────────────────────►◄
```

The *StopIt* method is for internal use only. It is the counterpart to the *BaseDialog* class *StopIt* method to remove the Windows object.

Protected: This method is protected and cannot be called from outside the instance. It can be overwritten, although that is not recommended.

ResDialog Class

The *ResDialog* class is designed to be used together with a binary (compiled) resource. A binary dialog resource is linked to a DLL (that is, a file with the extension .DLL).

Requires: Resdlg.cls is the source file of this class. Use the tokenized version of OODialog, oodialog.cls, to shorten your dialog's startup time.

        ::requires 'oodialog.cls'

Subclass: The *ResDialog* class is a subclass of *BaseDialog* (see page 322).

Instance Methods

This section describes the methods of the *ResDialog* class, grouped by their usage.

Init

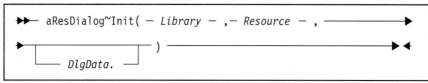

The *Init* method of the parent class, *BaseDialog*, has been overwritten.

Arguments: The arguments you have to pass to the *new* method of the class when creating a new dialog instance are:

    Library   The file name of the DLL where the resource is located.

    Resource   The ID of the resource. This is a unique number you assigned to the (dialog) resource while creating it.

    DlgData.   A stem variable (don't forget the trailing period) that contains initialization data. See *Init* [page 328] of the *BaseDialog* class for more details.

Example: This sample code creates a new dialog object from the *ResDialog* class. It uses dialog resource 100 in the MYDLG.DLL file. The dialog is initialized with the values of the *MyDlgData.* stem variable.

```
MyDlgData.101="1"
MyDlgData.102="Please enter your password."
MyDlgData.103=""
dlg = ResDialog~new("MYDLG.DLL", 100, MyDlgData.)
```

StartIt

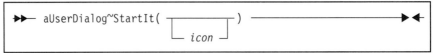

The *StartIt* method is for internal use only. It is necessary to create a real Windows object based on the dialog template.

Protected: This method is protected and cannot be called from outside the instance. It can be overwritten, although that is not recommended.

Arguments: There is only one argument:

    icon This argument has no impact at this time.

CategoryDialog Class

The *CategoryDialog* class creates and controls a dialog that has more than one panel. It is similar to the *notebook* control available in OS/2 or the tabbed dialogs available in the Windows 95 user interface.

Depending on the style you choose, you can switch among different pages by either clicking radio buttons or selecting an item from a drop down list. Each page has its own window controls.

Requires: Catdlg.cls is the source file of this class. Use the tokenized version of OODialog, oodialog.cls, to shorten your dialog's startup time.

        ::requires 'oodialog.cls'

Subclass: The *CategoryDialog* class is a subclass of *UserDialog* (see page 391).

Attributes: Instances of the *CategoryDialog* class have the following attributes:

        Catalog   A directory describing the layout and behavior of the dialog. This directory is usually set up in the *InitCategories* method [page 425] of the dialog.

        StaticID   An internal counter.

Methods: Instances of the *CategoryDialog* class implement the methods listed in Table 34.

    In fact, most of the methods do the same as the methods in the parent class, *UserDialog*, except that they are enabled to work with a category dialog.

Table 34. (Part 1 of 3) CategoryDialog Instance Methods

Methods...	...on page
AddCategoryComboEntry	432
AddCategoryListEntry	433
CategoryComboAddDirectory	433
CategoryComboDrop	433
CategoryListAddDirectory	435
CategoryListDrop	435
CategoryPage	426
ChangeCategoryComboEntry	433
ChangeCategoryListEntry	434
ChangePage	427
CreateCategoryDialog	426

Table 34. (Part 2 of 3) CategoryDialog Instance Methods

Methods...	...on page
CurrentCategory	427
DefineDialog	426
DeleteCategoryComboEntry	432
DeleteCategoryListEntry	434
DisableCategoryItem	435
EnableCategoryItem	435
FindCategoryComboEntry	432
FindCategoryListEntry	434
GetCategoryAttrib	431
GetCategoryCheckBox	431
GetCategoryComboItems	432
GetCategoryComboLine	430
GetCategoryEntryLine	429
GetCategoryListItems	434
GetCategoryListLine	429
GetCategoryMultiList	431
GetCategoryRadioButton	430
GetCategoryValue	431
GetCurrentCategoryComboIndex	432
GetCurrentCategoryListIndex	434
GetSelectedPage	427
HideCategoryItem	435
Init	423
InitCategories	425
InitDialog	427
InsertCategoryComboEntry	432
InsertCategoryListEntry	434
NextPage	427
PageHasChanged	428
PreviousPage	427
SetCategoryAttrib	431
SetCategoryCheckBox	431
SetCategoryComboLine	430
SetCategoryEntryLine	429

Table 34. (Part 3 of 3) CategoryDialog Instance Methods	
Methods...	**...on page**
SetCategoryListLine	430
SetCategoryListTabulators	435
SetCategoryMultiList	430
SetCategoryRadioButton	431
SetCategoryStaticText	429
SetCategoryValue	431
SetCurrentCategoryComboIndex	433
SetCurrentCategoryListIndex	434
ShowCategoryItem	435
StartIt	420

Instance Methods of Class CategoryDialog

The methods of the *CategoryDialog* class are grouped by their usage in this section (an alphabetical list was in Table 34).

Setting Up the Dialog

The methods listed below are used to set up the pages of the dialog and start it.

Init

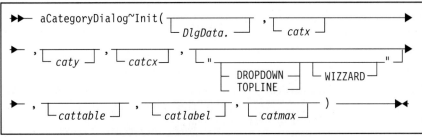

The *Init* method initializes the category dialog object.

Arguments: The arguments are:

> **DlgData.** A stem variable (don't forget the trailing period) that contains initialization data for some or all dialog items. If the dialog is terminated using the **OK** button, the values of the dialog's data fields are copied to this variable. The ID of the dialog items is used to name the entry within the stem.

catx, caty The position of the category selection control group (radio buttons or combo box). The defaults are 10 and 4.

catcx This argument sets the length of one item of the control group (calculated if omitted).

style This argument determines the style of the category dialog:

DROPDOWN Creates a drop-down list at the top (useful if there are many categories).

TOPLINE Draws a horizontal radio button group at the top of the client area.

WIZZARD Adds *Backward* and *Forward* buttons with IDs 11 and 12 to switch between category pages.

Without *DROPDOWN* or *TOPLINE*, the default category selection is done by a vertical radio button group, with the dialog pages to the right of the radio buttons.

cattable This argument can be used to set the category names separated by blanks. If omitted, set the category names in the *InitCategories* method [page 425].

catlabel This argument defines the label for the combo box in *DROPDOWN* style (default is "Page:")

catmax This argument sets the split point of the radio button group in default style, or the number of entries in the combo box drop-down list.

Example: This example creates a category dialog, using a combo box as the selection control:

```
dlg = MyCategoryDialog~new(MyData.,,,,"DROPDOWN", ,
        "Movies Cinemas Days Ticket","Dialog panel:")
dlg~createCenter(200, 180, "Let's Go to the Movies")
dlg~execute("SHOWTOP")
   ...
::class MyCategoryDialog subclass CategoryDialog
   ...
::method Movies     /* define the Movies page */
```

InitCategories

```
▶▶── aCategoryDialog~InitCategories ──────────────────────▶◀
```

The *InitCategories* method is called by *Init* to set the characteristics of the category dialog.

Protected: This method is protected.

Catalog: The *InitCategories* method should set up the *Catalog* directory with information about the layout and the behavior of the dialog. The directory entries are:

names   Array containing the names of the categories. The array is initialized with the names given in the *Init* method (argument *cattable*). These names are used as labels for selection control and as messages sent to the object to define the single pages. You have to provide a method for each category page—with the same name as the label in this directory—to define the dialog page using a resource or *Add...* methods. This is the only value of *Catalog* you have to set.

count   Number of categories.

handles   For internal use only.

id   For internal use only.

category   For internal use only.

page   A directory with the following entries:

font   Name of the font used for the dialog.
fsize   Size of the font.
style   Style of the dialog, see *Create* [page 394].
expected   Total number of expected dialog items of each category page (200).
btnwidth   Width of *Backward* and *Forward* push buttons (see *WIZZARD* option in *Init* method).
leftbtntext   Alternate label of *Backward* button.
rightbtntext   Alternate label of *Forward* button.

The next 4 entries should not be modified:
x   Horizontal position of the category pages relative to the parent dialog.
y   Vertical position of the category pages relative to the parent dialog.
w   Width of the category pages.
h   Height of the category pages.

Example: This example sets the category names to *Editor, Compiler, Linker*, and *Debugger*. The subclass of *CategoryDialog* must define four methods named after them.

```
::class MyCategoryDialog subclass CatergoryDialog

::method InitCategories
    self~catalog['names']= .array~of("Editor","Compiler",,
                                     "Linker","Debugger")
    self~catalog['page']['leftbtntext'] = "&Previous"
    self~catalog['page']['rightbtntext'] = "&Next"

::method Editor
    ...
::method Compiler
    ...
```

DefineDialog

The *DefineDialog* method is called after the dialog has been created. This method must not be overwritten in a subclass because it defines the layout of the window and calls the single page definition methods.

Protected This method is protected.

CategoryPage

The *CategoryPage* method adds controls to the base window of a Category Dialog. It is used to define the layout of the parent dialog that contains the single pages.

Protected This method is protected and should not be overwritten or called. Use the *InitCategories* method [page 425] to set up the dialog.

CreateCategoryDialog

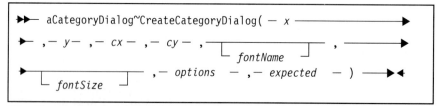

The *CreateCategoryDialog* method creates a single category page.

Protected This method is protected. It is called by another method and usually does not have to be called manually.

InitDialog

The *InitDialog* method is called after the Windows dialog has been created. It is useful for setting data fields and initializing combo and list boxes.

Protected   This method is protected.

GetSelectedPage

The *GetSelectedPage* method is used internally to return the currently selected page using the combo box or radio buttons (1 indicates the first page).

CurrentCategory

The *CurrentCategory* method returns the number of the current dialog page. The first page is numbered 1.

Example: This example tests the current page number:

```
if MyCategoryDialog~CurrentCategory=2 then do ...
```

NextPage

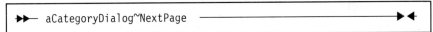

The *NextPage* method switches the dialog to the next category page.

PreviousPage

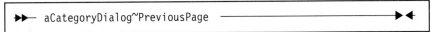

The *PreviousPage* method switches the dialog to the previous category page.

ChangePage

The *ChangePage* method switches the dialog to another page and returns the new page number. It is called by selection control, *Next-Page*, and *PreviousPage* to activate the selected page. *ChangePage* invokes *PageHasChanged* after the new page is activated.

Arguments: The only argument is:

newpage The page number of the new page (default is the page selected by the combo box or radio button).

Example: This example activates the second category page:

```
MyCategoryDialog~ChangePage(2)
```

PageHasChanged

```
▶▶── aCategoryDialog~PageHasChanged( ─ oldpage ─ , ─ newpage ─ ) ──▶◀
```

The *PageHasChanged* method is invoked whenever a new page is activated. The default implementation returns without an action. The user can overwrite this method to react to page changes.

Arguments: The arguments are:

oldpage The page number of the previous page.

newpage The page number of the new page.

StartIt

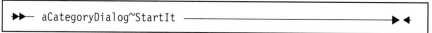

```
▶▶── aCategoryDialog~StartIt ──────────────▶◀
```

The *StartIt* method is called by the *Execute* method [page 329] to create a real Windows object based on the dialog template. You might overwrite it in your subclass, but be sure to forward the message to the parent method.

Protected This method is protected.

Connect... Methods

```
▶▶── aCategoryDialog~Connect...( ─ id, ─ fname ── ) ──────────▶◀
```

The *Connect...* methods connect dialog elements of certain types with an attribute or method. The *Connect...* methods should be placed into the user defined methods with the names of the categories defined in *InitCategories* [page 425]. The *Connect...* methods are defined for the *BaseDialog* class. For more information, see *Connect Methods* on page 333.

Arguments: The arguments are:

id The ID of the dialog item.

fname The name of the object attribute.

Example: This example connects an entry line in the *Movies* page with the *FIRSTNAME* object attribute:

```
::method InitCategories
  self~catalog['names'] = .array~of("Movies", ...)
...
::method Movies
  self~ConnectEntryLine(101, "FIRSTNAME")
```

Note: IDs for dialog elements need not be unique across all pages. However, IDs for buttons and list boxes that are connected to a method must be unique for the whole category dialog.

Methods for Dialog Items

The methods listed in this section deal with individual dialog items on one of the pages of the category dialog.

The methods correspond to methods with similar names of the *Base-Dialog* class; the word *Category* is inserted between the verb and the dialog item in the method name. For example, *AddCategoryComboEntry* for the *CategoryDialog* class has the same function as *AddComboEntry* of the *BaseDialog* class.

Note: The methods listed here have the same parameters as the corresponding methods of the *BaseDialog* class, with the number of the category page as an extra parameter.

Get and Set Methods

SetCategoryStaticText

```
▶▶── aCategoryDialog~SetCategoryStaticText( ────────────────────▶
▶── id, ─ data, ─ category ─  ) ──────────────────────────▶◀
```

For more information, see *SetStaticText* method [page 343].

GetCategoryEntryLine

```
▶▶── aCategoryDialog~GetCategoryEntryLine( id, ─ category ─) ───▶◀
```

For more information, see *GetEntryLine* method [page 344].

SetCategoryEntryLine

```
▶▶── aCategoryDialog~SetCategoryEntryLine( ─────────────────────▶
▶── id, ─ data, ─ category ─  ) ──────────────────────────▶◀
```

For more information, see *SetEntryLine* method [page 344].

GetCategoryListLine

For more information, see *GetListLine* method [page 344].

SetCategoryListLine

```
▶▶─ aCategoryDialog~SetCategoryListLine(─ id,─────────────────▶
▶─ data, ─ category ─  )  ─────────────────────────▶◀
```

For more information, see *SetListLine* method [page 345].

GetCategoryMultiList

```
▶▶─ aCategoryDialog~GetCategoryMultiList( ─ id,─ category ─)  ─▶◀
```

For more information, see *GetMultiList* method [page 345].

SetCategoryMultiList

For more information, see *SetMultiList* method [page 345].

GetCategoryComboLine

```
▶▶─ aCategoryDialog~GetCategoryComboLine(─ id,─ category ─)  ─▶◀
```

For more information, see *GetComboLine* method [page 346].

SetCategoryComboLine

For more information, see *SetComboLine* method [page 346].

GetCategoryRadioButton

```
▶▶─ aCategoryDialog~GetCategoryRadioButton( ─ id,─ category ─)  ─▶◀
```

For more information, see *GetRadioButton* method [page 346].

SetCategoryRadioButton

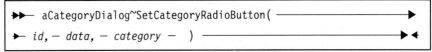

For more information, see *SetRadioButton* method [page 346].

GetCategoryCheckBox

For more information, see *GetCheckBox* method [page 346].

SetCategoryCheckBox

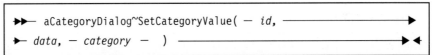

For more information, see *SetCheckBox* method [page 347].

GetCategoryValue

For more information, see *GetValue* method [page 347].

SetCategoryValue

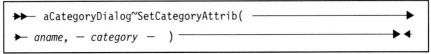

For more information, see *SetValue* method [page 347].

GetCategoryAttrib

```
▶▶─ aCategoryDialog~GetCategoryAttrib( ─ id, ─ category ─ ) ───▶◀
```

For more information, see *GetAttrib* method [page 348].

SetCategoryAttrib

```
▶▶─ aCategoryDialog~SetCategoryAttrib( ─────────────────▶
▶─ aname, ─ category ─ )  ──────────────────────────▶◀
```

For more information, see *SetAttrib* method [page 348].

Combo Box Methods

AddCategoryComboEntry

For more information, see *AddComboEntry* method [page 349].

Arguments: The arguments are:

    id   The ID of the combo box.

    data   The text string that is added to the combo box.

    category The category page number where the combo box is located.

Example: This example adds a text string to the list of the combo box 101 in the third category page.

```
MyCategoryDialog~AddCategoryComboEntry(101, ,
                    "I'm one of the choices", 3)
```

InsertCategoryComboEntry

For more information, see *InsertComboEntry* method [page 350].

DeleteCategoryComboEntry

For more information, see method *DeleteComboEntry* method [page 350].

FindCategoryComboEntry

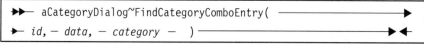

For more information, see *FindComboEntry* method [page 350].

GetCategoryComboItems

For more information, see *GetComboItems* method [page 351].

GetCurrentCategoryComboIndex

For more information, see *GetCurrentComboIndex* method [page 351].

SetCurrentCategoryComboIndex

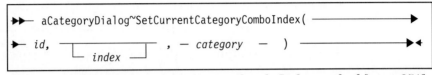

For more information, see *SetCurrentComboIndex* method [page 351].

ChangeCategoryComboEntry

For more information, see *ChangeComboEntry* method [page 352].

CategoryComboAddDirectory

For more information, see *ComboAddDirectory* method [page 352].

CategoryComboDrop

For more information, see *ComboDrop* method [page 353].

List Box Methods

AddCategoryListEntry

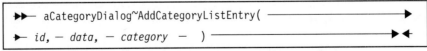

For more information, see *AddListEntry* method [page 353].

InsertCategoryListEntry

```
►►──  aCategoryDialog~InsertCategoryListEntry( ──────────────────►
►──  id, ─ item,  ─ data,  ─ category   ─  ) ──────────────────►◄
```

For more information, see *InsertListEntry* method [page 353].

DeleteCategoryListEntry

```
►►──  aCategoryDialog~DeleteCategoryListEntry( ──────────────────►
►──  id, ─ index,  ─ category   ─  ) ──────────────────────────►◄
```

For more information, see *DeleteListEntry* method [page 354].

FindCategoryListEntry

```
►►──  aCategoryDialog~FindCategoryListEntry( ────────────────────►
►──  id, ─ data,  ─ category   ─  ) ───────────────────────────►◄
```

For more information, see *FindListEntry* method [page 354].

GetCategoryListItems

```
►►──  aCategoryDialog~GetCategoryListItems(   ─ id, ─  category  ─) ─►◄
```

For more information, see *GetListItems* method [page 354].

GetCurrentCategoryListIndex

```
►►──  aCategoryDialog~GetCurrentCategoryListIndex(  ─ id, ─ category ─  )─►◄
```

For more information, see *GetCurrentListIndex* method [page 355].

SetCurrentCategoryListIndex

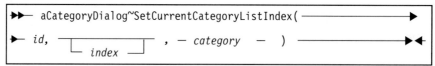

```
►►──  aCategoryDialog~SetCurrentCategoryListIndex( ──────────────►
►──  id, ─┬──────────┬─ , ─ category   ─  ) ──────────────────►◄
          └─ index ──┘
```

For more information, see *SetCurrentListIndex* method [page 355].

ChangeCategoryListEntry

```
►►──  aCategoryDialog~ChangeCategoryListEntry( ──────────────────►
►──  id, ─ item, ─ data, ─ category  ─  ) ───────────────────►◄
```

For more information, see *ChangeListEntry* method [page 355].

SetCategoryListTabulators

For more information, see *SetListTabulators* method [page 356].

CategoryListAddDirectory

For more information, see *ListAddDirectory* method [page 356].

CategoryListDrop

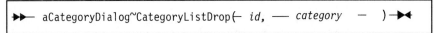

For more information, see *ListDrop* method [page 356].

Enable/Disable and Show/Hide Methods

EnableCategoryItem

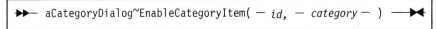

For more information, see *EnableItem* method [page 382].

DisableCategoryItem

For more information, see *DisableItem* method [page 382].

ShowCategoryItem

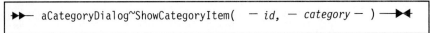

For more information, see *ShowItem* method [page 383].

HideCategoryItem

For more information, see *HideItem* method [page 383].

Standard Dialog Classes and Functions

The standard dialog classes are:

❑ TimedMessage
❑ InputBox
❑ PasswordBox
❑ IntegerBox
❑ MultiInputBox
❑ ListChoice
❑ MultiListChoice
❑ CheckList
❑ SingleSelection

Requires: Stddlg.cls is the source file for the standard dialog classes. Use the tokenized version of OODialog, oodialog.cls, to shorten your dialog's startup time.

```
::requires 'oodialog.cls'
```

Preparation: Standard dialogs are prepared by using the *new* method of the class, which in turn invokes the *Init* method. The parameters are described for the *Init* method of each class.

Execution: The dialog is then run by using the *Execute* method. *Execute* returns the user's input if the **OK** button is clicked and the null string if the **Cancel** button is clicked to terminate the dialog. If there is more than one return value, *Execute* returns the value 1 and stores the results in an attribute.

Functions: Each standard dialog is also available as a callable function.

Examples: See *Standard Dialog Classes* on page 154 and *Standard Dialogs* on page 312 for examples.

TimedMessage Class

The *TimeMessage* class shows a message window for a defined duration.

Requires: oodialog.cls is required to use this class.

Subclass: This class is a subclass of *UserDialog* (see page 391).

Execute: Returns 1.

The methods and function listed below are defined by this class.

Init

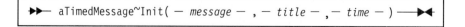

```
▶▶── aTimedMessage~Init( ─ message ─ , ─ title ─ , ─ time ─ ) ──▶◀
```

The *Init* method prepares the dialog.

Arguments: The arguments are:

    message A string that is displayed inside the window as a message.

    title A string that is displayed as the window title in the title bar of the dialog.

    time A number that determines how long (in milliseconds) the window is shown.

Example: This example shows a window with the *Information* title for a duration of three seconds:

```
dlg = .TimedMessage~New("Application will be started,",
                        "please wait", "Information", 3000)
dlg~Execute
drop dlg
```

DefineDialog

```
▶▶── aTimedMessage~DefineDialog ──────────────────────▶◀
```

The *DefineDialog* method is called by the *Create* method of the parent class, *UserDialog*, which in turn is called at the very beginning of *Execute*. You do not have to call it. However, you may want to overwrite it in your subclass to add more dialog controls to the window. If you overwrite it, you have to forward the message to the parent class by using the keyword *super*.

Example: This example shows how to subclass the *TimedMessage* class and how to add a background bitmap to the dialog window:

```
::class MyTimedMessage subclass TimedMessage
::method DefineDialog
    self~DefineDialog:super()
    self~BackgroundBitmap("mybackg.bmp", "USEPAL")
```

Execute

```
▶▶── aTimedMessage~Execute ──────────────────────────▶◀
```

The *Execute* method creates and shows the message window. After the given time (see *Init* method), it destroys the dialog automatically.

TimedMessage Function

OODialog provides a shortcut function to invoke a *TimedMessage* dialog as a function:

```
ret = TimedMessage("We are starting...","Please wait",3000)
```

The parameters are described in the *Init* method.

InputBox Class

The *InputBox* class provides a simple dialog with a title, a message, one entry line, an **OK**, and a **Cancel** push button.

Requires: Oodialog.cls is required to use this class.

Subclass: This class is a subclass of *UserDialog* (see page 391).

Execute: Returns the user's input.

The methods and function listed below are defined by this class.

Init

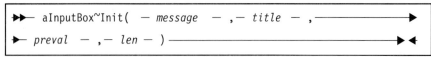

The *Init* method prepares the input dialog.

Arguments: The arguments are:

message   A text string that is displayed in the dialog.

title   A string that is displayed as the dialog's title in the title bar.

preval   A string to initialize the entry line. If you do not want to put any text in the entry line, just pass an empty string.

len   The width of the entry line in dialog units.

Example: This example shows a dialog with the *Input* title and an entry line:

```
dlg = .InputBox~New("Please enter your email address", ,
                    "Input", "user@host.domain", 150)
value = dlg~Execute
say "You entered:" value
drop dlg
```

DefineDialog

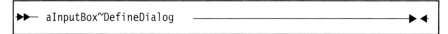

The *DefineDialog* method is called by the *Create* method of the parent class, *UserDialog*, which in turn is called at the very beginning of *Execute*. You do not have to call it. However, you may want to overwrite it in your subclass to add more dialog controls to the window. If you overwrite it, you have to forward the message to the parent class by using the keyword *super*.

AddLine

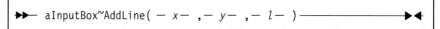

The *AddLine* method is used internally to add one entry line to the dialog.

Execute

The *Execute* method creates and shows the dialog. After termination, the value of the entry line is returned if the user clicks the **OK** button; a null string is returned if the user clicks on **Cancel**.

InputBox Function

OODialog provides a shortcut function to invoke an *InputBox* dialog as a function:

```
say "Your name:" InputBox("Please enter your name","Personal Data")
```

The parameters are described in the *Init* method.

PasswordBox Class

The *PasswordBox* class is an *InputBox* dialog with an entry line that echoes the keys with asterisks (*) instead of characters.

Requires: oodialog.cls is required to use this class.

Subclass: This class is a subclass of *InputBox* (see page 438).

Execute: Returns the user's password.

The methods are the same as for *InputBox*, with the exception of *AddLine*.

AddLine

The *AddLine* overwrites the same method of the parent class, *Input-Box*, by using a password entry line instead of a simple entry line.

PasswordBox Function

OODialog provides a shortcut function to invoke a *PasswordBox* dialog as a function:

```
pwd = PasswordBox("Please enter your password","Security")
```

The parameters are described in the *Init* method of the *InputBox* class.

IntegerBox Class

The *IntegerBox* class is an *InputBox* dialog whose entry line allows only numerical data.

Requires: oodialog.cls is required to use this class.

Subclass: This class is a subclass of *InputBox* (see page 438).

Execute: Returns the user's numeric input.

The methods are the same as for *InputBox*, with the exception of *Validate*.

Validate

The only method this subclass overwrites is *Validate*, which is one of the automatically called methods of *UserDialog*. It is invoked by the *OK* method, which in turn is called in response to a push button event. This method checks whether or not the entry line contains a valid numerical value. If the value is invalid, a message window is displayed.

IntegerBox Function

OODialog provides a shortcut function to invoke an *IntegerBox* dialog as a function:

```
say "Your age:" IntegerBox("Please enter your age","Personal Data")
```

The parameters are described in the *Init* method of the *InputBox* class.

MultiInputBox Class

The *MultiInputBox* class is a dialog that provides a title, a message, and one or more entry lines. After execution of this dialog you can access the values of the entry lines.

Requires: oodialog.cls is required to use this class.

Subclass: This class is a subclass of *UserDialog* (see page 391).

Execute: Returns 1 (if **OK** was clicked). The values entered by the user are stored in attributes matching the labels of the entry lines.

The methods are the same as for the *InputBox Class* method [page 438] class, with the exception of *Init*.

Init

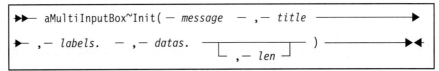

The *Init* method is called automatically whenever a new instance of this class is created. It prepares the dialog.

Arguments: The arguments are:

message A text string that is displayed on top of the entry lines. Use it to give the user advice on what to do.

title A text string that is displayed in the title bar.

labels. A stem variable containing strings that are used as labels on the left side of the entry lines. *Labels.1* becomes the label for the first entry line, *labels.2* for the second, and so forth.

datas. A stem variable (do not forget the trailing period) containing strings that are used to initialize the entry lines. *Datas.101* is the data for the first entry line.

len The length of the entry lines. All entry lines get the same length.

Example: This example creates a four-line input box. The data entered is stored in the object attributes that are displayed after dialog execution.

```
lab.1 = "&First name"  ;     lab.2 = "&Last name "
lab.3 = "&Street and City" ; lab.4 = "&Profession"
addr.101 = "Ingo Holder" ; addr.102 = "" ; addr.103 = ""
addr.104 = "Developer in the GSDL Boeblingen"
dlg = .MultiInputBox~new("Please enter your address", ,
                         "Your Address", lab., addr.)
if dlg~execute = 1 then do
  say "The address is:"
  say dlg~firstname dlg~lastname
  say dlg~StreetandCity
  say dlg~Profession
end
```

MultiInputBox Function

OODialog provides a shortcut function to invoke a *MultiInputBox* dialog as a function:

```
res = MultiInputBox('Enter your address','Personal Data', ,
             .array~of("&First name","Last &name","&City"), ,
             .array~of("Ueli","Wahli",'San Jose'), 100)
```

```
              if res \= .NIL then do entry over res
                          say 'Address-line[]= ' entry
              end
```

The parameters are described in the *Init* method, but, instead of stems, arrays are passed into and returned from the function.

ListChoice Class

The *ListChoice* class provides a dialog with a list box, an **OK**, and a **Cancel** button. The selected item is returned if the **OK** push button is used to terminate the dialog.

Requires: oodialog.cls is required to use this class.

Subclass: This class is a subclass of *UserDialog* (see page 391).

Execute: Returns the user's choice or a null string.

The method and function listed below is defined by this class.

Init

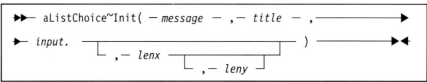

The *Init* method is used to initialize a new instance of this class.

Arguments: The arguments are:

message   A text string that is displayed on top of the list box. Use it to give the user advice on what to do.

title   A text string for the dialog's title.

input.   A stem variable (do not forget the trailing period) containing string values that are inserted into the list box.

lenx, leny The size of the list box in dialog units.

Example: This example creates a list choice dialog box where the user can select exactly one dessert:

```
lst.1 = "Cookies"
lst.2 = "Pie"; lst.3 = "Ice cream"; lst.4 = "Fruit"
dlg = .ListChoice~new("Select the dessert please", ,
                    "YourChoice",lst.)
say "Your ListChoice data:" dlg~execute
```

ListChoice Function

OODialog provides a shortcut function to invoke a *ListChoice* dialog as a function:

```
day = ListChoice('Select a day','My favorite day', ,
                .array~of("Monday","Tuesday","Wednesday","Thursday", ,
                    "Friday","Saturday","Sunday") )
say "Your favorite day is" day
```

The parameters are described in the *Init* method, but instead of an input stem, an array is passed into the function.

MultiListChoice Class

The *MultiListChoice* class is an extension of the *ListChoice* class. It makes it possible for the user to select more than one line at a time. The *Execute* method returns the selected items' indexes separated by blank spaces. The first item has index 1.

Requires: oodialog.cls is required to use this class.

Subclass: This class is a subclass of *ListChoice* (see page 442).

Execute: Returns the index numbers of the entries selected.

The methods are the same as for *ListChoice*, except that *Execute* returns the index numbers of the selected entries.

Example: This example creates a multiple list choice box where the user can select multiple entries:

```
lst.1 = "Monday" ;   lst.2 = "Tuesday" ; lst.3 = "Wednesday"
lst.4 = "Thursday" ; lst.5 = "Friday" ;  lst.6 = "Saturday"
lst.7 = "Sunday"
dlg = .MultiListChoice~new("Select the days you are" ,
                "working this week", "YourMultipleChoice",lst.)
s = dlg~execute
if s \= 0 then do while s \= ''
                parse var s res s
                say lst.res
            end
```

MultiListChoice Function

OODialog provides a shortcut function to invoke a *MultiListChoice* dialog as a function:

```
days = MultiListChoice('Select days','My TV Days', ,
                .array~of("Monday","Tuesday","Wednesday", ,
                    "Thursday","Friday","Saturday","Sunday") )
if days \= .NIL then do day over days
                say 'TV day =' day
            end
```

The parameters are described in the *Init* method, but, instead of stems, arrays are passed into and returned from the function. The return array contains the values of the selected items.

CheckList Class

The *CheckList* class is a dialog with a group of one or more check boxes.

Requires: oodialog.cls is required to use this class.

Subclass: This class is a subclass of *UserDialog* (see page 391).

Execute: Returns 1 (if **OK** was clicked). The check boxes selected by the user are marked in a stem variable with the value 1.

The method and function listed below is defined by this class.

Init

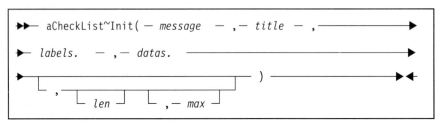

The *Init* method is used to initialize a new instance of this class.

Arguments: The arguments are:

message A text string that is displayed on top of the check box group. Use it to give the user advice on what to do.

title A text string for the dialog's title.

labels. A stem variable (do not forget the trailing period) containing all the labels for the check boxes.

datas. This argument is a stem variable (do not forget the trailing period) that contains the result of execution. You can also use it to preselect the check boxes. The first check box relates to stem item 101, the second to 102, and so forth. A value of 1 indicates *selected*, and a value of 0 indicates *deselected*.

For example, *Datas.103=1* indicates that there is a check mark on the third box.

len Determines the length of the check boxes and labels. If omitted, the size is calculated to fit the largest label.

max	The maximum number of check boxes in one column. If there are more check boxes than *max*—that is *labels.* has more items than the value of *max*—this method continues with a new column.
Example:	This example creates and shows a dialog with seven check boxes:

```
lst.1 = "Monday" ;  lst.2 = "Tuesday"; lst.3 = "Wednesday"
lst.4 = "Thursday"; lst.5 = "Friday";  lst.6 = "Saturday"
lst.7 = "Sunday"
do i = 101 to 107
   chk.i = 0
end
dlg = .CheckList~new("Please select a day!", ,
                    "Day of week",lst., chk.)
if dlg~execute = 1 then do
   say "You selected the following day(s): "
   do i = 101 to 107
      a = i-100
      if chk.i = 1 then say lst.a
   end
end
```

CheckList Function

OODialog provides a shortcut function to invoke a *CheckList* dialog as a function:

```
weekdays = .array~of("Monday","Tuesday","Wednesday", ,
                    "Thursday","Friday","Saturday","Sunday")
days = CheckList('Check the days','Working Days',weekdays)
if days \= .NIL then do i = 1 to days~items
                     if days[i] then say 'Working day =' weekdays[i]
              end
```

The parameters are described in the *Init* method, but, instead of stems, arrays are passed into and returned from the function.

SingleSelection Class

The *SingleSelection* class shows a dialog that has a group of radio buttons. The user can select only one item of the group.

Requires:	oodialog.cls is required to use this class.
Subclass:	This class is a subclass of *UserDialog* (see page 391).
Execute:	Returns the number of the radio button selected.

The method and function listed below is defined by this class.

Init

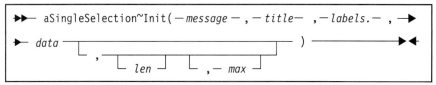

The *Init* method is used to initialize a new instance of this class.

Arguments: The arguments are:

message A text string that is displayed on top of the radio button group. Use it to give the user advice on what to do.

title A text string for the title bar.

labels. This argument is a stem variable containing all labels for the radio buttons.

data You can use this argument to preselect one radio button. A value of 1 selects the first radio button; 2 the second; and so forth.

len Determines the length of the check boxes and labels. If omitted, the size is calculated to fit the largest label.

max The maximum number of radio buttons in one column. If there are more radio buttons than *max*—that is, *labels.* has more items than the value of *max*—this method continues with a new column.

Example: This example creates and executes a dialog that contains a two-column radio button group. The fifth radio button (the button with the label *May*) is preselected.

```
mon.1 = "January" ; mon.2 = "February" ; mon.3 = "March"
mon.4 = "April"   ; mon.5 = "May"      ; mon.6 = "June"
...
dlg = .SingleSelection~new("Please select a month!", ,
                           "Single Selection", mon., 5, , 6)
s = dlg~execute
say  "You Selected the month: " mon.s
```

SingleSelection Function

OODialog provides a shortcut function to invoke a *SingleSelection* dialog as a function:

```
months = .array~of("Jan","Feb","Mar","Apr","May","Jun",,
                   "Jul","Aug","Sep","Oct","Nov","Dec")
m = SingleSelection('Check it','Born in',months,12,,6)
say "Born in month" m '=' months[m]
```

The parameters are described in the *Init* method, but, instead of a stem, an array is passed into the function.

AnimatedButton Class

The *AnimatedButton* class provides the methods to implement an animated button within a dialog.

The attributes and methods are described briefly here. A sample program, oowalker.rex, is provided with the OODialog sample programs. See *Animation Demonstration* on page 311.

ParentDlg   Attribute holding the handle of the parent dialog.

Stopped   Animation ends when set to 1 (see *Stop* method).

Init   Initialize the animation parameters:

```
but = .AnimatedButton~new(buttonid,from,to, ,
                    movex,movey,sizex,sizey,delay, ,
                    startx,starty,parentdialog)
```

These values are stored in a stem variable:

sprite.buttonid ID of animation button.

sprite.from   Array of in-memory bitmap handles, or a bitmap resource ID in a DLL.

sprite.to   0 if *sprite.from* is an array, or a bitmap resource ID in a DLL.

sprite.movex   Size of one move horizontally (pixels).
sprite.movey   Size of one move vertically.
sprite.sizex   Horizontal size of all bitmaps (pixels).
sprite.sizey   Vertical size of all bitmaps.
sprite.delay   Time delay between moves (ms).

Startx and *starty* are the initial bitmap position, and *parentdialog* is stored in the *ParentDlg* attribute.

Two other values are initialized in the stem variable:

sprite.smooth   Set to 1 for smooth edge change (can be changed to 0 for a bouncy edge change).
sprite.step   Set to 1 as the step size between *sprite.from* and *sprite.to* for bitmaps in a DLL.

SetSprite   Set all *sprite.* animation values using a stem:

```
mysprite.from = .array~of(bmp1,bmp2,...)
mysprite.to = 0
mysprite.movex = ...
...
self~setSprite(mysprite.)
```

GetSprite   Retrieve the animation values into a stem:

```
self~getSprite(mysprite.)
```

SetFromTo   Set bitmap information (*sprite.from* and *sprite.to)*:

```
self~setFromTo(bmpfrom, bmpto)
```

SetMove	Set size of one move (*sprite.movex* and *sprite.movey*): ```self~setMove(movex, movey)```
SetDelay	Set delay between moves in milliseconds (*sprite.delay)*: ```self~setDelay(delay)```
SetSmooth	Set smooth (1) or bouncy (0) edges (*sprite.smooth)*: ```self~setSmooth(0)```

SetStep	Set the step size (*sprite.step)* between *sprite.from* and *sprite.to* for bitmaps in a DLL, for example, if bitmap resources are numbered 202, 204, 206, and so forth:
	```self~setFromTo(202,210)```
	```self~setStep(2)```

Run	Run the animation by going through all of the bitmaps until the dialog is stopped; invokes *MoveSeq:* ```self~run```
MoveSeq	Animate one sequence through all bitmaps in the given move steps; invokes *MovePos:* ```self~moveSeq```
MovePos	Move the bitmaps by the arguments: ```self~movePos(movex, movey)```
MoveTo	Move the bitmaps in the predefined steps to the given position; invokes *MoveSeq:* ```self~moveTo(posx, posy)```
SetPos	Set the new starting position of the bitmaps: ```self~setPos(newx, newy)```

GetPos	Retrieve the current position into a stem:
	```self~getPos(pos.)```
	```say 'pos=' pos.x pos.y```

ParentStopped	Check the parent dialog window and return its finished attribute (1 means finished).
Stop	Stop animation by setting the *stopped* attribute to 1.
HitRight	Invoked by run when the bitmap hits the right edge (returns 1 and bitmap starts at left again; you can return 0 and set the new position yourself).
HitLeft	Invoked when the bitmap hits the left edge (default action is to start at right again).
HitBottom	Invoked when the bitmap hits the bottom edge (default action is to start at top again).
HitTop	Invoked when the bitmap hits the top edge (default action is to start at bottom again).

To use an animated button, a dialog has to:

❑ Define an owner-drawn button, for example, in a resource file

❑ Load the bitmaps of the animation into memory using an array

❑ Initialize the animated button with the animation parameters

❑ Invoke the run method of the animated button

❑ Stop the animation and remove the bitmaps from memory

The dialog can also dynamically change the parameters (for example, the size of a move, or the speed) and overwrite actions, such as hitting an edge.

See the `oowalker.rex` and `oowalk2.rex` examples in `OODIALOG\SAMPLES`.

16

Windows Program Manager and Registry

Object REXX ships a file with two classes to access Windows system information:

WindowsProgramManager   Interacts with the Program Manager to create and delete program groups and shortcuts

WindowsRegistry   Interacts with the Registry to query, modify, add, and delete entries

The classes are defined in the `WINSYSTM.CLS` file in the Object REXX directory.

Windows Program Manager Class and Methods

You can use the ***WindowsProgramManager*** class to create program groups and shortcuts to access your programs.

The class is defined in the WINSYSTM.CLS file. Use a *::requires* statement to activate its function:

```
::requires "winsystm.cls"
```

The ***WindowsProgramManager*** class provides the following methods:

Init   Create an instance and load the required external function package:

```
mgr = .WindowsProgramManager~new
```

AddGroup   Add a program group to the *Programs* group of the desktop. If the group already exists, it is opened. The only argument is the name of the program group:

```
mgr~addGroup(name)
mgr~addGroup("Object REXX Redbook")
```

DeleteGroup Delete a program group from the desktop. The only argument is the name of the program group:

```
mgr~deleteGroup(name)
```

ShowGroup   Open a program group. The arguments are the name of the group, and, optionally, the style (*MIN*, *MAX*). If the style is omitted, the group is opened in normal size:

```
mgr~showGroup(name, ['MIN' | 'MAX'])
mgr~showGroup("Object REXX Redbook")
```

AddItem   Add a shortcut to a program group. The only required arguments are the name of the shortcut and the program to be invoked. Optional arguments are the name of an icon file, the icon number (default 0), and the working directory. The shortcut is placed in the last group used with either *AddGroup* or *ShowGroup*.

```
mgr~addItem(name,program,[iconfile],[iconno],[workdir])
mgr~addItem('OODialog Samples', ,
            'rexx oodialog\samples\sample.rex', ,
            'oodialog\samples\oodialog.ico ')
```

DeleteItem Delete a shortcut from the most recently used program group. The name of the shortcut is the only argument:

```
mgr~deleteItem(name)
mgr~deleteItem('OODialog Samples')
```

A sample program, desktop.rex, is provided in the OBJREXX\SAMPLES directory.

Windows Registry Class and Methods

You can use this **WindowsRegistry** class to query the registry and modify, add, and delete entries.

The class is defined in the WINSYSTM.CLS file. Use a *::requires* statement to activate its function:

```
::requires "winsystm.cls"
```

The **WindowsRegistry** class provides the following methods:

Init   Create an instance and load the required external function package. The current key is set to *HKEY_LOCAL_MACHINE*:

```
rg = .WindowsRegistry~new
```

Local_Machine Attribute containing the handle of root key *HKEY_LOCAL_MACHINE*:

```
locmach = rg~local_machine
```

Current_User Attribute containing the handle of root key *HKEY_CURRENT_USER*:

```
curuser = rg~current_user
```

Users   Attribute containing the handle of root key *HKEY_USERS*:

```
usrkey = rg~users
```

Classes_Root Attribute containing the handle of root key *HKEY_CLASSES_ROOT*:

```
usr = rg~classes_root
```

CurrentKey Attribute containing the handle of the current key. The current key is set by *Init*, *Create*, and *Open*:

```
key = rg~current_key
```

The *CurrentKey* is used if the key is omitted in other methods.

Create   Add a new subkey to the registry and return its handle. The arguments are the parent key and the new subkey. The parent key can be a root key or a key retrieved by using *Open*. If the parent key is omitted, the *CurrentKey* is used:

```
newkey = rg~create([parent],subkey)
objectrexxkey = rg~create(, 'OBJECTREXX')
newkey = rg~create(rg~local_machine, 'MyOwnKey')
```

Open   Open a subkey and return its handle. The arguments are the parent key (see *Create* for more information), the subkey, and access. Possible values for access are *ALL* (default)*; WRITE* (create subkeys, set values); *READ* (query subkeys and values); *QUERY* (values);

EXECUTE (key access, no subkey access); *NOTIFY* (change notification); and *LINK* (create symbolic links). More than one value can be specified, separated by a blank:

```
key = rg~open([parent],subkey,[access])
syskey = rg~open(rg~local_machine,'SYSTEM')
```

Close

Close a previously opened key. The only argument is the handle of the key:

```
rg~close([key])
rg~close(objectrexxkey)
```

It might take several seconds before all data is written to disk; use *Flush* to empty the cache.

List

Retrieve the list of subkeys for a given key in a stem variable. The parameters are the key handle and the name of the stem variable (including the period). The keys are returned as stem.1, stem.2, and so forth:

```
rg~list([key],stem.)
rg~list(objectrexxkey,orexxkeys.)
do i over orexxkeys.
    say orexxkeys.i
end
```

Query

Retrieve the values of a given key and return them in a stem variable. The suffixes are *class* (class name); *subkeys* (number of subkeys); *values* (number of value entries); and *date* and *time* (of last modification):

```
var. = rg~query([key])
myquery. = rg~query(objectrexxkey)
say "class="myquery.class "at" myquery.date
say "subkeys="myquery.subkeys "values="myquery.values
```

Delete

Delete a given subkey and all its subkeys and values:

```
rg~delete([key])
rg~delete(obectrexxkey)
```

ListValues

Retrieve all value entries of a given key and store them in a compound variable. The arguments are the key and the name of a compound variable (including the period). The suffixes of the compound variable are numbered starting with 1, and for each number the three values are the name (var.*i.name*), the data (var.*i.data*), and the type (var.*i.type*). The type is *NORMAL* for alphabetic values, *EXPAND* for expandable strings (for example, a PATH), *NONE* for no specified type, and *OTHER* for any other type (for example, binary):

```
rg~listValues([key],var.)
qstem. = rg~query(objectrexxkey)
rg~listvalues(objectrexxkey,lv.)
```

```
do i = 1 to qstem.values
    say "name of value:" lv.i.name "(type="lv.i.type")"
    if lv.i.type = 'NORMAL' then
        say "data of value:" lv.i.data
end
```

GetValue   Retrieve the data and type for the default or a named value of a given key. The arguments are the key and the name of the value. The result is a stem variable with suffixes *data* and *type*. The default value is returned if the name is blank or omitted:

```
var. = rg~getValue([key],[name])
myval. = rg~getvalue(,'filesystem') /* current key */
say "Type is" myval.type
if myval.type = 'NORMAL' then say "Value is" myval.data
myval. = rg~getvalue(mykey)
say "my default value is:" myval.data
```

SetValue   Set the default or a named value of a given key. The arguments are the key, the name of the value (omit or blank for the default value), the value itself, and the type (*NORMAL, EXPAND, NONE, OTHER*):

```
rg~setValue([key],[name],value,[type])
rg~setvalue(objectrexxkey,, 'My default','NORMAL')
rg~setvalue(objectrexxkey,'VERSION','1.0')
```

DeleteValue   Delete the default or a named value for a given key. The arguments are the key and the name (or blank for the default value):

```
rg~deleteValue([key],[name])
rg~deletevalue(objectrexxkey)
```

Connect   Open a key, either *HKEY_LOCAL_MACHINE* or HKEY_USERS, on a remote computer. The arguments are the key and the computer name:

```
rg~connect([key],computername)
```

Save   Save the entries of a given key into a file. The arguments are the key and the name of the file:

```
rg~save([key],filename)
rg~save(objectrexxkey, '\objrexx\orexx')
```

Do not use a file extension on a FAT file system.

Load   Load the entries of a given key under *HKEY_USER* or *HKEY_LOCAL_MACHINE* from a file. Registry information is stored in the form of a hive; that is, a discrete body of keys, subkeys, and values that is rooted at the top of the registry hierarchy. A hive is backed by a single file. The arguments are the key and the name of the file:

```
rg~load([key],filename)
rg~load(aKey, 'xxxxxxx')
```

Restore   Restore a key from a file. The arguments are a key, the name of the file, and optionally the *VOLATILE* keyword:

```
rg~restore([key],filename,['VOLATILE'])
rg~restore(objectrexxkey,'\objrexx\orexx')
```

The *VOLATILE* keyword creates a new memory-only set of registry information that is valid only until the system is restarted.

Replace   Replace the backup file of a subkey with a new file. The values in the new file become active when the system is restarted. The arguments are a key, a subkey, the name of the new file, and the name of the old file:

```
rg~replace([key],subkey,newfilename,oldfilename)
```

Unload   Remove a subkey and its dependents from the registry but do not modify the file containing the registry information. The arguments are a parent key and the subkey to be removed:

```
rg~unload([key],subkey)
```

Flush   Force the system to write the cache buffer of a given key to disk:

```
rg~flush([key])
```

Two sample programs, reg_nt.rex and reg_95.rex, are provided in the OBJREXX\SAMPLES directory.

17

Object REXX Demonstration Workbench

Object REXX provides a workbench that can be used to debug Object REXX programs. You can interactively run programs, watch and modify values of variables, set breakpoints, and trace programs.

The workbench is included with Object REXX on the CD as a demonstration version, without the full function that will be included in a future Object REXX for Windows product.

Starting the Object REXX Workbench

You can invoke the workbench program, ORXWB.EXE, directly or through the shortcut provided in the Object REXX program group.

Figure 160 show the initial layout of the workbench.

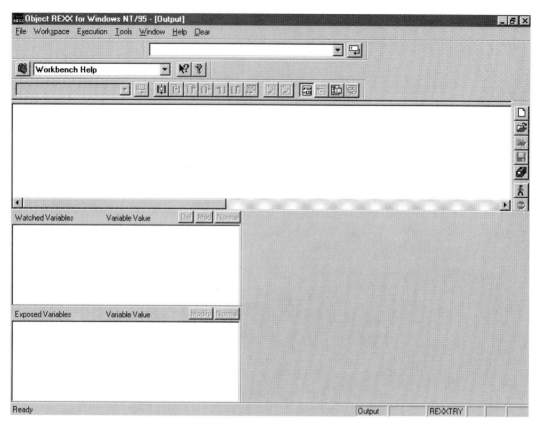

Figure 160. *Object REXX Workbench Layout*

You can tailor the layout of the windows and button bars (Tools, Input, Edit, Help, and Trace) by moving them to another position. Figure 161 shows the button bars floating freely in the window.

Figure 161. *Object REXX Workbench Button Bars*

Debugging a Program with the Workbench

Open a program, using the *File* pull-down, and load it into the edit window. Now you can debug the program:

❑ Place the cursor in front of a line and set a breakpoint, using the *Execution* pull-down or the push button in the trace bar.

❑ Highlight a variable, modify its value, or add it to the watch window (right mouse button or *Execution* pull-down).

❑ Set trace on or off (trace output is in a separate window).

❑ Place the cursor on a program line and start execution, using *Run to Cursor* (*Execution* pull-down or trace bar push button).

Figure 162 shows the program source with a breakpoint set (triangle) and the current point of execution (circle). Watched variables and currently exposed variables are displayed in windows at the bottom.

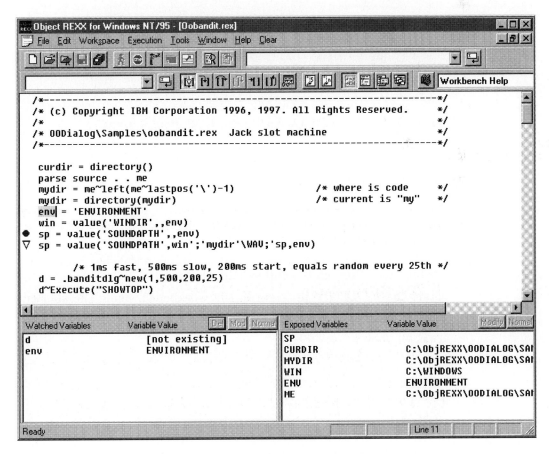

Figure 162. *Object REXX Workbench Program Execution*

When debugging OODialog programs, you can use the nontokenized version of `oodialog.cls` by setting an additional path in *Execution Settings* (see Figure 163).

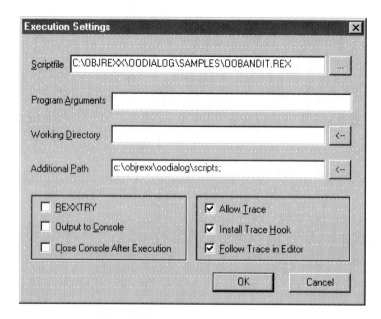

Figure 163. *Object REXX Workbench Execution Settings*

Workbench Function

The demonstration version of the workbench does not include the functions of saving the source after modifications and saving the workbench layout.

Explore the workbench, using small programs and learn more about its functions through the online help facility.

Start the *REXXTRY* program in the workbench, using the shortcut provided in the Object REXX program group. The scrolling and recall facilities of the workbench make *REXXTRY* easier to use than in a DOS window.

Part 6

Appendixes

A

New Features in Object REXX and Migration

Object REXX for Windows NT and Windows 95 is a superset of classic REXX and is compatible with Object REXX for OS/2. Therefore, most REXX programs will run unchanged using Object REXX. Some small incompatibilities that may arise when migrating existing programs are discussed at the end of this chapter, in *Migration Considerations* on page 485.

Many enhancements have been built into Object REXX. The sample applications presented in this book demonstrate in detail the OO support. In this chapter, we summarize the OO support and discuss the other enhancements in detail.

Object REXX provides the following enhancements:

❏ A full set of OO facilities

➢ Classes and methods with inheritance and polymorphism
➢ Metaclasses and Mixin classes
➢ A new operator, ~, to invoke methods

> ➤ Concurrency—the ability to run code easily in parallel
> ➤ New special variables (*self, super*)
> ➤ Special and built-in objects

❑ A set of directives that permit

> ➤ Definition of classes and methods (*::class* and *::method*)
> ➤ Embedding of source files (*::requires*)
> ➤ Creation of improved subroutines with private variables (*::routine*)

❑ The *REXXC* utility, which can be used to distribute programs without source and to speed up load time

❑ New and enhanced instructions

❑ New and enhanced built-in functions

❑ New condition traps

❑ New REXX utilities, including a set of Windows specific functions (*SysSystemDirectory, SysVolumeLabel,* and *SysPulseEventStem*)

❑ An Object REXX class for the Windows **Program Manager** to create program groups and icons

❑ An Object REXX class for the Windows **Registry** to query and update the content

Syntax diagrams are used extensively to describe the detailed parameters of the new and enhanced instructions. The structure of the syntax diagrams is explained in Appendix C, *Definition for Syntax Diagram Structure,* on page 529.

Object-Oriented Facilities

The set of object-oriented facilities is so large that we cannot describe them all in detail here. Our intention is to add a few concepts and facilities not described in the earlier chapters of this book. We encourage study of the chapters on OO facilities in the Object REXX Reference manual.

New Special Variables

There are two new special variables:

self   The object of the currently running method. Used to invoke other methods on the same object (*self~display*) or to pass as a parameter to a method of another object (*.Customer~addVehicle(self)*).

super   The superclass (parent in inheritance hierarchy) of the current object. Used to invoke a method in the superclass, in many cases the method of the same name. For example, in the *init* method of a class it is common to invoke the *init* method of the parent (*self~init:super*).

Special and Built-In Objects

Object REXX provides a set of objects that are always available:

.environment

The global environment object. It contains all predefined class objects (*.Object*, *.String*, etc.) and some other objects (*.true*, *.false*, *.nil*). It can be used for communication within one process in a Windows system.

.nil   The *NIL* object, an object that does not contain any data. It can be used to test for nonexistent data—for example, in an array:

```
if myarray[i] = .nil then ...
```

.local   The local environment object. It contains default input/output streams (*.input*, *.output*, *.error*) and can be used for communicating among parts of the application within one process (see *The Local Directory* on page 225).

.methods   A directory of methods defined in the current program using *::method* directives without an associated class.

.rs   The return code from any executed command, with values of -1 (failure), 1 (error), 0 (OK).

Directives

Object REXX provides four directives, two to define classes and methods, one to define external routines, and one to implement dependencies between source files.

Directives are nonexecutable and must be placed at the end of the source file. They are processed first to set up a program's classes, methods, and routines.

Class Directive

The *::class* directive defines a new class. Several options are available:

public   Makes the class available in all programs that have a *::requires* directive for this program

subclass   Inherits from a parent class

inherit	Inherits from other mixin classes
mixinclass	Defines a mixin class for inheritance
metaclass	Defines a meta class for additional class methods

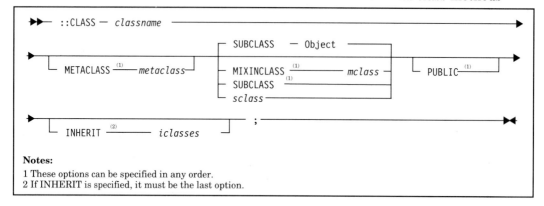

Notes:

1 These options can be specified in any order.
2 If INHERIT is specified, it must be the last option.

Method Directive

The *::method* directive defines a method. Multiple method directives are usually placed directly after the class directive. All options except *protected* are described in this redbook. The protected option deals with the Security Manager, an Object REXX feature that has not been used in this redbook.

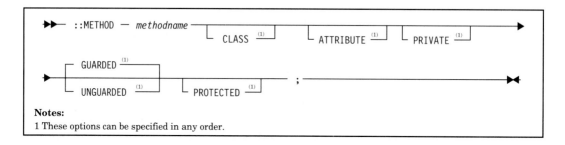

Notes:

1 These options can be specified in any order.

Routine Directive

The *::routine* directive defines a callable subroutine. Such routines behave like external routines but are in the search order before external routines (after internal ones). The only option is *public*, which makes the routine available to all programs with a *::requires* directive for this program.

Requires Directive

The *::requires* directive specifies that a program requires access to another source program. In many cases, the other program contains class definitions needed for execution. The *::requires* directive allows the building of libraries of reusable code and the implementation of configuration management of REXX programs (see Chapter 11, *Configuration Management with Object REXX,* on page 215). The *::requires* directives must precede all other directives.

```
▶▶── ::REQUIRES ─────── programname ─────── ; ─────────────────────────────▶◀
```

The REXXC Utility

The *REXXC* utility can be used to transform a source program into an executable image that can be distributed without the source code:

```
REXXC inputfile outputfile
```

When there are multiple programs that call each other, it is necessary to keep the same file names after transformation. There are basically two approaches:

❑ Use the same names for the output files but place them in a different matching directory structure.

❑ Transform the source into an output file and, when successful, save the source under a different name and rename the output to the name of the original source. (With long names support, the source can be saved as *filename.ext.rxc*, for example, as implemented in the *REXXCX* command in the Xamples subdirectory of the car dealer application.)

See *Tokenizing Object REXX Programs* on page 75 for more information.

New and Enhanced Instructions

The new instructions added to Object REXX are:

❑ EXPOSE
❑ FORWARD
❑ GUARD
❑ RAISE
❑ REPLY
❑ USE

The parameters for four old instructions have been enhanced:

- ❑ CALL
- ❑ DO
- ❑ PARSE
- ❑ SIGNAL

The new and changed instructions are discussed in alphabetical order.

CALL (Enhanced)

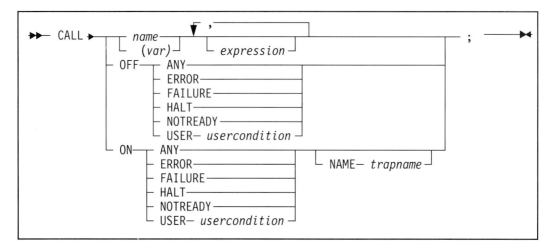

The first new feature on the CALL instruction is that (*var*) can now be used instead of *name* to specify the routine to be called. The variable is evaluated first, and the resulting value is used as the target of the CALL instruction. Observe that this value is not changed to upper-case, so it must exactly match the label to be called. In this small example, there are three different ways of calling internal and external routines:

```
/* TstCALL.CMD - Test of "CALL (var)" instruction */
Call label calldata        /* label is a symbol (constant) */
label = 'label'
Do 2
    Call (label) calldata  /* label is a variable */
    label = 'newlabel'     /* - that changes */
End
Call "label" calldata      /* label is a string */
exit
label:
    Say "The first call was made to label - label:"
    return
"label":
    Say 'The second call was made to label - "label":'
    return
"newlabel":
    Say 'The third call was made to label - "newlabel":'
    return
```

The last call to "label" bypasses any search for an internal routine and calls an external command file named LABEL.CMD:

```
/* LABEL.CMD - test with external routine */
    Say 'The fourth call was made to external routine - LABEL.CMD'
    return
```

Running the TstCALL.CMD gave the expected result. The little *do* loop (Do 2) caused the same call statement to call two different routines. The variable *label* was evaluated correctly.

```
[C:\]TstCALL
The first call was made to label -> label:
The second call was made to label -> "label":
The third call was made to label -> "newlabel":
The fourth call was made to external routine -> LABEL.CMD
```

Also, the CALL instruction has two new conditions, *ANY* and *USER*, added. They are explained in *SIGNAL (Enhanced)* on page 474, and we will come back to these in connection with the rest of the new condition traps in *New Condition Traps* on page 480.

DO (Enhanced)

The DO instruction has a new repetitor function added that will make it possible to loop through all values of a stem object or any other collection that provides a *makearray* method. The repetitor is coded as *control2 OVER collection* in the syntax diagram below.

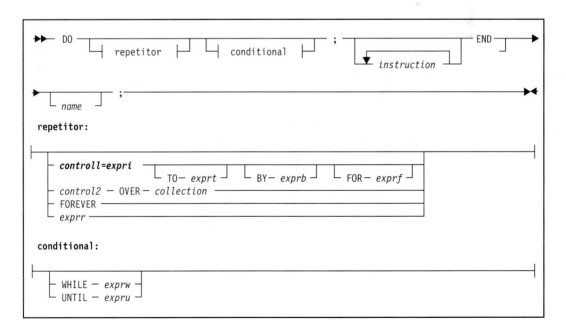

The *DO xvar OVER Stemx.* sets the variable *xvar* to each one of the member names of the *Stemx.* stem object. This is very useful because we no longer have to know the names of the tails in a stem variable. The *DO .. OVER* gives all the tails, but in any order, so do not rely on the order.

DO OVER works very well with the collection classes of Object REXX, such as lists, arrays, sets, tables, bags, and relations. The car dealer application uses it extensively.

EXPOSE (New)

The *EXPOSE* instruction is new for Object REXX. Before, we had the *EXPOSE* option on the *PROCEDURE* instruction. The *PROCEDURE* instruction protected the variables of the calling routine. If the routine needed access to some of those variables, we used the *EXPOSE* option to make them available. The new *EXPOSE* instruction has a very similar function for the variables of an object. It is used to expose the instance or class variables of a method from the object's variable pool. The *EXPOSE* instruction can be used only in a method and, if used, it must be the first instruction after the *::method* directive.

FORWARD (New)

This new instruction is used to forward a message that caused the currently active method to start running. Parts of the forwarded message can be changed by the different options on the *FORWARD* instruction. Target object, arguments, and even the message name can be changed.

One use of *FORWARD* is to pass on a message to the superclass if the current method is overriding a method of that class but still wants that method to run. The *CONTINUE* option decides whether a return should be made to the forwarding method. It also decides how any result should be handled. The *FORWARD* instruction causes no concurrency—the forwarding method waits for the return (if *CONTINUE* is specified) or exits directly after forwarding the message.

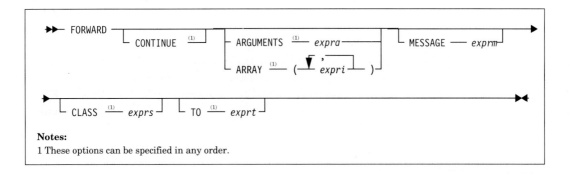

Notes:
1 These options can be specified in any order.

GUARD (New)

The *GUARD* instruction is used to control access to an object's variable pool. The normal state for an object is that it is guarded from concurrent use by different methods. Sometimes we want to let multiple methods share the use of one object's variable pool. This is done by using either *methodname~setunguarded* or *::method methodname unguarded*. The GUARD instruction can now be used to temporarily lock out concurrent use of the object's variable pool. The option *when expression* can make it conditional.

An example of GUARD is used in the fork class of the philosophers' forks (see Figure 131 on page 275).

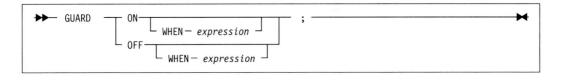

PARSE (Enhanced)

The *PARSE* instruction has two small enhancements. The *upper* option is now complemented with a *lower* option; thus, any character string to be parsed is first translated to lowercase. The other new option—*caseless*—causes any matching done during parsing to be independent of case; a letter in uppercase is thus equal to the same letter in lowercase.

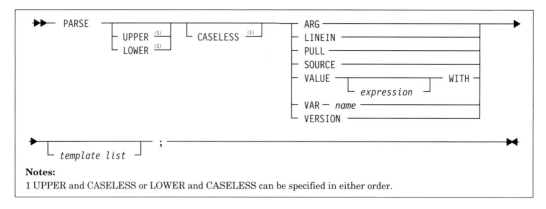

Notes:

1 UPPER and CASELESS or LOWER and CASELESS can be specified in either order.

Examples:

```
parse value 'AbCdEfGhIjKlM' with p1 'FgH' p2
  ===> p1 = 'AbCdEfGhIjKlM', p2 = ''
parse caseless value 'AbCdEfGhIjKlM' with p1 'FgH' p2
  ===> p1 = 'AbCdE', p2 = 'IjKlM'
```

RAISE (New)

Traps are normally created totally involuntarily. *RAISE* is a new instruction that enables the programmer to create traps in a controlled way.

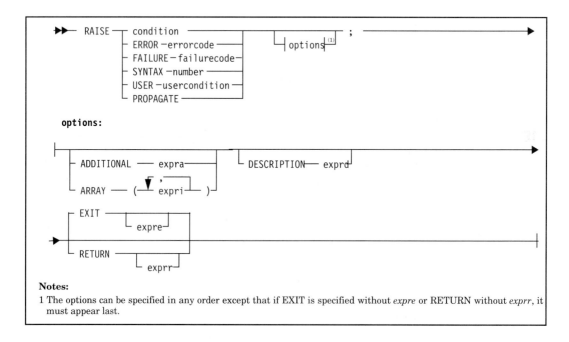

Notes:

1 The options can be specified in any order except that if EXIT is specified without *expre* or RETURN without *exprr*, it must appear last.

One nice use of the *RAISE* instruction is to have a routine for catching condition traps for methods without having to add a lot of code to each method.

The following is an example of *raise propagate*:

```
/* TstRaise.Cmd - Test the new RAISE instruction */
   signal on any
   tm = .myTest~new
   say tm~myMethod
   exit
any:
   signal off any
   if .local["M.SIGL"] <> .nil then do
      sigl = .local["M.SIGL"]
      .local["M.SIGL"] = .nil
      end
   if var('rc')
      then say 'REXX ['condition("C")'] error' rc 'in line' sigl':' ,
               "ERRORTEXT"(rc)
      else say 'REXX ['condition("C")'] error in line' sigl
   say 'The Source Line is:'"SOURCELINE"(sigl)
   exit
::class myTest
::method init
   return
::method myMethod
   signal on any
   a = 'xyz'
   c = a+2     /* This line causes SYNTAX error */
   return
any:
   .local["M.SIGL"] = sigl
   raise propagate
===> Result:
   REXX [SYNTAX] error 41 in line 25: Bad arithmetic conversion
   The Source Line is:   c = a+2
```

REPLY (New)

REPLY is used to send an early reply from a method to the caller, removing the method from the current activity stack and letting it run concurrently with the caller. This is one of the ways to cause concurrency under Object REXX. See *Examples of Early Reply with Unguarded and Guarded Methods* on page 270. Observe that *REPLY* can be used only within methods, and it can be executed only once within a method.

```
>>──REPLY──┬──────────────┬──;──────────────────────────────><
           └─ expression ─┘
```

SIGNAL (Enhanced)

SIGNAL is used to cause an *abnormal* change in the flow of control or, if *ON* or *OFF* is specified, it controls the trapping of specific conditions. In Object REXX, some new conditions have been added:

❏ *ANY*—traps any condition not specifically enabled by the other condition settings

❏ *LOSTDIGITS*—detects when a number in an arithmetic operation has more digits than the current setting of *NUMERIC DIGITS*

❏ *NOMETHOD*—detects when an object receives an unknown message and there is no *unknown* method to receive it

❏ *NOSTRING*—detects when a string value is required from an object and it is not supplied

❏ *USER usercondition*—allows the setup of user conditions invokable by the *RAISE* instruction that specifies the same *usercondition* name.

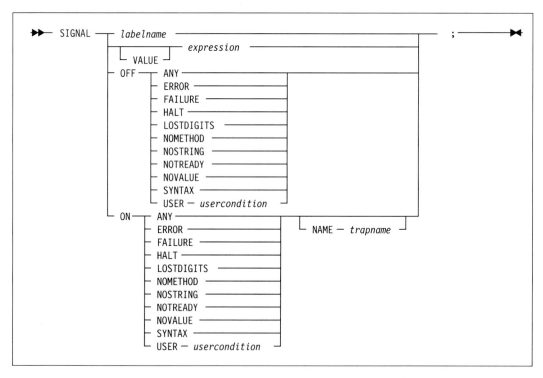

For more information on conditions and *SIGNAL*, see *CALL/SIGNAL (Enhanced)* on page 480.

USE (New)

USE ARG retrieves the argument objects provided to a program, routine, function, or method. The objects are assigned into variables.

The difference between *USE ARG* and *PARSE ARG* is that *PARSE ARG* (and *ARG*) accesses and parses the string values of the arguments, but *USE ARG* allows nonstring arguments and does a one-to-one assignment of arguments to REXX variables. This is the way we pass objects (not only strings) between routines.

New and Enhanced Built-In Functions

Object REXX has three new built-in functions and some changes to nine old ones.

ARG (Enhanced)

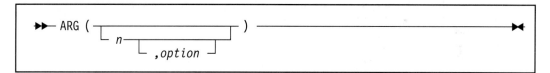

ARG has two new options. The first is *array*, which returns the arguments in the form of an array object. The array index corresponds with the argument position. If the option *n* is used, the index starts at the specified position. If any argument is omitted, the corresponding index is absent. The second new option is *normal*, which returns the *nth* argument, if it exists, or the null string otherwise.

CHANGESTR (New)

CHANGESTR returns a copy of *haystack*, in which *newneedle* replaces all occurrences of *needle*.

CONDITION (Enhanced)

```
►►─ CONDITION (─┬─────────┬─ ) ─────────────────────────────────►◄
                └ option ┘
```

CONDITION has two new options. The *additional* option makes it possible to get some additional object information on certain conditions (*NOMETHOD, NOSTRING, NOTREADY, SYNTAX,* and *USER*). The second new option, *object*, returns an object containing all the information about the current trapped condition. This can be used to create a generalized trap-and-debug routine, as described in *CALL/SIGNAL (Enhanced)* on page 480.

COUNTSTR (New)

```
►►─ COUNTSTR (needle,haystack ) ─────────────────────────────────►◄
```

COUNTSTR returns a count of the nonoverlapping occurrences of *needle* in *haystack*. Here is one example:

```
countstr('11','101111101110')   --> 3   /* observe - no overlap */
```

DATATYPE (Enhanced)

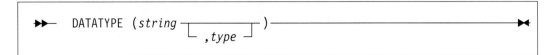

```
►►─ DATATYPE (string ─┬──────┬─ ) ───────────────────────────────►◄
                      └ ,type ┘
```

DATATYPE has two new types. The first one is *variable*. As an example, *DATATYPE(xyz,'v')* would return 1 if *xyz* could be on the left-hand side of an assignment without causing a *SYNTAX* condition.

The second new type is *9 Digits*. The description specifies that this type returns 1 if *DATATYPE(string,'w')* would return 1 when *NUMERIC DIGITS* is set to 9. Thus if *NUMERIC DIGITS* is larger than 9, type *9* returns 0 for any whole number larger than 9 digits. Here is an example:

```
numeric digits 12
datatype('1234567890,'W')   --> 1   /* less than digits() */
datatype('1234567890,'9')   --> 0   /* more than 9 digits */
```

DATE (Enhanced)

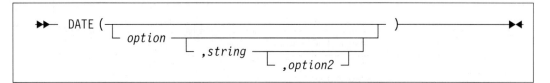

DATE is now enhanced so that it is possible to work with a date other than the current one. The *string* allows input of a date to translate from one form to another. If the input string is not in the default format (*dd mon yyyy*), *option2* can be used to specify the format to Object REXX. For example, if you want to know how many days it is to your next birthday, enter the following statement in a *REXXTRY* window (*96/mm/dd* is your birthday):

```
say date('B','96/mm/dd','O') - date('B') 'days'
```

Two of the old options have different names. *Basedate* is now only *base* and *sorted* is changed to *standard*.

STREAM (Enhanced)

In Object REXX, input and output can be handled two ways. The old way is to use the built-in functions (*STREAM, LINES, LINEIN, LINEOUT, CHARIN,* and *CHAROUT*), which still work. *STREAM* has a lot of new command strings that we will look at, but we will not go through them all in detail. The new way is to use the new stream class (*.Stream*) in Object REXX, in which all of the built-in functions are available through methods.

Whichever we choose, we must remember not to mix the two ways for the same stream object. When we use the built-in I/O functions, the language processor creates a stream object and maintains it for us. If we use the *new* method to create a stream object, the object is returned to and maintained by our own program.

Because of this, when Object REXX stream methods and stream built-in functions refer to the same file from the same program, there are two separate stream objects with different read and write pointers. This will cause unpredictable results if the stream is written to by using both methods and built-in functions.

So what are the changes to *STREAM* that both methods and functions can use:

1. *OPEN* has some new options. First, Object REXX now supports separate pointers for read and write. The default is to open for both read and write. That can also be specified by option *both*, in case we want to point it out or add one of the new position options, *append* or *replace*. The position options are also valid if we open for *WRITE*.

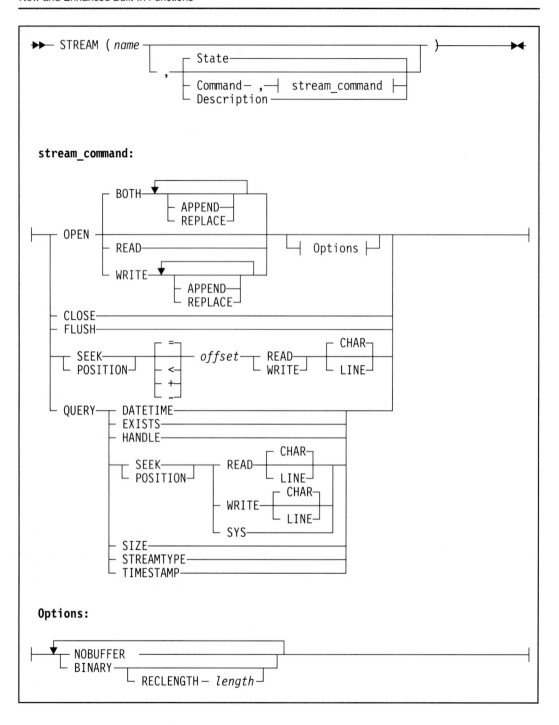

Option *nobuffer* turns off buffering of the stream. This forces all data written to the stream to be physically written immediately to the media.

Binary makes it possible to handle data without regard to any line-end characters, and *reclength* makes it possible to define a fixed record length so that line operations can be used.

2. *FLUSH* is a new command that forces any data currently buffered for writing to be written to this stream.

3. *SEEK* now has a synonym called *POSITION*. Since we now have two pointers, we have to choose between the *read* pointer (default) and the *write* pointer. *Char* (default) specifies that we are seeking in terms of character position, and *line* in terms of lines.

4. *QUERY* is enhanced by four new options:

   - *Handle*—returns the handle associated with the open stream.

   - *Seek/position*—returns the current read or write position of the file, as qualified by *read*, *write*, *char,* and *line*.

   - *Streamtype*—returns the type of stream (*persistent, transient,* or *unknown*).

   - *Timestamp*—returns the date and time stamps of a stream in the form *yyyy-mm-dd hh:mm:ss*.

TIME (Enhanced)

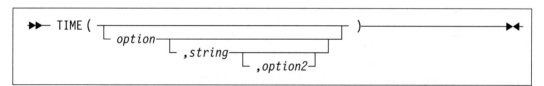

TIME is now enhanced so that it is possible to work with a time other than the current one. The *string* allows input of a date to translate from one form to another. If the input string is not in the default format (*hh:mm:ss*), *option2* can be used to specify the format to Object REXX.

VAR (New)

VAR is a new built-in function. It returns 1 if *name* is the name of a variable (that is, a symbol that has been assigned a value), or 0 otherwise.

New Condition Traps

New condition traps are implemented in both the *CALL* and *SIGNAL* instructions.

CALL/SIGNAL (Enhanced)

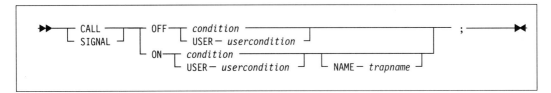

The new conditions are explained in *SIGNAL (Enhanced)* on page 474. Note that the *RAISE condition* does not trap on the level issued. It shows up as a trap on the calling statement in the parent routine.

The code examples below show the use of a generalized trap routine. A main program requires the class definition and a generalized trap routine. It creates an object and runs a method that causes a syntax error.

The main program:

```
/* TstRaise.Cmd - Test the new RAISE instruction */
   signal on any
   tm = .myTest~new
   say tm~myMethodA
   exit
   any: interpret .local["M.TRAPDSP"]
::requires 'TstRaise.CaM'    /* myTest class and methods */
::requires 'TrapDisp.Cmd'    /* generalized trap routine */
```

The program containing the Object REXX class and methods:

```
/* TstRaise.CaM - Class & Method directives for TstRaise.Cmd */
::class myTest public
::method init
   return
::method myMethodA
   signal on any
   x = self~myMethodB
   return x
   any: interpret .local["M.TRAPRTN"]
::method myMethodB
   signal on any
   a = 'xyz'
   c = a+2                      /* this line will cause SYNTAX error */
   return c
   any: interpret .local["M.TRAPRTN"]
```

The generalized trap routine:

```
/* TrapDisp.Cmd - Error condition trap and display routines */
.local["M.TRAPRTN"] = 'trace "o"; ',
   'if .local["M.SIGL"] = .nil then do; ',
   '   .local["M.SIGL"] = sigl; ',
   '   .local["M.COBJ"] = condition("O"); ',
   '   PARSE SOURCE with . sourceid; ',
   '   .local["M.COBJ"]["M.MODULE"] = sourceid; ',
   '   .local["M.COBJ"]["M.LINE"] = sourceline(sigl); ',
   'end; ',
   'raise propagate; '
.local["M.TRAPDSP"] = 'trace "o"; ',
   'signal off any; ',
   'if .local["M.SIGL"] <> .nil then do; ',
   '   sigl = .local["M.SIGL"]; ',
   '   .local["M.SIGL"] = .nil; ',
   '   CObj = .local["M.COBJ"]; ',
   'end; ',
   'else do; ',
   '   CObj = condition(o); ',
   '   CObj["M.MODULE"] = CObj["PROGRAM"]; ',
   '   CObj["M.LINE"] = sourceline(sigl); ',
   'end; ',
   'if var("rc"); ',
   '   then say "REXX ["CObj["CONDITION"]"] error" rc ',
   '                "in line" sigl":" "ERRORTEXT"(rc); ',
   '   else say "REXX ["CObj["CONDITION"]"] error in line" sigl; ',
   'say "The Source Module is: "CObj["M.MODULE"]; ',
   'say "Source line is:" CObj["M.LINE"]; ',
   'exit; '
```

Sample execution:

```
[C:\]TstRaise
REXX [SYNTAX] error 41 in line 16: Bad arithmetic conversion
The Source Module is: C:\TstRaise.CaM
Source line is:    c = a+2    /* this line will cause SYNTAX error */
```

New REXX Utilities

A set of new REXX utilities has been added in Object REXX. These are
described in detail in the Object REXX manuals; therefore, we include
only a short description here.

Utilities for Semaphores

If the system API functions do not return a value, the *GetLastError()*
return code is returned to the caller.

SysCreateEventSem
> Creates or opens a Windows event semaphore. Returns an
> event semaphore handle that can be used with the
> **SysOpenEventSem**, **SysCloseEventSem**, **SysRe-
> setEventSem**, **SysPostEventSem**, **SysWaitEvent-
> Sem,** and **SysPulseEventSem** functions. Returns a null
> string if the semaphore cannot be created or opened.

SysOpenEventSem
> Opens a Windows event semaphore and returns the
> **OpenEvent** return codes.

SysPostEventSem
> Posts an Windows event semaphore and returns the **Set-
> Event** return codes.

SysWaitEventSem
> Waits on an Windows event semaphore and returns the
> **WaitForSingleObject** return codes.

SysResetEventSem
> Resets an Windows event semaphore and returns the **Sys-
> ResetEventSem** return codes.

SysCloseEventSem
> Closes an Windows event semaphore and returns the
> **CloseHandle** return codes.

SysCreateMutexSem
> Creates or opens a Windows mutex semaphore. Returns a
> mutex semaphore handle that can be used with the
> **SysOpenMutexSem**, **SysCloseMutexSem**, **SysRe-
> questMutexSem**, and **SysReleaseMutexSem** functions.
> Returns a null string if the semaphore cannot be created
> or opened.

SysOpenMutexSem
> Opens a Windows mutex semaphore and returns the
> **OpenMutex** return codes.

SysRequestMutexSem
> Requests a Windows mutex semaphore and returns the
> **WaitForSingleObject** codes.

SysReleaseMutexSem

Releases a Windows mutex semaphore and returns the **ReleaseMutex** return codes.

SysCloseMutexSem

Closes an Windows mutex semaphore and returns the **CloseHandle** return codes.

SysPulseEventSem

Posts and immediately resets an event semaphore, and returns the **PulseEvent** return code.

Utilities for REXX Macros

SysAddRexxMacro

Adds a routine to the REXX macrospace and returns the **RexxAddMacro** return codes.

SysQueryRexxMacro

Queries the existence of a macrospace function. Returns either the placement order of the macrospace function or a null string if the function does not exist in the macrospace.

SysReorderRexxMacro

Changes the search-order position of a loaded macrospace function. The new search-order position could be either before or after any registered functions and external REXX files. **SysReorderRexxMacro** returns the **RexxReorderMacro** return codes.

SysDropRexxMacro

Removes a routine from the REXX macrospace and returns the **RexxDropMacro** return codes.

SysClearRexxMacroSpace

Removes all loaded routines from the REXX macrospace and returns the **RexxClearMacro** return codes.

SysLoadRexxMacroSpace

Loads all functions from a file created with the **SysSaveRexxMacroSpace** utility. If any of the functions already exists in the macrospace, the entire load request is discarded and the macrospace remains unchanged. **SysLoadRexxMacroSpace** returns the **RexxLoadMacro** return codes.

SysSaveRexxMacroSpace

Saves all REXX macrospace functions to a file. Observe that saved macrospaces can be loaded only with the same interpreter level that created the image. **SysSaveRexxMacroSpace** returns the **RexxSaveMacro** return codes.

Utilities for Windows Systems

SysBootDrive

Returns the drive used to boot Windows, for example, C:.

SysFileSystemType

Returns the name of the file system for a drive (FAT, HPFS, LAN, etc.). If the drive is not accessible, a null string is returned.

SysLoadFuncs

Loads all RexxUtil functions (or other packages). After a REXX program calls **SysLoadFuncs**, the RexxUtil functions are available in all Windows sessions:

```
call RxFuncAdd 'SysLoadFuncs', 'RexxUtil', 'SysLoadFuncs'
call SysLoadFuncs
```

SysSetPriority

Changes the priority of the current process and returns the **SysSetPriority** return codes.

SysSwitchSession

Makes the named application the foreground application.

SysSystemDirectory

Returns the Windows system directory.

SysVolumeLabel

Returns the label of the specified or current drive.

Migration Considerations

Migration considerations are described in the Object REXX Reference manual. Here we provide a short extract:

Stems   Stems behave a little differently in Object REXX. The symbol functions return *VAR* (not *LIT*) because a stem object is automatically created the first time used, and a *NOVALUE* condition is never raised. Stems can be assigned to each other (*a. = z.*), and they point to the same object.

In many cases, it may be desirable to use some of the new collections provided by Object REXX, instead of a stem variable.

Parse version

Return *n.nn*, the current version.

Streams   Avoid mixing methods (*aStream~linein*) and functions (*linein(aStream)*) because they work on different objects representing the same file. For nonexisting files *LINEIN* and *CHARIN* return the null string, and *LINES* and *CHARS* return 0.

Earlier error detection

Before the program is started, Object REXX performs some syntax checking and the program might never get control. For example, missing *END* statements and missing parameters are detected before starting the program.

Global environment

The global environment directory **.environment** is not global across processes in a Windows system. It cannot be used to communicate between multiple processes.

B

Car Dealer Source Code

This appendix describes the location of all the source code of the sample applications and contains an extract of the source code of the car dealer application.

The following sections of the car dealer source code are listed in this appendix:

- ❏ Sample data
- ❏ Classes and methods
- ❏ Running the car dealer programs

Note: Only an extract of the programs is listed here. All the programs are available on the CD, and on your hard drive once the sample applications have been installed.

Directory Structure

The sample applications are stored in two main directories, one for the car dealer application, and one for the OODialog sample applications.

Car Dealer Application

The car dealer application is available in the CARDEAL directory on the CD and in a directory of your choice when Object REXX is installed on your hard drive. The subdirectories and a description of their content are listed in Table 35.

Table 35. Subdirectories of the Car Dealer Application

Subdirectory	Description	Details
(main)	Master directory of car dealer application	Table 19 on page 300
SampData	Master files with sample data	Table 20 on page 300
Base	Base class definitions for objects in storage	Table 21 on page 301
FAT	Class definitions for persistent objects in files	Table 22 on page 301
DB2	Class definitions for persistence in DB2	Table 23 on page 301
RAM	Class definitions for objects in RAM	Table 24 on page 302
AUI	Class definitions for ASCII interface	Table 25 on page 302
Media	Multimedia files	Table 26 on page 302
Ood	GUI definitions and executable for OODialog	Table 27 on page 302
StorProc	Sample commands for stored procedures in a DB2 client/server environment	Table 28 on page 303
WWW	Car dealer on the World Wide Web	Table 29 on page 303
Xamples	Additional small examples	Table 30 on page 303
Install	Installation programs and DB2 setup	Table 31 on page 304
Src	Source code of REXX programs of the main directory	
....\Src	Subdirectory in above directories with source code of REXX programs	

Philosophers' Forks and OODialog Samples

The philosophers' fork and the other OODialog sample applications are available in the OBJREXX\OODIALOG\SAMPLES directory on the CD and in the OODIALOG\SAMPLES subdirectory of Object REXX when installed on your hard drive.

Sample Data

The original sample data files are stored in the SAMPDATA subdirectory of the car dealer application. The actual files in use with persistent file storage are stored in the FAT\DATA subdirectory. You can restore the original data at any time by copying the files from SAMPDATA into FAT\DATA.

Note: The not signs (¬) represent tab characters in the sample data listings below.

Sample Customer Data

```
/*------------------------------------------------------------------*/
/* SampData\customer.dat CarDealer - Customer data file    ITSO-SJC */
/*------------------------------------------------------------------*/
/*number name              address                                  */
/*------------------------------------------------------------------*/
101¬Senator, Dale      ¬Washington
102¬Akropolis, Ida     ¬Athens
103¬Dolcevita, Felicia ¬Rome
104¬DuPont, Jean       ¬Paris
105¬Deutsch, Hans      ¬Stuttgart
106¬Helvetia, Toni     ¬Zurich
107¬Rising Star        ¬Hollywood
108¬Zabrowski, Russkie ¬Moscow
109¬Valencia, Maria de ¬Barcelona
601¬Wahli, Ueli        ¬ITSO San Jose
602¬Turton, Trevor     ¬Johannesburg
603¬Holder, Ingo       ¬Boeblingen
/*------------------------------------------------------------------*/
999¬New and used cars  ¬For sale
```

Figure 164. *Sample Customer Data (sampdata\customer.dat)*

Sample Vehicle Data

```
/*--------------------------------------------------------------------*/
/* SampData\vehicle.dat  CarDealer - Vehicle data file      ITSO-SJC */
/*--------------------------------------------------------------------*/
/*serial make       model      year customer                        */
/*--------------------------------------------------------------------*/
123456¬Ford       ¬T          ¬1931¬101
297465¬Volkswagen ¬Camper     ¬1971¬102
111111¬Porsche    ¬Targa      ¬1989¬102
222222¬Lamborghini ¬Countach  ¬1992¬103
398674¬Cadillac   ¬Allante    ¬1991¬103
334455¬Chevrolet  ¬Impala     ¬1985¬104
456456¬Toyota     ¬Camry      ¬1988¬105
543543¬Pontiac    ¬Firebird   ¬1979¬106
911911¬Chrysler   ¬Le Baron   ¬1982¬106
298653¬Mercury    ¬Sable      ¬1987¬106
176549¬Olsmobile  ¬Aurora     ¬1993¬107
199999¬Acura      ¬Legend     ¬1990¬107
777777¬Mercedes   ¬380S       ¬1990¬108
666888¬Lincoln    ¬Towncar    ¬1986¬109
601001¬Audi       ¬5000-Wagon¬1984¬601
602002¬BMW        ¬735S       ¬1991¬602
603003¬Porsche    ¬944 S2Conv¬1989¬603
/*----------------------------------------------new/used cars----*/
999001¬Ford       ¬Windstar   ¬1995¬999
999002¬Audi       ¬V8 Quattro¬1990¬999
999003¬Volvo      ¬860 Wagon  ¬1995¬999
999004¬Honda      ¬Civic      ¬1994¬999
999005¬MixedStuff ¬Fun        ¬1995¬999
/*----------------------------------------------not a car!-------*/
999666¬ThinkPad   ¬701        ¬1995¬999
999777¬Airplane   ¬Tumble     ¬1993¬999
999999¬ORexxRedbook¬Team      ¬1995¬999
```

Figure 165. *Sample Vehicle Data (sampdata\vehicle.dat)*

Sample Work Order Data

```
/*--------------------------------------------------------------------*/
/* SampData\workord.dat  CarDealer - WorkOrder data file    ITSO-SJC */
/*--------------------------------------------------------------------*/
/*number date cost complete custmr serial serv.items               */
/*--------------------------------------------------------------------*/
1¬09/06/95¬-1 ¬0¬101¬123456¬1
2¬09/07/95¬-1 ¬0¬103¬398674¬10¬9¬4
3¬09/08/95¬-1 ¬0¬106¬911911¬7¬6
4¬09/09/95¬-1 ¬0¬108¬777777¬11
5¬08/01/95¬100¬1¬107¬199999¬2¬3
```

Figure 166. *Sample Work Order Data (sampdata\workord.dat)*

Sample Service Item Data

```
/*----------------------------------------------------------------*/
/* SampData\service.dat  CarDealer - ServiceItem data file   ITSO-SJC */
/*----------------------------------------------------------------*/
/*number description labor part quant part quan                     */
/*----------------------------------------------------------------*/
1 ¬Brake job            ¬110¬21¬1¬22¬2¬23¬2¬24¬2
2 ¬Check fluids         ¬25 ¬10¬5¬11¬1¬31¬1
3 ¬Tire rotate/balance¬20
4 ¬Tires new Sedan      ¬0  ¬51¬4
5 ¬Tires new Sport      ¬10 ¬52¬4
6 ¬Starter              ¬75 ¬71¬1
7 ¬Alternator           ¬90 ¬72¬1
8 ¬Heating system       ¬45 ¬61¬1¬62¬1¬81¬1¬82¬1
9 ¬Electrical           ¬85 ¬45¬3¬91¬1
10¬Exhaust system       ¬85 ¬1 ¬1
11¬Fenders              ¬45 ¬41¬2
```

Figure 167. *Sample Service Item Data (sampdata\service.dat)*

Sample Part Data

```
/*----------------------------------------------------------------*/
/* SampData\part.dat       CarDealer - Part data file        ITSO-SJC */
/*----------------------------------------------------------------*/
/*number description cost stock                                     */
/*----------------------------------------------------------------*/
1 ¬Muffler           ¬120¬3
10¬Oil 10-40 quart¬5  ¬30
11¬Oil filter        ¬22 ¬15
21¬Brake cylinder ¬120 3
22¬Brake fluid       ¬7  ¬13
23¬Brake drum        ¬28 ¬6
24¬Brake disk        ¬35 ¬9
31¬Steering fluid ¬8  ¬40
41¬Fender            ¬67 ¬2
45¬Light bulb        ¬2  ¬20
51¬Tire 185-70       ¬57 ¬8
52¬Tire 205-60       ¬73 ¬12
61¬Belt              ¬12 ¬2
62¬Radiator          ¬133¬1
71¬Starter           ¬189¬4
72¬Alternator        ¬165¬2
81¬Water pump        ¬97 ¬1
82¬Heating control¬43 ¬1
91¬Cruise control ¬54 ¬2
```

Figure 168. *Sample Part Data (sampdata\part.dat)*

Multimedia Setup

Multimedia Data Definition File

```
/*-------------------------------------------------------------------*/
/* Media\media.dat         CarDealer - Multi-media definition   ITSO-SJC */
/*-------------------------------------------------------------------*/
/* serial, title of file         , filename                          */
/*-------------------------------------------------------------------*/
   999001, Fact-sheet             , ford.fac
   999001, Side picture           , fordsid.bmp
   999001, Front picture          , fordfrt.bmp
   999001, Back picture           , fordbck.bmp
   999001, Angle picture          , fordang.bmp
   999001, Audio                  , ford.wav
   999002, Fact-sheet             , audi.fac
   999002, Side picture           , audisid.bmp
   999002, Front picture          , audifrt.bmp
   999002, Back picture           , audibck.bmp
   999002, Audio                  , audi.wav
   999003, Fact-sheet             , volvo.fac
   999003, Side picture           , volvosid.bmp
   ...
   999005, Fact-sheet             , mixed.fac
   999005, Tow truck              , towtruck.bmp
   999005, Truck                  , truck.bmp
   999005, Pickup                 , pickup.bmp
   999005, Fire engine            , fireeng.bmp
   999005, Motor cycle            , motocycl.bmp
   999005, Audio                  , mixed.wav
   999666, Fact-sheet             , ibm701i.fac
   999666, ThinkPad 701           , ibm701i.bmp
   999666, Video                  , ibm701i.avi
   999777, Fact-sheet             , tumble.fac
   999777, The plane              , tumble1.bmp
   999777, Straight ahead         , tumble2.bmp
   999777, Upside down!           , tumble3.bmp
   999777, Video                  , tumble1.avi
   999999, Facts: Redbook team    , orexxred.fac
   999999, Ueli Wahli             , ueli1.bmp
   999999, Ingo Holder            , ingo1.bmp
   999999, Trevor Turton          , trevor.bmp
   999999, Audio                  , orexxred.wav
   601001, Facts: Ueli Wahli      , wahli.fac
   601001, Ueli's portrait        , ueli.bmp
   601001, Ueli's car             , audi.bmp
   601001, License plates         , licenses.bmp
   601001, Cactus garden          , cactus.bmp
   601001, Facts: Boxie (cat)     , boxie.fac
   601001, Boxie the cat          , boxie.bmp
   601001, Boxie in trouble       , cat.bmp
   601001, Audio                  , wahli.wav
   602002, Facts: Trevor Turton,  turton.fac
   602002, Trevor's portrait      , trevor2.bmp
   603003, Facts: Ingo Holder     , holder.fac
   603003, Ingo's portrait        , ingo2.bmp
   603003, Facts: Porsche         , porsche.fac
   603003, Porsche front view     , porsche1.bmp
   603003, Porsche side view      , porsche2.bmp
   603003, Audio                  , ingo.wav
```

Figure 169. *Multimedia Data Definition File (media\media.dat)*

Base Classes

Base Customer Class

```
/*------------------------------------------------------------------*/
/* Base\carcust.cls    CarDealer - Customer class (base)   ITSO-SJC */
/*------------------------------------------------------------------*/

::class CustomerBase public

/*----- class methods ----------------------------------------------*/

::method initialize class                  /* preprare class          */
   expose extent
   extent = .set~new                       /* - keep track of cust.   */
   self~persistentLoad                     /* - and load into memory  */

::method add class                         /* add new customer        */
   expose extent
   use arg custx
   if custx~class = self then do           /* - check if already there*/
      do custo over extent
         if custo~number = custx~number then return
      end
      extent~put(custx)                    /* - add to extent         */
   end

::method remove class                      /* remove customer from    */
   expose extent                           /*    extent               */
   use arg custx
   if custx~class = self then
      extent~remove(custx)

::method findNumber class                  /* find customer by number */
   expose extent
   parse arg custnum
   do custx over extent                    /* - search extent         */
      if custx~number = custnum then return custx /* - return when found */
   end
   return .nil

::method findName class                    /* find customer by name   */
   arg custsearch
   custnames = .list~new                   /* - prepare result list   */
   do custx over self~extent               /* - check extent          */
      if abbrev(translate(custx~name),custsearch) then do
         custstring = custx~number~right(3) || ,
                    '-'custx~name'-'custx~address
         custnames~insert(custstring)      /* - add a match           */
      end
   end
   return custnames~makearray              /* - return result array   */
```

Figure 170. *(Part 1 of 4) Base Customer Class (base\carcust.cls)*

```
::method findAddress class                         /* find customer by address*/
   arg custsearch
   do custx over self~extent                       /* - check extent          */
      if custx~address = custsearch then
         return custx~number                        /* - return customer number*/
   end
   return ''                                        /* - return not found      */

::method extent class                              /* return extent of cust.  */
   expose extent
   return extent~makearray                          /* - as an array           */

::method heading class                             /* return a heading        */
      return 'Number        Name             Address'

/*----- instance methods --------------------------------------*/

::method init                                      /* initialize new customer */
   expose customerNumber name address cars orders
   self~init:super                                  /* - call parent           */
   use arg customerNumber, name, address
   cars = .set~new                                  /* - prepare cars/orders   */
   orders = .set~new
   if arg() < 3 | arg() > 4 then return self~setnil
   if \datatype(customerNumber,'W') then return self~setnil
   if customerNumber<100 | customerNumber>999 then return self~setnil
   self~class~add(self)                             /* - add to extent         */
   if arg() = 4 then self~persistentInsert          /* - a real new customer   */

::method setnil private                            /* set customer data nil   */
   expose customerNumber name address cars orders
   self~class~remove(self)                          /* - remove from extent    */
   cars = .nil
   orders = .nil
   customerNumber = 0
   name = '-none-'
   address = '-none-'
   return .nil

::method delete                                    /* delete a customer       */
   expose cars orders
   do carx over cars                                /* - delete all cars       */
      carx~delete
   end
   do workx over orders                             /* - delete all workorders */
      workx~delete
   end
   self~class~remove(self)                          /* - remove from extent    */
   self~persistentDelete                            /* - delete permanent stor */
   self~setnil

::method number unguarded                          /*                         */
   expose customerNumber
   return customerNumber

::method name attribute                            /* customer's name         */

::method address attribute                         /* customer's address      */
```

Figure 170. *(Part 2 of 4) Base Customer Class (base\carcust.cls)*

```
::method update                                   /* update customer data    */
   expose name address
   if arg() = 2 then do
      use arg name, address
      self~persistentUpdate                        /* - update persistent stor*/
   end

::method addVehicle                               /* add a vehicle           */
   expose cars
   use arg newcar
   owner = newcar~getowner                         /* - check its owner       */
   if owner = self | owner = .nil then do
      cars~put(newcar)                             /* - add if no owner       */
      if owner = .nil then
         newcar~setowner(self)                     /* - set new owner         */
   end
   else do                                         /* - error if other owner  */
      say 'Cannot add car' newcar~makemodel 'to customer' self~name
      say '  it belongs to' newcar~getowner~name
   end

::method removeVehicle                            /* remove vehicle from cust*/
   expose cars
   use arg oldcar
   oldcar~deleteOwner                              /* - delete owner          */
   cars~remove(oldcar)                             /* - remove from cars      */

::method checkVehicle                             /* check if car in set     */
   expose cars
   use arg somecar
   if cars~hasindex(somecar) then return 1         /* - yes it is             */
   else return 0

::method getVehicles                              /* return array of cars    */
   expose cars
   return cars~makearray

::method findVehicle                              /* find car by serial      */
   expose cars
   use arg serial
   do carx over cars                               /* - check all cars        */
      if carx~serial = serial then return carx
   end
   return .nil

::method addOrder                                 /* add order to customer   */
   expose orders
   use arg newwork
   orders~put(newwork)                             /* - add order to set      */

::method removeOrder                              /* remove order from cust. */
   expose orders
   use arg oldwork
   orders~remove(oldwork)                          /* - remove order from set */

::method getOrders                                /* return all orders       */
   expose orders
   return orders~makearray                         /* - as an array           */
```

Figure 170. *(Part 3 of 4) Base Customer Class (base\carcust.cls)*

```
::method detail                                    /* return a detail line    */
   expose customerNumber name address
   return customerNumber~right(5) '      ' name~left(20) ' ' address~left(20)

::method makestring                                /* default string output   */
   expose customerNumber name
   return 'Customer:' customerNumber name

::method display                                   /* display customer data    */
   expose customerNumber name address cars orders
   say '-'~copies(78)
   say self~class~heading
   say self~detail
   if cars~items > 0 then
      do carx over cars
         say '   Vehicle:' carx~detail
      end
   if orders~items > 0 then do
      do orderx over orders
         say ' WorkOrder:' orderx~detail
      end
   end
```

Figure 170. *(Part 4 of 4) Base Customer Class (base\carcust.cls)*

Base Vehicle Class

```
/*-----------------------------------------------------------------*/
/* Base\carvehi.cls      CarDealer - Vehicle class (base)    ITSO-SJC */
/*-----------------------------------------------------------------*/

::class VehicleBase public

/*----- class methods ---------------------------------------------*/

::method initialize class                          /* prepare class           */
   self~persistentLoad                             /* - load into memory      */

/*----- instance methods ------------------------------------------*/

::method init                                      /* initialize new vehicle */
   expose serialNumber make model year owner
   self~init:super
   use arg serialNumber, make, model, year, owner
   if arg() < 5 | arg() > 6 then self~setnil
   if owner \= .nil then
      owner~addVehicle(self)                       /* - add car to customer   */
   if arg() = 6 then self~persistentInsert         /* - insert real new car   */

::method setnil private                            /* set vehicle data nil    */
   expose serialNumber make model year owner
   if owner \= .nil then
         owner~removeVehicle(self)                 /* - remove from customer  */
   serialNumber = 0
   make = '-none-'
```

Figure 171. *(Part 1 of 2) Base Vehicle Class (base\carvehi.cls)*

```
   model = '-none-'
   year = 0
   owner = .nil

::method delete                             /* delete a vehicle      */
   expose serialNumber make model year owner
   if owner \= .nil then do
      do workx over owner~getOrders         /* - remove work orders  */
         if workx~getVehicle = self then workx~delete
      end
      owner~removeVehicle(self)             /* - remove car from cust. */
   end
   self~persistentDelete                    /* - from permanent stor  */
   self~setnil

::method serial                             /* return serial number  */
   expose serialNumber
   return serialNumber
::method make attribute                     /* vehicle's make         */
::method model attribute                    /* vehicle's model        */
::method year attribute                     /* vehicle's year         */

::method update                             /* update vehicle data    */
   expose make model year
   if arg() = 3 then do
      use arg make, model, year
      self~persistentUpdate                 /* - in permanent storage */
   end

::method makemodel unguarded                /* return make and model  */
   expose make model
   return make~strip'-'model~strip          /* - as string            */

::method getOwner unguarded                 /* return owner (customer) */
   expose owner
   return owner
::method setOwner                           /* set a new owner (cust) */
   expose owner
   use arg newowner
   if owner = .nil then
      if newowner~checkVehicle(self) then   /* - if its the proper one */
         use arg owner
::method deleteOwner                        /* delete the owner (cust) */
   expose owner
   owner = .nil

::method detail                             /* return a detail line   */
   expose serialNumber make model year
   return serialNumber~right(8) ' ' make~left(12) ' ' model~left(10) ,
         ' ' year
::method makestring                         /* default string output  */
   expose serialNumber make model
   return 'Vehicle:' serialNumber make model
::method display                            /* display vehicle data   */
   expose serialNumber make model year owner
   if owner = .nil then ownerst = '-no owner-'
                   else ownerst = owner~number
   say serialNumber~right(8) ' ' make~left(12) ' ' model~left(10) ,
         ' ' year ' ' ownerst
```

Figure 171. *(Part 2 of 2) Base Vehicle Class (base\carvehi.cls)*

Base Work Order Class

```
/*------------------------------------------------------------------*/
/* Base\carwork.cls     CarDealer - WorkOrder class (base)  ITSO-SJC */
/*------------------------------------------------------------------*/

::class WorkOrderBase public

/*----- class methods ----------------------------------------------*/

::method initialize class                        /* prepare the class      */
   expose extent WorkServRel
   extent = .list~new                            /* - extent of work orders */
   if .local['Cardeal.WorkServRel'] = .nil then  /* - prepare relation to   */
      .local['Cardeal.WorkServRel'] = .Relation~new
   WorkServRel = .local['Cardeal.WorkServRel']   /* - service items         */
   self~persistentLoad                           /* - load into memory      */

::method getWorkServRel class                    /* return the relation     */
   expose WorkServRel
   return WorkServRel

::method add class                               /* add workorder to extent */
   expose extent
   use arg workx
   if workx~class = self then do
      do worko over extent                       /* - check if already there*/
         if worko~number = workx~number then return worko~getindex
      end
      return extent~insert(workx, .nil)          /* - insert new at start   */
   end

::method remove class                            /* remove order from extent*/
   expose extent
   use arg indx, workx
   if extent~at(indx) = workx then               /* - ckeck and remove      */
      extent~remove(indx)

::method findNumber class                        /* find workorder by number*/
   expose extent
   use arg worknum
   do workx over extent                          /* - check the extent      */
      if workx~number = worknum then return workx
   end
   return .nil

::method findStatus class                        /* find workorder by status*/
   expose extent
   use arg xstatus
   worklist = .list~new                          /* - prepare result        */
   xstat1 = 0                                     /* - 0 is incomplete       */
   xstat2 = 1                                     /* - 1 is complete         */
   if xstatus = 0 then xstat2=0
   if xstatus = 1 then xstat1=1
   do workx over extent                          /* - go over all orders    */
      xstatus = workx~getstatus                   /* - and check the status  */
      if xstatus >= xstat1 & xstatus <= xstat2 then do
```

Figure 172. *(Part 1 of 5) Base Work Order Class (base\carwork.cls)*

```
                    if xstatus = 0 then statusx = 'Incomplete'
                              else statusx = 'Complete'
               workstring = workx~number~left(3) '' workx~date ,
                          workx~cost~right(6) statusx~left(11) ,
                          (workx~getvehicle~make~strip || ,
                            '-'workx~getvehicle~model~strip)~left(20) ,
                          workx~getcustomer~name
               worklist~insert(workstring,.nil)           /* - add to result        */
           end
       end
       return worklist~makearray                          /* - return result as array*/

::method newNumber class                                  /* return a new number     */
    expose extent
    if extent~items = 0 then return 1
    newnum = 0
    do workx over extent                                  /* - find maximum number   */
        newnum = max(newnum, workx~number)
    end
    return newnum + 1                                      /* - return next higher    */

::method extent class
    expose extent                                         /* return extent as array  */
    return extent~makearray

/*----- instance methods -------------------------------------------*/

::method init                                             /* initialize new workorder*/
    expose orderNumber cost date status customer car listindex
    self~init:super
    status = 0                                            /* - incomplete            */
    cost = -1                                             /* - unknown cost          */
    orderNumber = 0
    if arg() = 3 then do                                  /* - new work order        */
        use arg date, customer, car
        orderNumber = self~class~newNumber                /* - find new number       */
        listindex = self~class~add(self)                  /* - add to extent         */
        customer~addOrder(self)                           /* - add to customer       */
        self~persistentInsert                             /* - add to persistent stor*/
        end
    else if arg() = 6 then do                             /* - load from persistent  */
        use arg orderNumber, date, cost, status, customer, car
        listindex = self~class~add(self)                  /* - add to extent         */
        customer~addOrder(self)                           /* - add to customer       */
        end
    else self~setnil

::method setnil private                                   /* set workorder data nil  */
    expose orderNumber cost date status customer car listindex
    customer~removeOrder(self)
    self~class~remove(listindex,self)                     /* - remove from extent    */
    status = 0
    cost = -1
    orderNumber = 0
    date = '00/00/00'
    customer = .nil
    car = .nil
    listindex = 0
    return .nil
```

Figure 172. *(Part 2 of 5) Base Work Order Class (base\carwork.cls)*

```
::method delete                                /* delete a work order    */
   expose orderNumber cost date status customer car listindex
   self~class~remove(listindex,self)           /* - remove from extent    */
   self~persistentDelete                       /* - delete persistent stor*/
   self~setnil

::method number unguarded                      /* return workorder number */
   expose orderNumber
   return orderNumber

::method cost unguarded                        /* return cost of workorder*/
   expose cost
   return cost

::method date unguarded                        /* return date of workorder*/
   expose date
   return date

::method setstatus                             /* change the status       */
   expose status
   use arg newstatus
   if newstatus = 0 | newstatus = 1 then do    /* - change peristent stor */
      if status \= newstatus then self~persistentUpdate
      status = newstatus
   end

::method getstatus unguarded                   /* return the status       */
   expose status
   return status

::method getstatust unguarded                  /* return status as text   */
   expose status
   if status = 0 then return 'incomplete'
   else              return 'complete'

::method getindex unguarded private            /* return index in extent  */
   expose listindex
   return listindex

::method getCustomer unguarded                 /* return the customer     */
   expose customer
   return customer

::method getVehicle unguarded                  /* return the vehicle      */
   expose car
   return car

::method getServices                           /* return all services     */
   return self~class~getWorkServRel~allat(self)

::method addServiceItem                        /* add service to workorder*/
   expose cost status
   use arg itemx
   workserv = self~class~getWorkServRel        /* - get the relation      */
   if workserv~hasitem(itemx,self) then return /* - cannot add same item  */
   workserv[self] = itemx                      /* - record in relation    */
   if status = 0 then cost = -1
   if arg() = 2 then return self~persistentInsertServ(itemx~number)
```

Figure 172. *(Part 3 of 5) Base Work Order Class (base\carwork.cls)*

```
::method removeServiceItem                      /* remove a service      */
   expose cost status
   use arg itemx
   workserv = self~class~getWorkServRel
   workserv~removeitem(itemx,self)              /* - remove in relation   */
   if status = 0 then cost = -1
   if arg() = 2 then return self~persistentDeleteServ(itemx~number)

::method getTotalCost                           /* compute total cost     */
   expose cost
   totalcost = 0
   do servx over self~getServices               /* - sum up all services  */
      totalcost = totalcost + servx~laborcost + servx~getPartsCost
   end
   if cost \= totalcost then do                 /* - update cost attribute */
      cost = totalcost
      self~persistentUpdate
   end
   return totalcost

::method checkAndDecreaseStock                  /* check if enough parts  */
   expose status
   if status = 1 then return 0                  /* - not for complete ones */
   enough = 1
   do servx over self~getServices               /* - check all services   */
      partsx = servx~getparts
      do partx over partsx                       /* - and parts in service  */
         quan = servx~getquantity(partx)
         partno = partx~number                   /* - get part number      */
         if symbol("stock."partno) = 'LIT' then  /* - record stock         */
            stock.partno = partx~stock
         stock.partno = stock.partno - quan
         if stock.partno < 0 then do             /* - check temporary stock */
            enough = 0
            say ''servx
            say ' --> Not enough stock for' partx
         end
      end
   end
   if enough then do                            /* - all stocks are OK    */
      do servx over self~getServices             /* - go over all services  */
         partsx = servx~getparts
         do partx over partsx                    /* - and all parts        */
            quan = servx~getquantity(partx)
            x = partx~decreaseStock(quan)        /* - decrease stock of part*/
         end
      end
      status = 1
      x = self~getTotalCost                      /* - and compute total cost*/
   end
   return enough

::method generateBill                           /* prepare the bill       */
   expose orderNumber date customer car
   separ = '-'~copies(78)
   bill = .list~new                             /* - result lines         */
   bill~insert('Bill for work order' orderNumber left(' ',30) 'Date:' date)
   bill~insert(separ)
   bill~insert('   Customer:' customer~name)
```

Figure 172. *(Part 4 of 5) Base Work Order Class (base\carwork.cls)*

```
      bill~insert('    Vehicle:' car~makemodel)
      bill~insert(separ)
      bill~insert('Description           Parts           Unit        ' ,
                  'Partcost  Laborcost')
      bill~insert(separ)
      do servx over self~getServices                 /* - over all services     */
         bill~insert(servx~description~left(54) servx~getPartsCost~right(8) ,
                     servx~laborcost~right(10))
         partsx = servx~getparts
         do partx over partsx                         /* - and parts in service  */
            quan = servx~getquantity(partx)
            costx = quan * partx~price
            bill~insert('  '~left(18) quan~right(3) partx~description~left(16) ,
                        '$'partx~price~right(4) '=' costx~right(5))
         end
      end
      bill~insert(separ)
      bill~insert('Total cost of work order'~left(65) self~getTotalCost~right(8))
      bill~insert(separ)
      return bill~makearray

::method detail                                      /* return a detail line     */
   expose orderNumber cost date status
   return orderNumber~right(3) '  Date:' date~left(8) '  Cost:' ,
          cost~right(5) '  Status: ' self~getstatust

::method detailcust                                  /* return cust/vehicle      */
   expose customer car
   return '  Customer:' customer~name~left(20) ,
          '  Vehicle:' car~makemodel~left(20)

::method makestring                                  /* return default string    */
   expose orderNumber cost date status customer car
   return 'Workorder:' orderNumber date self~getstatust ,
          '('customer~name~left(10)'/'car~makemodel~left(10)')'

::method makeline                                    /* return a short line      */
   expose orderNumber cost date status customer car
   return orderNumber~left(3) '' date cost~right(6) ,
          self~getstatust~left(11) car~makemodel customer~name

::method display                                     /* display work order data */
   expose orderNumber cost date status customer car
   separ = '-'~copies(78)
   say workx~detail
   say workx~detailcust
   first = 1
   do servx over self~getServices
      if first then say '  Services:' servx~number~right(3) servx~description
      else          say '          ' servx~number~right(3) servx~description
      first = 0
      lines = lines + 1
   end
```

Figure 172. *(Part 5 of 5) Base Work Order Class (base\carwork.cls)*

Base Service Item Class

```
/*--------------------------------------------------------------------*/
/* Base\carserv.cls     CarDealer - ServiceItem class(base) ITSO-SJC */
/*--------------------------------------------------------------------*/

::class ServiceItemBase public

/*----- class methods --------------------------------------------*/

::method initialize class                       /* prepare the class       */
   expose extent WorkServRel
   extent = .list~new                           /* - extent as a list      */
   if .local['Cardeal.WorkServRel'] = .nil then /* - prepare relation      */
      .local['Cardeal.WorkServRel'] = .Relation~new
   WorkServRel = .local['Cardeal.WorkServRel']  /* - to work orders        */
   self~persistentLoad                          /* - load into memory      */

::method getWorkServRel class                   /* return the relation     */
   expose WorkServRel
   return WorkServRel

::method add class                              /* add service to extent   */
   expose extent
   use arg servx
   if servx~class = self then                   /* - add to extent         */
      return extent~insert(servx)

::method remove class                           /* remove service from ext.*/
   expose extent
   use arg indx, servx
   if extent~at(indx) = servx then              /* - remove ffrom extent   */
      extent~remove(indx)

::method findNumber class                       /* find service by number  */
   expose extent
   parse arg servnum
   if extent~items > 0 then                     /* - check the extent      */
      do servx over extent
         if servx~number = servnum then return servx
      end
   return .nil

::method extent class                           /* return extent as array  */
   expose extent
   return extent~makearray

::method heading class                          /* return a heading line   */
   return 'Item  LaborCost  Description  Quantity  Part'
```

Figure 173. *(Part 1 of 3) Base Service Item Class (base\carserv.cls)*

```
/*----- instance methods ------------------------------------*/

::method init                                    /* initialize new service */
    expose itemNumber description laborCost parts quantity. listindex
    self~init:super
    use arg itemNumber, description, laborCost
    parts = .set~new                             /* - set of parts         */
    quantity. = ''                               /* - with quantity        */
    if arg() \= 3 then self~setnil
    else listindex = self~class~add(self)        /* - add to extent list   */

::method setnil private                          /* set service data nil   */
    expose itemNumber description laborCost parts listindex
    self~class~remove(listindex,self)            /* - remove from extent   */
    itemNumber = 0
    description = '-none-'
    laborCost = 0
    parts = .nil
    quantity. = ''
    listindex = 0
    return .nil

::method delete                                  /* delete a service item  */
    expose listindex
    self~class~remove(listindex,self)            /* - remove from extent   */
    /* self~persistentDelete */
    self~setnil

::method number unguarded                        /* return service number  */
    expose itemNumber
    return itemNumber

::method laborcost unguarded                     /* return labor cost      */
    expose laborCost
    return laborCost

::method description unguarded                    /* return description     */
    expose description
    return description

::method usesPart                                /* record used part       */
    expose parts quantity.
    if arg() \= 2 then return
    use arg partx, quan
    parts~put(partx)                             /* - add to parts list    */
    quantity.partx = quan                        /* - with quantity        */

::method getParts                                /* return all parts       */
    expose parts
    return parts~makearray                       /* - as an array          */

::method getQuantity                             /* return quantity        */
    expose quantity.
    use arg partx
    return quantity.partx                        /* - of a part            */
```

Figure 173. *(Part 2 of 3) Base Service Item Class (base\carserv.cls)*

```
::method getPartsCost                           /* calculate cost of parts */
   expose parts quantity.
   partcost = 0
   do partx over parts                          /* - over all parts        */
      partcost = partcost + partx~price * quantity.partx
   end
   return partcost

::method getWorkOrders                          /* return workorders       */
   return self~class~getWorkServRel~allindex(self)/* - using this service  */

::method detail                                 /* return detail line      */
   expose itemNumber description laborCost
   return itemNumber~right(3) laborCost~right(11) '' description~left(20)

::method makestring                             /* return default string   */
   expose itemNumber description laborCost
   return 'ServiceItem:' itemNumber '($'laborCost')' description

::method display                                /* display service data    */
   expose itemNumber description laborCost parts quantity.
   say '-'~copies(78)
   say self~class~heading
   say self~detail
   do partx over parts
      say ' '~left(30) quantity.partx~right(6) ' ' ,
          partx~number~right(3) partx~description
   end
   do workx over self~getWorkOrders
      say '-' workx
   end
```

Figure 173. *(Part 3 of 3) Base Service Item Class (base\carserv.cls)*

Base Part Class

```
/*------------------------------------------------------------------*/
/* Base\carpart.cls      CarDealer - Part class (base)      ITSO-SJC */
/*------------------------------------------------------------------*/

::class PartBase public

/*----- class methods ----------------------------------------------*/

::method initialize class                       /* prepare the class       */
   expose extent
   extent = .set~new                            /* - extent of parts       */
   self~persistentLoad                          /* - load into memory      */

::method add class                              /* add new part to extent  */
   expose extent
   use arg partx
   if partx~class = self then                   /* - add to extent         */
      extent~put(partx)
```

Figure 174. *(Part 1 of 3) Base Part Class (base\carpart.cls)*

```
::method remove class                              /* remove part from extent */
   expose extent
   use arg partx
   if partx~class = self then                      /* - remove               */
      extent~remove(partx)

::method findNumber class                          /* find part by number    */
   expose extent
   parse arg partnum
   do partx over extent                            /* - check the extent     */
      if partx~number = partnum then return partx
   end
   return .nil

::method extent class                              /* return extent as array */
   expose extent
   return extent~makearray
::method heading class                             /* return a heading line  */
   return 'Partid   Description            Price    Stock'

/*----- instance methods --------------------------------------------*/

::method init                                      /* initialize a new part  */
   expose partid description price stock
   self~init:super
   use arg partid, description, price, stock
   if arg() \= 4 & arg() \= 5 then self~setnil
   else self~class~add(self)                       /* - add to extent        */
   if arg() = 5 then self~persistentInsert         /* - add to persistent    */

::method setnil private                            /* set part data nil      */
   expose partid description price stock
   self~class~remove(self)                         /* - remove from extent   */
   partid = 0
   description = '-none-'
   price = 0
   stock = 0
   return .nil

::method delete                                    /* delete a part          */
   self~class~remove(self)                         /* - remove from extent   */
   /* self~persistentDelete */                     /* - not implemented      */
   self~setnil

::method number unguarded                          /* return parts number    */
   expose partid
   return partid

::method price unguarded                           /* return price of part   */
   expose price
   return price

::method description unguarded                     /* return description     */
   expose description
   return description

::method stock unguarded                           /* return stock of part   */
   expose stock
   return stock
```

Figure 174. *(Part 2 of 3) Base Part Class (base\carpart.cls)*

```
::method increaseStock                          /* increase stock of part  */
   expose stock
   parse arg stockchange
   stock = stock + stockchange                  /* - add change            */
   return self~persistentUpdate                 /* - store persistently    */

::method decreaseStock                          /* decrease stock of part  */
   expose stock
   parse arg stockchange
   if stockchange > stock then return -1         /* - check if possible     */
   stock = stock - stockchange                  /* - subtract change       */
   return self~persistentUpdate                 /* - store persistently    */

::method detail                                 /* return a detail line    */
   expose partid description price stock
   return partid~right(5) ' ' description~left(15) ' ',
          price~right(8) ' ' stock~right(5)

::method makestring                             /* return default string   */
   expose partid description
   return 'Part:' partid description

::method display                                /* display part data       */
   expose partid description price stock
   say partid~right(5) ' ' description~left(15) ' ',
       price~right(8) ' ' stock~right(5)
```

Figure 174. *(Part 3 of 3) Base Part Class (base\carpart.cls)*

Persistent Class

```
/*-------------------------------------------------------------------*/
/* Base\persist.cls     CarDealer - Persistent class      ITSO-SJC */
/*-------------------------------------------------------------------*/

::class Persistent public mixinclass Object

/*----- class methods ---------------------------------------------*/
::method persistentLoad class                   /* default load into memory*/
   return 0
::method persistentStore class                  /* default store back      */
   return 0


/*----- instance methods ------------------------------------------*/
::method persistentInsert                       /* default new object      */
   return self~class~persistentStore
::method persistentDelete                       /* default delete object   */
   return self~class~persistentStore
::method persistentUpdate                       /* default update object   */
   return self~class~persistentStore
::method persistentInsertServ                   /* new work-serv relation  */
   return self~class~persistentStore
::method persistentDeleteServ                   /* delete work-serv relat. */
   return self~class~persistentStore
```

Figure 175. *Persistent Class (base\persist.cls)*

Cardeal Class

```
/*------------------------------------------------------------------*/
/* Base\cardeal.cls      CarDealer - Cardeal class          ITSO-SJC */
/*------------------------------------------------------------------*/

    .local['Cardeal.Cardeal.class'] = .Cardeal

::class Cardeal public

/*----- class methods ----------------------------------------------*/

::method initialize class                       /* prepare the class     */
    expose env envir
    parse source env .                          /* - where are we running */
    if env = 'OS/2' then envir = 'OS2ENVIRONMENT'
                    else envir = 'ENVIRONMENT'
    if RxFuncQuery('SysLoadFuncs') then do      /* - load rexx utilities  */
        call RxFuncAdd 'SysLoadFuncs', 'RexxUtil', 'SysLoadFuncs'
        call SysLoadFuncs
    end
    x = RxFuncDrop('PlaySoundFile')             /* - drop multimedia funct.*/
    self~mciRxInit                              /* - init multimedia funct.*/
    .local['Cardeal.Part.class']~initialize     /* - initialize all classes*/
    .local['Cardeal.ServiceItem.class']~initialize
    .local['Cardeal.Customer.class']~initialize
    .local['Cardeal.Vehicle.class']~initialize
    .local['Cardeal.WorkOrder.class']~initialize
    return 0

::method terminate class                        /* application terminate   */
    expose envir
    if .local['Cardeal.Data.type'] = 'DB2' then do /* - check if DB2        */
        call sqlexec "CONNECT RESET"            /* - disconnect            */
        if arg() = 0 then do
            temp = value('TMP',,envir)
            if temp = '' then temp = directory()
            call SysFileTree temp"\t*.*", tempfiles, 'FO'
            do i=1 to tempfiles.0               /* - erase temp files      */
                parse upper value substr(tempfiles.i,lastpos('\',tempfiles.i)+1) ,
                    with fn '.' fx
                if pos('.'fx'.',',.BMP.WAV.AVI.')>0 & fn~right(1)~datatype('W')=1
                    then "@erase" tempfiles.i
            end
        end
    end
    do localx over .local~makearray             /* - delete all local      */
        if localx~left(8) = 'Cardeal.' then .local~remove(localx)
    end

::method playaudio class                        /* play an audio file      */
    expose MultiMedia
    arg filename
    if filename = '' | Multimedia = 0 then return
    call PlaySoundFile filename, "YES"
```

Figure 176. *(Part 1 of 2) Cardeal Class (base\cardeal.cls)*

```
::method playvideo class                          /* play a video file       */
   expose MultiMedia env
   arg filename
   if filename = '' | Multimedia = 0 then return
   parse var filename fanme '.' ext
   select
      when ext = 'AVI' & env = 'Windows95' then "mplayer /PLAY" filename
      when ext = 'AVI' & env = 'WindowsNT' then "mplay32 /PLAY" filename
      when ext = 'MOV' then "play32" filename
      otherwise nop
   end

::method mciRxInit class private                   /* initialize multimedia   */
   expose done MultiMedia
   if symbol('done') = 'VAR' then return MultiMedia
   if RxFuncQuery('PlaySoundFile') then            /* - load rex functions     */
       MultiMedia = (RXFUNCADD('PlaySoundFile','OODIALOG','PlaySoundFile')=0)
   else MultiMedia = 1
   done = 1
   return MultiMedia
```

Figure 176. *(Part 2 of 2) Cardeal Class (base\cardeal.cls)*

Persistence in Files

Configuration for File Storage

```
/*-------------------------------------------------------------------*/
/* FAT\carmodel.cfg      CarDealer - Model Config. (FAT)     ITSO-SJC */
/*-------------------------------------------------------------------*/

   Parse source . . me
   maindir = me~left(me~lastpos('\')-1)      /* main cardeal directory */
   if stream(maindir'\base\cardeal.cls',c,'query exists') = '' then
       call carerror maindir

   .local['Cardeal.Data.type'] = 'FAT'               /* Data in Files  */
   .local['Cardeal.Data.dir']  = maindir'\FAT\Data'/* Data directory   */
   .local['Cardeal.Media.dir'] = maindir'\Media'   /* Media directory  */

::requires 'base\cardeal.cls'

::requires 'fat\carcust.cls'
::requires 'fat\carvehi.cls'
::requires 'fat\carpart.cls'
::requires 'fat\carserv.cls'
::requires 'fat\carwork.cls'
```

Figure 177. *Configuration for File Storage (fat\carmodel.cfg)*

File Customer Class

```
/*----------------------------------------------------------------*/
/* FAT\carcust.cls        CarDealer - Customer class (FAT)    ITSO-SJC */
/*----------------------------------------------------------------*/

   .local['Cardeal.Customer.class'] = .Customer

::requires 'base\carcust.cls'
::requires 'base\persist.cls'

::class Customer public subclass CustomerBase inherit Persistent

/*----- class methods ------------------------------------------*/

::method persistentLoad class                   /* load customers from file*/
   expose file
   file = .local['Cardeal.Data.dir']'\customer.dat'
   call stream file, 'c', 'open read'
   do i = 0 by 1 while lines(file)              /* - read the file        */
      parse value linein(file) with customerNumber '9'x name '9'x address
      if left(customerNumber,2) = '/*' then iterate
      self~new(strip(customerNumber), strip(name), strip(address))
   end
   call stream file, 'c', 'close'
   return i

::method persistentStore class                  /* store customers in file */
   expose file
   call stream file, 'c', 'open write replace'
   do custx over self~extent                    /* - run over extent      */
      x = lineout(file,custx~fileFormat)
   end
   call stream file, 'c', 'close'
   return 0

/*----- instance methods ---------------------------------------*/

::method fileFormat                             /* prepare record for file */
   return strip(self~number)'9'x || left(self~name,20)'9'x || ,
          left(self~address,20)
```

Figure 178. *File Customer Class (fat\carcust.cls)*

File Vehicle Class

```
/*---------------------------------------------------------------*/
/* FAT\carvehi.cls       CarDealer - Vehicle class (FAT)    ITSO-SJC */
/*---------------------------------------------------------------*/

   .local['Cardeal.Vehicle.class'] = .Vehicle

::requires 'base\carvehi.cls'
::requires 'base\persist.cls'

::class Vehicle public subclass VehicleBase inherit Persistent

/*----- class methods ---------------------------------------*/

::method persistentLoad class                   /* load vehicles from file */
   expose file
   file = .local['Cardeal.Data.dir']'\vehicle.dat'
   custclass = .local['Cardeal.Customer.class']
   call stream file, 'c', 'open read'
   do i = 0 by 1 while lines(file)               /* - read the file        */
      parse value linein(file) ,
            with serialNumber '9'X make '9'X model '9'X year '9'X owner
      if left(serialNumber,2) = '/*' then iterate
      self~new(strip(serialNumber), strip(make), strip(model), strip(year), ,
            custclass~findNumber(owner))
   end
   call stream file, 'c', 'close'
   return i

::method persistentStore class                   /* store vehicle in file   */
   expose file
   call stream file, 'c', 'open write replace'    /* - run over customers    */
   do custx over .local['Cardeal.Customer.class']~extent
      do carx over custx~getVehicles             /* - and their vehicles    */
         x = lineout(file,carx~fileFormat)
      end
   end
   call stream file, 'c', 'close'
   return 0

/*----- instance methods ---------------------------------------*/

::method fileFormat                              /* prepare record for file */
   return strip(self~serial)'9'x || left(self~make,12)'9'x || ,
         left(self~model,10)'9'x || strip(self~year)'9'x || ,
         strip(self~getowner~number)
```

Figure 179. *(Part 1 of 2) File Vehicle Class (fat\carvehi.cls)*

```
::method getmedianumber                            /* return number of media  */
   expose medianumber mediacontrol picfile
   if symbol('medianumber') = 'VAR' then return medianumber
   medianumber = 0
   mediacontrol = ''
   picfile = .array~new
   mediafile = .local['Cardeal.Media.dir']'\media.dat'
   do i=1 by 1 while lines(mediafile)>0              /* - read media controlfile*/
     line = linein(mediafile)
     if left(line,2) = '/*' then iterate
     parse var line serial ',' title ',' file
     if self~serial = strip(serial) then do         /* - check for serial      */
        medianumber = medianumber + 1
        picfile[medianumber] = strip(file)          /* - build control info    */
        mediacontrol = mediacontrol''left(strip(title),20)',file     ;'
     end
   end
   x = stream(mediafile,'c','close')
   return medianumber

::method getmediacontrol                            /* return media controlinfo*/
   expose medianumber mediacontrol
   if symbol("medianumber") = 'LIT' then return ''
   return mediacontrol

::method getmediainfo                               /* return a media file     */
   expose medianumber mediacontrol picfile
   if symbol("medianumber") = 'LIT' then return ''
   arg medianum
   if medianumber = 0 | mediacontrol = '' | ,
      medianum > medianumber | medianum <= 0 then return ''
   mediatitle  = substr(mediacontrol,medianum*30-29,20)
   vfacts = .local['Cardeal.Media.dir']'\'picfile[medianum]
   if left(mediatitle,4) = 'Fact' then do
     factdata = linein(vfacts)
     x = stream(vfacts,'c','close')
     vfacts = factdata
   end
   return mediatitle'::'vfacts
```

Figure 179. *(Part 2 of 2) File Vehicle Class (fat\carvehi.cls)*

File Work Order Class

```
/*------------------------------------------------------------------*/
/* FAT\carwork.cls      CarDealer - WorkOrder class (FAT)   ITSO-SJC */
/*------------------------------------------------------------------*/

   .local['Cardeal.WorkOrder.class'] = .WorkOrder

::requires 'base\carwork.cls'
::requires 'base\persist.cls'


::class WorkOrder public subclass WorkOrderBase inherit Persistent

/*----- class methods ----------------------------------------------*/

::method persistentLoad class                   /* load work orders file   */
   expose file
   file = .local['Cardeal.Data.dir']'\workord.dat'
   custclass = .local['Cardeal.Customer.class']
   servclass = .local['Cardeal.ServiceItem.class']
   call stream file, 'c', 'open read'
   do i = 0 by 1 while lines(file)              /* - read the file         */
      parse value linein(file) with orderno '9'x date '9'x cost ,
                  '9'x status '9'x owner '9'x car '9'x items
      if left(orderno,2) = '/*' then iterate
      custx = custclass~findNumber(owner)        /* - create new work order */
      wo = self~new(strip(orderno), strip(date), strip(cost), ,
                  strip(status), custx, custx~findVehicle(car))
      do while items \= ''                        /* - add services to order */
         parse var items itemx '9'x items
         wo~addServiceItem(servclass~findNumber(itemx))
      end
   end
   call stream file, 'c', 'close'
   return i

::method persistentStore class                  /* store workorders in file*/
   expose file
   call stream file, 'c', 'open write replace'
   do ordrx over self~extent                     /* - run over extent       */
      x = lineout(file,ordrx~fileFormat)
   end
   call stream file, 'c', 'close'
   return 0

/*----- instance methods --------------------------------------------*/

::method fileFormat                             /* prepare record for file */
   out = strip(self~number)'9'x || strip(self~date)'9'x || ,
         strip(self~cost)'9'x || strip(self~getstatus)'9'x || ,
         strip(self~getcustomer~number)'9'x || strip(self~getvehicle~serial)
   workserv = self~class~getWorkServRel
   do servx over workserv~allat(self)
      out = out'9'x || servx~number
   end
   return out
```

Figure 180. *File Work Order Class (fat\carwork.cls)*

File Service Item Class

```
/*------------------------------------------------------------*/
/* FAT\carserv.cls      CarDealer - ServiceItem class (FAT) ITSO-SJC */
/*------------------------------------------------------------*/

   .local['Cardeal.ServiceItem.class'] = .ServiceItem

::requires 'base\carserv.cls'
::requires 'base\persist.cls'

::class ServiceItem public subclass ServiceItemBase inherit Persistent

/*----- class methods --------------------------------------------*/

::method persistentLoad class                  /* load service from file  */
   expose file
   file = .local['Cardeal.Data.dir']'\service.dat'
   partclass = .local['Cardeal.Part.class']
   call stream file, 'c', 'open read'
   do i = 0 by 1 while lines(file)             /* - read the file         */
      parse value linein(file) with ,
            itemNumber '9'x description '9'x laborCost '9'x parts
      if left(itemNumber,2) = '/*' then iterate
      si = self~new(strip(itemNumber), strip(description), strip(laborCost))
      do while parts \= ''                      /* - add parts to service  */
         parse var parts partnum '9'x quant '9'x parts
         si~usesPart(partclass~findNumber(partnum), strip(quant))
      end
   end
   call stream file, 'c', 'close'
   return i

::method persistentStore class                 /* store services in file  */
   /* no change in data ever */
   return 0

/*----- instance methods -----------------------------------------*/

::method fileFormat                            /* prepare record for file */
   /* never used since service items are not updated */
   out = strip(self~number)'9'x || left(self~description,20)'9'x || ,
         strip(self~laborcost)
   do partx over parts
      out = out'9'x || right(partx~number,2) || ,
               '9'x || right(self~getquantity(partx),2)
   end
   return out
```

Figure 181. *File Service Item Class (fat\carserv.cls)*

File Part Class

```
/*----------------------------------------------------------------*/
/* FAT\carpart.cls        CarDealer - Part class (FAT)      ITSO-SJC */
/*----------------------------------------------------------------*/

   .local['Cardeal.Part.class'] = .Part

::requires 'base\carpart.cls'
::requires 'base\persist.cls'


::class Part public subclass PartBase inherit Persistent

/*----- class methods -------------------------------------------*/

::method persistentLoad class                    /* load parts from file    */
   expose file
   file = .local['Cardeal.Data.dir']'\part.dat'
   call stream file, 'c', 'open read'
   do i = 0 by 1 while lines(file)               /* - read the file         */
      parse value linein(file) with ,
           partid '9'x description '9'x price '9'x stock
      if left(partid,2) = '/*' then iterate
      self~new(strip(partid), strip(description), strip(price), strip(stock))
   end
   call stream file, 'c', 'close'
   return i

::method persistentStore class                   /* store parts in file     */
   expose file
   call stream file, 'c', 'open write replace'
   do partx over self~extent                      /* - run over extent       */
      x = lineout(file,partx~fileFormat)
   end
   call stream file, 'c', 'close'
   return 0

/*----- instance methods -----------------------------------------*/

::method fileFormat                              /* prepare record for file */
   return strip(self~number)'9'x || left(self~description,15)'9'x || ,
          strip(self~price)'9'x  || strip(self~stock)
```

Figure 182. *File Part Class (fat\carpart.cls)*

Persistence in DB2

Configuration for DB2 Storage

```
/*--------------------------------------------------------------*/
/* DB2\carmodel.cfg      CarDealer - Model Config. (DB2)    ITSO-SJC */
/*--------------------------------------------------------------*/

   Parse source . . me
   maindir = me~left(me~lastpos('\')-1)     /* main cardeal directory */
   if stream(maindir'\base\cardeal.cls',c,'query exists') = '' then
      call carerror maindir

   call rxdb2con                            /* Rexx DB2 connect      */
   if result>0 then exit 16

   .local['Cardeal.Data.type'] = 'DB2'     /* Data in DB2          */
   .local['Cardeal.Data.dir']  = '-none-'  /* Data in DB2          */
   .local['Cardeal.Media.dir'] = '-none-'  /* Media in DB2         */

::requires 'base\cardeal.cls'

::requires 'db2\carcust.cls'
::requires 'db2\carvehi.cls'
::requires 'db2\carpart.cls'
::requires 'db2\carserv.cls'
::requires 'db2\carwork.cls'
```

Figure 183. *Configuration for DB2 Storage (db2\carmodel.cfg)*

DB2 Customer Class

```
/*--------------------------------------------------------------*/
/* DB2\carcust.cls       CarDealer - Customer class (DB2)    ITSO-SJC */
/*--------------------------------------------------------------*/

   .local['Cardeal.Customer.class'] = .Customer

::requires 'base\carcust.cls'

::class Customer public subclass CustomerBase

/*----- class methods --------------------------------------------*/

::method persistentLoad class                 /* null, load by demand  */
   return 0
```

Figure 184. *(Part 1 of 3) DB2 Customer Class (db2\carcust.cls)*

```
::method findNumber class                             /* load customer by number */
   use arg custnum
   vehiclass = .local['Cardeal.Vehicle.class']
   workclass = .local['Cardeal.WorkOrder.class']
   custx = self~findNumber:super(custnum)             /* - check if in memory    */
   if custx \= .nil then return custx
   stmt = 'select c.custname, c.custaddr' ,
          ' from cardeal.customer c' ,
          ' where c.custnum =' custnum
   call sqlexec 'PREPARE s1 FROM :stmt'
   call sqlexec 'DECLARE c1 CURSOR FOR s1'
   call sqlexec 'OPEN c1'
   call sqlexec 'FETCH c1 INTO :xcustn, :xcusta'
   if sqlca.sqlcode = 0 then do
       custx = self~new(custnum, xcustn, xcusta)
       vehiclass~persistentLoadByCust(custx)          /* - load vehicles of cust.*/
       workclass~persistentLoadByCust(custx)          /* - load workorders       */
       end
   else custx = .nil
   call sqlexec 'CLOSE c1'
   return custx

::method findName class                               /* find customer by name   */
   use arg custsearch
   custnames = .list~new                              /* - prepare result list   */
   stmt = "select c.custnum, c.custname, c.custaddr" ,
          "  from cardeal.customer c" ,
          " where c.custname like ?  order by 2"
   call sqlexec 'PREPARE s1 FROM :stmt'
   call sqlexec 'DECLARE c1 CURSOR FOR s1'
   xsearch = "'"custsearch"%'"
   call sqlexec "OPEN c1 USING :xsearch"
   do icust=0 by 1 until rcc \= 0                      /* - search table with LIKE*/
      call sqlexec 'FETCH c1 INTO :xcustno, :xcustn, :xcusta'
      rcc = sqlca.sqlcode
      if rcc = 0 then do
         custstring = xcustno~right(3)'-'xcustn'-'xcusta
         custnames~insert(custstring)
      end
   end
   call sqlexec 'CLOSE c1'
   return custnames~makearray                          /* - return result array   */

::method findAddress class                             /* find customer by address*/
   use arg custsearch
   stmt = "select c.custnum, c.custname, c.custaddr" ,
          "  from cardeal.customer c" ,
          " where c.custaddr = ?"
   call sqlexec 'PREPARE s1 FROM :stmt'
   call sqlexec 'DECLARE c1 CURSOR FOR s1'
   xsearch = "'"custsearch"'"
   call sqlexec "OPEN c1 USING :xsearch"
      call sqlexec 'FETCH c1 INTO :xcustno, :xcustn, :xcusta'
      rcc = sqlca.sqlcode
   call sqlexec 'CLOSE c1'
   if rcc = 0 then return xcustno                      /* return customer number  */
   else return ''
```

Figure 184. *(Part 2 of 3) DB2 Customer Class (db2\carcust.cls)*

```
/*----- instance methods -------------------------------------------*/

::method persistentInsert                        /* store new customer    */
   insertstmt = "insert into cardeal.customer" ,
                "   values("self~number","'"self~name"'",'"self~address"')"
   call sqlexec 'EXECUTE IMMEDIATE :insertstmt'
   if sqlca.sqlcode \= 0 then do
      say 'cust insert' sqlca.sqlcode sqlmsg
      self~setnil
      end
   else call sqlexec 'COMMIT'
   return sqlca.sqlcode

::method persistentUpdate                        /* update a customer     */
   updatetstmt = "update cardeal.customer" ,
                "   set custname = '"self~name"'", custaddr ='"self~address"'" ,
                " where custnum =" self~number
   call sqlexec 'EXECUTE IMMEDIATE :updatetstmt'
   if sqlca.sqlcode \= 0 then say 'customer update' sqlca.sqlcode sqlmsg
   else call sqlexec 'COMMIT'
   return sqlca.sqlcode

::method persistentDelete                        /* delete a customer     */
   delstmt = 'delete from cardeal.customer where custnum =' self~number
   call sqlexec 'EXECUTE IMMEDIATE :delstmt'
   if sqlca.sqlcode \= 0 then say 'cust delete' sqlca.sqlcode sqlmsg
   else call sqlexec 'COMMIT'
   return sqlca.sqlcode
```

Figure 184. *(Part 3 of 3) DB2 Customer Class (db2\carcust.cls)*

DB2 Vehicle Class

```
/*------------------------------------------------------------------*/
/* DB2\carvehi.cls       CarDealer - Vehicle class (DB2)     ITSO-SJC */
/*------------------------------------------------------------------*/

   .local['Cardeal.Vehicle.class'] = .Vehicle

::requires 'base\carvehi.cls'

::class Vehicle public subclass VehicleBase

/*----- class methods ---------------------------------------------*/

::method persistentLoad class                    /* null, load by demand   */
   return 0
::method persistentLoadByCust class              /* load vehicle of customer*/
   use arg custx
   customerNumber = custx~number
   stmt = 'select v.serialnum, v.make, v.model, v.year' ,
          ' from cardeal.vehicle v  where v.custnum =' customerNumber
   call sqlexec 'PREPARE s2 FROM :stmt'
   call sqlexec 'DECLARE c2 CURSOR FOR s2'
   call sqlexec 'OPEN c2'
```

Figure 185. *(Part 1 of 3) DB2 Vehicle Class (db2\carvehi.cls)*

```
    do until rcv \= 0                                  /* - run over vehicles    */
        call sqlexec 'FETCH c2 INTO :xserial, :xmake, :xmodel, :xyear'
        rcv = sqlca.sqlcode
        if rcv = 0 then
            carx = self~new(xserial, xmake, xmodel, xyear, custx)
    end
    call sqlexec 'CLOSE c2'
    return 0

/*----- instance methods -------------------------------------------*/

::method persistentInsert                              /* store new vehicle      */
    custnum = self~getowner~number
    insertstmt = "insert into cardeal.vehicle" ,
                 " (serialnum, custnum, make, model, year)" ,
                 "   values("self~serial","custnum",'"self~make"'," ,
                 "'"self~model"','"self~year")"
    /* say 'created' self 'in DB2' */
    call sqlexec 'EXECUTE IMMEDIATE :insertstmt'
    if sqlca.sqlcode \= 0 then do
        say 'vehicle insert' sqlca.sqlcode sqlca.sqlerrmc
        self~setnil
    end
    call sqlexec 'COMMIT'

::method persistentUpdate                              /* update vehicle data    */
    updatetstmt = "update cardeal.vehicle" ,
                  "   set make ='"self~make"', model ='"self~model"'," ,
                  "year =" selfyear ,
                  " where serialnum =" self~serial
    call sqlexec 'EXECUTE IMMEDIATE :updatetstmt'
    if sqlca.sqlcode \= 0 then say 'customer update' sqlca.sqlcode sqlmsg
    else call sqlexec 'COMMIT'
    return sqlca.sqlcode

::method persistentDelete                              /* delete a vehicle       */
    delstmt = 'delete from cardeal.vehicle where serialnum =' self~serial
    call sqlexec 'EXECUTE IMMEDIATE :delstmt'
    if sqlca.sqlcode \= 0 then say 'vehicle delete' sqlca.sqlcode sqlmsg
    else call sqlexec 'COMMIT'
    return sqlca.sqlcode

::method getmedianumber                                /* number of media files  */
    expose medianumber mediacontrol                    /* - in the BLOB          */
    if symbol("medianumber") = 'VAR' then return medianumber
    medianumber = 0
    mediacontrol = ''                                  /* - prepare control info */
    stmt = 'select substr(v.pictures,1,3)' ,
           '  from cardeal.vehicle v  where v.serialnum =' self~serial
    call sqlexec 'PREPARE s2 FROM :stmt'
    if sqlca.sqlcode \= 0 then return 0
    vpicind = -1
    call sqlexec 'DECLARE c2 CURSOR FOR s2'
    call sqlexec 'OPEN c2'
        call sqlexec 'FETCH c2 INTO :vpic :vpicind'
    call sqlexec 'CLOSE c2'
    if vpicind >=0 then medianumber = vpic
    return medianumber
```

Figure 185. *(Part 2 of 3) DB2 Vehicle Class (db2\carvehi.cls)*

```
::method getmediacontrol                              /* return media controlinfo*/
   expose medianumber mediacontrol
   if symbol("medianumber") = 'LIT' then return ''
   if medianumber <= 0 then return ''
   stmt = 'select substr(v.pictures,5,30*'medianumber')' ,
          '  from cardeal.vehicle v  where v.serialnum =' self~serial
   call sqlexec 'PREPARE s2 FROM :stmt'
   call sqlexec 'DECLARE c2 CURSOR FOR s2'
   call sqlexec 'OPEN c2'
      call sqlexec 'FETCH c2 INTO :vpic :vpicind'
      rcv = sqlca.sqlcode
   call sqlexec 'CLOSE c2'
   if rcv = 0 & vpicind >= 0 then mediacontrol = vpic
   return mediacontrol

::method getmediainfo                                 /* return one media file   */
   expose medianumber mediacontrol
   parse source env .
   if env = 'OS/2' then env = 'OS2ENVIRONMENT'
                    else env = 'ENVIRONMENT'
   if symbol("medianumber") = 'LIT' then return ''
   if mediacontrol = '' then self~getmediacontrol
   arg medianum
   if medianumber = 0 | medianum > medianumber | medianum <= 0 | ,
      mediacontrol = '' then return ''
   mediatitle  = substr(mediacontrol,medianum*30-29,20)
   medialength = substr(mediacontrol,medianum*30- 8, 8)
   mediastart = 7 + 30 * medianumber
   do i=1 to medianum -1
      blg = substr(mediacontrol,i*30-8,8)
      mediastart = mediastart + blg
   end
   call sqlexec 'CLEAR SQL VARIABLE DECLARATIONS'
   call sqlexec 'DECLARE :vpic3 LANGUAGE TYPE BLOB FILE'
   vpic3.file_options = 'OVERWRITE'
   temp = value('TMP',,env)
   if temp = '' then temp = directory()
   tnam = 't'self~serial''medianum
   shorttitle = mediatitle~left(4)
   select
      when shorttitle = 'Fact' then vpic3.name = ''
      when shorttitle = 'Audi' then vpic3.name = temp'\'tnam'.WAV'
      when shorttitle = 'Vide' then vpic3.name = temp'\'tnam'.AVI'
      otherwise                      vpic3.name = temp'\'tnam'.BMP'
   end
   vfacts = vpic3.name
   stmt = 'select substr(v.pictures,'mediastart','medialength')' ,
          '  from cardeal.vehicle v  where v.serialnum =' self~serial
   call sqlexec 'PREPARE s2 FROM :stmt'
   call sqlexec 'DECLARE c2 CURSOR FOR s2'
   call sqlexec 'OPEN c2'
      if vfacts = '' then call sqlexec 'FETCH c2 INTO :vfacts'
                     else call sqlexec 'FETCH c2 INTO :vpic3 :vpicind3'
      if sqlca.sqlcode \= 0 then vfacts = ''
   call sqlexec 'CLOSE c2'
   call sqlexec 'CLEAR SQL VARIABLE DECLARATIONS'
   return mediatitle'::'vfacts
```

Figure 185. *(Part 3 of 3) DB2 Vehicle Class (db2\carvehi.cls)*

DB2 Work Order Class

```
/*------------------------------------------------------------------*/
/* DB2\carwork.cls     CarDealer - WorkOrder class (DB2)   ITSO-SJC */
/*------------------------------------------------------------------*/

   .local['Cardeal.WorkOrder.class'] = .WorkOrder

::requires 'base\carwork.cls'

::class WorkOrder public subclass WorkOrderBase

/*----- class methods -------------------------------------------*/

::method persistentLoad class                 /* null, load by demand    */
   return 0

::method findNumber class                     /* find workorder by number*/
   use arg worknum
   custclass = .local['Cardeal.Customer.class']
   workx = self~findNumber:super(worknum)      /* - check in memory first */
   if workx \= .nil then return workx          /* - return if found       */
   stmt = 'select w.custnum' ,
          '  from cardeal.workorder w  where w.ordernum =' worknum
   call sqlexec 'PREPARE s3 FROM :stmt'
   call sqlexec 'DECLARE c3 CURSOR FOR s3'
   call sqlexec 'OPEN c3'
   call sqlexec 'FETCH c3 INTO :xcustnum'
   rcw = sqlca.sqlcode
   call sqlexec 'CLOSE c3'
   if rcw = 0 then do
      custx = custclass~findNumber(xcustnum)
      if custx \= .nil then
         do workx over self~extent
            if workx~number = worknum then return workx
         end
   end
   return .nil

::method findStatus class                     /* find workorder by status*/
   use arg xstatus
   worklist = .list~new                        /* - prepare result list   */
   stmt = 'select w.ordernum, w.orderdate, w.cost, w.status,' ,
          '       c.custname, v.make, v.model' ,
          '  from cardeal.workorder w, cardeal.customer c, cardeal.vehicle v' ,
          ' where w.custnum = c.custnum and w.serialnum = v.serialnum' ,
          '   and w.status in (?, ?)' ,
          ' order by 1'
   hostvar = ':xordno, :xdate, :xcost, :xstatus, :xcustn, :xmake, :xmodel'
   call sqlexec 'PREPARE s3 FROM :stmt'
   call sqlexec 'DECLARE c3 CURSOR FOR s3'
   xstat1 = 0
   xstat2 = 1
   if xstatus = 0 then xstat2=0
   if xstatus = 1 then xstat1=1
   call sqlexec 'OPEN c3 USING :xstat1, :xstat2'
```

Figure 186. *(Part 1 of 3) DB2 Work Order Class (db2\carwork.cls)*

```
   do iwork = 0 by -1 until rcw \= 0
      call sqlexec 'FETCH c3 INTO' hostvar
      rcw = sqlca.sqlcode
      if rcw = 0 then do
         if xstatus = 0 then statusx = 'Incomplete'
                         else statusx = 'Complete'
         workstring = xordno~left(3) '' xdate xcost~right(6) statusx~left(11)  ,
                     (xmake~strip'-'xmodel~strip)~left(20) xcustn
         worklist~insert(workstring,.nil)
      end
   end
   call sqlexec 'CLOSE c3'
   return worklist~makearray

::method newNumber class                          /* create new order number */
   stmt = 'select max(ordernum) from cardeal.workorder'
   call sqlexec 'PREPARE s3 FROM :stmt'
   call sqlexec 'DECLARE c3 CURSOR FOR s3'
   call sqlexec 'OPEN c3'
   call sqlexec 'FETCH c3 INTO :xmax'
   call sqlexec 'CLOSE c3'
   return xmax + 1

::method persistentLoadByCust class               /* load workorders of cust.*/
   use arg custx
   servclass = .local['Cardeal.ServiceItem.class']
   customerNumber = custx~number
   stmt = 'select w.ordernum, w.cost, w.orderdate, w.status, w.serialnum' ,
          ' from cardeal.workorder w  where w.custnum =' customerNumber
   call sqlexec 'PREPARE s4 FROM :stmt'
   call sqlexec 'DECLARE c4 CURSOR FOR s4'
   call sqlexec 'OPEN c4'
   do until rcw \=  0                              /* - run over orders      */
      call sqlexec 'FETCH c4 INTO :xorder, :xcost, :xdate, :xstatus, :xserial'
      rcw = sqlca.sqlcode
      if rcw = 0 then do
         cars = custx~getVehicles
         do carx over cars                         /* - find matching car    */
            if carx~serial = xserial then do       /*   for work order       */
               orderx = self~new(xorder, xdate, xcost, xstatus, custx, carx)
               servitems = servclass~extent
               stmt2 = 'select r.itemnum' ,
                       ' from cardeal.workserv r  where r.ordernum =' xorder
               call sqlexec 'PREPARE s5 FROM :stmt2'
               call sqlexec 'DECLARE c5 CURSOR FOR s5'
               call sqlexec 'OPEN c5'
               do until rcs \=  0                   /* - and add rels to serv, */
                  call sqlexec 'FETCH c5 INTO :xitem'
                  rcs = sqlca.sqlcode
                  if rcs = 0 then
                     do servx over servitems
                        if servx~number = xitem then
                           orderx~addServiceItem(servx)
                     end
               end
               call sqlexec 'CLOSE c5'
            end
         end /*cars*/
```

Figure 186. *(Part 2 of 3) DB2 Work Order Class (db2\carwork.cls)*

```
      end   /*rcw=0*/
   end
   call sqlexec 'CLOSE c4'
   return 0

/*----- instance methods --------------------------------------*/

::method persistentInsert                         /* store new work order    */
   custnum = self~getcustomer~number
   carserial = self~getvehicle~serial
   insertstmt = "insert into cardeal.workorder" ,
              "    values("self~number","custnum","carserial"," ,
              self~cost",'"self~date"',"self~getstatus")"
   call sqlexec 'EXECUTE IMMEDIATE :insertstmt'
   if sqlca.sqlcode \= 0 then do
      say 'workorder insert' sqlca.sqlcode sqlmsg
      self~setnil
      end
   else call sqlexec 'COMMIT'
   return sqlca.sqlcode

::method persistentDelete                         /* delete work order       */
   delstmt = 'delete from cardeal.workorder where ordernum =' self~number
   call sqlexec 'EXECUTE IMMEDIATE :delstmt'
   if sqlca.sqlcode \= 0 then say 'order delete' sqlca.sqlcode sqlca.sqlerrmc
   delstmt = 'delete from cardeal.workserv where ordernum =' self~number
   call sqlexec 'EXECUTE IMMEDIATE :delstmt'
   if sqlca.sqlcode \= 0 & sclca.sqlcode \= 100 then
      say 'order-serv delete' sqlca.sqlcode sqlmsg
   else call sqlexec 'COMMIT'
   return sqlca.sqlcode

::method persistentInsertServ                     /* add service item        */
   use arg itemnum
   insertstmt = 'insert into cardeal.workserv values('self~number',' itemnum')'
   call sqlexec 'EXECUTE IMMEDIATE :insertstmt'
   rci = sqlca.sqlcode
   if rci \= 0 then say 'workserv insert' sqlca.sqlcode sqlmsg
   else call sqlexec 'COMMIT'
   return sqlca.sqlcode

::method persistentDeleteServ                     /* delete service item     */
   use arg itemnum
   deletestmt = 'delete from cardeal.workserv' ,
              ' where ordernum =' self~number 'and itemnum =' itemnum
   call sqlexec 'EXECUTE IMMEDIATE :deletestmt'
   if sqlca.sqlcode \= 0 then say 'workserv delete' sqlca.sqlcode sqlca.sqlerrmc
   else call sqlexec 'COMMIT'
   return sqlca.sqlcode

::method persistentUpdate                         /* update work order data  */
   updatestmt = 'update cardeal.workorder' ,
              '   set cost =' self~cost', status =' self~getstatus ,
              ' where ordernum =' self~number
   call sqlexec 'EXECUTE IMMEDIATE :updatestmt'
   if sqlca.sqlcode \= 0 then say 'workorder update' sqlca.sqlcode sqlmsg
   else call sqlexec 'COMMIT'
   return sqlca.sqlcode
```

Figure 186. *(Part 3 of 3) DB2 Work Order Class (db2\carwork.cls)*

DB2 Service Item Class

```
/*----------------------------------------------------------------------*/
/* DB2\carserv.cls       CarDealer - ServiceItem class (DB2) ITSO-SJC */
/*----------------------------------------------------------------------*/

    .local['Cardeal.ServiceItem.class'] = .ServiceItem

::requires 'base\carserv.cls'

::class ServiceItem public subclass ServiceItemBase

/*----- class methods ---------------------------------------------------*/

::method persistentLoad class                     /* load all service items  */
    partclass = .local['Cardeal.Part.class']
    stmt = 'select s.itemnum, s.labor, s.description' ,
           '  from cardeal.service s' ,
           ' order by 1'
    hostvar = ':xitem, :xlabor, :xdesc1'
    call sqlexec 'PREPARE s1 FROM :stmt'
    if sqlca.sqlcode \= 0 then
       say 'sqlerror service items prepare:' sqlca.sqlcode sqlmsg
    call sqlexec 'DECLARE c1 CURSOR FOR s1'
    call sqlexec 'OPEN c1'
    if sqlca.sqlcode \= 0 then
       say 'sqlerror service items open:' sqlca.sqlcode sqlmsg
    do iserv = 0 by 1 until sqlca.sqlcode \= 0      /* - run over service table*/
       call sqlexec 'FETCH c1 INTO' hostvar
       if sqlca.sqlcode \= 0 & sqlca.sqlcode \= 100 then
          say 'sqlerror service items fetch:' sqlca.sqlcode sqlmsg
       else if sqlca.sqlcode = 0 then do
          /* say 'creating service item' xitem */
          servx = self~findNumber(xitem)
          if servx = .nil then
             servx = self~new(xitem, xdesc1, xlabor)
       end
    end
    call sqlexec 'CLOSE c1'
    if sqlca.sqlcode \= 0 then
       say 'sqlerror service items close:' sqlca.sqlcode sqlmsg
    /* say 'Loaded' self~getextent~items 'service items' */
                                                 /* - add service-part rels */
    stmt = 'select r.itemnum, r.quantity, r.partnum' ,
           '  from cardeal.servpart r'
    hostvar = ':xitem, :xquan, :xpartid'
    call sqlexec 'PREPARE s1 FROM :stmt'
    if sqlca.sqlcode \= 0 then
       say 'sqlerror service-parts prepare:' sqlca.sqlcode sqlmsg
    call sqlexec 'DECLARE c1 CURSOR FOR s1'
    call sqlexec 'OPEN c1'
    if sqlca.sqlcode \= 0 then
       say 'sqlerror service-parts open:' sqlca.sqlcode sqlmsg
```

Figure 187. *(Part 1 of 2) DB2 Service Item Class (db2\carserv.cls)*

```
      do iservprt = 0 by 1 until sqlca.sqlcode \= 0  /* - run over servpart tab.*/
         call sqlexec 'FETCH c1 INTO' hostvar
         if sqlca.sqlcode \= 0 & sqlca.sqlcode \= 100 then
            say 'sqlerror service-parts fetch:' sqlca.sqlcode sqlmsg
         else if sqlca.sqlcode = 0 then do
            /* say 'creating service-part' xitem xpartid */
            partx = partclass~findNumber(xpartid)
            if partx = .nil then
               say 'Service item' xitem 'uses non-existing part' xpartid
            servx = self~findNumber(xitem)
            if servx = .nil then
               say 'Service item' xitem 'not in service table'
            else
               servx~usesPart(partx, xquan)
         end
      end
      call sqlexec 'CLOSE c1'
      if sqlca.sqlcode \= 0 then
         say 'sqlerror service-parts close:' sqlca.sqlcode sqlmsg
      /* say 'Loaded' partclass~getextent~items 'parts' */
      /* say 'Loaded' iservprt 'service/part relationships' */
      /* say 'All sample data read'                        */
      return iserv
```

Figure 187. (Part 2 of 2) DB2 Service Item Class (db2\carserv.cls)

DB2 Part Class

```
/*----------------------------------------------------------------------*/
/* DB2\carpart.cls      CarDealer - Part class (DB2)      ITSO-SJC */
/*----------------------------------------------------------------------*/

   .local['Cardeal.Part.class'] = .Part

::requires 'base\carpart.cls'

::class Part public subclass PartBase

/*----- class methods ---------------------------------------------*/

::method persistentLoad class                  /* load all parts from DB2 */
   stmt = 'select p.partnum, p.price, p.stock, p.description' ,
          '  from cardeal.part p' ,
          ' order by 1'
   hostvar = ':xpartid, :xprice, :xstock, :xdesc2'
   call sqlexec 'PREPARE s1 FROM :stmt'
   if sqlca.sqlcode \= 0 then
      say 'sqlerror parts prepare:' sqlca.sqlcode sqlmsg
   call sqlexec 'DECLARE c1 CURSOR FOR s1'
   call sqlexec 'OPEN c1'
   if sqlca.sqlcode \= 0 then
      say 'sqlerror parts open:' sqlca.sqlcode sqlmsg
```

Figure 188. (Part 1 of 2) DB2 Part Class (db2\carpart.cls)

```
    do ipart = 0 by 1 until sqlca.sqlcode \= 0      /* - run over all parts   */
        call sqlexec 'FETCH c1 INTO' hostvar
        if sqlca.sqlcode \= 0 & sqlca.sqlcode \= 100 then
           say 'sqlerror parts fetch:' sqlca.sqlcode sqlmsg
        else if sqlca.sqlcode = 0 then do
            partx = self~findNumber(xpartid)
            if partx = .nil then
               partx = self~new(xpartid, xdesc2, xprice, xstock)
        end
    end
    call sqlexec 'CLOSE c1'
    if sqlca.sqlcode \= 0 then
        say 'sqlerror parts close:' sqlca.sqlcode sqlmsg
    return ipart

/*----- instance methods ---------------------------------------*/

::method persistentUpdate                          /* update a part          */
    use arg quant
    updatestmt = 'update cardeal.part set stock =' self~stock ,
                 ' where partnum =' self~number
    call sqlexec 'EXECUTE IMMEDIATE :updatestmt'
    if sqlca.sqlcode \= 0 then say 'part-update' sqlca.sqlcode sqlmsg
    else call sqlexec 'COMMIT'
    return sqlca.sqlcode

::method persistentInsert                          /* store new part         */
    insertstmt = "insert into cardeal.part" ,
                 "   values("self~number","self~price","self~stock"," ,
                       "'"self~description"')"
    call sqlexec 'EXECUTE IMMEDIATE :insertstmt'
    if sqlca.sqlcode \= 0 then say 'part-insert' sqlca.sqlcode sqlmsg
    else call sqlexec 'COMMIT'
    return sqlca.sqlcode
```

Figure 188. *(Part 2 of 2) DB2 Part Class (db2\carpart.cls)*

Running the Car Dealer Application

Program to Run the Car Dealer Application

```
/*--------------------------------------------------------------------*/
/* car-run.rex            CarDealer - Run Car Dealer        ITSO-SJC */
/*                        (AUI or GUI, File or DB2)                   */
/*--------------------------------------------------------------------*/

parse source . . me
sourcedir = me~left(me~lastpos('\')-1)
curdir = directory()           /* save current directory        */
new = directory(sourcedir)   /* make CARDEAL current directory */

arg p1 p2 p3 '(' quiet
if quiet \= '' then talk = 0
else talk = 1

if p1 = '' | p1 = '?' then do
    say 'Syntax: CAR-RUN  [F | D | M] [A | G ]'
    say '   first  parm:  F = File, D = DB2/2, M = in Memory only'
    say '   second parm:  A = Ascii window, G = GUI'
    say '   parameters :  in any sequence, blank separated'
    say '                 setup F|D|M is saved'
    return
end

opt = left(strip(p1),1)''left(strip(p2),1)''left(strip(p3),1)

/* setup data storage */

select
    when pos('F',opt)>0 then do; "copy FAT\carmodel.cfg     >nul"
                                 if talk then say 'Setup for FAT data'; end
    when pos('D',opt)>0 then do; "copy DB2\carmodel.cfg     >nul"
                                 if talk then say 'Setup for DB2 data'; end
    when pos('M',opt)>0 then do; "copy RAM\carmodel.cfg     >nul"
                                 if talk then say 'Setup for Memory data'; end
    otherwise nop
end

/* Run program in AUI or GUI mode */

select
    when pos('A',opt)>0 then     call "AUI\car-aui"
    when pos('G',opt)>0 then     call "OOD\car-ood"
    otherwise if talk then
                 say 'You can now run any Car Dealer application (ASCII or GUI)'
end

curdir = directory(curdir)   /* restore current directory     */
return
```

Figure 189. *Command to Run the Car Dealer (\car-run.rex)*

C

Definition for Syntax Diagram Structure

Throughout this book, syntax is described using the structure defined below:

❑ Syntax diagrams are read from left to right, top to bottom, following the path of the line.

The ▶▶— symbol indicates the beginning of a statement.

The ——▶ symbol indicates that the statement syntax is continued on the next line.

The ▶—— symbol indicates that a statement is continued from the previous line.

The ——◀ symbol indicates the end of a statement.

Diagrams of syntactical units other than complete statements start with the ▶—— symbol and end with the ——▶ symbol.

Required items appear on the horizontal line (the main path).

```
▶▶── STATEMENT─ required_item ──────────────────────────────▶◀
```

Optional items appear below the main path.

```
▶▶── STATEMENT ──────────────────────────────────────────────▶◀
                 └─ optional_item ─┘
```

Choices appear vertically, in a stack. If one item *must* be chosen, it will appear on the main path.

```
▶▶── STATEMENT ──┬─ required_choice1 ─┬──────────────────────▶◀
                 └─ required_choice2 ─┘
```

If choosing one of the items is optional, the entire stack appears below the main path.

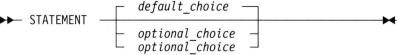

```
▶▶── STATEMENT ──────────────────────────────────────────────▶◀
                 ├─ optional_choice1 ─┤
                 └─ optional_choice2 ─┘
```

If one of the items is the default, it appears above the main path, and the remaining choices are shown below it.

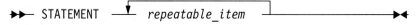

```
                 ┌─ default_choice ─┐
▶▶── STATEMENT ──┼──────────────────┼────────────────────────▶◀
                 ├─ optional_choice ─┤
                 └─ optional_choice ─┘
```

An arrow returning to the left above the main line indicates an item that can be repeated.

```
                 ┌◀─────────────────┐
▶▶── STATEMENT ──┴─ repeatable_item ─┴────────────────────────▶◀
```

A repeat arrow above a stack indicates that the items in the stack can be repeated.

Keywords appear in uppercase (for example, PARM1). They must be spelled exactly as shown but can be entered in lowercase. Variables appear in all lowercase letters (for example, *parmx*). They represent user-supplied names or values.

If punctuation marks, parentheses, arithmetic operators, or such symbols are shown, they must be entered as part of the syntax.

D

Special Notices

This publication is intended to help programmers use the new Object REXX language to create object-oriented applications. The information in this publication is not intended as the specification of any programming interfaces that are provided by Object REXX for Windows NT and Windows 95.

References in this publication to IBM products, programs or services do not imply that IBM intends to make these available in all countries in which IBM operates. Any reference to an IBM product, program, or service is not intended to state or imply that only IBM's product, program, or service may be used. Any functionally equivalent program that does not infringe on any of IBM's intellectual property rights may be used instead of the IBM product, program or service.

Information in this book was developed in conjunction with use of the equipment specified, and is limited in application to those specific hardware and software products and levels.

IBM may have patents or pending patent applications covering subject matter in this document. The furnishing of this document does not give you any license to these patents. You can send license inquiries, in writing, to the IBM Director of Licensing, IBM Corporation, 500 Columbus Avenue, Thornwood, NY 10594 USA.

E

Related Publications

The publications listed in this section are considered particularly suitable for a more detailed discussion of the topics covered in this document.

International Technical Support Organization Publications

- ❑ *OS/2 REXX: From Bark to Byte*, GG24-4199
- ❑ *Object-Oriented Databases, ObjectStore, Introduction and Sample Application*, GG24-4128

  (This book is based on the same car dealer application that we use in our book.)

- ❑ Object REXX for OS/2, SG24-4586, ISBN 0-13-273467-2

  (The original book on Object REXX, following a similar structure and content.)

A complete list of International Technical Support Organization publications, known as *redbooks*, with a brief description of each, may be found in:

International Technical Support Organization Bibliography of Redbooks, GG24-3070.

Other Publications

These publications are also relevant fur further information sources:

❑ *Object REXX Reference* [ORXW_REF.INF]

❑ *Object REXX Programming Guide* [ORXW_PRG.INF]

❑ *OODialog Method Reference* [OODIALOG.INF]

The first two books listed above are not available in hardcopy, but are shipped in online format with Object REXX.

❑ *The REXX Language, A Practical Approach to Programming*, by Mike Cowlishaw, published by Prentice Hall, 1990, ZB35-5100-01, ISBN 0-13-780651-5.

❑ *The Essential Client/Server Survival Guide*, by Robert Orfali, Dan Harkey, and Jeri Edwards, published by John Wiley & Sons, Inc., 1994, SR28-5572-00, ISBN 0-471-13119-9.

❑ *The Essential Distributed Objects Survival Guide*, by Robert Orfali, Dan Harkey, and Jeri Edwards, published by John Wiley & Sons, Inc., 1995, SR28-5898-00, ISBN 0-471-12993-3.

How to Get ITSO Redbooks

This section explains how both customers and IBM employees can find out about ITSO redbooks, CD-ROMs, workshops, and residencies. A form for ordering books and CD-ROMs is also provided.

This information was current at the time of publication, but is continually subject to change. The latest information may be found at URL:

http://www.redbook.ibm.com/redbooks

How IBM Employees Can Get ITSO Redbooks

Employees may request ITSO deliverables (redbooks, BookManager BOOKs, and CD-ROMs) and information about redbooks, workshops, and residencies in the following ways:

❑ **PUBORDER** — to order hardcopies in the United States

❑ **GOPHER link to the Internet** - type:

```
GOPHER.WTSCPOK.ITSO.IBM.COM
```

❑ **Tools disks**

To get LIST3820s of redbooks, type one of the following commands:

```
TOOLS SENDTO EHONE4 TOOLS2 REDPRINT GET SG24xxxx PACKAGE
TOOLS SENDTO CANVM2 TOOLS REDPRINT GET SG24xxxx PACKAGE
      (second line for Canadian users only)
```

To get lists of redbooks:

```
TOOLS SENDTO USDIST MKTTOOLS MKTTOOLS GET ITSOCAT TXT
TOOLS SENDTO USDIST MKTTOOLS MKTTOOLS GET LISTSERV PACKAGE
```

To register for information on workshops, residencies, and redbooks:

```
TOOLS SENDTO WTSCPOK TOOLS ZDISK GET ITSOREGI 1996
```

For a list of product areas specialists in the ITSO:

```
TOOLS SENDTO WTSCPOK TOOLS ZDISK GET ORGCARD PACKAGE
```

❑ **Redbooks Home Page on the World Wide Web**

```
http://w3.itso.ibm.com/redbooks/redbooks.html
```

❑ **IBM Direct Publications Catalog on the World Wide Web**

```
http://www.elink.ibmlink.ibm.com/pbl/pbl
```

IBM employees may obtain LIST3820s of redbooks from this page.

❑ **ITSO4USA category on INEWS**

❑ **Online** — send orders to:
   USIB6FPL at IBMMAIL or DKIBMBSH at IBMMAIL

❑ **Internet Listserver**

With an Internet E-mail address, anyone can subscribe to an IBM Announcement Listserver. To initiate the service, send an E-mail note to announce@webster.ibmlink.ibm.com with the keyword subscribe in the body of the note (leave the subject line blank). A category form and detailed instructions will be sent to you.

How Customers Can Get ITSO Redbooks

Customers may request ITSO deliverables (redbooks, BookManager BOOKs, and CD-ROMs) and information about redbooks, workshops, and residencies in the following ways:

❏ **Online Orders** (Do not send credit card information over the Internet) — send orders to:

	IBMMAIL	**Internet**
In United States:	usib6fpl at ibmmail	usib6fpl@ibmmail.com
In Canada:	caibmbkz at ibmmail	lmannix@vnet.ibm.com
Outside North America:	dkibmbsh at ibmmail	bookshop@dk.ibm.com

❏ **Telephone orders**

United States (toll free)	1-800-879-2755
Canada (toll free)	1-800-IBM-4YOU
Outside North America:	(long distance charges apply)

(+45) 4810-1320 - Danish	(+45) 4810-1020 - German
(+45) 4810-1420 - Dutch	(+45) 4810-1620 - Italian
(+45) 4810-1540 - English	(+45) 4810-1270 - Norwegian
(+45) 4810-1670 - Finnish	(+45) 4810-1120 - Spanish
(+45) 4810-1220 - French	(+45) 4810-1170 - Swedish

❏ **Mail Orders** — send orders to:

IBM Publications	IBM Publications	IBM Direct Services
Customer Support	144-4th Avenue, S.W.	Sortemosevej 21
P.O. Box 29570	Calgary, Alberta T2P 3N5	DK-3450 Aller/d
Raleigh, NC 27626-0570	Canada	Denmark
USA		

❏ **Fax** — send orders to:

United States (toll free)	1-800-445-9269	
Canada	1-403-267-4455	
Outside North America	(+45) 48 14 2207	(long distance charge)

❏ **1-800-IBM-4FAX (United States)** or **(+1) 415 855 43 29 (Outside USA)** — ask for:

Index # 4421 Abstracts of new redbooks
Index # 4422 IBM redbooks
Index # 4420 Redbooks for last six months

❏ **Direct Services** - send note to softwareshop@vnet.ibm.com

❏ **On the World Wide Web**

Redbooks Home Page:	http://www.redbooks.ibm.com
IBM Direct Publications:	http://www.elink.ibmlink.ibm.com/pbl/pbl

❏ **Internet Listserver**

With an Internet E-mail address, anyone can subscribe to an IBM Announcement Listserver. To initiate the service, send an E-mail note to announce@webster.ibmlink.ibm.com with the keyword subscribe in the body of the note (leave the subject line blank).

IBM Redbook Order Form

Please send me the following:

Title	Order Number	Quantity

☐ **Please put me on the mailing list for updated versions of the IBM Redbook Catalog**

First name _____ Last name _____

Company _____

Address _____

City _____ Postal code _____ Country _____

Telephone number _____ Telefax number _____ VAT number _____

☐ Invoice to customer number _____

☐ Credit card number _____

Credit card expiration date _____ Card issued to _____ Signature _____

We accept American Express, Diners, Eurocard, Master Card, and Visa. Payment by credit card not available in all countries. Signature mandatory for credit card payment.

DO NOT SEND CREDIT CARD INFORMATION OVER THE INTERNET

Sample Code on the Internet

If you do not have World Wide Web access, you can obtain the list of all current redbooks through the Internet by anonymous FTP:

```
ftp ftp.almaden.ibm.com
cd /redbooks
get itsopub.txt
```

This FTP server also stores the sample code developed for this redbook. To retrieve the sample files, issue the following commands from the redbooks directory:

```
lcd d:\carinst  <=== any local directory for installation files
binary
cd SG244825
mget *.*
ascii
get read.me
```

For IBM people without access to the external FTP server, the code is also available as RXREDWIN PACKAGE on the PCTOOLS conference disk.

To install the sample code, follow the directions in the read.me file, in conjunction with *Installing Object REXX, DB2, and the Sample Applications* on page 287.

Index

Special Characters

A

B

C

LOB 188
local directory 225, 465
loop 11
    bottom-driven loop 12
    repetitive loop 12
    top-driven loop 12

M

MakeArray 348
menu 103
    data file 104
    loop 104
    object 103
    operations 103
message object 268
meta class 70
method 58, 68
    class 69
    directive 59, 65, 466
    init 67
    instance 69
    new 67
    private 69
    reference manual 317
    unguarded 269
migration considerations 485
mixin 117
Move 386
MoveItem 385
movies 313
MultiInputBox 156, 319, 440, 441
MultiListChoice 158, 319, 443
multimedia 98, 192, 291
    BLOB 185
    files 492
    World Wide Web 255
multiple input box 156
multiple list choice 158
multiple selection 17

N

nested dialogs 144
Netscape Navigator 235
new
    method 67
NextPage 427
NoAutoDetection 334

O

object
    concurrency 267
    cooperation 53
    creation 67, 91
    destruction 68, 91
    file persistence 107
    instance 67
    instance management 92
    message 268
    methods 58
    model 93
    persistence 107
    relationships 89
    stream (file) format 111
object management group 54
Object REXX
    class library 73
    concurrency 267
    configuration management 215
    DB2 stored procedures 207
    dialog classes 126
    enhanced instructions 467
    GUI builder 122
    installation 289
    migration 485
    new features 463
    new instructions 467
    program group 291
    security 203
    shared objects 208
    tokenizing 161
    using BLOBs 188
    why 55
    workbench 457
    World Wide Web 233
object-oriented
    benefits 46
    languages 49
    why 46
ObjectToDC 377
OK 388
OMG 54
OODialog
    base dialog 322
    car dealer add services window 167
    car dealer bill window 169
    car dealer customer window 163
    car dealer main window 162
    car dealer part list window 170
    car dealer service items window 171
    car dealer simple installation
        window 228

P

ASCII 97
GUI 121
UserDialog 126, 130, 145, 318, 391
utilities
    new 482

V

Validate 389, 440
VAR
    new built-in function 479
variable
    methods and 84
    pool 65
    special 464
video 98, 192
    World Wide Web 256
video archive 306

W

waterfall method 48
Web , See World Wide Web
which 307
Windows 95 98
Windows Program Manager 452, 485
Windows Registry 453
Windows utilities 484
WinTimer 320
workbench 457
World Wide Web
    audio 256
    browser 234
    car dealer 261
    home page 235
    Internet Connection Server 235
    Internet name 236
    multimedia 255
    Object REXX 233
    pictures 255
    server 235
    video 256
Write 371
WriteDirect 369
WriteToButton 371
WriteToWindow 370

Y

YesNoMessage 319

IBM OBJECT REXX FOR WINDOWS EVALUATION LICENSE

IBM RESOURCE WORKSHOP, ILINK, IVIEW, AND OODIALOG
EVALUATION LICENSE

BEFORE USING THIS PROGRAM YOU SHOULD CAREFULLY READ THE FOLLOWING TERMS AND CONDITIONS. USING THE PROGRAM INDICATES YOUR ACCEPTANCE OF THE FOLLOWING TERMS AND CONDITIONS.

IBM Resource Workshop, ILINK, IVIEW, and OODialog ("Program") is copyrighted and licensed, not sold. The term "Program" means the original and all whole or partial copies of it. International Business Machines Corporation or one of its subsidiaries ("IBM") owns or has licensed from the owner copyrights in the Program.

IBM grants you free of charge a non-exclusive, nontransferable license to download the Program and use it to enable you to evaluate the potential usefulness of the Program to you.

You may copy the Program for back-up purposes only. You may not distribute, sublicense, lease or rent the Program, or create derivative works, reverse compile, reverse assemble or otherwise attempt to translate or seek to gain access to the Program's source code, except as permitted by law without the possibility of contractual waiver.

The term of your License will be one year from your first use. You must destroy and/or delete the Program within ten (10) days after the expiration of this one year period.

You may terminate this license at any time. IBM may terminate this license at any time if you are in breach of any of its terms. In either event, you must destroy all copies of the Program.

IBM IS PROVIDING THE PROGRAM TO YOU "AS IS", WITHOUT ANY WARRANTIES (EXPRESS OR IMPLIED) OR SUPPORT WHATSOEVER, INCLUDING BUT NOT LIMITED TO ANY IMPLIED WARRANTIES OF MERCHANTABILITY, OR FITNESS FOR ANY PARTICULAR PURPOSE.

IN NO EVENT WILL IBM BE LIABLE FOR ANY DAMAGE WHATSOEVER, INCLUDING, BUT NOT LIMITED TO, LOST PROFITS, LOST SAVINGS, INCIDENTAL OR INDIRECT DAMAGES OR OTHER ECONOMIC CONSEQUENTIAL DAMAGES, EVEN IF IBM HAS BEEN ADVISED OF THE POSSIBILITY OF SUCH DAMAGES. IN ADDITION, IBM WILL NOT BE LIABLE FOR ANY DAMAGES CLAIMED BY YOU BASED ON ANY THIRD-PARTY CLAIM.

The above limitation of remedies also applies to any developer and/or supplier of the Program. Such developer and/or supplier is an intended beneficiary of these limitation terms.

As your testing and evaluation of this Program is important to IBM, this license is granted without charge. You agree that IBM may use all suggestions, improvements and written materials you may furnish IBM in connection with your use of this Program, and that IBM may include them in any IBM product without accounting to you.

If you acquire the Program in the United States, this license is governed by the laws of the State of New York. If you acquire the Program in Canada, this license is governed by the laws of the Province of Ontario. Otherwise, the license is governed by the laws of the country in which you acquire the Program.

Note to U.S. Government Users -- Documentation related to Restricted Rights -- Use, duplication, or disclosure is subject to restrictions set forth in GSA ADP Schedule Contract with IBM Corporation.

IBM EVALUATION AGREEMENT
FOR DB2 FOR WINDOWS NT AND WINDOWS 95

This is a no charge Evaluation License ("License") between you and International Business Machines Corporation ("IBM") for the evaluation of IBM's software and related documentation ("Program").

IBM grants you a non-exclusive, non-transferable license to the Program only to enable you to evaluate the potential usefulness of the Program to you. You may not use the Program for any other purpose and you may not distribute any part of it, either alone or with any of your software products.

IBM retains ownership of the Program and any copies you make of it. You may use the Program on one (1) machine only.

You may not decompile, disassemble or otherwise attempt to translate or seek to gain access to the Program's source code.

The term of your License will be from the date of first use of the Program, and will terminate 60 days later, unless otherwise specified. THE PROGRAM WILL STOP FUNCTIONING WHEN THE LICENSE TERM EXPIRES. You should therefore take precautions to avoid any loss of data that might result. You must destroy and/or delete all copies you have made of the Program within ten (10) days of the expiry of your License.

If you are interested in continuing to use the Program after the end of your License, you must place an order for a full license to the Program and pay the applicable license fee. In that event, your use of the Program will be governed by the provisions of the applicable IBM license for the Program.

IBM accepts no liability for damages you may suffer as a result of your use of the Program. In no event will IBM be liable for any indirect, special or consequential damages, even if IBM has been advised of the possibility of their occurrence.

YOU UNDERSTAND THAT THE PROGRAM IS BEING PROVIDED TO YOU "AS IS", WITHOUT ANY WARRANTIES (EXPRESS OR IMPLIED) WHATSOEVER, INCLUDING BUT NOT LIMITED TO ANY IMPLIED WARRANTIES OF MERCHANTABILITY, QUALITY, PERFORMANCE OR FITNESS FOR ANY PARTICULAR PURPOSE. Some jurisdictions do not allow the exclusion or limitation of warranties or consequential or incidental damages, so the above may not apply to you.

IBM may terminate your License at any time if you are in breach of any of its terms.

This License will be governed by and interpreted in accordance with the laws of the State of New York.

This License is the only understanding and agreement we have for your use of the Program. It supersedes all other communications, understandings or agreements we may have had prior to this License.

LICENSE AGREEMENT AND LIMITED WARRANTY

READ THE FOLLOWING TERMS AND CONDITIONS CAREFULLY BEFORE OPENING THIS CD PACKAGE. THIS LEGAL DOCUMENT IS AN AGREEMENT BETWEEN YOU AND PRENTICE-HALL, INC. (THE "COMPANY"). BY OPENING THIS SEALED CD PACKAGE, YOU ARE AGREEING TO BE BOUND BY THESE TERMS AND CONDITIONS. IF YOU DO NOT AGREE WITH THESE TERMS AND CONDITIONS, DO NOT OPEN THE CD PACKAGE. PROMPTLY RETURN THE UNOPENED CD PACKAGE AND ALL ACCOMPANYING ITEMS TO THE PLACE YOU OBTAINED THEM FOR A FULL REFUND OF ANY SUMS YOU HAVE PAID.

1. **GRANT OF LICENSE:** In consideration of your purchase of this book, and your agreement to abide by the terms and conditions of this Agreement, the Company grants to you a nonexclusive right to use and display the copy of the enclosed software program (hereinafter the "SOFTWARE") on a single computer (i.e., with a single CPU) at a single location so long as you comply with the terms of this Agreement. The Company reserves all rights not expressly granted to you under this Agreement.

2. **OWNERSHIP OF SOFTWARE:** You own only the magnetic or physical media (the enclosed CD) on which the SOFTWARE is recorded or fixed, but the Company and the software developers retain all the rights, title, and ownership to the SOFTWARE recorded on the original CD copy(ies) and all subsequent copies of the SOFTWARE, regardless of the form or media on which the original or other copies may exist. This license is not a sale of the original SOFTWARE or any copy to you.

3. **COPY RESTRICTIONS:** This SOFTWARE and the accompanying printed materials and user manual (the "Documentation") are the subject of copyright. The individual programs on the CD are copyrighted by the authors of each program. Some of the programs on the CD include separate licensing agreements. If you intend to use one of these programs, you must read and follow its accompanying license agreement. You may not copy the Documentation or the SOFTWARE, except that you may make a

single copy of the SOFTWARE for backup or archival purposes only. You may be held legally responsible for any copying or copyright infringement which is caused or encouraged by your failure to abide by the terms of this restriction.

4.   **USE RESTRICTIONS:** You may <u>not</u> network the SOFTWARE or otherwise use it on more than one computer or computer terminal at the same time. You may physically transfer the SOFTWARE from one computer to another provided that the SOFTWARE is used on only one computer at a time. You may <u>not</u> distribute copies of the SOFTWARE or Documentation to others. You may <u>not</u> reverse engineer, disassemble, decompile, modify, adapt, translate, or create derivative works based on the SOFTWARE or the Documentation without the prior written consent of the Company.

5.   **TRANSFER RESTRICTIONS:** The enclosed SOFTWARE is licensed only to you and may <u>not</u> be transferred to any one else without the prior written consent of the Company. Any unauthorized transfer of the SOFTWARE shall result in the immediate termination of this Agreement.

6.   **TERMINATION:** This license is effective until terminated. This license will terminate automatically without notice from the Company and become null and void if you fail to comply with any provisions or limitations of this license. Upon termination, you shall destroy the Documentation and all copies of the SOFTWARE. All provisions of this Agreement as to warranties, limitation of liability, remedies or damages, and our ownership rights shall survive termination.

7.   **MISCELLANEOUS:** This Agreement shall be construed in accordance with the laws of the United States of America and the State of New York and shall benefit the Company, its affiliates, and assignees.

8.   **LIMITED WARRANTY AND DISCLAIMER OF WARRANTY:** The Company warrants that the SOFTWARE, when properly used in accordance with the Documentation, will operate in substantial conformity with the description of the SOFTWARE set forth in the Documentation. The Company does not warrant that the SOFTWARE will meet your requirements or that the operation of the SOFTWARE will be uninterrupted or error-free. The Company warrants that the media on which the SOFTWARE is delivered shall be free from defects in materials and workmanship under normal use for a period of thirty (30) days from the date of your purchase. Your only remedy and the Company's only obligation under these limited warranties is, at the Company's option, return of the warranted item for a refund of any amounts paid by you or replacement of the item. Any replacement of SOFTWARE or media under the warranties shall not extend the original warranty period. The limited warranty set forth above shall not apply to any SOFTWARE which the Company determines in good faith has been subject to misuse, neglect, improper installation, repair, alteration, or damage by you.

EXCEPT FOR THE EXPRESSED WARRANTIES SET FORTH ABOVE, THE COMPANY DISCLAIMS ALL WARRANTIES, EXPRESS OR IMPLIED, INCLUDING WITHOUT LIMITATION, THE IMPLIED WARRANTIES OF MERCHANTABILITY AND FITNESS FOR A PARTICULAR PURPOSE. EXCEPT FOR THE EXPRESS WARRANTY SET FORTH ABOVE, THE COMPANY DOES NOT WARRANT, GUARANTEE, OR MAKE ANY REPRESENTATION REGARDING THE USE OR THE RESULTS OF THE USE OF THE SOFTWARE IN TERMS OF ITS CORRECTNESS, ACCURACY, RELIABILITY, CURRENTNESS, OR OTHERWISE.

IN NO EVENT, SHALL THE COMPANY OR ITS EMPLOYEES, AGENTS, SUPPLIERS, OR CONTRACTORS BE LIABLE FOR ANY INCIDENTAL, INDIRECT, SPECIAL, OR CONSEQUENTIAL DAMAGES ARISING OUT OF OR IN CONNECTION WITH THE LICENSE GRANTED UNDER THIS AGREEMENT, OR FOR LOSS OF USE, LOSS OF DATA, LOSS OF INCOME OR PROFIT, OR OTHER LOSSES, SUSTAINED AS A RESULT OF INJURY TO ANY PERSON, OR LOSS OF OR DAMAGE TO PROPERTY, OR CLAIMS OF THIRD PARTIES, EVEN IF THE COMPANY OR AN AUTHORIZED REPRESENTATIVE OF THE COMPANY HAS BEEN ADVISED OF THE POSSIBILITY OF SUCH DAMAGES. IN NO EVENT SHALL LIABILITY OF THE COMPANY FOR DAMAGES WITH RESPECT TO THE SOFTWARE EXCEED THE AMOUNTS ACTUALLY PAID BY YOU, IF ANY, FOR THE SOFTWARE.

SOME JURISDICTIONS DO NOT ALLOW THE LIMITATION OF IMPLIED WARRANTIES OR LIABILITY FOR INCIDENTAL, INDIRECT, SPECIAL, OR CONSEQUENTIAL DAMAGES, SO THE ABOVE LIMITATIONS MAY NOT ALWAYS APPLY. THE WARRANTIES IN THIS AGREEMENT GIVE YOU SPECIFIC LEGAL RIGHTS AND YOU MAY ALSO HAVE OTHER RIGHTS WHICH VARY IN ACCORDANCE WITH LOCAL LAW.

ACKNOWLEDGMENT

YOU ACKNOWLEDGE THAT YOU HAVE READ THIS AGREEMENT, UNDERSTAND IT, AND AGREE TO BE BOUND BY ITS TERMS AND CONDITIONS. YOU ALSO AGREE THAT THIS AGREEMENT IS THE COMPLETE AND EXCLUSIVE STATEMENT OF THE AGREEMENT BETWEEN YOU AND THE COMPANY AND SUPERSEDES ALL PROPOSALS OR PRIOR AGREEMENTS, ORAL, OR WRITTEN, AND ANY OTHER COMMUNICATIONS BETWEEN YOU AND THE COMPANY OR ANY REPRESENTATIVE OF THE COMPANY RELATING TO THE SUBJECT MATTER OF THIS AGREEMENT.

Should you have any questions concerning this Agreement or if you wish to contact the Company for any reason, please contact in writing at the address below.

Robin Short
Prentice Hall PTR
One Lake Street
Upper Saddle River, New Jersey 07458